The Making of the New Negro

American Studies

AMERICAN STUDIES publishes monographs and edited volumes on American history, society, politics, and culture. The series is a forum for groundbreaking approaches and areas of research, as well as pioneering scholarship that adds new insights into relatively established fields in the study of America.

Series Editors:
Derek Rubin and Jaap Verheul,
Utrecht University

Published in this Series

Derek Rubin and Jaap Verheul (eds.)
American Multiculturalism after 9/11: Transatlantic Perspectives
2009 (ISBN 978 90 8964 1441)

Sebastian Reyn
Atlantis Lost: The American Experience with De Gaulle, 1958-1969
2010 (ISBN 978 90 8964 214 1)

The Making of the New Negro

Black Authorship, Masculinity, and Sexuality in the Harlem Renaissance

Anna Pochmara

Amsterdam University Press

The publication of this book was made possible by a financial contribution from the Institute of English Studies, the University of Warsaw.

Cover illustration: Author Langston Hughes [far left] with [left to right:] Charles S. Johnson; E. Franklin Frazier; Rudolph Fisher and Hubert T. Delaney, on the roof of 580 St. Nicholas Avenue, Harlem, on the occasion of a party in Hughes' honor, 1924. Photographs and Prints Division, Schomburg Center for Research in Black Culture, The New York Public Library, Astor, Lenox and Tilden Foundations
Cover design: Neon, design and communications, Sabine Mannell, Amsterdam, the Netherlands
Design: JAPES, Amsterdam, the Netherlands

ISBN   978 90 8964 319 3
e-ISBN   978 90 4851 423 6
NUR   632

© Anna Pochmara / Amsterdam University Press, 2011

A part of Chapter 1 has already been published as "The Black Man's Burden: Dilemmas of Black Masculinity in Booker T. Washington's Up from Slavery." The Americanist 25 (2009): 97-110

Table of contents

Acknowledgements

This book has been an intellectual adventure that would not be possible without the contribution and help from a number of scholars and friends. All my academic teachers have left a significant mark on my analytical approach and scholarly interests. I would especially like to thank Professors Piotr Skurowski, Agnieszka Graff, and Cynthia Dominik. I am also very grateful to Professor Agata Preis-Smith for her guidance as my M.A. thesis supervisor as well as for her astute review of this text, which was very helpful in the process of revision. The most substantial part of this book was written during my stay at Yale University in 2007-2008, where Professor Hazel V. Carby, as my Fulbright mentor, enhanced my research with her warm, friendly, and inspiring guidance. I also wish to express my gratitude to the Chair of American Literature Section, Dr. Marek Paryż, who actively encouraged me to publish my manuscript as a book. Additionally, I want to thank a number of my friends for their intellectual and emotional support. Most notably, I am grateful to my dear friend Anna B. Ross for her careful and constructive proofreading of the draft version of this study, help with archival sources in German, and companionship during our American expedition. I am also deeply indebted to Filip Lipiński, who has helped me with visual references and, as a fellow Fulbrighter, greatly facilitated my research at the New York archives. I was fortunate to find support in many other young scholars, especially Dr. Ewa Nowik, Dr. Agnieszka Szarkowska, Dr. Justyna Wierzchowska, and Dr. Joanna Ziarkowska, whose exemplary academic commitment have inspired me. Finally, I want to thank my parents and my husband for their generous support for this academic project as well as other life choices.

Introduction

...The Negro began that revelation and vindication of himself,
that impassioned study of his accomplishments,
the declaration of his future that creates
the masculine literature of the 'New Negro.'[1]
J. Saunders Redding, *To Make a Poet Black*

If there is ever a Negro literature, it must disengage itself
from the weak, heinous elements of the culture that spawned it.[2]
Leroi Jones (Amiri Baraka), "The Myth of a 'Negro Literature'"

This book sets out to analyze gender and sexuality constructions in selected texts of New Negro Renaissance discourse.[3] One of the main aims of this book is to examine the production of literary and cultural history as an ongoing dialogic process that is mediated through the notions of gender and sexuality. Such a dialogue is exemplified by the opening epigraphs. J. Saunders Redding and Amiri Baraka refer to the same period of black literary history and yet their assessments are diametrically opposed. More significantly, both views are expressed in a gender-marked way – on the one hand, the New Negro Renaissance is praised as "masculine" and, on the other, represented as the abject – condemned as "weak," "heinous," and femininely able to "spawn." Following the logic revealed in this example, this study will explore how aesthetic evaluations and representations of the New Negro Renaissance are diversely entangled in the tropes of gender and sexuality. In the main body, this gender-marked dialogue will be analyzed on the example of the two leading figures of the movement, Wallace Thurman and Alain Locke. In the Prologue and the Epilogue, this synchronic perspective will be complemented with a focus on the public debates preceding and immediately following the Renaissance.

The examination of these dialogical rhetorics will demonstrate that the role of masculinity is especially significant in historical narratives of black literature. Both levels of analysis, diachronic and synchronic, will examine how the tropes loaded with gendered and sexual connotations serve either to celebrate or to repudiate rival black leaders. Consequently, a discussion of relations among towering black authors needs the explanatory potential of two theoretical paradigms: Harold Bloom's anxiety of influence and Susan Gilbert and Susan Gubar's anxiety of authorship.[4] The black male writer is caught in a double bind between the need to engage in "heroic warfare" with his strong predecessors and the need to establish a legitimate patrilineal lineage, which will both validate black male authorship and set off the specters of social illegitimacy resulting from white men's symbolic and biological fathering of black children. These two conflicting endeavors are differently entangled in the politics of masculinity. The anxiety of influence is resolved by rhetorical emasculation of strong rivals, whereas the anxiety of authorship leads to a celebration of forefathers and masculinization of black history. Both concepts will be applied to analyze the production of black literary tradition, strategic self-fashioning, and self-positioning of black authors within this tradition, rather than to diagnose the personal psychological condition of the authors. These contradictory forces behind the creation of patrilineal black history will also shed light on fundamental black feminist projects, such as Alice Walker's *In Search of Our Mothers' Gardens: Womanist Prose* (1984) or Hazel V. Carby's *Reconstructing Womanhood: The Emergence of the Afro-American Woman Novelist* (1987), which aim to undo this masculinization and to rewrite black literary history. Their endeavors are more complicated than white feminists' search for literature of their own, since they not only face exclusion from authorship but also have to respond to the persistent attempts to forge and strengthen male historical bonds stemming from black men's anxiety of authorship.

The Making of the New Negro is also interested in how black writers appropriate and rewrite dominant gender ideologies to construct their masculine identity.[5] These black assertions of masculinity inevitably pose a challenge to white constructions, yet they most frequently retain their sexist dimension. On the other hand, modern hegemonic (white middle-class) masculinity is permeated with a constant anxiety and a need to be revived, reasserted, and contrasted with groups that are unmanly, including black men, which makes the relation between hegemonic masculinity and black masculinity complex and contradictory. I will explore this dialectic with reference to the concepts of Victorian manliness and modern masculinity as defined by Gail Bederman in her *Manliness and Civilization: A Cultural History of Gender and Race in the United States, 1880-1917* (1995). Bederman analyzes the turn of the twentieth century as a critical moment for the remaking of American manhood, in which manliness based on self-restraint and self-sacrifice was gradually being superseded with a more assertive and virile ideology of masculinity. Despite this shift in hegemonic ideologies, both manliness and masculinity exploit the presence of other races. Victorian manliness draws privilege from the position of patronage over uncivilized non-white races, whereas modern masculinity appropriates the imaginary primitive vitality of other races to revitalize itself. Bederman's insights into history of American masculinity will be complemented with references to the work of Michael S. Kimmel. I will apply his concept of the preindustrial "Genteel Patriarch," whose identity was stably based on land ownership, and "Marketplace Manhood," an ideology which, according to Kimmel, emerged in the 1830s and was based on an endless process of proving one's manhood in the sphere of economic competition. Both Bederman's concept of modern masculinity and Kimmel's Marketplace Manhood are haunted by a sense of instability, constant anxiety, and the need to be endlessly proven time and again. Both are also exclusionary and parasitical in relation to representations of black masculinity, which is constructed as their Other.[6] Yet, although hegemonic ideologies exclude black men, they inevitably must appropriate them to assert their own masculine agency. I will analyze in detail how each of the discussed writers draws on one or more dominant masculinities. In the case of Booker T. Washington, it will be Victorian manliness and the figure of the Genteel Patriarch, which are in dialogue with the more modern and militant masculinity of W. E. B. Du Bois. Locke's texts will be discussed with reference to Marketplace Manhood and the term "producerist masculinity," introduced by Martin Summers to define masculine ideology centered on productivity and activity in the public sphere. This construction of masculinity is in stark contrast to Thurman's nonproductive, leisure ideology of dandyism, which also to some extent fits Summers's notion of "consumerist masculinity." Finally, Richard Wright's texts champion the virile working-class masculinity, which flirts with the dominant mythology of aggressive black men.

As hegemonic masculinity is predicated not only on the exclusion of black men but also of the working class, another thematic thread that will be woven throughout this project is the relationship between the leader and the masses.[7] This study will approach the issue of the working class analogously to Marlon B. Ross, who, on the one hand, claims that "the ongoing debate over black male models, mentors, and tokens ensures that the analysis of prominent figures will always be needed" and, on the other, is interested in the relationship between "token leader and folk masses."[8] The tension between the black elite and the black masses is a problem encountered by all the leaders and writers who intend to forge a collective black identity. The perennial dilemma faced by representatives of the underprivileged stems from the fact that the privilege entailed in the leading position distances them from the community they represent. They are forced to strategically balance between an assertion of agency through disidentification from the masses, on the one hand, and legitimization of racial identity, on the other, whose authenticity is frequently established through identification with the folk or with the working class. Thus the masses are either celebrated, as it is in the case of Washington's and Wright's writings, or condemned, mostly due to their violation of respectability, as in the case of Du Bois's works. The lower classes can also be gendered as masculine, which is mostly visible in Wright's texts, or pacified as feminine, which will be explored in Du Bois's and Locke's rhetorics. The class issue is also at the heart of Thurman's works; however, his identification is ambiguous and contradictory. On the one hand, he celebrates the virility of the black masses; on the other hand, he distances himself from them to assert his radical individuality.

Another interest of *The Making of the New Negro*, which is analogous to the black leaders-black masses dialectic, is the correlation between the black agency and black women. This relationship is largely dependent on the hegemonic ideologies appropriated by male authors in their self-fashionings. The more assertive and militant ideology is adopted, the less space for black women's agency is left, which is visible primarily in the texts of Du Bois and Wright. In contrast, Washington, who adopts a more patient and acquiescent ideology of Victorian manliness, provides ample space for black women's activity in the public sphere in the anthology he co-edits – *A New Negro for a New Century: An Accurate and Up-to-Date Record of the Upward Struggles of the Negro Race* (1900). Even more conspicuously, Thurman's espousal of the passive and non-productive dandy enables him to depict black "superwomen" who are economically successful and sexually active. Another correlation that emerges from my analysis is the absence of female voices in the projects that are primarily intent on constructing collective black identity as either race or nationality. Since such projects emphasize the similarity and features that bind together the diverse black community, frequently they do it at the cost of obliterating the gender difference. Here, the most representative examples that will be analyzed are Du Bois's talented tenth, Locke's New Negro, and Wright's collective black subject in *12 Million Black Voices*.

As this study's interest in history and stratification of masculinities suggests, the theoretical framework it adopts is that of social constructivism, which assumes that gender identity is culturally determined and inherently connected with other categories of difference that stratify American society, such as race, class, sexual orientation, or nationality. Thus no single masculinity or femininity will be discussed but rather different constructions varying according to other identity positions. Moreover, these positionalities are fluid and context dependent, i.e. they are situationally performed and processual rather than fixed and unchangeable. Consequently, even the concept of hegemonic masculinity is considered to be a dynamic situational process. The constructed character of black masculinity, which is assumed in this study, is accurately expressed by Isaac Julien and Kobena Mercer in their text "True Confessions":

> Social definitions of what it is to be a man, about what constitutes "manliness," are not "natural" but are historically constructed and this construction is culturally variable...Patriarchal culture constantly redefines and adjusts the balance of male power and privilege and the prevailing system of gender roles by negotiating psychological and personal identity through a variety of material, economic, social and political structures such as class, the division of labor and the work/home nexus at the point of consumption. Race and ethnicity mediate this at all levels, so it's not as if we could strip away the "negative images" of black masculinity created by Western patriarchy and discover some "natural" black male identity which is good, pure and wholesome. The point is

that black male gender identities have been culturally constructed through complex dialectics of power.[9]

Apart from the conceptualization of black male identity as constructed and variable, Mercer and Julien emphasize that the longings for authentic black male identity are illusive. This contention is significant since such tendencies have constituted an important element of black struggle, especially when it conflated the promise of freedom with the idealized vision of African roots and racial authenticity. As other scholars argue, not only are such cravings illusory, but they also tend to be dangerously linked to masculinism and exclusion of female voices.[10]

The temporal scope of this study encompasses the decades that have attracted much scholarly attention, yet relatively few works have examined the New Negro Renaissance with a focus on masculinities and non-normative sexuality.[11] The Making of the New Negro draws on the findings from these pioneering studies, which notably include Hazel V. Carby's Race Men (1998), B. Christa Schwarz's Gay Voices of the Harlem Renaissance (2003), and Summers's Manliness and Its Discontents: The Black Middle Class and the Transformation of Masculinity, 1900-1930 (2004). The most relevant precursor of this book, however, is Ross's epic work Manning the Race: Reforming Black Men in the Jim Crow Era (2004). In his study, he claims that "the so-called New Negro Renaissance represents one of the best arenas in which to investigate the individual and institutional dynamics constructing black manhood identity in the early twentieth century."[12] This assumption is the driving force behind The Making of the New Negro. Ross analyzes a plethora of projects devoted to the construction of black agency dating from the beginning of the century to the late days of the Renaissance. In his analysis of the movement, he concentrates on the sexual politics of patronage and the precarious relationships among white patrons, black patrons, and black protégés. My book focuses in detail on two of the dozens of black writers, sociologists, and activists analyzed by Ross and thus it complicates some of his findings. Nevertheless, it wholeheartedly supports his thesis about the utmost significance of gender ideologies and sexualized imagery in New Negro discourse.

The first chapter of this study, serving as a prologue to the main body, will present the socio-historical context and ideological dynamics that dominated the American collective imagination on the eve of the New Negro Renaissance. Both historical processes that contributed to the emergence of the movement and the ideological framework in which it was entangled will be discussed on the example of the debate between Washington and Du Bois. The scope of analysis will focus on the texts central to the debate. Yet it will also include Du Bois's texts from the 1920s due to their temporal coincidence with the emergence of the New Negro movement. This chapter will introduce cultural logics that constitute the frame of reference for the participants of the New Negro Renaissance. It will primarily focus on the lynch logic, which is an ideological construct structured as a dynamic triangle of the black rapist, the white female victim, and the white avenger. The lynch logic forcefully interlocks race, gender, and sexuality, and it haunts the writings of all authors analyzed in this book. The traumatic and long-lasting impact of lynch mythology is tellingly expressed by Wright, who, referring to his boyhood in the 1920s in the South, claims that "I had never in my life been abused by whites, but I had already become as conditioned to their existence as though I had been the victim of a thousand lynchings."[13] The second significant cultural paradigm I will analyze is the dynamic of civilization and the white man's burden. As Bederman argues, the white man's burden was an ideology that reinforced the dominant position of Victorian hegemonic masculinity by drawing privilege from the position of the patron of the non-white races. Black authors openly challenge it, which will be analyzed on the example of Du Bois, appropriate it, which is most exemplarily performed by Washington, or rewrite it, which will be discussed with reference to Locke's peculiar modernist primitivism. Apart from illustrating different approaches to race relations of the day, the Washington-Du Bois debate will be read as a dialogue between two different visions of black masculinity.

The opening chapter will be followed by two main parts of the study. Each of the parts will be dedicated to a figure regarded as leading and influential for the entire movement by both the contemporaneous participants and later literary histories of the New Negro Renaissance. The first part will examine texts by Locke, the editor of the seminal *The New Negro: An Interpretation* (1925), whereas the second part will be devoted to Thurman, the editor of the movement's younger generation magazine *Fire!!* (1926). The decision to juxtapose the two figures stems from their acknowledged central role in the movement as well as the fact that they both were the driving forces behind collective ventures intended to define and guide black cultural self-expression. Their analogous positions, respectively within the older and the younger generation, make a dialogic reading of their output particularly productive. The similarity between Locke and Thurman is additionally reinforced by their corresponding explorations of the possibility of representing alternative sexuality in writing.

The juxtaposition of the two leaders will reveal a set of polarizations which stem from their competing visions of collective black identity and of the artistic movement. As the titles of the respective parts indicate, this dichotomy can be summarized in the contrast between Locke's New Negro and Thurman's Niggerati. Whereas Locke fashions the movement as the renaissance, Thurman rebelliously celebrates the decadence of black artists. Whereas Locke affirms black production, procreation, and cultural regeneration, Thurman foregrounds black infertility and degeneration. *The Making of the New Negro* will explore the implications of this fundamental distinction on different rhetorical levels. It will also examine the ways in which Locke and Thurman appropriate diverse European discourses of same-sexuality. Consequently, the New Negro and Niggerati can be analyzed as two contending visions of non-normative masculinity, which are articulated with different rhetorics. Locke creates a private language shared by a closed circle of friends, a peculiar *idioglossia*, which includes only a particular version of masculinist same-sexuality; whereas Thurman's novelistic representations form a *heteroglossia* of pluralist and multiple voices.

Locke's vision will be discussed in Part 1, consisting of two chapters. Chapter 2 will analyze the central tropes of the movement: "The New Negro" and "The Renaissance." Socio-linguistic echoes implicated in these terms will lead the examination back to both the American and the European Renaissances. The exploration of transatlantic intertextual references will focus on close analogies between Locke's rhetoric and the contemporaneous, predominantly German, discourses of the *Jugendkultur*, youth movements, and homosexual liberation institutions. These links will be read as reinforced by the presence of the philosophy of German individualism and classical Greek ideals of love in both the above-mentioned diverse European liberation discourses and Locke's texts. This intertextual reading will illuminate the ways in which the construction of black subjectivity is connected to the representation of gender relations and alternative sexualities in Locke's vision of the New Negro Renaissance. Chapter 3 will analyze texts that outline Locke's vision of the black aesthetic. The primary focus will fall on gender implications of his aesthetic prescriptive guidelines and judgments. The tropes analyzed in this section will include the triad of decadence, sentimentalism, and modernist realism. Gender politics of Locke's aesthetics will also be exemplified by his distinctive delineation of black primitivism as a strategy to draw from historical African cultures, which at the time were recognized by European modernism as rich sources of inspiration. The analysis will focus on the way Locke masculinizes the black artist and the new black aesthetic.

Part 2 will examine the writings of Thurman, whose presence in the academic discourse is less pronounced than Locke's. The subsequent, fourth chapter of this study will focus on Thurman's embrace of and rebellion against the (black) American bourgeoisie and its gender constructions. Particular attention will be devoted to Thurman's trespassing of the boundaries inherent in the ideologies of separate spheres and Jim Crow segregation. In the course of this reading, Thurman's appropriation of working-class cultural codes will come into focus, which will further illuminate the gendered dimensions of Thurman's counter-bourgeois project. Chapter 5 will analyze Thurman's appropriation of the European discourse of decadence. This reading will primarily focus on the figure of the dandy and its potential for expression of alternative masculinities and sexualities. The discrepancy arising between the racialized subject positions in Thurman's fiction and the dandyist philosophy of the aesthetics of the self will be elucidated with reference to the cultural phenomenon of the Harlem "sweetback." The implications of the transatlantic transplantations in Thurman's writings will shed light on complex and paradoxical entanglements of race, gender, and sexuality in American Jim Crow imagination.

Whereas the Prologue of the study is devoted to the two leading figures preceding the New Negro Renaissance, Washington and Du Bois, the Epilogue will be dedicated to the person who was almost unanimously recognized as the leading voice of black American letters immediately following the movement: Richard Wright. The concluding chapter will analyze the ways in which Wright's early texts dialogize, rewrite, and interrogate the tropes and cultural logics introduced in the preceding parts. It will also explore Wright's representation of the New Negro. The author of *Native Son* criticizes the Negro Renaissance and rhetorically emasculates it, primarily through connotations with same-sexuality. This analysis will shed light on the processes of representation of the New Negro movement by later generations and their gendered and sexualized character.

The initial aim of my study was to examine the interconnections among the constructions of race, gender, sexuality, class, and nationality in the New Negro discourse. In the preliminary research for the book, the issues of black masculinities and alternative male sexualities emerged as especially significant elements of this discourse. It is in the light of this fact that the choice of only black male voices must be read. The study intends to problematize and comment on the domination of male voices in the New Negro Renaissance discourse rather than to perpetuate the exclusion of female voices. It aims to develop the body of scholarship represented by masculinity studies and whiteness studies, which examine culturally hegemonic positions. The assumption behind this project is that it is productive to explore the normative non-marked gender-less character of masculine subjectivity. Since the concept of hegemonic masculinity is defined in opposition to black masculinities, which occupy marginalized positions in relation to it, an analysis of black masculinities reveals an elaborate interplay of hegemonic and marginalized positions. This dynamic is further complicated by the significant presence of same-sexuality in the discourse of the movement. I will explore the ways in which the non-normative sexualities and black masculinities challenge and rewrite hegemonic masculinity. The equally important question, however, will be the absence and presence of the New Negro Woman.

Chapter 1
Prologue: The Question of Manhood in the Booker T. Washington-W.E.B. Du Bois Debate

Whether at last the Negro will gain full recognition
as a man...is the present Negro problem of America.
W.E.B. Du Bois, "The Negro Race in the United States of America"[1]

The greatest thing that can be done for the Negro at the present time
is to make him the most useful and indispensable man in his community.
Booker T. Washington, "The American Negro and His Economic Value" [2]

"It seems to me," said Booker T.,
"That all you folks have missed the boat
Who shout about the right to vote,
And spend vain days and sleepless nights
In uproar over civil rights.
Just keep your mouth shut, do not grouse,
But work, and save, and buy a house."
"I don't agree," said W.E.B.,
"For what can property avail
If dignity and justice fail.
Unless you help to make the laws,
They'll steal your house with a trumped-up clause.
A rope's as tight, a fire as hot,
No matter how much cash you've got.
Speak soft, and try your little plan,
But as for me, I'll be a man"
"It seems to me," said Booker T.–
"I don't agree,"
Said W.E.B.
Dudley Randall, "Booker T. and W. E. B."[3]

The emergence of the New Negro movement was entangled in powerful dynamics and paradigms involving race, gender, and sexuality that defined Jim Crow America. The opening chapter presents these ideological constructs, and the following chapters explore how they were echoed and rewritten in New Negro discourse. As I have indicated, the main focus is the debate between Booker T. Washington and W. E. B. Du Bois, which has shaped modern African American discourse in general and the New Negro Renaissance in particular. Both participants of the dispute are numerously referred to in the discussions of the politics and rhetoric of the movement. Alain Locke chooses to include the two principal texts of the debate, The Souls of Black Folk and Up from Slavery, in his study of black self-expression in the 1920s, even though they considerably predate the Roaring Twenties decade, "because within this period in which we are interested they have established themselves as Negro classics and come in to the prime of their influence."[4] I contend that these two symbolic progenitors of black liberation stand not only for two different visions of black emancipation and leadership but also for two competing visions of masculinity.

Washington and Du Bois's dispute has been interpreted in a number of critical texts, yet very few scholars have focused on the intricate correlations between race and gender assertions that underlie it.[5] The significance of the gender question in the debate is visible in the epigraphs to this chapter. In the first one, Du Bois rewrites the race issue into a gender dilemma – black emancipation is identified with, and hence reduced to, the problem of black manhood. The citation from Washington's text signals that, although the issue of "being a man" is significant for black uplift, it will be approached in a more tentative manner. The last epigraph comes from a contemporary poem by Dudley Randall, where Du Bois's conflation of race and masculinity is manifestly echoed and the question of manhood is positioned as the central issue of the emancipatory struggle. The verse is ironic, yet the fact that Du Bois has the last word in the debate suggests that the text sympathizes with his militantly asserted black masculinity. Prevalent contemporary discourses on the debate share Randall's identification with Du Bois's strategy.[6] The analysis of gender constructions within the debate might shed light on the reasons behind the perception of Du Bois's arguments as more successful.

Race Relations in Post-Reconstruction America: Socio-cultural Context of the Debate

Since, as Ross argues, "the Jim Crow regime itself is a sexual system of oppression," I will begin with an introduction of the essential historical and cultural phenomena and indicate how they shaped representations of race, gender, and sexuality at the turn of the century.[7] Economic, political, legal, and physical repressions of Jim Crow America produced and perpetuated ideologies that were deeply preoccupied with gender issues. What is particularly significant from the point of view of this study is that the dynamic between black and white masculinity emerges as especially prominent in Jim Crow mythology, which is exemplified by its central constructs such as the myth of uncontrollable black male sexual violence and white men's noble duty to protect women and assume a paternal role towards the non-white races.

The 1880s and 1890s witnessed the failure of racial emancipation initiated during the Civil War, which directly led to a sense of emasculation experienced by black men. Economically, the emergence of the sharecropping system, which in many cases bound black laborers to plantations, de facto reinstated slave-like dependence. Politically, black people suffered increasing disfranchisement in the Southern states, implemented through measures such as the infamous "grandfather clause."[8] Economic and political oppression was reinforced by the introduction of segregation in a variety of local and state codes. These local laws gained a nationwide buttress in the landmark decision of the Supreme Court in the case Plessy v. Ferguson in 1896, which established the "separate but equal" doctrine. The economic and political exclusion from the public sphere, additionally fortified with racial segregation, denied black men access to the markers of hegemonic masculinity, which in the nineteenth century was primarily performed in the public realm and defined against feminine domesticity.

Economic and legal emasculation was reinforced with physical violence primarily in the form of the lynching practice. According to Tuskegee statistics, between 1882 and 1901, 1,914 black people were lynched, which indicates that most Southern black communities witnessed a lynching and no black individual could feel safe from it.[9] Although the phenomenon of lynching predates both Reconstruction and the Civil War, post-Reconstruction lynchings were characterized by new features, several of which are particularly relevant for a gender analysis. First of all, a systemic shift – from the white ownership of black bodies to the segregation of the two social groups – explains the increased frequency and intensity of violence exercised on black bodies, which were no longer privately owned. Even more significantly, the 1880s was the period when lynchings began to be strongly associated with rape charges. Although the prevailing majority of crime allegations accompanying lynchings were not related to sexual assaults, this connection was powerfully established in the collective imagination, which is visible in public debates at the time.[10] In the late 1880s, this obsession with black male sexuality led to the emergence of the myth of the black rapist.[11] Frederick Douglass, referring to the sudden change in the perception of Negro men, claims that it is hardly believable that blacks had been transformed in a few years into "a criminal people." He persuasively argues that a new justification for violence against the black community emerged when the old tales of black insurrection or of black political supremacy were no longer convincing in the context of massive political disempowerment of black people in the South.[12] This contemporaneous interpretation accurately accounts for the way the structural changes – disfranchisement and the newly emerged sharecropping system – resulted in a sudden shift in the ideology of race: the rebellious Nat Turners and servile Uncle Toms were substituted with the black brute.

The black brute is not only a racial myth but, more particularly, a forceful ideology of black masculinity. In the collective imagination, it developed into a powerful and complex lynch logic, according to which pure white womanhood needs to be protected from uncontrollable black male sexuality by white noble manhood. The significance of black masculinity in this narrative is highlighted by the absence of the black woman from the triangular scenario comprising the black rapist, the pure white woman, and the white avenger. Since this ideological logic remained one of the most terrible and persuasive justifications of racial violence at least for the next century, its reverberations are present in all the corpora of texts examined in this study.

The emergent lynch logic was inherently connected with the peculiar structure of post-Reconstruction lynching practices, which complexly intersected race with gender and sexuality. One of their recurrent characteristics was the frequent nudity of victims, which highlighted the corporeality of their bodies and sexualized their position as objects of the white gaze. Referring to the lynching practice, Robin Wiegman states that "the de-commodification of the African-American body that accompanies the transformation from chattel to citizenry is mediated through a complicated process of sexualization and gendering." What lent additional impact to the visual control of the lynch victim was a peculiar combination of the panoptic control of the modern prison and the spectacular control of the premodern scaffold. As Wiegman argues, "the black subject is disciplined in two powerful ways: by the threat of always being seen and by the specular scene." The emphasis on the corporeal and sexual character of the lynch victim was further reinforced with the practice of dismemberment and collecting "trophies." Although various body parts were collected, literary, political, and scholarly discourses have tended to focus on castrations of lynch victims as the most symbolic form of mutilation. On the one hand, such a practice was ideologically justified by a need to contain and appropriate black male sexuality; on the other, according to Wiegman, it symbolically denied the privilege of the phallus and political citizenship to black men. It animalistically sexualized the black male and simultaneously excluded him from the masculine political privilege.[13] Thus, with regard to their numbers, ideological justifications, and specific practices, post-Reconstruction lynchings rigidly controlled and disempowered black masculinity.

Even though the ghastly impact of Southern lynch mythology spread to the North, there was considerable divergence between the levels of disempowerment and physical terror above and below the Mason-Dixon Line, which was one of the factors behind the Great Migration of black people. As historians August Meier and Elliot Rudwick claim in From Plantation to Ghetto, already by 1910, "Negroes were mainly an urban population, almost two-thirds of them being city dwellers."[14] Apart from the push factors represented by the oppressive Jim Crow re-gime in the South, a critical pull factor emerged with American involvement in World War I and the resulting demand for cheap industrial labor, which seriously accelerated the migratory process. As a result, by 1920, "the North and West had over 470,000 more Negroes than...in 1910."[15] Migration, industrialization, and urbanization of the black community had a profound impact on black gender relations, which were confronted with hegemonic paradigms of separate spheres and modern masculinity defined by performance in the public realm. This shift also resulted in the emergence of new race ideologies that complemented the Southern lynch logic and that were national in scope.

Thereby emergent rhetorical concepts also complexly interlocked race and sexuality. For example, additional justification for racial oppression was readily provided by social and philosophical thought of Darwinism. By 1896, Jim Crow politics together with racialist philosophy created a nationwide system of dual citizenship. This system affirmed the "natural hierarchy of races," the concept which was to find its most powerful expression in *The Passing of the Grand Race* by Madison Grant (1916). As Bederman claims, the central ideal guiding such a vi-sion was the concept of *civilization*. Non-white ethnicities were defined in contrast to the civilized white man. They were at best represented as "adolescent races," which are either backward in the progress of civilization or incapable of assimila-tion to white civilization altogether.[16] Such an approach to race implicated that any interracial intimacy would lead to the degeneration of either of the groups, which further strengthened the anxiety concerning black sexuality aroused by the lynching ideology.

The discourse of civilization was intricately linked to the idea of manliness. As Bederman argues, Victorian manliness was the ideology of masculinity that pre-vailed in the mid-nineteenth century. Webster's *The New International Dictionary of the English Language* (1863) defines "manly" as "becoming to a man" and lists qua-lities such as either "firm, brave, undaunted" or "dignified, noble, stately" in con-trast to "masculine" which means simply "having the qualities of a man." Analo-gously, *The Century Dictionary* (1889) states that "manly...is the word into which have been gathered the highest conceptions of what is noble in man or worthy of his manhood." "Manly" was the "character or conduct worthy of a man." The ideology of manliness was based on self-mastery and restraint, which served as primary features defining recently emerged middle-class masculinity. Manliness was also deeply rooted in the genteel tradition of bourgeois respectability. White self-controlled manliness was contrasted with uncivilized races represented as in-capable of taming their primitive passions. The white man assumed a responsi-bility for the enlightenment and protection of the uncivilized peoples. "The white man's burden" emerged as a rhetorical tool which simultaneously justified colo-nization and advocated the paternalistic ideology of manliness. In addition, the notions of civilization, race, and gender were conflated in an assumption that the progress of civilization coincides with the progress in gender differentiation and separation of masculine and feminine spheres, which was supported by one of the most influential champions of social evolution of the era: Herbert Spencer.[17]

According to Bederman, the concept of manliness as the source of male privilege began to be replaced with a new vision of masculinity in the 1890s. The genteel Victorian ideology reached a critical point when middle-class ideals were tested in the changing market conditions, under the challenge of new immigration, and by the end of the frontier. In a more demanding environment, in which new immigrants, freedmen, and women challenged the privileged position of white middle-class men, a more assertive gender ideology was necessary. Thus, at the end of the century, an ideology of more virile masculinity appeared; it celebrated ideals such as aggressiveness, physical force, and male sexuality.[18] The ideological shift was reflected in the lexical definitions. The term "manly," defined as "having qualities becoming to a man;...esp. brave, courageous, resolute, noble" was supplanted by "masculine," defined as "having the qualities of a man; suitable to, or characteristic of, a man; virile; not feminine or effeminate; strong; robust."[19] The behavior that had earlier stood for manliness and self-possession began to be perceived in the 1890s as effeminate and labeled with newly coined terms such as "overcivilized," "sissy," "pussy-foot," "stuffed shirt." This remaking of hegemonic masculinity attempted to revitalize the weakened civilized manliness and to simultaneously retain the hierarchy of civilizations in terms of racial domination.[20]

The black discourse of racial uplift and the white rhetoric of civilization interestingly interacted with each other. The emancipatory discourse necessarily addressed the issues of disfranchisement, economic deprivation, segregation, and physical violence of the lynch mob. Black leaders were concerned with securing political and economic rights as well as bodily security. On the other hand, surprisingly similar anxieties underlay the issue of remaking white civilized manliness: retaining political power in the cities, succeeding in the new corporate reality, and reviving the bodily strength of white masculinity. What makes the connection between the two even more significant is that the discourse of manliness was parasitical in relation to blackness – it projected the repressed and the "unmanly" onto black masculinity, whether submission before Reconstruction or bestiality afterwards. Thus, the ideologies of race, civilization, citizenship, and masculinity were powerfully intertwined and constituted a fundamental contextual network of references for black emancipatory discourse.

Booker T. Washington's Strategic Evasion of Violence

Following the death of Frederick Douglass in 1895, the next leading figure entangled in the post-Reconstruction ideologies of Jim Crow and civilization was Booker T. Washington. Washington's politics have remained controversial since its most prominent articulation in his Atlanta convention speech. He is assessed simultaneously as "the most powerful and influential black leader ever to have existed before or since his advent" and "the Great Compromiser."[21] Washington's autobiography has attracted some attention from masculinity scholars. Donald Gibson, in his analysis of the first chapter of Up from Slavery, claims that Washington strategically feminizes himself in order to achieve his goals with the support of white patronage. Maurice O. Wallace, analyzing the same text, admits that Washington's self-creation is feminized, yet he maintains that there are subversive spaces which allow for the expression of heteronormative masculine sexual desire.[22] In my analysis, I argue that Washington, rather than feminize his persona, seeks ways to assert his masculine agency and construct black national identity within the tradition of civilized manliness.

Gibson claims that Washington "wanted his audience to feel that his voice was not threatening but calm and placid" and, in order to achieve it, he feminized his autobiographical persona.[23] Whereas it is hard to disagree with the former claim, the latter argument does not take into consideration the possibility of asserting one's masculinity in a self-possessed way. Undoubtedly, Washington's choice of a conciliatory voice constituted a strategic rhetorical gesture addressed at his white Southern audience, as the tone of his personal letters was much more indignant.[24] The published text carefully omits any elements of violence, black male sexuality, or resentment against whites. These omissions are especially visible when Up from Slavery is contrasted with the urtext of African American autobiography, Narrative of the Life of Frederick Douglass, an American Slave (1845). The two texts have been frequently compared, since Washington's text positions him as Douglass's successor after his death. As far as the plot is concerned, both autobiographies trace the way from plantation slavery to freedom. Yet, Washington chooses to depict plantation idyll rather than plantation trauma, which is epitomized by the central scene in Douglass's Narrative representing his Aunt Hester's flogging. Washington persistently repeats in his text that "there was no feeling of bitterness" toward the white people.[25] Instead, there was sorrow and sympathy for the war wounds and deaths of Confederate soldiers. Reconstruction is characteristically the period that is assessed in the text as most violent. Washington compares Ku Klux Klan night raids with slave patrols and claims that the former were far more brutal. He does not provide any space for the black responses to white violence, which were taking place according to historical records.[26] Additionally, he constructs his depictions of aggression with careful tentativeness. While historians write of terror, assault, and oppression, Washington introduces Ku Klux Klan vigilante as men who "joined themselves together for the purpose of regulating the conduct of the colored people."[27] When he describes open confrontation between white and black people, the only man defending blacks and standing up to whites is a white Southerner, General Ruffner. The choice of Reconstruction as the symbol of white violence is a conscious strategy on the part of the author.

This depiction is not a call for retribution or black defense, as according to Washington, this "darkest part of the Reconstruction days" is just an "*unpleasant* part of the history of the South." He concludes that "to-day there are no such organizations in the South, and their existence is almost forgotten by both races. There are few places in the South now where public sentiment would permit such organizations to exist." White violence in these passages is "regulatory," "unpleasant," and "almost forgotten." Washington's strategy is to forget, move on, and enjoy the contemporary bliss of interracial relations. This also results in his persistent critique of the black exodus to the North. He openly states that "by far the greatest part of the Negro race is better off in the country districts and should continue to live there."[28] In addition, his famous slogan "cast your buckets where you are" can be read not only as advocacy of conservative politics but also as a geopolitical reference to the increasing black migration. It is not surprising that Washington's reactionary narrative aroused protests at its very publication, since his depiction of the peaceful stage of race relations in the 1890s is in stark contrast to the historical data about lynchings, which are also provided by Washington's Tuskegee Institute.

Washington briefly mentions lynchings two times in the text. At first he does not even name the term itself but indirectly speaks of "the practice to which the people in certain sections of the South have felt themselves compelled to resort, in order to get rid of the force of the Negroes' ballot." This "practice" causes "permanent injury to the morals of white man" and only temporary wrong to the Negro. At the end of the text, he refers to the incidents of turn-of-the-century lynchings as "superficial and temporary signs," whereas, according to historians, these incidents greatly outnumbered Ku Klux Klan raids during Reconstruction.[29] Washington is hopeful because he received "warm and hearty" support from the Southern newspapers in regard to the "evil habit of lynching." As historical record shows, mainstream media support was limited and they misrepresented Washington's anti-lynch claims. When he spoke to the National Negro Business League, he openly stated that "the crime of lynching everywhere and at all times should be condemned." Yet, what the *Atlanta Constitution* reported was a story with the headline "Law-breaking Negroes Worst Menace to Race." Also, Northern newspapers preferred to publish his conciliatory calls in which Washington expressed "very deep grief on account of the death of so many innocent men of both races because of the deeds of a few despicable criminals."[30] Thus, even though the tone of his private letters to Oswald Villard or Francis Garrison reveals outrage at "unspeakably cruel acts" and "criminal negligence" of the police, in his *Up from Slavery* persona, Washington chooses to diminish the influence of lynchings and represent black men as reconciled with the status quo and devoid of any kind of bitterness or aggression.[31] As the similarities between *Up from Slavery* and the records from the Southern newspapers indicate, Washington's narrative was addressed at and intended to appease white public opinion in the South.

Up from Slavery, however, cannot be reduced solely to the function of satisfying the white South. When read in the context of the powerful lynch ideology, it can be interpreted as a particular strategy to rebuke the Southern myth of the black rapist used to justify lynchings. By advocating black self-control and restraint from retaliation and representing black people in a peaceful way, Washington argues that black men are devoid of aggression and do not have any reasons for retaliation. Thus, he undermines the myth that projects black males to be aggressive and sexually unrestrained.

Washington indirectly refutes the charges of black male sexual aggression by constructing the persona of a devoted and loyal slave:

> In order to defend and protect women and children who were left on the plantations when white males went to war, the slaves would have laid down their lives. The slave who was selected to sleep in the "big house" during the absence of the males was considered to have the place of honour. Anyone attempting to harm "young Mistress" or "old Mistress" during the night would have had to cross the dead body of the slave to do so.[32]

This passage represents the black male as devoid of sexual desire for white womanhood. The scene argues that black men, far from being rapists, are loyal protectors of white women. Yet, it also provides a space for exemplification of black bravery and honor. Even though Washington does not mention the slaves who joined the army, the black protector of women is also courageous and self-sacrificing as he is willing to give his life for the honor of white womanhood. Hence, within the triangular lynch logic, Washington's loyal slave assumes the position typically occupied by the white noble defender, whereas the role of the rapist is filled by the Union soldier.

Black Manliness and the Protestant Work Ethic

Depicting black men as non-aggressive, patient, and stoical in their attitude towards whites, Washington challenges the myth of the black rapist. In addition, this strategy can also be interpreted as drawing on the tradition of civilized manliness, which enables him to translate passive non-resistance into manly self-possession and restraint. The values that are celebrated in Washington's text run parallel to the Victorian tradition of white genteel masculinity.

This is visible in the very choice of the author's name, which pays tribute to the tradition of white nobility. Washington informs the reader that an ex-slave boy without a surname typically would choose Lincoln or Sherman as his symbolic father. Young Booker, during a school roll, chooses "Washington" as his new surname and, emblematically, as his father figure.[33] In this way he claims his right to genteel manliness and privilege. The gentility of George Washington is reinforced later in the text. The author of Up from Slavery quotes an anecdote in which President Washington lifts his hat to a black man to avoid being impolite, which according to the text makes him "a true gentleman."[34] Later, Booker adds his middle name, Taliaferro, which was given to him by his mother. Thus, the composition of his final name comprises: a slave first name, Booker; a mother-given name, Taliaferro; and a symbolically chosen white father's name, Washington. It neatly reflects his origins: a black mother and a white (slave-owning) father. It also manifests his choice of a particular model of antebellum gentlemanly masculinity.

The model of masculinity advocated in the text is most accurately illustrated by the descriptions of two other exemplary men: General Armstrong and President McKinley. Washington devotes a considerable part of the chapter on education to the head of Hampton Institute. He is "a perfect man," clearly a paragon of masculinity that Washington wishes to follow. The terms in which General Armstrong is depicted exemplify the nineteenth-century manliness as defined by Bederman. Armstrong is "the noblest human being," a "great character," hardworking, self-sacrificing, "Christlike," high, and pure.[35] He represents a model of a noble patriarch full of self-restraint, whose genteel manners and self-restraint evoke awe and respect in all Hampton students and teachers.

Another example of masculinity that ideally fits this concept of manliness can be found in Washington's reference to President McKinley. This passage is slightly shorter than the three pages devoted to the celebration of General Armstrong, yet it also perfectly reflects the essence of manliness. Referring to his fund-raising experiences, Washington shares his reflections about men of success:

> I have observed that those who have accomplished the greatest results are those who "keep under the body"; are those who never grow excited or lose self-control, but are always calm, self-possessed, patient, and polite. I think that President William McKinley is the best example of a man of this class I have ever seen. In order to be successful in any kind of undertaking, I think the main thing is for one to grow to the point where one completely forgets himself.[36]

This depiction is parallel to the characterization of Armstrong in its emphasis on self-sacrifice, which here is linked with the most characteristic features of manliness – self-control and patience. Praise for such ideals recurs in many other passages. For example, Washington's "faithful secretary," Mr. Scott, is eulogized for his "tact, wisdom, and hard work." The difficulties faced when founding Tuskegee Institute make Washington realize that patience, earnest effort, and endurance guarantee success in every kind of task, independently of one's race. Thus, also the ideals that are valued and taught at Tuskegee are "industry, thrift, and economy."[37] Washington proposes a noble, self-controlled manliness as a role model to follow for black men on their path to civilized humanity.

Although Washington privileges white models of manhood, his attempt to become the successor of Frederick Douglass makes it necessary for him to acknowledge Douglass as a race leader. He is, however, selective in his representation of the most famous nineteenth-century black abolitionist. Instead of the militant race leader and intellectual, Washington's Douglass accepts segregation in a stoical and gentlemanly manner.[38] Thus he does not contradict the model of black masculinity signified by President Washington. The representation of Douglass in Up from Slavery interestingly resonates with Wallace Thurman's depiction of "Fred" Douglass, who bludgeoned the skulls of his opponents, which is discussed in Chapter 4. Such dramatic disparity between two representations of the same historical figure suggests that for black men who attempt to resolve the anxiety of authorship and to create a patrilineal heritage, the choice of exemplary heroes from the past is less important than the contemporaneous ideologies in which their representations are donned.

The narrative uplift scenario in Washington's autobiography clearly parallels the Horacio Alger "rags-to-riches" dime novel tradition. Yet his narrative can be traced back even further, to Benjamin Franklin's Autobiography – the text acknowledged as a secularized version of the Protestant work ethic. Washington, too, emphasizes a strenuous work ethic and discipline, with a focus on the material level of life. Moreover, Washington consciously alludes in the text to the very genre of (auto)biography in a manner that lends an air of authenticity to his own testimony: "I have a great fondness for...biography. I like to be sure that I am reading about a real man or a real thing."[39] Thus he legitimizes his "rags-to-riches" story in which from being "A Slave among the Slaves" in the title of the first chapter, he emerges as the leader of black people who meets the president, travels to Europe, organizes Negro conferences, and is the head of one of the most influential black educational institutions. The text makes it clear that his success is due to his hard work and patience, which makes Up from Slavery an autobiographical embodiment of the Protestant work ethic. Washington's application of the core American doctrines of individualism, success, and the work ethic – as well as references to Presidents Washington and McKinley – position black identity in the mainstream of American national discourse.

Characteristically, the head of Tuskegee strongly emphasizes his point of departure in the success story, when he is a "crying," "frightened child," fed like "dumb animals."[40] Thus, he does not present himself as an extraordinary character. Quite on the contrary, he tends to stress his petty fears and minor deceptions. His autobiographical persona is easy to identify with even for the lowest strata of the black population. According to Washington, it is not courage or intellect but hard work, patience, and restraint that lead to success. He praises the blessed influence of menial labor as a necessary element of education. The timetable that he designed for Tuskegee strongly reminds one of Franklin's routine. The students are occupied with useful activities from 5 a.m. until 9.30 p.m., and the day is carefully divided into studying, working, cleaning, and praying. The epitome of the moralizing success story is found at the very end:

> As I write the closing words of this autobiography I find myself – not by design – in the city of Richmond, Virginia; the city...where, about twenty-five years ago, because of my poverty I slept night after night under a sidewalk. This time I am in Richmond as the guest of the coloured people of the city; and came at their request to deliver an address last night to both races in the Academy of music, the largest and finest audience room in the city.[41]

Washington's real-life advancement from the lower class to the top of black social strata is a persuasive argument for his ideology of self-denial, endurance, and restraint. Moreover, his success is also a gendered success – as a leader of the black community, just like General Armstrong, he becomes a role model of manliness for other black men to follow.

In the light of Washington's persistent opposition to black migration and urbanization, Michael Kimmel's concept of the premodern Genteel Patriarch can be used to classify the black subject and manhood as championed by the head of Tuskegee Institute. The Genteel Patriarch represents a pre-industrial ideology of masculinity, which is defined by rural existence and whose privilege is rooted in land ownership. By echoing this traditional mythology of American masculinity, Washington evades the anxieties of modern, predominantly urban, Marketplace Manhood as theorized by Kimmel. Washington's rural manliness can also be read as an attempt to appropriate the potent image of the yeoman farmer and, connected with it, the pastoral ideal central to the American myth of origin. His pastoral model of black manhood, however, is dramatically undercut by the social reality of the day. The dominant pattern of employment in the South was the infamous sharecropping system, which was rural and far from modern industrial economy, but it prevented black people from access to land ownership, which is the fundamental element of both the Genteel Patriarch and the yeoman farmer myths. Accordingly, despite the potential for empowerment inherent in these concepts, social reality drastically defied Washington's rhetoric. His black subject aspires to the Genteel Patriarch, but he remains "du most gentlemanfied man" ironically mocked in Zora Neale Hurston's classic narrative, which exposes the failed and fatal mimicry of white middle-class respectability.[42]

Another factor that complicates Washington's appropriation of Victorian manliness is the problematic position he assigns to the black woman. Structural conditions of sharecropping do not allow for the necessary complement to Victorian manliness – genteel femininity put on a pedestal. What sharecropper farming requires instead is an ideology of womanhood based on hard physical work. In his paradigm, praising menial work, industrial education, and rural life in the South, Washington tries to strike a balance between hard work and purity as markers of ideal black femininity. The situation of black women is used as a peculiar argument supporting technical education in opposition to "liberal education." Both in Up from Slavery and in his text "Industrial Education for the Negro," Washington claims that liberal education constitutes a threat to black femininity. He argues that it is increasingly common and manifestly absurd when a (black) woman can converse intelligently about theoretical chemistry and cannot cook, iron, or launder. In his autobiography, he openly states that with liberal education and no practical skills, "the girls went to the bad."[43] Thus, according to the logic of the text, liberal education for women, together with migration or urbanization related to it, is a straight path to prostitution, whereas menial work is correlated with respectability. In this peculiar line of reasoning, Washington uses the concept of feminine purity as an argument to challenge Du Bois's advocacy of higher education, which will be elaborated on further in the chapter.

Black Man's Burden

Washington's work-ethic gospel is intertwined not only with the concept of manliness but also with the discourse of civilization, which, as Bederman argues, powerfully intersects ideologies of race and gender. Washington, in his autobiography, appropriates the Euro-American rhetoric of civilization with its most potent figure of the white man's burden. This image from Kipling's poem became the central myth in the imperial ideology and poetically justified colonization with benevolence and civilizational progress. According to Bederman, "the white man's burden...linked white supremacy, male dominance, and evolutionary advancement in one powerful figure."[44] Washington's rewriting of the white man's burden scenario in his autobiography is a significant element of his assertion of masculinity which reinforces and legitimizes his ethic of manliness and masculine privilege.

As the text is devoted to the history of Tuskegee Institute, the concept of civilization is primarily evoked in the context of the educational process. Washington accepts the prevailing hegemonic assumptions concerning the hierarchy of races and civilizations. He argues that black people in any other place in the world are not nearly as civilized as American freedmen after "the school of American slavery." "African heathens," turned into black slaves, became "stronger...materially, intellectually, morally, and religiously." Thanks to the slave experience, they gained the "spirit of self-reliance and self-help."[45] These valuable qualities could be developed through the educational system at Tuskegee. The experience of slavery in Washington's narrative is positioned as a necessary step in the racial uplift.

Apart from this general support for the Euro-American civilizing process, the white man's burden scenario itself is adopted and reenacted in the chapter "Black

Race and Red Race," in which Washington experiments with educating Indians.[46] Over one hundred "wild and for the most part perfectly ignorant Indians" were taken to Hampton to be civilized under the guidance of young Booker as their "house father." The Indians are represented as considering themselves "above the white man" and "far above the Negro," on the one hand, and unable to be civilized, on the other.[47] In Washington's text, Indians are proud savages who nevertheless are behind black people in the civilizational progress. This representation echoes the words of Frederick Douglass, who, in a letter to Harriet Beecher Stowe, claims that "the black man (un-like the Indian) loves civilization."[48] Both leaders construct black identity as civilized and closer to mainstream American culture by contrasting it with American Indians. "The Negro students gladly took the Indians as room-mates, in order that they might teach them to speak English and to acquire civilized habits." The process of civilizing is based on cutting their hair, changing their clothes, and teaching them the rules of "absolute" hygiene.[49] Ross correctly argues that Washington appropriates another race for self-empowerment; however, he reads the relationship mainly through the lens of the spoils system and its patronage politics. "The Indians represent the 'spoils' that Washington must manage."[50] I suggest that this episode also powerfully mirrors the white man's burden. Washington accepts his place in the hierarchy beneath the white man and eagerly takes fatherly advice from respectable white role models. Yet, he establishes his own civilized position by assuming "the black man's burden," the role of the "house father," consisting of civilizing Indians. Such logic is explicitly stated in the text: "they [the students] lift themselves up in proportion as they help to lift others, and the more unfortunate the race, the lower in the scale of civilization, the more does one raise one's self by giving the assistance."[51] The confrontation with another race, which can be represented as uncivilized and wild, enables Washington to construct himself as a noble civilizing man in the tradition of Victorian manliness. He appropriates this potent ideology in order to uplift himself in the progress to civilization and civilized manhood.

Yet the fact that Washington positions the civilizational "burden" in the sphere of cleanliness and domesticity voids his rhetoric of the authority and dominance inherent in the original concept. Not only in this episode but throughout the whole autobiography, Washington frequently uses metaphors and images of domestic chores and hygiene to depict the schooling process.[52] The text vigorously promotes slogans and concepts such as: "the most valuable lesson...was in the use and value of the bath," "The use of the tooth-brush" directly leads to "a higher degree of civilization among the students," or "the gospel of the toothbrush."[53] As these quotes show, Washington's representations of cleaning interestingly conflate education, missionary work, and civilizational advancement.

The conflation of the discourse of civilization with obsessive cleaning has a number of implications. First of all, in terms of the nineteenth-century separate spheres, it positions the black civilizing process chiefly in the domestic sphere of housekeeping and hygiene, which in the nineteenth century was coded as strictly feminine. Consequently, Washington's civilizing mission constitutes the intersection of the white man's burden and the myth of female attempts at domination most memorably embodied by Widow Douglass and Aunt Sally's civilizing influence in *Huckleberry Finn*. Moreover, a persistent desire for "absolute cleanliness" and "whitewashing" might be interpreted as reinforcing the association of black people with impurity, which evokes a compulsory reaction of cleaning.[54] The association of impurity and non-white races was a significant element in nineteenth-century racialist thought and the logic of eugenics. Thus, Washington's obsessive preoccupation with cleaning can be read as an element of internalized eugenic ideology.

Despite these connotations, such a strategy enables Washington to represent blacks as civilized, successful, and worthy of respect, without challenging the position of the white man within the public sphere. It is representative of Washington's autobiography as a whole. *Up from Slavery* proposes a strategic project for black subjectivity and masculinity, which is largely determined and limited by his intended audience, the white South. Washington carefully chooses his role models, who construct an interesting patriarchal lineage. Namely, both George Washington and Frederick Douglass are celebrated as the symbolic fathers in the text. The former stands for (white) noble manliness, while references to the latter position the head of Tuskegee as Douglass's successor in the leadership of the black community.[55] Its form of the success story, the role models it eulogizes, and the doctrines they represent all position black identity in *Up from Slavery* in the mainstream American discourse of individual success, work ethic, and imperial uplift of the less civilized. The strategic choice of the most distinctive American doctrines enables Washington to represent the black community as an inherent element of American society.

In the context of the post-Reconstruction South, the strategy of constructing black manhood in terms of Victorian tradition devoid of any signs of resentment or militant tone enabled Washington to become an influential leader and effective educator with the support of white public opinion and its sponsorship. In his autobiography, he does not feminize his position but rather walks a tightrope to construct a vision of civilized black manliness, which does not openly challenge the white man's status. This strategy might be also interpreted as a rebuttal of the myth of the black rapist and an attempt to rewrite the lynch triangle. Throughout the text black men are devoid of aggression or sexuality. *Up from Slavery* represents black men as protectors rather than aggressors in relation to white womanhood. Thus instead of the black brute, the white female victim, and the white protector, Washington represents black men as protectors of white femininity, whereas the sexual threat is projected onto the Northern soldier. Additionally, the purity of black womanhood is endangered by liberal education, which is intimately connected to immigration, urbanization, and the industrial North. This danger, however, is only implicitly signaled in Washington's texts; what is foregrounded is pastoral interracial coexistence.

In contrast to American Indians, black men are paragons of noble self-restrained manliness. The comparison with Indians enables Washington to claim the privileged position of uplifting the savage peoples and, to some extent, appropriate the power dynamic of the white man's burden. Self-restraint combined with the Protestant work ethic also provides the basis for a vision of a successful self-made man. Washington draws on American respect for hard menial work in order to advocate a strenuous path to respectable working manhood. This is the only entrance into the public sphere that exists in the text, as he trades civil rights for the right to industrial education. Nevertheless, even this sphere of performance is limited, since the civilization and black men's working opportunities are rooted in domesticity and cleanliness. Thus Washington's appropriation of the late-nineteenth-century hegemonic discourses of civilization lacks the authority and privilege intrinsic in its original version. However, a closer reading reveals the implicit presence of more virile representations of black manhood in his project.

Subversive Spaces in Washington's Rhetoric

Even though Up from Slavery represents a model of manhood that is defined by its lack of virility and sexual assertion, Washington finds a way to enhance his masculine attractiveness in a way that would be acceptable to his white Southern audience. In order to simultaneously construct his auto-creation as humble and yet manifestly successful, he resorts to quoting selected accounts from Southern newspapers. This strategy allows him to remain unassuming and clearly avoid any traits of the conceited educated coon stereotype and yet to assert his success in a manner that gives an impression of ultimate objectivity. The selected fragments include depictions of Washington that emphasize his masculine virility and thus transcend the limits of Victorian manliness. In the report from the Atlanta Exposition address, which he chooses to cite, Washington is likened to "a Negro Moses" and "a Sioux chief." He is represented as "a remarkable figure, tall, bony, straight, muscular,...high forehead, straight nose, heavy jaws, and strong, determined mouth, with big white teeth, piercing eyes, and a commanding manner." His speech evokes an enthusiastic response from the audience: "The fairest women of Georgia stood up and cheered. It was as if the orator had bewitched them."[56] This description constructs Washington's persona in terms that belong to the tradition of the more assertive ideology of late-nineteenth-century masculinity rather than gentlemanly manliness. The author of the article focuses on the powerful bodily features of Washington, depicting him in assertively masculine terms such as "strong," "tall," "straight," "commanding," and "piercing." The reference to Native American identity serves here not as a contrast to assert the civilized status of black people, but, on the contrary, its function is to endow Washington's image with virile "primitive" masculinity. The description of the women's reaction also constitutes an indicator of the sexual appeal of Washington. Since the Atlanta Compromise speech was delivered to an interracial audience, it can be assumed that the phrase "the fairest women of Georgia" not only includes but even prevailingly refers to white women. Moreover, since the article Washington refers to is authored by a white man, the white gaze directed at Washington can be read as charged with homoerotic desire, which is just mediated through the figure of "the fairest women of Georgia." The latent presence of same-sexuality and being the object of the desiring gaze links Washington's auto-creation to the constructions of masculinity in the New Negro Movement, especially to Thurman's dandy and his performative self-display.

In the context of the haunting myth of the black rapist, it would not be possible for Washington himself to state that white women were "bewitched" by his speech. A minor remark about willful relations between white women and black men in a black newspaper in Wilmington in 1898 was a pretext for violent riots, which were later recorded in the novel *The Marrow of Tradition* (1901) by Charles Chesnutt. The ventriloquist strategy of depicting one's virile masculinity and sexual appeal with the use of the white voice is not only safe but endows the narration with authority and objectivity. Thus, Washington manages to find a space for a more vigorous assertion of masculinity in the text which on the surface constructs black manhood in terms of gentle, self-possessed, and self-restrained manliness.

W.E.B. Du Bois's Black Manhood and Its Anxieties

Washington's vision as represented in the Atlanta Compromise was challenged not only by modern critics but also by his contemporaries, such as John Hope and William Monroe Trotter. It also had its supporters, including a young black intellectual, W. E. B. Du Bois, who congratulated the Atlanta orator on "a word fitly spoken."[57] Yet, in the course of eight years Du Bois would become Washington's chief opponent with a competing project of racial uplift, black leadership, and, intimately connected with them, black masculinity. During the eight years dividing the Atlanta Compromise and the review of *Up from Slavery* in *The Dial*, Du Bois devoted himself to sociological research and the struggle against segregation. An episode that is acknowledged to be central to the development of his militant vision of emancipation is the case of Sam Hose's lynching and the lack of a fair trial for which Du Bois had campaigned.[58] Finally, he joined a group of more radical black intellectuals, including Trotter, who rejected Washington's accommodationist politics. Thus, at the point of the publication of *The Souls of Black Folk* (1903), Du Bois's persona and rhetoric are in open opposition to Washington. It is interpreted by Houston Baker as a *phaneric mask* – meant to advertise and distinguish rather than securely conceal, like Washington's approach.[59] This difference in both his personal auto-creation and political construction of the collective black subject notably influences the project of black masculinity that Du Bois advances.

The significance of Du Bois's persona and writings is hard to overestimate. In a eulogy by Cornel West, Du Bois is described as "the towering black scholar of the twentieth century." "The scope of his interests, the depth of his insights, and the sheer majesty of his prolific writings," writes West, "bespeak a level of genius unequaled among modern black intellectuals."[60] This assessment reflects the most important aspects of this black Renaissance man's prominence. First of all, West emphasizes the variety of Du Bois's writings, ranging from sociological research, political propaganda, and literary criticism to poetry and fiction. This versatility is matched by the wide extent of intellectual and political projects he was engaged in, including the civil rights struggle and an interest in Ethiopianism, African cultures, Pan-Africanism, as well as American nationalism. The significance of Du Bois's genius and prolific output are further intensified by the almost one-hundred-year span of his life during which he could remember the last days of Radical Reconstruction, the days of the New Negro Renaissance, the Depression, World War II, as well as the 1960s Civil Rights Movement.

Such a multitude of writings demands that this analysis be selective and restricted to the relevant period. The examination will primarily focus on the writings engaged in the debate with Washington and those directly influencing the New Negro Renaissance period. The selected works include Du Bois's most influential anthologies – the seminal text *The Souls of Black Folk* (1903) and *Darkwater: Voices From Within the Veil* (1920) published on the eve of the Renaissance. Apart from these volumes, my analysis will be supported with references to a number of sociological studies written between 1896 and 1910 and articles published in *The Crisis* between 1910 and 1929. There are many continuities in the texts; however, there is also a visible change in Du Bois's perspective in the span of over twenty years outlined above. The most relevant difference is a shift from the embrace of the American creed in *The Souls of Black Folk* to a more Afro-centric perspective and an open critique of Western civilization in "The Souls of White Folk" from *Darkwater*.

Du Bois's project for black masculinity is much more openly asserted and central to his vision of racial uplift than it is in the case of Washington. Yet, even though Du Bois's writings are intended for a Northern rather than Southern audience, they are entangled in a parallel network of concepts, including civilization, nation, citizenship, and segregation. My discussion will firstly focus on the persistent preoccupation with the problem of manhood in his rhetoric. This concern with masculinity leads to an inevitable exclusion of female subjects from the body politic of black leaders and citizens. Apart from the exclusion of women, I will also identify other thematic strategies of constructing the black subject as masculine. Finally, I will read Du Bois's texts as advancing a particular masculinist tradition and ideology of assertive yet intellectually endowed black masculinity.

As Hazel V. Carby argues in her analysis of black manhood in *Race Men*, Du Bois completely failed to "imagine black women as intellectuals and race leaders."[61] The community that he imaginatively brings into being as the symbolic *talented tenth* is gender-specific and constructed in masculine terms only. Carby's thesis can be supported with the very terms used to refer to the black community. In order to show the prominence of masculinist rhetoric in Du Bois's writings, his construction of the black subject will be contrasted with the one in Washington's text. Washington, when referring to his community, predominantly uses the term "people" – it appears 342 times in the text. The term "men" is used less than half as often – only 143 times. In order to make the comparison more representative, the analysis examines the two texts written by Du Bois in the span of twenty years – *The Souls of Black Folk* and *Darkwater*. In both publications, the black subject is almost exclusively referred to by the phrase "black men" – the term "men" is used 210 times in *The Souls of Black Folk* and 249 times in *Darkwater*.[62] The ratio of "men" to "people" is reverse in comparison to Washington's text; the term "people" is used only 109 times in *The Souls of Black Folk* and 132 times in *Darkwater*. Thus, the black community as constructed in Du Bois's texts is imagined to consist of "men" rather than "people." Significantly, this is visible even in the texts that advocate women's suffrage, such as "The Ruling of Men" in *Darkwater*.

At the turn of the century, according to Webster's *The New International Dictionary of the English Language* (1913), the terms "men" and "people" were parallel in their meaning of human beings. "Man" is defined as "a human being; opposed to beast," "the human race, mankind," whereas "people" is defined as "the body of persons who compose a community," "human beings as distinguished from animals." The key difference is that the second meaning of "man" denoted an "adult male person," whereas "people" denotatively was a gender-neutral term. Apart from this gender difference, there used to be a class distinction between the two terms. It is only indicated in the turn-of-the-century dictionary, where the third definition of "people" is "the mass of community as distinguished from a special class," but in *The American Dictionary of the English Language* (1863), the second definition of the entry "people" is "the vulgar; the mass of illiterate persons" and the third is "the commonalty, as distinct from men of rank." These residual mid-nineteenth-century meanings could have influenced Du Bois's lexical choice. Thus his marked preference for the term "men" can be read as both implying masculine gender and detaching the black subject from the lower classes. Class identification with "men of rank" rather than "low down folk" parallels the elitism of the talented tenth notion.

Du Bois's masculinist rhetoric is visible not only in the sheer statistics of use. As Stuart Hall argues, referring to Roland Barthes, when analyzing discourse, one needs to take into account also the connotative field of reference, since it is the primary domain through which ideology enters a language.[63] An analysis of the connotative fields of the terms "people" and "men" in *The Souls of Black Folk* reveals striking differences. In the language of *The Souls*, "people" are accompanied by connotations such as "poverty and ignorance," "ruder souls," "lowly," "voluntarily surrender," "weaker," "untaught," "backward," "defenseless," "patent weaknesses and shortcomings," "undeveloped," "stolen and oppressed," "slavery and servitude."[64] These connotations visibly reflect the residual meaning of the "people" as the "illiterate mass." The other uses are either neutral or with the use of positive connotations such as "honest-hearted," "generous," or "decent."[65] At the same time, the term "men" occurs in the vicinity of "able-bodied," "toiling, sweating," "cursing," "angry silence," "thoughtful," "marvelous hindsight," "striv[ing] to know," "angry and revengeful," "eager striving," "successful," "exceptional," "thinking," "of the sturdier make," "armed," "honorable," "reputable," or "swarthy."[66] Such divergence in the connotative fields of the two concepts, which were semantically equivalent at the time, points to their different positioning in Du Bois's vision of race. The term "people" signifies oppression of the black race and its disadvantaged social position, whereas "men" calls into being a masculine-gendered powerful group, whose destiny is the struggle for the emancipation and empowerment of black people. This duality of passive "people" and active "men" enables Du Bois to identify with the black community and the discrimination suffered by its subaltern strata and, at the same time, to reinvent himself as a free, active leader.

The polarization between black leadership and the masses is revoked in Du Bois's seminal essay "The Talented Tenth" (1903). Although the wording of the title concept seems to be gender neutral, it is constructed in masculinist terms from the very beginning of the text. The essay opens with the following prophesy: "The Negro race, like all races, is going to be saved by its *exceptional men*."[67] Subsequently, the exceptional race "men" are contrasted with "people," who are "common," "ignorant," and "unskilled." "Negro people need social leadership more than most groups," and the leading position is embodied by the talented tenth modeled on the black "men [who] strove to uplift their people," "the masses of the Negro people." The connotative field of "men" includes: "brave," "intelligent," "college-bred," "educated," and "gifted." The contrast between "people" and the elite is even starker and more explicit than in *The Souls* – it juxtaposes the ignorant masses and the "exceptional" and "distinguished" men, whose task is "to civilize and elevate their less fortunate fellows."[68] This dynamic is also manifest in Du Bois's later references to his classical concept: "I believed in the higher education of a Talented Tenth who through their knowledge of modern culture could guide the American Negro *into a higher civilization*."[69]

These quotes indicate that, like Washington, Du Bois appropriates the rhetoric of civilization and the dynamic of the white man's burden. Here, however, the place of the "primitive" racial other is occupied by the lower classes. Moreover, whereas Washington's process of civilizing and education primarily consists in hygiene training in the feminine realm of domesticity, Du Bois asserts the significance of masculinity in a gendered vision of human development. He proposes that "the object of all true education is not to make men carpenters, it is to make carpenters men" and asserts that "men we shall have only as we make manhood the object of the work of the schools."[70] Thus, even though Du Bois uses the same dynamic of the authority legitimized by the civilizing mission that is appropriated by Washington, Du Bois's position is much more masculinist elitist, and rooted in class rather than race difference.

In order to compensate for the elitism of the masculinist talented tenth and to avoid complete estrangement from the lower strata, Du Bois, in his autobiographical writings, highlights his ties with the black masses. At the opening of The Souls, he represents himself as "bone of the bone and flesh of the flesh of them that live within the Veil," which positions him as a representative of "black folk" in biological terms.[71] Du Bois, predicting the possible critique of his persona as detached from the Southern reality of the Negro, devotes a chapter to record his personal experiences in Tennessee. In order to find a job there, young Du Bois walks miles in "the burning July sun" until he finally finds a job in a "log hut" school with a desk made of three boards.[72] In Darkwater, the strategy of constructing himself as a legitimate descendant of the oppressed group is visible when he evokes the figure of his maternal, hence undoubtedly blood related, great grandmother, singing a Bantu song for him.[73] Through such claims, Du Bois emphasizes his biological, hereditary, and personal belonging to the disadvantaged black community. By mediating between the two positions – the leader and the subaltern – he tries to solve the perennial predicament of being a privileged representative of an underprivileged group.

Du Bois's compulsive preoccupation with black masculinity is also manifest in his use of the expression "manhood" instead of "civil rights" or "citizenship." "Manhood" is even more inextricably linked to the male gender than "men." Whereas the term "men" was ambiguous and was used just as frequently to denote mankind as male human beings, the primary meaning of "manhood" at the time was "the state of being a man...as distinguished from a child or a woman" (The New International Dictionary of the English Language, 1913). At the turn of the century, the term "manhood suffrage" was used to denote only the "suffrage of all male citizens" (The New International Dictionary of the English Language, 1913). Yet in the political discourse of the day, the term "civil rights" was predominant, which is manifest for instance in the names of two acts intended to reinforce the emancipation of freed black people, the Civil Rights Act of 1866, which extended the rights of emancipated slaves, and the Civil Rights Act of 1871, which illegalized early Ku Klux Klan activity. Against the dominant political lexicon and despite his support for women's franchise, Du Bois repeatedly expresses his outrage at "the denial of manhood rights" – rather than gender-neutral "civil rights" – to black people. In "Of the Ruling of Men," he claims that were it not for their disfranchisement, "black men in the South would have their...manhood rights recognized."[74] Similarly, in "The Negro Race in the United States," the ideal path to liberation would be "to give the Negroes the power of self-protection by insisting on their full manhood suffrage." In response to Washington's accommodationist policy, he claims that "the systematic denial of manhood rights to black men in America is the crying disgrace of the century." "Manhood rights," in Du Bois's texts, most literally signify civil rights, as they are sometimes explicated as franchise and self-protection. More significantly, in phrases such as "the worst foes of Negro manhood," "manhood" on its own is used to mean civil rights or citizenship in general. In an article criticizing a speech made by President Harding, he makes a claim that "no system of social uplift which begins by denying the manhood of a man can end by giving him a free ballot, a real education, and a just wage." In an open letter to the newly elected President Wilson, Du Bois's first demand is: "We want to be treated as men."[75] The metonymical transfer of meaning from manhood/civil rights to "manhood" univocally identifies the cause of black citizenship with the right to assert black masculinity.

Du Bois's excessive preoccupation with masculinity reveals his deep sense of anxiety over the condition of black manhood. Apart from the frequency with which he mentions this issue, his anxiety is visible in Du Bois's use of the term "real man," a hegemonic concept which always contains an exclusionary logic and depends on the groups excommunicated from it. Du Bois uses it to challenge his opponents. In "Of Booker T. Washington and Others," he argues that "those black men, *if they are really men*, are called...to oppose such a course."[76] He depicts the head of Tuskegee as a "submissive," "surrendering," and "silent" person who lacks "true manhood" and whose policy "is bound to sap the manhood of any race." Washington's persona is constructed against a patrilineal tradition of great black leaders who are "terrible," "fierce," "revolting," "revenging," "intellectual," and "self-assertive." Douglass emerges as "the greatest of Negro leaders," yet, unlike in Washington's account, he does not accept segregation but unflinchingly advocates struggle for "the manhood rights of the Negro by himself."[77] Thus, Du Bois undermines Washington's claims to Douglass's heritage and paints a picture of citizenship deeply invested in militant masculinity. The anxiety of authorship and the need to form black male lineage coexist with the anxiety of influence manifest in Du Bois's challenge to a strong predecessor in the person of Washington. He asserts his own masculine agency by rhetorically emasculating the head of Tuskegee.

Du Bois urges his male readers to become "real men" – that is, to assert their courage, pride, and self-confidence as signifiers of their gender identity. The sense of threat to black manhood can be read as a strategic construction, which is supposed to mobilize black people to more active engagement in emancipation. This is a potentially productive strategy, since, as David Gilmore claims, a need to validate one's masculinity is an inherent feature of most ideologies of masculine identity.[78] More specifically, Du Bois's persistent preoccupation with black manhood reflects the hegemonic "crisis" of masculinity at the turn of the century. He chooses a dominant, assertive, and modern, ideology of manhood rather than the secure Victorian manliness espoused by Washington, yet it comes with the price of the anxieties that define it. At the time, modern hegemonic masculinity was threatened by the first wave of women's movement and by new waves of non-Anglo-Saxon immigration, which challenged white man's dominance in the public sphere, hitherto protected by the separate spheres divide and class stratification. As Bederman argues, "turn-of-the-century middle-class men seem to have been unusually interested in – even obsessed with manhood."[79] Thus Du Bois's insecurity regarding political privilege mirrors contemporaneous hegemonic anxieties and the sense of "crisis," which was a crucial phenomenon of the day. That his compulsive preoccupation with manhood appears to exceed white anxieties stems from the unequal Jim Crow conditions in which white men exercised their civil rights in contrast to post-Reconstruction black men, whose franchise was curtailed with legislation.

Du Bois's claim to dominant masculinity is further complicated because American hegemonic ideologies of manhood at the time were constructed not just in opposition to women and new immigrants but also to black men, whose emancipation threatened white men's political privilege. Thus black manhood in Du Bois's vision is endangered not only due to the denial of voting rights, but also because he is conscious that the ideology he espouses is built on the exclusion of black males. The tense and innate discrepancy between being black and being a man is revealed in the passage introducing Du Bois's grandfather, who "held his head high, took no insults, made few friends. He was not a 'Negro'; he was a man!" A parallel image recurs in another mention of Dr. James Du Bois, when he "had to fight hard to be a man and not a lackey."[80] The fact that blackness is at odds with manhood is revealed also in Du Bois's reference to the stereotype of "old-time Negro" who "stood for the earlier religious age of submission and humility. With all his laziness and lack of many elements of true manhood."[81] The clash between being black and being a man parallels Du Bois's concept of "two warring ideals in one dark body," one of the most often cited definitions of double-consciousness. However, if racial double-consciousness can be read as potentially empowering, in the case of masculine identity Du Bois univocally strives to reconcile blackness and manhood. If "dogged strength alone keeps [the dark body] from being torn asunder" by double-consciousness, such "dogged strength" rhetorically serves to prove that the black subject is a "real man." Analogous to his conceptualization of double-consciousness, Du Bois's attempts to bridge the gap between black race and hegemonic manhood are also manifest in his espousals of the American tradition. He erects an interracial patrilineal heritage which obligates black males to "strive for *the rights which the world accords to* men, clinging unwaveringly to those great words which *the sons of the Fathers* would fain forget [Declaration of Independence]."[82]

Despite the dilemmas of class elitism, racial authenticity, and deep anxiety over the condition of black men, Du Bois advances his vision of black leadership in masculinized terms, with reference to a patriarchal lineage of black and white revolutionaries. The masculinization of race leadership is Du Bois's chief strategy of empowerment. A fragment from his 1912 resolutions published in *The Crisis* will serve as the final example of his assertion of masculinity:

> I am resolved in this New Year to play the man – to stand straight, look the world squarely in the eye, and walk to my work with no shuffle or slouch. I am resolved to be satisfied with no treatment which ignores my manhood and my right to be counted as one among men.[83]

These opening sentences of the editorial reveal a performative effort entailed in the process of becoming a man. Male identity is not essential and natural here but it is rather "played" by assertion of self-confidence and self-respect, which can be read as illuminating Du Bois's strategic appropriations of hegemonic masculinity and the logic of the white man's burden. "Manhood" and "being a man" both precede "absolute equality of the Negro race" and are the path to this equality. These two causes – manhood rights and racial equality – are inseparable in Du Bois's texts. As the opening epigraph of this chapter states: "Whether at last the Negro will gain full recognition as a man...is the present Negro problem of America."[84]

The Function of Women and Femininity

Apart from the masculinization of the elite destined to uplift the black race, Du Bois's rhetoric also simply excludes women from the community of black citizens. Du Bois uses the collective subject "we" with reference to black people; however, it is in some cases followed by "our" or "your" women. This phrasing denies black women the subject position indicated by "we." Such use of possessive pronouns can be found in the most important texts, including "The Niagara Movement Statement" (1906), where Du Bois states as the primary objective: "freedom, manhood, the *honor of your wives, chastity of your daughters*." Thus, the honorable and chaste women are excluded from "the divine brotherhood of all men, white and black."[85] In this text, Du Bois also evokes a line of race activists, who include white men such as John Brown and Robert Gould Shaw next to Douglass and Turner. Such inclusion further emphasizes the reinforcement of masculine "divine brotherhood," from which Sojourner Truth is missing. This exclusion can be largely accounted for by Du Bois's embrace of Victorian white gender ideals. In "The Conservation of Races" (1897), the Negro people are resolved to strive "for the development of *strong manhood* and *pure womanhood*."[86] Over twenty years later, in *Darkwater*, the denial of the universal franchise beats back "the love of women and strength of men."[87] Thus, for Du Bois, model men are strong, whereas women are loving and pure.

Preoccupation with the purity of women recurs in a number of Du Bois's writings, including *The Souls* and *Darkwater*, as well as his sociological and political essays. Whereas for Washington, women's purity is endangered by liberal education, according to Du Bois this problem is inextricably linked to the sexual violence persisting since slavery. Du Bois focuses on white male violence against black women, a theme that is carefully erased from Washington's account.[88] In *The Souls*, "the burden" on the back of the black man is:

> The red stain of bastardy, which two centuries of systematic defilement of Negro women had stamped upon his race, meant not only the loss of ancient African chastity, but also the hereditary weight of a mass of corruption from white adulterers, threatening almost the obliteration of the Negro home.[89]

In this passage the subject bearing the burden of his race is the black man, frustrated, as Carby claims, because he "could not control sexual reproduction of black women."[90] The sexual violence against black women is represented as a black men's problem and a menace to the black family rather than an assault against black females. This anxiety over female purity is voiced in a number of other texts. In his sociological essay "The Negro Race in the United States" (1901), Du Bois writes about the early days of slavery: "Family life was impossible, there being few women imported, and sexual promiscuity and concubinage ensued."[91] Here, promiscuity is linked to the scarcity of women. The non-normative sexual relations and lack of control over black female sexuality constitute a threat to black emancipation, the black family, and black manhood.

This outrage at the historical "defilement" is mirrored in Du Bois's sociological analyses and political essays concerning the contemporary situation of the black family and black women. In "The Conservation of Races," Du Bois calls on black men to "*guard the purity of black women* and to reduce *the vast army of black prostitutes* that is marching today to hell."[92] In "The Problem of Amusement" (1897), he criticizes the black community for "allowing our daughters, unattended and unwatched, to be escorted at night, through great cities or country districts by chance acquaintances."[93] He draws attention to the dangers of city life, which are due to "an abnormal excess of women" in Philadelphia and New York.[94] The larger than expected number of single women:

> leads to two evils – illicit sexual intercourse and restricted influence of family life. When among any people a low inherited standard of sexual morals is co-incident with an economic situation tending to prevent early marriage and to

promote abnormal migrations to the irresponsibility and temptations of city life, then the inevitable result is prostitution and illegitimacy.[95]

Thus, both the scarcity of women and their "abnormal excess" are held responsible for immorality and illegitimacy standing in the way of the black men's path to respectable manhood. In the above fragment, just as in numerous other passages, Du Bois constructs the city as the source of temptations and dangers. At the same time, it is linked with the excess of women, which metonymically makes the women a significant part of the city temptations.

The "defilement" and anxiety over the purity of black womanhood is interestingly intertwined with the issue of slavery. As I have indicated, the oppressed subject position is depicted by Du Bois with the gender-neutral "people" rather than "men." Accordingly, slavery is symbolized in The Souls by a disloyal and immoral mammy-like figure. In a disturbing image, a mother-like figure with an "awful black face" "had aforetime quailed at that masters command, had bent in love over the cradles of his sons and daughters...and at his behest had laid herself low to his lust."[96] Carby claims that such representation "compromises the black man's masculinity because it does not recognize his control over her sexual being."[97] This depiction of slavery relations enables Du Bois not only to place the blame for black lack of masculine power on women but also to represent slavery in feminine terms. Black men are free from the stigma of "quailing at the master's command" as it is projected onto the defiled black femininity.

In an essay dedicated to the cause of women's – and, in particular, black women's – emancipation, "The Damnation of Women" (1920), Du Bois at first pays tribute to brave black women in the past and then gives the floor to his sociological voice to discuss the contemporary situation of women. He states that instead of getting married, black women are "called to the city," where they "fight for their daily bread like men; independent and approaching economic freedom." Yet their economic success does not seem to contribute to the racial uplift. On the contrary, "the family group..., which is the ideal of culture with which these folk have been born, is not based on the idea of an economically independent working mother." This situation inevitably results in "broken families" and "cheap women," who outnumber the men in the cities.[98]

In this peculiar analysis, on the one hand, Du Bois seems to admit that the American family with the cult of true womanhood is not a universal ideal and that the new economic freedom for women cannot be abolished. Yet he cannot entertain a vision in which this economic privilege of black women is compatible with racial uplift. Black women in this passage are not only immoral "cheap women," they also threaten the masculinity of black males by "fighting...like men," having "sturdier minds," and by the sheer fact of outnumbering them. In the essay, he represents the situation in which black women are "strong, fertile, muscled, and able to work," and yet he eulogizes the black women who are "sweetly feminine, ...unswervingly loyal,...desperately earnest, and...instinctively pure in body and in soul."[99] Thus, even though Du Bois appreciates the achievement of racial heroines such as Harriet Tubman and Sojourner Truth, in his vision of uplift, the black woman should conform to the respectable Victorian femininity. Tubman and Truth represent "strong, primitive types of Negro womanhood," whereas contemporary black women should be rather "sweetly feminine" and "pure."[100] Although he claims that their combination "has deep meaning," racial emancipation and women's suffrage are not compatible for Du Bois. He argues that the liberation of women is the greatest cause, but the political priority is ascribed to the problem of the color line and peace. Thus, despite Du Bois's support for women's suffrage, black independent women not only do not fit his vision of racial progress but are castrating figures that challenge black masculine empowerment.

This construction of fatal femininity is pointed out also by Carby in her reading of Du Bois's "The Wings of Atlanta," where Atlanta stands for gold lust. According to Carby, "a greed for gold becomes entwined with a narrative of sexual lust, a mark that stains the city."[101] Thus, femininity, temptation, sexual impurity, and the city are powerfully interconnected in Du Bois's writings. This conflation is also characteristic of hegemonic nineteenth-century discourses. Kimmel claims that the projection of sexual temptation on the figure of the urban woman was a way to deal with the sense of crisis in hegemonic masculinity partly stemming from the rearrangements in gender relations caused by urbanization and industrialization.[102] Even though Du Bois unreservedly supported black migration to the North as a necessary step to black emancipation, his representations of the city reveal anxieties possibly resulting from economic hardships and unemployment connected with the process of mass urbanization. Du Bois's text resolves urban anxieties by projecting the danger posited by city life as sexual rather than economic. This urban menace constitutes a challenge to black respectability and is signified either by uncontrolled black female sexuality, "the vast masses of prostitutes marching to hell," or sexual assaults on black womanhood, which requires the protection of militant black manhood. These sentiments parallel Washington's logic according to which liberal education in the Northern city made "the girls [go] to the bad."

Gender and family relations are the main focus of Du Bois's sociological essays. In these peculiar texts, he analyzes different strata of the black community both as a detached observer who impersonally explains crime with the lack of employment opportunities and as an engaged representative who pronounces ethical judgments on black morality. His assessment of the black community, coming from the study "The Negroes of Dougherty County, Georgia" (1902), parallels the nineteenth-century vision of civilizational hierarchy rather than a typical economically-based class stratification:

In the first grade I put people who correspond to the ordinary middle class of people in New England – good honest people who are getting along well, who are thrifty and thoroughly honest and without any trace of any immorality of any sort. In the second grade were those who were getting on well but usually did not own their homes but were at the same time honest and upright people. In the third grade I put the mass of laborers – all the laborers that had no criminal tendencies and were not distinctly lewd. Of course, there were some I put in that grade who as to morality would not pass in New England, but they were not bad people and lewdness was not conspicuous. There were some of those I put in the third class, those that were cohabiting without marriage ceremony but cohabitation was practically permanent. In the fourth class I put all the rest; that is the lowest grade of the loafers and...those that live in all sorts of loose relationships.[103]

This lengthy quotation reveals several significant features of Du Bois's sociological and political thought. First of all, even though at times he acknowledges that Anglo-Saxon civilization standards are not universal, he assumes here the New England middle class as the measuring rod of social status. Secondly, the upper class of the black community seems to correspond to the Anglo-Saxon middle class, which positions black people as being backward in relation to American society as a whole. Yet the most interesting aspect of Du Bois's hierarchy is a peculiar combination of income and morality that determines a place in his stratification. In his vision of racial uplift, not only should the black community succeed economically, but it is equally important that it follows the ideals of middle-class respectability, primarily concerning sexual conduct. Characteristically, the standards of morality are almost exclusively defined by sexual relations rather than any other social activity. The lowest classes are characterized by "cohabitation" and "loose relationships," which, as is visible in his other analyses, lead to one of the greatest problems of the black community – illegitimacy. In turn, this social sin, in Du Bois's writings, is connected with the defilement and impurity of black femininity. Ross, in his analysis of The Philadelphia Negro (1899), comes to parallel conclusions and claims that "Du Bois bases class on a scale of moral worthiness and social conformity that links ever-lower rank with ever-increasing deviance" and "focuses on 'sexual looseness' as the core of the 'Negro problem' and the 'monogamic ideal' as its solution."[104] Thus Du Bois rewrites the economic category of class into a notion determined by sexuality and gender relations.

The above-quoted stratification advocates white middle-class ideals as a path to the social uplift of black people. This assumption can also be induced from a later study, "The Negro American Family" (1909), in which several families are described and assessed. In the family depicted as the most successful, "the father is the head, and what he says is the law," while "the mother stays at home, cooks, and looks after the children." The family with the lowest income, which is represented in predominantly negative terms, consists of a single mother, an illiter-ate and unclean washerwoman, and her two daughters.[105] This juxtaposition, along with the above-cited representations of black femininity, reveals Du Bois's commitment to the middle-class ideology of respectability. As George L. Mosse convincingly claims, the roots of modern citizenship are inextricably linked to the formation of normative masculinity and the exclusion of non-normative sexual behaviors and ethnic otherness.[106] Du Bois, in his quest for the recognition of black citizenship and nationality, echoes the links between masculinity, citizen-ship, and respectability that were formed in the eighteenth century.

The images of black women in Du Bois's writing reveal a deep anxiety over strong black womanhood, which is associated with the residual myth of the mammy, haunting the American imagination of the day. He does not attempt to take advantage of the strength represented by this ideological concept in his vi-sion of racial emancipation and perceives it solely as an inheritance of slavery days and a path to broken families in the contemporary society. On the contrary, he avoids images of strong women and frequently projects racial oppression, im-morality, and sexual non-normativity on black females. Not only the text of The Souls of Black Folk but also a gender analysis of his sociological writings and Dark-water exemplify Carby's thesis that Du Bois excludes women from the black avant-garde that is meant to lead the race.

Rewriting the Lynch Ideology

Du Bois's anxiety over strong black womanhood is complexly interconnected with his concern with black manhood and the problem of the cultural and literal emas-culation of black men in post-Reconstruction America. The threat of emascula-tion inherent in the myth of the black rapist was an issue that no black emancipa-tory discourse was able to avoid. As I argued in the first part of this chapter, Washington reacts to the lynch ideology by outlining a vision of black civilized manliness that is devoid of violence in general and sexual aggression towards the white womanhood in particular. He entirely erases violent conflict from his pas-toral vision. Du Bois's rendering of this problem is quite different; not only does he not avoid the issue of lynching, but he foregrounds it. Both in The Souls and in Darkwater, he rewrites the hegemonic lynch scenario so that it empowers the black man and positions the white man as the sexual aggressor.

The scene of lynching culminates the triad of chapters in The Souls that are most relevant to Du Bois's representation of black manhood in the text: "Of the Passing of the First-Born," "Of Alexander Crummel," and "Of the Coming of John." Du Bois counters here the myth of the black rapist by positioning an educated young man as the target of the lynch mob. The threat of lynching is evoked early in the chapter, when black John, having completed his education in the North, comes back home and is instructed by a white judge in the essence of the lynch law logic:

> In this country the Negro must remain subordinate, and can never expect to be the equal of white men. In their place, your people can be honest and respectful...But when they want to reverse nature, and rule white men, and marry white women, and sit in my parlor, then, by God! We'll hold them under if we have to lynch every Nigger in the land.[107]

Here, in the words of the judge, Du Bois represents the gist of late-nineteenth-century white supremacy: it is based on the irreversible laws of nature and combines the residual Reconstruction ideology of black domination with the post-Reconstruction ideology of the black rapist. In the last sentence we see a sudden change in the judge, from a benevolent white patriarch into a lynch mob leader, which undermines the myth that only the lowest classes of Southern society were responsible for lynch crimes. The ending of the chapter proves that the policy of being "honest and respectful," which is strongly reminiscent of Washington's emancipatory strategy, is not enough to avoid lynching. Du Bois rearranges the lynching triangle of the black rapist, the pure white woman, and the honorable white avenger. In "The Coming of John," a pure black woman is assaulted by an idle rich white man and protected by her brother, who seizes "fallen limb" and strikes "him with all the pent up hatred of his great black arm." In a stark contrast to Washington's black men, who hold no bitterness, here, the black man is full of hatred and masculine physical prowess signified by his "great black arm." Since the white man dies, it is not long before John can hear the thundering gallop of horsemen led by the judge, "whose eyes flash with fury" and who probably holds "the coiling twisted rope."[108] It remains unclear whether John dies as a victim of the lynch mob or jumps off the cliff to the sea, but death as the ending is inevitable. John's death is the price paid for the dignity of black manhood. Just as in Du Bois's sociological essays, racial emancipation and the honor of black manhood depend on the control of black women's sexuality. The hegemonic lynch triangle is rewritten into the paradigm of the pure black woman, the white rapist, and the black protector.

Whereas The Souls and the early sociological texts reveal Du Bois's embrace of American civilization and politics, in Darkwater, he shifts toward a relativist position and challenges the primacy of white American civilization. Moreover, he approaches the oppressors systemically and points out parallels in the discourses of American racism and imperialism. This is most clearly visible when Du Bois criticizes a powerful myth of civilization rhetoric – the white man's burden. Despite the shift in his politics, Du Bois's rewriting of this concept closely resembles the above-discussed triangle from The Souls. In one of the Darkwater poems, "The Riddle of the Sphinx," black womanhood signifies the conquered darker races and continents. The darker race is not able to advance because:

> the burden of white men bore her back and the white world
> stifled her sighs.
> The white world's vermin and filth:
> All the dirt of London,
> All the scum of New York;
> Valiant spoilers of women
> And conquerors of unarmed men;
> Shameless breeders of bastards,
> Drunk with the greed of gold,
> Baiting their blood-stained hooks
> With cant for the souls of the simple;
> Bearing the white man's burden
> Of liquor and lust and lies![109]

The white man's burden ideology is deconstructed here into a graphic image of rape. The symbolic figure of the dark woman as Africa and the oppressed black race is raped by a white man, whose burden presses her back to the ground. Bederman argues that the burdened white man combined both racial and gender domination. Du Bois's image also explicitly exploits the gender specificity of this figure and represents imperial domination in terms of male sexual violence. White men are "spoilers of women" and "breeders of bastards." The white world, in the poem, is incapable of civilizing any "lower" races, as it stands for "vermin and filth," "dirt," "scum," "liquor and lust and lies." Rather than representing the measuring rod of morality, as is suggested in Du Bois's sociological writings, here white civilization is criminalized and characterized by non-normative sexuality. The poem ends with a prophecy of the coming of the black Christ and a masculinized image of the black race. At the moment of racial awakening "shall our burden be manhood" – the challenge to imperial domination is combined with the assertion of masculinity in contrast to the conquered and raped femininity.[110] "The Riddle of the Sphinx" repeats the scenario of "The Coming of John," with the white rapist, the black woman in need of protection, and the black avenger, here to be born as the Christ figure. The image of violated black womanhood also parallels the disturbing figure of the enslaved mammy from *The Souls*. Black race under white imperial or American supremacy is represented in terms of violated femininity, whereas racial uplift and liberation depend on the formation of strong militant black masculinity.

Thus in his writings, Du Bois rewrites the concept of the white man's burden in two ways. It is echoed in the mission of "exceptional men" to "civilize and elevate" the ignorant masses, where it accepts the gender implications of male dominance and appropriates it to provide the masculinist elite of the talented tenth with an opportunity to assert their authority over the passive people. On the other hand, the original imperial narrative is explicitly deconstructed in terms of sexual violation in "The Riddle of the Sphinx." The white patriarch becomes the rapist, which undermines the concept of civilized and benevolent white male patronage.

The fact that Du Bois refutes the charges of black sexual aggression by focusing on the threat to the purity of black womanhood can be interestingly interpreted in the light of arguments advanced by the historian Jacquelyn Hall, who claims that the white lynch logic was aimed to discipline not only the black community but also white women, who at the time were becoming actively involved in the suffrage movement. The myth of the black brute and the threat of rape functioned as "a fantasy of aggression against the boundary-transgressing women."[111] Hall's insights can be productively applied to Du Bois's deconstruction of the lynch ideology into the image of the white rapist. If interpreted according to Hall's argumentation, this strategy serves not only to refute the charges of uncontrolled black sexuality but also to discipline black womanhood, which is positioned as endangered and in need of manly protection. Such a representation of women encourages their passivity and dependence on black men, whose role in turn is constructed in terms of militant yet noble manhood.

Black Christ and His Mother

A significant complement to Du Bois's rewritings of the lynch ideology and exclusion of black women can be found in his figure of the revenging Christ, which serves as a unifying motif for the diverse texts collected in Darkwater.[112] As "The Riddle of the Sphinx" illustrates, the noble black avenger is intimately related to Christ imagery, whereas the victimized black woman is structurally positioned as his mother. Du Bois uses the religious and spiritual significance of the Holy Family in order to challenge the myth of black brutality, ennoble the specters of illegitimacy, and empower black masculinity.

The symbol of the suffering Christ had been a popular theme in the representation of the plight of black people. The most influential example comes from Harriet Beecher Stowe's Uncle Tom's Cabin (1852), where the title character submissively accepts his suffering, which symbolizes the salvation of the black race. This symbolism, although appreciated by the contemporary black leaders, including even militant Frederick Douglass, has been frequently criticized for its passive submission ideology, most notably by James Baldwin in "Everybody's Protest Novel" (1949). Yet Du Bois, already 50 years before Baldwin, rejected the ideology of Uncle Tom's Cabin as the source of fatalistic faith that results either in "dumb suffering" or its opposite – moral laxity.[113] In "The Religion of the American Negro" (1900), he argues that Christian doctrines of passive submission constituted useful propaganda for the slave masters. The suffering in this world offered a promise of otherworldly redemption. In the light of this critical assessment of Christian doctrines in black history, Du Bois's use of the black Christ needs to be read as conscious of its nineteenth-century connotations and constructed in opposition to them.

Eric Sundquist claims that in the early twentieth century, the figure of a submissive Christ was substituted by the figure of a militant and resisting black Christ. "Lynching, poverty, and discrimination were his crucifixion, and resistance, not docility, was the message of his new parables."[114] According to Sundquist, the figure of Christ as constructed in Du Bois's works was both pioneering and radical. It forged a link to the African church and, simultaneously, was a key influence on Negro Renaissance incarnations of this figure. The *Darkwater* Christ accurately exemplifies the new incarnation of this symbolic figure. In "Jesus Christ in Texas" and in "The Prayers of God," he is crucified by white people and crucifixion is represented as lynching. Although Sundquist's study does not primarily focus on gender dimensions, the black Christ is read as a reaction to the tradition of white supremacist "manly Christianity" epitomized by white Southerners such as Robert E. Lee and Jefferson Davis. Sundquist furthermore argues that "the Black Christ was therefore a figure born of the African American tradition of resistance latent in black religious orthodoxy, and now reborn…as an assertion of black masculinity and the castrating threat of the lynch mob." The days of "feminine" submission were succeeded by "masculine" resistance.[115] Sundquist's allusion to manly Christianity can be elaborated with yet another cultural reference. The post-Reconstruction decades (the 1880s to the 1920s), on which this chapter is focused, are analyzed by Clifford Putney as the time when American religiosity was being remade into muscular Christianity. One of the elements of this shift was a renewed representation of Jesus as a "man's man" about whom "there was nothing mushy, nothing sweetly effeminate." Arguments that his apprenticeship in carpentry inevitably lent him a muscular physique reinvented Jesus Christ as a superman figure.[116] Echoes of muscular Christianity endow Du Bois's representations of the black Christ with even more assertive masculine potential.

Another gender insight made by Sundquist refers to the figure of the mother of the black Christ represented for example by the black woman raped by a white colonizer and avenged by the black Christ figure in "The Riddle of the Sphinx." So far I have discussed this image as a deconstruction of the white lynch triangle. Sundquist interprets this construct as an ingenious intersection of race and sexuality, in which the lynched black man emerges as a redeeming Christ, while the black woman raped by the white man becomes his mother. This powerful image directly links Christ's revolutionary avenging attitude to his illegitimacy.[117] Sundquist claims that this scenario renders the black woman pure and inviolate. Yet this reading is not thoroughly convincing due to the strong resemblance between the crucifixion scenario in *Darkwater* and the gender pattern represented in *The*

Souls, in which the woman stands for the slave past, sexual oppression, and the "defilement" of the black race. Thus, Christ's mother figure does not have the kind of resistance potential that is located in the masculine Christ. She remains a passive victim, and thus she may even be interpreted as the counterpart of the earlier embodiment of the "feminine" submissive Christ personas.

The exclusion of the black woman from *Darkwater*'s messianic vision is clearly visible in the final element of the text, "The Comet." In this short story, a black man, interpreted by Sundquist as the embodiment of the black Christ, and a white woman assume that they are the only people left on earth after a comet disaster. They are "primal woman, mighty mother of all men to come and Bride of Life," and "Son of God and great All-Father of the race to be."[118] This prophecy turns out to be an illusion, as other white survivors quickly change the black man's status back to that of the "nigger." Yet the story positions black masculinity as the hope for humanity liberated from the stigma of race, whereas the black woman does not even appear in the narrative. Having given birth to the Christ figure, she is erased from the episodic plot of *Darkwater*. Consequently, not only does the black Christ serve to assert militant black masculinity, but the focus on the redemption as revenge excludes black women from Du Bois's prophetic vision. The dichotomy of the black Messiah and his mother echoes the polarization of black subject positions inherent in the earlier discussed contrasts between "men" and "people," the talented tenth and the masses, or "manhood rights" and feminized images of oppression.

Another significant function of the Christ imagery is that it strategically ennobles the vengeance and violence by thematizing it in terms of redemption and salvation. The construction of racial resistance with allusions to the figure of Christ legitimizes the militant position and refutes the possible accusations of bestial and barbaric aggression. The *Darkwater* narrative does not subscribe to the doctrine of passive submission which clearly would contradict Du Bois's concept of black manhood; however, it represents black resistance in spiritual and religious terms, which prevents this stance from being identified with the stereotypical aggressive black brute.

Intellectual Militancy

Another thematic leitmotif relevant for Du Bois's assertion of black masculinity is to be found in his profuse celebrations of black soldiers and use of military images. Analogous to the noble Christ avenger figure, Du Bois's war tropes engage in an inescapable dialogue with the dominant mythology. They challenge the ideology of black barbarity on the one hand, and celebrate militant masculinity on the other. Among the large body of texts devoted to black military effort, *The Crisis* editorial "Returning Soldiers" (1919) is one of the most noteworthy. The significance of this text for the New Negro Renaissance is manifested by the fact that in *The Portable Harlem Renaissance Reader* (1994) it is used as the opening text of the movement. In a highly explicit way, Du Bois pays tribute to the courage of black soldiers, who "fought to the last drop of blood," and announces a new attitude of black men who "stand again to look America squarely in the face and call a spade a spade." He overtly names America's vices of lynching, disfranchisement, theft, and insult, and declares war on American democracy: "we are cowards and jackasses if now that the war is over, we do not marshal every ounce of our *brain and brawn* to fight a sterner, longer, more unbending battle against the forces of hell in our own land. We return. We return from fighting. We return fighting."[119] He constructs a sense of community and identification with the black soldiers by the use of "we." The rhetoric of the text is deeply charged with masculinist imagery of phrases such as "stern," "unbending battle," and repudiation of the unmanly "jackasses and cowards." The phrase "battle against the forces of hell" evokes the militant Christ imagery to be developed in *Darkwater*. The black collective subject in the text is Negro and American at the same time. It unites intellectuals such as Du Bois with common soldiers. Yet this community is not all-inclusive; due to the masculine-gendered imagery, it excludes women from the participation in this battle of "Soldiers of Democracy." There is one more important element in the rhetoric of this text. The above-quoted fragment, where "brain" complements "brawn," is emblematic of Du Bois's balancing between militant assertion and intellectual polemic. In his depictions of black leadership, he walks a tightrope between nobility and belligerence.

That such a search for the precarious balance between the intellectual and the combatant is at the center of Du Bois's vision is manifest also in his much later speech, "The Negro College" (1932), whose rhetoric closely resembles the one from "Returning Soldiers." After advocating education based on black experience in America as an answer to the oppression of African American people, Du Bois ends by thematizing black education in terms of militancy and struggle. He represents the race problem in radical images: "America proposed the *murder* of this group, its moral descent into *imbecility and crime* and its utter loss of *manhood, self-assertion, courage*." The words here echo his concerns expressed in sociological studies. However, here it is white society that threatens the Negro with criminalization leading to physical annihilation. He refers to the famous line by Claude McKay, "if we must die, let it not be like hogs," to inspire a reaction against the emasculation of the black community. Yet, in his militant vision, black people "conquer the world by thought and brain and plan" rather than like "snarling dogs." Black industry and, foremost, black artistic expression constitute core elements of the struggle and are opposed to "fear and cowardice."[120] In this way, Du Bois manages to construct a strong militant counter-hegemonic stand, yet the battle is supposed to take place primarily on the level of political and artistic discourse. He thereby avoids the animal barbarism of "snarling dogs" and envisions the black struggle as simultaneously black civilizational progress. Such a strategy to assert a militant attitude and avoid associations with barbarity is frequently used in black emancipatory discourses. It is discussed in Chapter 3 in the example of Locke's aesthetic writings, which employ a plethora of militant imagery, and in Chapter 6 in Wright's essays depicting black literature as a deadly weapon.

The representation of black struggle as civilized and noble is accompanied by Du Bois's claims about the uncivilized behavior of white society. This strategy is manifest in his lyrical deconstruction of the white man's burden in "The Riddle of the Sphinx." In order to challenge white America's right to the status of civilization, he also refers to the earlier-mentioned pre-modern character of lynching spectacles. He claims that:

> You have created here, in the United States, which today pretends to the moral leadership of the world, a situation where on the last night of the old year you can slowly and publicly burn a human being alive for amusement of Americans,...in the great place, Mississippi, which has done so much for the civilization of the world.[121]

This quote argues that the "barbaric" elements of lynching – its public character and torture as an amusement – clash with "the moral leadership" and "civilization." The paradox exposed here is analogous to Wiegman's claim about the combination of pre-modern and modern disciplinary regimes in lynch culture. Du Bois highlights the uncivilized public violence of the lynch mob to challenge the myth of noble white patronage and to justify black militancy.

Du Bois's militant black manhood is constructed in opposition to white barbarity and black spinelessness. In the light of his earlier attacks against Washington, black "fear and cowardice" can metonymically be read as targeted at the head of Tuskegee and his embracement of non-aggressive manliness. Yet not all of Du Bois's texts that use military imagery and praise militancy directly challenge Washington's assertion of masculinity. Since their debate ends with Washington's death and Du Bois's eulogy of him, in the last words of their dialogue, the editor of *The Crisis* depicts the author of *Up from Slavery* as "a great figure" and "the greatest Negro leader since Frederick Douglass." In the text, Du Bois expresses a balanced opinion of Washington's contributions and mistakes. He admits that Washington is the most distinguished man, "white or black who has come out of the South since the Civil War," which seems to attribute his failures to the Southern context. Significantly, among his services to the race, Du Bois lists "compelling of the white South to at least think of the Negro as a possible man." A reference to black manhood appears also at the end of the obituary, which closes with a military call for the black community to "close ranks and march steadily on" and "never to swerve from their great goal: "the right to stand as men among men throughout the world."[122] On his death, Washington is strategically used as a figure contributing to the emergence of black militant manhood and positioned as another illustrious predecessor in the patrilineal black history.

Conclusion

My analysis has aimed to demonstrate that Washington and Du Bois proposed competing projects for black liberation not only with regard to the generally acknowledged points of contention, such as slavery, segregation, citizenship, and education, but also with regard to the construction of black manhood. Both leaders were entangled in parallel racial and gender ideologies; however, a number of divergences in their discourses stem from different geo-sociological contexts. Washington strived to become a powerful speaker for the black community and to gain the support of the white South for his project. This necessarily limited his vision, as it could not threaten the dominant position of white men in the public sphere. He chose to invest his persona in Victorian manliness, Genteel Patriarchy, and the Protestant work ethic. In this way, he challenged the myth of black violence and uncontrolled sexuality inherent in the powerful stereotype of the lynching ideology. This strategy proved to be successful with the white community. Yet, in the long run, it was not a wholly satisfactory project for black manhood, since Victorian manliness was already in decline at the time and was being replaced by a more assertive hegemonic mythology of modern masculinity. The ideals of manly self-control, self-sacrifice, and restraint were suitable for the mid-nineteenth-century white men, whose privilege was not yet challenged by any significant changes or other groups aspiring to power. At the end of the nineteenth century, the position of white men was contested by new immigrants, women, and black freedmen, and the hegemonic ideology of manhood accordingly changed into the ideal of more aggressive and virile masculinity. Washington's choice of a reactionary, conservative, and residual rather than dominant ideology for a group that tried to challenge the status quo and gain privilege was not a successful tactic in the long run. Yet it is important to stress that even in such an appeasing project, there is space for a challenge to the lynch ideology and a tactical expression of sexual appeal of Washington's autobiographical persona. In *Up from Slavery*, the representation of self-controlled black manhood rewrites the black brute into a civilized protector of female chastity. In addition, this civilized position enables the black man to assume the "burden" of uplifting the less advanced Indians, which further enhances his status of masculine authority. Washington's vision of noble black manliness is interrupted by the subversive image of his persona as a virile object of sexual desire legitimized by quotes from white male journalists.

Du Bois addressed his texts to a different audience – black and white Northerners. This enabled a more explicit preoccupation with the construction of black masculinity, which is persistently expressed in his outrage at the denial of black manhood. Du Bois's vision is linked to the emergent ideology of a more assertive masculinity rather than to stoical manliness. Thus, he outlines the concept of the *talented tenth* comprising "exceptional men," which is contrasted with the passive, subordinate, discriminated, subaltern "people." Yet he is conscious of the myth of the black brute, which haunts black masculinity at the time, and he carefully balances his militant masculinity with intellectual effort and spiritual engagement.

Despite their differences, both visions are invested in the ideals of middle-class respectability, which is manifest in Du Bois's family models represented in his sociological writings and in Washington's preoccupation with decency and hygiene. The notion of respectability is inextricably linked to the exclusion of non-normative sexual behaviors, which in both visions primarily manifests itself as anxiety over the control of black female sexuality. According to Washington, the moral purity of black womanhood can be endangered by the policy advocated by his opponent – accessible liberal education and urban migration. Du Bois expresses his anxiety much more abundantly, and the threats to black feminine purity are more varied. Both disproportionally small and large numbers of black women in relation to black men constitute a menace to black female respectability. In his rewritings of the lynch ideology, black womanhood is primarily endangered by the white rapist. Du Bois strategically positions black women as passive and vulnerable or uses them to represent oppression and violation in order to contrast these positions with noble black avengers or black citizens with manhood rights. In both cases, they serve as foils that enable him to assert black masculinity. Thus, even if Du Bois's project of an open assertion of black civil rights seems to be more effective in challenging the status quo, as far as the status of black women is concerned, it remains conservative. The fact that his preoccupation with the gender issue is more persistent makes his reactionary position even more intense than Washington's.

The two leaders competed for the leadership of the black community on the eve of the New Negro Renaissance. Many of the issues that they addressed, such as migration, urbanization, disenfranchisement, or physical violence, continued to be determining social forces for the next generation. The New Negro movement was also entangled in an analogous network of race ideologies including the lynch logic and the rhetoric of civilization. Additionally, the polarization of the two approaches to race uplift, which emerged in the Washington-Du Bois debate, was profoundly echoed in Renaissance discourse. The next chapter will investigate how the issues of race, gender, and sexuality were approached by another leader and a figure competing with Du Bois for the position of spokesperson for the black community and the midwife of the New Negro Renaissance movement – Alain Locke.

Part 1

Alain Locke and the New Negro

Chapter 2
Midwifery and Camaraderie: Alain Locke's Tropes of Gender and Sexuality

Youth speaks, and the voice of the New Negro is heard.[1]
Alain Locke, "Negro Youth Speaks"

I see myself as a...philosophical midwife to a generation of younger Negro poets.[2]
Alain Locke

He wanders about seeking beauty that he may beget offspring...when he finds a fair and noble and well-nurtured soul,...he tries to educate him...and they are married by a far nearer tie and have a closer friendship than those who beget mortal children, for the children who are their common offspring are fairer and more immortal.[3]
Plato, "The Symposium"

I wish more race men were as concerned with younger fellows.[4]
Countee Cullen to Alain Locke

"Alain Locke was best known for his espousal and *fathering* of the 'New Negro Movement,'" as Eugene C. Holmes puts it in his tribute to the famous Howard professor.[5] Since not only Holmes but also other prominent historians of the era perpetuate the image of Locke as a *parental* figure, his relation to the Negro Renaissance encourages an examination that focuses on gender and sexuality in his rhetoric. A strong tendency to conceptualize the patronage politics of the movement as a procreative filial relationship and more particularly midwifery is pointed out by Ross, who claims that "a crucial figure of blood filiation emerges in the debate over who 'midwifed' the renaissance, with Carl Van Vechten, Alain Locke, Charles S. Johnson, James Weldon Johnson, Walter White, and Jessie Fauset (the lone female) vying for this honor in the scholarship."[6] Although Ross admits that it is Locke who rhetorically manages to assume the midwife position most successfully, his analysis focuses mostly on the pathological relation between "the black male as midwife and the white woman as godmother of black renaissance talent."[7] My reading of Locke's self-fashioning also explores his pro-creative tropes, and it unreservedly supports Ross's claim about the significance of sexual politics and non-normative sexualities in the rhetoric of the New Negro Renaissance. Yet, since my main focus is Locke's textual representations of his relations with black artists rather than with white patrons, my conclusions are less pessimistic than Ross's claim that the respectable filial images of white patronage suppress its emasculating effect on black beneficiaries and the anxiety that it is "an intensely eroticized affair" which prostitutes black talent.[8]

The ideology of masculinity in Locke's writings is briefly analyzed by Summers, who states that "Locke employed masculinist language in order to claim a racialized manliness within the context of hegemonic, white, middle-class manhood that was defined through, and performed in, the marketplace." Summers argues that the 1920s was the time when black manhood was reinvented and Victorian manliness defined by production was superseded by modern masculinity characterized by virility and consumption.[9] Such a reading is convincing if one focuses on the dichotomies of production versus consumption and the respectable suppression of sexuality into the private sphere versus sexualized masculinity, yet it is not able to explain the differences that I pointed out in the previous chapter between Washington's respectable gentility and Du Bois's respectable militancy. Therefore I will use Kimmel's concept of Marketplace Manhood, defined by a need to prove one's manhood in the sphere of economic competition and production, to discuss both Du Bois's and Locke's constructions of respectable black manhood, and I reserve Victorian manliness to refer to Washington's black gentleman. Moreover, even though the logic of production is decidedly manifest in Locke's writings, the construction of black masculinity emerging from his texts goes beyond Marketplace Manhood, which, for instance, does not explain the implicit but central presence of alternative sexualities in Locke's rhetoric.

But before moving on to non-normative sexualities in Locke's writing, I will examine the gender implications of two central concepts in the discourse of the movement – "the New Negro" and "the Renaissance." Locke fashions the movement as a regeneration and rebirth of black culture, which is inextricably related to his persistent celebration of youth as the source of cultural vitality. He thematizes black *cultural production* as *spiritual reproduction* ensuing from social and textual relations of male artists. Significantly, Locke's tropes of male intimacy are closely related to European homoerotic discourses of the day. I will argue that a particularly interesting intertextual connection arises from the reading of Locke's New Negro rhetoric and his correspondence with younger artists in the light of the German youth movement with which he was familiar due to his four-year-long stay in, and many later visits to, Berlin. This reading of Locke's texts will reveal a specific vision of male artistic bonding, which celebrates the relation between the older mentor and the younger protégé and is legitimized by a number of intertextual references. Locke's tributes to other strong authors transcend the anxiety of influence that underlies Du Bois's writing and his strategy to assert black masculinity. Locke's intertextual bonding with past artistic giants and present prodigies resolves his anxiety of authorship and is a strategy to legitimize his status as a cultural producer. I will claim that it is also intimately bound to tropes of same-sexuality.

This chapter will examine the rhetoric of both Locke's published writings and private letters to other artists of the period. The correspondence selected for this analysis intricately overlaps with the public discourse since, being addressed to other artists, it discusses the same cultural productions and events of the period that are the subject matter of Locke's magazine articles. In the letters, Locke fashions himself in relation to the other artists in a parallel way to the one found in his published texts. Moreover, in some letters there are indications that Locke censored the mail he archived and considered it possible that it would be read by the public. For example, Countee Cullen and Claude McKay suggest that Locke should destroy selected pieces of correspondence from them, since "sentiments expressed [in them] would be misconstrued by others."[10] Also, as early as 1941, the New Negro Renaissance was beginning to be officially archived with the establishment of the James Weldon Johnson collection at Yale University, and the process included collecting private correspondence. Carl Van Vechten, the founder of the collection, asked Locke among others to contribute to the project; consequently, the editor of The New Negro was conscious that his letters might become public in the future.[11] Not only public but also private sources can therefore be interpreted as texts in which Locke consciously constructs his public persona and develops his project of the black renaissance. The structural and thematic parallels between these two kinds of sources are highly significant, since personal correspondence illuminates the sexual and gendered dimension of the New Negro.

The Old New Negroes

There are few more influential constructions of the black subject than the concept of the New Negro advanced by Locke to depict the generation that came of age after World War I. All traditional literary histories of the Negro Renaissance contributed to positioning The New Negro (1925) as "the biblical text" of the Renaissance, to use Arnold Rampersad's phrasing.[12] Yet even if Locke's publications in the Harlem number of the Survey Graphic and the anthology following it constitute its most prominent reincarnation, the trope of the New Negro was not without its history.[13] According to Henry Louis Gates, a tendency to forge a renewed identity has been an omnipresent element of black history – "blacks seem to have felt the need to attempt to 'reconstruct' their image to whites probably since that dreadful day in 1619 when the first boatload of us disembarked in Virginia."[14] Consequently, Locke's essays necessarily resonate with the echoes of past "New Negroes."

The first influential use of the term dates back to a publication compiled by Booker T. Washington, Fannie Barrier Williams, and N. B. Wood: *A New Negro for a New Century* (1900). This text was not a relevant part of the debate discussed in the previous chapter because it is not solely Washington's publication, it does not refer to Du Bois, and it is not alluded to in the latter's writing. The representations of assertive but cultured black manhood in this collective race album position it closely to Du Bois's project of the masculinist talented tenth. In contrast to Washington's autobiography and his position in the debate with Du Bois, this enterprise emphasizes the militant dimension of black history – seven out of eighteen chapters are devoted to black involvement in American wars, with the primary focus on the Spanish-American War. In the introduction, J. E. MacBrady states that the book constitutes "an authentic statement of the *thrilling experiences and daring acts of the brave black men*, both regulars and volunteers, who *faced the perilous exploits of war with indomitable courage.*" The book fulfills this promise as it repeatedly underlines the courage and patriotism of black men.[15] Moreover, it constructs a patrilineal history in a chapter tellingly entitled "Fathers to the Race." Interestingly, the fathers include Frederick Douglass, Touissant L'Ouverture, as well as Phillis Wheatley and Sojourner Truth. Thus the book performs an ambiguous gesture – it acknowledges the central role of black women in the struggle for equality, yet simultaneously masculinizes Truth and Wheatley by referring to them as "fathers." This cross-dressing reveals the anxiety of black male authorship striving to form a legitimate patrilineal heritage to counter the illegitimacy haunting black filial relations and the recurrent absence of the legitimate black father.

The chapter on African American regulars in Cuba contains a fragment that seems to be especially interesting from the perspective of masculinity studies, since it makes a reference to Theodore Roosevelt's Rough Riders. According to Bederman, Roosevelt's persona was emblematic of the attempts at redefining American masculinity that took place at the turn of the twentieth century. Bederman argues that "Theodore Roosevelt, more than any man of his generation, embodied virile manhood for the American public."[16] In the light of this statement, it seems significant that the author engages in a polite dispute with Roosevelt's account of the performance of black soldiers. As Ross claims, "the anthologists of *A New Negro* need to point out Roosevelt's lies without antagonizing the war hero about to become president or damaging their larger campaign of presenting the Negro as a force for national unity and global progress."[17] The author of the chapter cites a longish speech delivered by the future president during his election campaign for the office of governor of New York, in which Roosevelt praises black soldiers as "brave men, worthy of respect" and emphasizes a sense of interracial comradeship "fighting side by side...under fire."[18] This speech is con-

trasted with Roosevelt's later account of the Rough Riders story, which undermines the courage of black soldiers. The chapter concludes with a testimony of
Sergeant Presley Holliday, a black soldier fighting with Roosevelt, who corrects
and explains the unfavorable statements written by Roosevelt. In this way, Washington's New Negro simultaneously receives confirmation of his masculine
bravery from the contemporaneous symbol of militant yet civilized white masculinity but also is assertive enough to confront and contradict Roosevelt's later narrative.

Apart from the inclusion of black women as "fathers to the race" mentioned
earlier, the involvement of Williams in the publication resulted in a considerable
space devoted to black female activists in her article "Club Movement among Colored Women." As Gates claims, Williams "places the black woman at the center
of the New Negro's philosophy of self-respect."[19] The influence and political significance of the Club Movement activity can be further illuminated with a quote
from Walter White's *Fire in the Flint*, in which the main character's sweetheart,
Jane Phillips, makes a link between black women's social activity and resistance
to racial oppression:

> Like all women, coloured women, she realized that most of the spirit of revolt
> against the wrongs inflicted on her race had been born in the breasts of co-
> loured women. She knew, and in that knowledge was content, that most of the
> work of churches and societies and other organizations which had done so
> much towards welding the Negro into a racial unit had been done by wo-
> men.[20]

White's female character depicts the social activity of black women as the main
source of "the spirit of revolt," and thus emphasizes its political and militant
character. This gives additional political impact to the leaders of the Club Movement presented in *A New Negro for a New Century*. Black female activists are depicted by Williams as self-assertive and endowed with agency. She claims that
"the woman thus portrayed is the *real new woman* in American life" and argues
that the progress achieved by black women is as great "as if a century elapsed
since the day of emancipation."[21] This phrasing is significant, as it closely parallels Locke's statement about the 1920s New Negro's "hurdl[ing] several generations of experience at a leap."[22] Williams provides the link between the New Negro and the New Woman, whose pronounced absence in Locke's discourse will
be discussed later in the chapter.

Thus, *A New Negro for a New Century* emerges as an interesting predecessor to
Locke's New Negro, especially in the light of its gender implications. Conceived in
parallel post-war circumstances, it positions the New Negro as a brave patriot
who is proud of the past progress and looks hopefully into the future. The considerable space provided for the discussion of black womanhood balances the

masculinist discourse of the first part of the book and includes black women under the umbrella of the New Negro.

Gates convincingly argues, however, that the most immediate influence on the 1925 incarnation of the New Negro can be ascribed to the post-war militant socialist articles published mainly in The Messenger, The Crusader, The Kansas City Call, and The Chicago Whip, where the "New Negro was a militant, card-carrying, gun-toting socialist who refused to turn the other cheek."[23] The strength of this link is conspicuous in the light of the fact that Claude McKay, one of the central figures of the movement's beginnings, was strongly connected with the socialist press, being the editor of The Liberator. One of the poems recognized as an inspiration for the Negro Renaissance – McKay's "If We Must Die" (first published in The Liberator in 1919) – can be interpreted as a poetic rendering of the attitudes ascribed to the New Negro and his reaction to post-war violence in general and the Red Summer of 1919 in particular. Barbara Foley and William J. Maxwell provide evidence that the link between radical left-wing politics and the New Negro goes beyond the figure of McKay, and it has not been given enough scholarly attention. They trace Marxist philosophy and politics in the writings of both the forgotten and the most eminent members of the New Negro Renaissance. Foley argues that in the way the term "Red Summer" is used in academic discourse, there is a "continual slippage between radical and black"; the label conflates the Red Scare and post-war violence against black people.[24]

Consequently, both in the light of Washington's publication as well as the post-war leftist sentiments, Locke's New Negro resonates with the past meanings of the concept signifying militancy and defiance. These intertextual reminiscences are not univocal. On the one hand, one cannot neglect Gate's observation that "Locke's New Negro...transformed the militancy associated with the trope and translated it into the romantic, apolitical movement of the arts."[25] Analogously, Foley agrees that, despite the residual presence of radical politics in the movement, "the New Negro class struggle warrior of 1919 reemerge[d] as the culture hero of the Harlem Renaissance."[26] On the other hand, one can argue that by choosing a trope loaded with militancy to name and announce his concept of the black subject and, at the same time, by translating it into the sphere of "apolitical" cultural productions, Locke militantly politicizes the arts as an alternative field of struggle for emancipation. This rhetorical strategy will be explored in detail in Chapter 3.

The Old Negro and the New

Distancing himself from the vision of harmonious continual progress of black people portrayed in A New Negro for a New Century, Locke constructs the New Negro primarily through a confrontation with the Old. The rhetoric used to build the dichotomy between the New and the Old is gender-marked; masculine and feminine connotations are repeatedly used to depreciate the Old and empower the New Negro. According to the texts from his anthology, the Old Negro was a myth created by "innocent sentimentalism, partly in deliberate reactionism" and perpetuated by black people as "protective social mimicry." Locke illustrates this construction with a list of stereotypes which include "'aunties,' 'uncles' and 'mammies,'" "Uncle Tom and Sambo," and "'Colonel' and 'George.'" The emergence of the New Negro is conditioned by "the repudiation of social dependence, and then the gradual recovery from hyper-sensitiveness and 'touchy' nerves, the repudiation of the double standard of judgment with its special philanthropic allowances"; the rejection of the position of "a social ward or minor" and "supine and humiliating submission."[27] In all these fragments, the fundamental principle underlying the shift from the Old to the New Negro is the change from passive submission to dynamic agency. "Protective social mimicry" is the antithesis of the active attitude, as it denies self-expression and creative power. The list of pervading stereotypes consists only of types submissive to the dominant white culture. For example, the text is silent about the black rapist, the stereotype embodying the opposite of submission and standing for threatening black action, whose ideological significance was explored in the previous chapter. By this significant omission, Locke further polarizes the difference between the passive Old and the assertive New Negro. This thematic polarization is also visible at the level of grammar. The structure of sentences reflects the passivity of the Old Negro, who is described as the object in the passive voice syntax; he is "a something to be argued about, condemned or defended, to be 'kept down,' or 'in his place,' or 'helped up,' to be worried with or worried over, harassed or patronized, a social bogey or a social burden."[28] Significantly, the features of the Old persona that Locke rejects are its "hyper-sensitiveness" and "'touchy' nerves," bringing to mind gender associations with neurasthenic womanhood of the turn of the century. Further gender meanings are produced by the exorcising of the Old Negro's dependencies, "charity," "help," "patronage," "philanthropy," "patronization," and "condescension." The link between charity and femininity stems from the fact that philanthropist activities were mainly organized by (white) women's organizations in the nineteenth century. Their influence, visible predominantly in teaching, is depicted by Du Bois in The Souls of Black Folk as "the crusade of the New England school ma'am."[29] Thus the Old Negro, representing also the past model of race relations, which Locke argues is no longer valid, emerges as a passive, dependent, and nervously feminine persona, who in addition needs (white female) charity.

As the effeminate figure haunting the past of the black community leaves the stage, Locke, in a performative speech act, calls for the energetic New Negro to enter. The fact that Locke polarizes the two figures significantly differs from Washington's vision of the New Negro as a step in the gradual process of race progress. Simultaneously, this dramatic gap between the old and the new reinforces the concept of the Renaissance as an unprecedented and revolutionary rebirth of black culture. In order to empower and legitimize the New Negro as the emerging black subject, Locke underlines its American character with allusions to American pluralism and stresses its modernity through his focus on rapid urbanization and migration. As I will show, the rhetoric conflating Americanness, modernity, and the urban context reinforces the masculinist character of Locke's black subject.

Locke emphasizes the all-American character of the New Negro in a number of ways.[30] Foley argues that this attempt to represent African Americans as "the pure products of America" was strengthened in the shift from the "Survey Graphic Harlem Number" to The New Negro, which is manifest in the omission of the Orientalist Mecca metaphor from the latter publication.[31] Foley's claim can also be supported with the fact that an analogous exclusion affects the comparison of "a railroad and a suitcase" to "a Baghdad carpet," which Locke used in his "Harlem" text in the Survey Graphic.[32] This Americanization is visible not only in the tropes but also in the politics and philosophy of The New Negro. Significant influences on Locke's writing are to be found in the contemporaneous attempts to redefine American culture, represented for example by the avant-garde group of Young America, who claimed in 1916 that "we are living in the first days of a renascent period." The parallels between this rhetorical gesture to remake American nationality and the remaking of black identity are intimately linked to the impact of cultural pluralism on Locke's philosophy. Locke's project for the collective black identity is indebted to Horace Kallen's non-assimilationist vision of a multicultural orchestra and Randolph Bourne's transnational diasporic America.[33] Thus in the final version of Locke's anthology, the emergence of the New Negro is determined by the very forces that shape contemporaneous American society.

Apart from these tropes, allusions, and potential inspirations, Locke explicitly states that the most prominent factor that serves to nationalize black people is rapid urbanization. Whereas in "The Survey Graphic Harlem Number" urbanization is discussed in an essay devoted to Harlem and not in "Enter the New Negro," a year later Locke decides that the two issues – the emergence of the New Negro and migration – are too closely interrelated to keep them separate. His emphatic representation of the difference between the country and the city transcends the sociological rendering of urbanization; the two polarized concepts stand respectively for the medieval and the modern, the regional and the national, the subaltern and the emancipated. "In the very process of being transplanted, the Negro is becoming transformed."[34] The actual migration to the Northern city seems to transform the Old Negro into the New. Significantly, Locke emphasizes that social push and pull factors are not of the utmost relevance:

The tide of Negro migration, northward and city-ward, is not to be fully explained as a blind flood started by the demands of war industry coupled with the shutting off of foreign migration, or by the pressure of poor crops coupled with increased social terrorism in certain sections of the South and South-west...The wash and rush of this human tide on the beach line of the northern city centers is to be explained primarily in terms of a new vision of opportunity, of social and economic freedom of a spirit to seize."[35]

Instead of social determinism, self-determination is identified as the main force behind the Great Migration, which parallels Locke's insistence on the activity and self-reliance of the New Negro. Black mobility is not "a blind flood" put into motion by social "pressures" and economic "demands" but is connoted with "freedom" and "a new vision of opportunity." Apart from the core American ideal of self-reliance, these concepts and the very insistence on mobility suggest that Manifest Destiny is another national myth appropriated by Locke. His celebration of urbanization is in stark contrast to Washington's strategy of uplift, which advocated the status quo of rural existence as advantageous for the black community. Locke's position here is closer to Du Bois's acknowledgement of migration as a necessary step to emancipation. There is, however, a significant difference. Du Bois's representations of rapid urbanization were not as hopeful as Locke's, primarily due to the former's apprehension concerning the purity of black womanhood. Locke does not focus on black female subjects in his text and thus avoids such anxieties, representing urbanization in unequivocally positive terms.

This is not the only gender implication of Locke's project. As was manifest in fragments analyzed earlier, the contrast between the Old and the New Negro is strongly gendered. The significance of urbanization for Locke can also be analyzed from a gender perspective. According to scholars, the industrial revolution, urbanization, and the rise of the capitalist workplace were decisive in the emergence of the separate sphere ideology.[36] The separate spheres dramatized the difference between feminine and masculine gender ideologies, which were segregated into separate realms – the private and the public. This divide was the target of many nineteenth-century women's reform movements, including the black women's Club Movement. The separate spheres were also central to the ideology of productive manliness to which Locke subscribed, according to Summers. Thus, the factor that is perceived by Locke to be the major emancipatory force historically is largely responsible for the exclusion of women from the public realms of economy and citizenship.

The masculinization of the New Negro is also manifest in its grammatical singular form. Locke's choice of the singular form stems from strategic pragmatism rather than substantial reasons, since Locke repeatedly emphasizes the pluralist character of the black community.[37] Conscious that the black community was becoming increasingly diversified and that the essential black subject was a social fiction, Locke pragmatically constructs the New Negro in the singular form to consolidate race consciousness and facilitate group identification. This gesture is repeated in his later publications, predominantly in the influential bronze booklets, which include for example *Negro in America* (1933), *Negro and His Music* (1936), or *Negro in Art: a Pictorial Record of the Negro Artist and of the Negro Theme in Art* (1940). The singular form has particular gendered implications – the New Negro is referred to only in the masculine form of the inclusive "he." This grammatical masculinization is even more conspicuous when it is contrasted with the only time Locke uses a feminine pronoun in "The New Negro" – "*she* is the home of the Negro's 'Zionism,'" where "she" refers to Harlem.[38] Since the single use of "she" is to denote "the home" of the New Negro, it can be argued that Locke perpetuates the paradigm of the masculine agency and the feminized space, which has been assessed by many scholars as instrumental in excluding women from American history and literature.[39]

The gendering of the New Negro is also visible in the metaphors used in the texts listed above, which represent him primarily as the cultural producer. For example, in a fragment from *Negro in Art*, Locke claims that "the Negro artist won world-wide recognition, won *his freedom in the world* of art or, so to speak, his *artistic spurs. After proving his prowess* and right to be an artist in the fullest sense of the word, he was next to start to *conquer a province* of his own."[40] The use of lexical items such as "proving his prowess" or "winning spurs" constructs the black artist in masculinist terms, which will be elaborated on in the following chapter. The allusions to the conquest of provinces and the winning of freedom position the New Negro within the tradition of the American Western expansion, a determining force shaping American masculine identity.[41] Locke's allusion to Manifest Destiny and the cowboy myth has been mentioned in relation to his account of black migrants as looking to freedom and opportunity. This link is explicitly articulated in the statement from "Harlem" that the Great Migration "can be compared only with the pushing back of the western frontier in the first half of the last century."[42] Black migrants are envisioned as manly pioneers conquering the city jungles of the North, and the only "she" in "The New Negro" is the feminized space of Harlem.

The excessive use of the masculine pronoun and masculinist metaphors in the depiction of the black subject are not the only ways in which the New Negro is masculinized. As Cheryl A. Wall claims in the introduction to *Women of the Harlem Renaissance*, "with its imagery drawn from industry, technology and war,...the essay takes on a masculinist cast."[43] When Locke depicts the diversification of the Harlem community, it is restricted to professions associated primarily with men:

> It has attracted the African, the West Indian, the Negro American; has brought together the Negro of the North and the Negro of the South; the man from the city and the man from the town and village; the peasant, the student, the business man, the professional man, artist, poet, musician, adventurer and worker, preacher and criminal, exploiter and social outcast.[44]

Not only is the word "man" repeated four times in the space of one sentence, but some professions mentioned, such as preacher, are restricted to men. Furthermore, Locke's text does not refer to nurses, domestics, and teachers, which are the professions identified as dominated by black women by Elise Johnson McDougald in her essay published in The New Negro. The absence of the female element seems even more conspicuous given that this excerpt is intended to celebrate the diversification of the black community.

McDougald's "The Task of Negro Womanhood" represents the space devoted to the women's issue within The New Negro. The article analyzes the social situation of black women in the North. Nevertheless, unlike Williams's text, it does not include the Negro woman in the concept of the New Negro. This exclusion is clearly visible when McDougald writes about the significance of the task of black women teachers, whose "inspiration is the belief that the hope of the race is in the New Negro student...[and] what he is determined to make of himself tomorrow." An analogous paradigm underlies the celebration of black women as "the mothers of the race." Even though McDougald acknowledges sex inequality, she claims that "the Negro woman's feminist efforts are directed chiefly toward the realization of the equality of the races, the sex struggle assuming the subordinate place."[45] Thus, although in comparison to black men, black women as represented in her text are better educated and their economic independence is growing faster, they are not positioned as the hope of the race and are not interpellated as New Negroes.

The New Negro and the New Woman

Characteristically, McDougald, unlike Williams, does not refer to the concept of the New Woman. Accordingly, this figure is missing from the whole anthology and Locke's vision of the New Negro.[46] This absence seems to be a persistent and tactical omission, since Locke emphasizes numerous other parallel social phenomena such as "a New World," "a New America," "the New South," "New Ireland," "the New Czechoslovakia," and "the New Poland."[47] The exclusion of the New Woman is even more striking when one realizes that the battle for black and female suffrage was fought concurrently and frequently by the same leaders – Frederick Douglass, William Lloyd Garrison, and Sojourner Truth, to mention just a few. The link between the two projects is acknowledged in A New Negro for a New Century and in Du Bois's articles on women's suffrage. It is also explicitly established in McKay's Soviet publication "The Negroes in America," where he argues that "the Negro question is inseparably connected with the question of woman's liberation."[48] The common past and shared experience of the two emancipatory struggles is recognized by Charles S. Johnson, Locke's rival to the status of the Renaissance midwife. In 1923, in Opportunity, the magazine with which Locke most intensely collaborated at the time, Johnson states that "it is more than a historical accident that Negro suffrage and woman suffrage were proposed and fought at the same time. And there is a most uncanny similarity between the charges made against the mentality of women and those made against the mentality of Negroes."[49] In the light of these references, Locke's silence can be read as a deliberate erasure of the reference to the New Woman.

This overall absence seems to be even more striking since there are many inherent analogies between the New Negro and New Woman that are at least as significant as the ones that Locke deliberately constructs with reference to the awakenings in Europe and in America. The history of the two terms runs in salient parallels. Both terms originated in the 1890s. Even though accounts of the exact year of origin differ, most scholars studying the concepts coincidentally agree on 1895 as the year that both "the New Woman" and "the New Negro" were coined.[50] As Gates claims, one of the hallmarks of the first New Negroes were their "education, refinement, and money," which strongly parallels the traits of the late-nineteenth-century New Women, whose "most salient characteristic – and...first self-conscious demand" was "education."[51] In addition, both concepts allude to the millennial hope for a better future. As Michelle Elizabeth Tusan claims, the concept of the New Woman was invented by the feminist press in the 1890s to signify "the political woman of the coming century," which neatly parallels the origins of the concept of the New Negro which date back to Booker T. Washington's anthology, A New Negro for a New Century.[52] Also, as I have mentioned, the New Negro was reinvented after the war as a militant fighter, which parallels claims about the significant influences of military imagery on the postwar reincarnation of the New Woman as a flapper with bobbed hair reminiscent of a combat helmet.

The reasons for Locke's silencing of the New Woman can be partly deduced from the public image of this figure at the time. A key feature that was ascribed to the post-war New Woman was her sexual liberation. According to Carroll Smith-Rosenberg, "for these later New Women, sexual autonomy...meant the right to sexual experimentation and self-expression."[53] This generally acknowledged characteristic of the 1920s New Woman is elaborated by Kevin J. Mumford in his Interzones: Black/White Sex Districts in Chicago and New York in Early Twentieth Century (1997). In a chapter meaningfully entitled "New Fallen Women," Mumford argues that the stylistics of the New Woman was profoundly shaped by the image of the prostitute. More particularly, he argues that one of the stylistic symbols of the 1920s New Woman – bobbed hair – is an appropriation of the image present in the houses of prostitution in Harlem and on the South Side of Chicago.[54] Thus it is possible that Locke omits the New Woman as a referent for the New Negro not only to reinforce the masculinization of the trope but also not to tint it with transgressive sexuality represented by the New Woman's free sexual expression and her debt to the stylistics of (black) prostitution. Such a reading enforces the theory of Locke's commitment to respectable middle-class manhood and confirms Summers's thesis about the significance of this masculine ideology in his texts. I discussed the concerns with the purity of black womanhood in the first chapter as a significant element in the Washington-Du Bois debate. The fact that the emerging black middle class in the 1920s was also deeply concerned with the control of black women's sexuality is discussed in the article "Policing the Black Woman's Body in an Urban Context" by Hazel V. Carby. Carby convincingly argues that uncontrolled black female sexuality was perceived as "a threat to the progress of the race; as a threat to the establishment of a respectable urban black middle class; as a threat to congenial black and white middle-class relations; and as a threat to the formation of black masculinity in an urban environment."[55] Consequently, Locke's silencing of the New Woman enables him to advance the identity of the New Negro without endangering black bourgeois respectability with allusions to unrestrained (black) female sexuality. Independently of the reasons, the erasure of the New Woman from Locke's discourse renders the New Negro as incompatible with the notion of emancipated femininity, especially black femininity. Locke, in his Renaissance rhetoric, seems to be incapable of conceiving of the New Negro Woman.

The Renaissance, Rebirth, and Ideologies of Masculinity

Even though Locke does not employ the New Woman trope, he strategically legitimizes the New Negro Renaissance through a large number of other cultural references. Apart from the earlier-mentioned national awakenings in Europe and Young America of 1916, Locke's vision of the New Negro strongly draws on the tradition of the American Renaissance. He constructs the New Negro as an active agent whose independence is manifested primarily in his right to self-representation and self-definition. "We shall let the Negro speak for *himself*," he announces in the foreword to *The New Negro*. Resonating with the echoes of Emersonian self-reliance, the newly emerged black consciousness is supposed to be emancipatory through a focus on the group's own experience rather than established knowledge. Locke repeatedly mentions the significance of "self-understanding," "self-respect," "self-dependence," "self-expression," "self-portraiture," "self-determination," and "self-reliance" itself.[56] Both at the level of politics and rhetoric, the American Renaissance emerges as one of the most powerful intertextual echoes in Locke's rhetoric. Its analysis will be elaborated in the remainder of the chapter, and it will illuminate Locke's representations of black masculinity and same-sexuality.

Locke's references to the discourse of the American Renaissance, and the concept of the Renaissance in general, are not free of gender connotations. As Charlene Avallone argues, male writers, literary critics, and scholars, in the process of constructing the movement, tended to exclude women writers. The discourse on the American Renaissance "serves to maintain male preeminence."[57] This exclusionary dynamic is visible not only on the level of marginalization of individual women writers in the academic narrative of the movement, but can also be observed in the rhetoric of the movement's founding texts. The canonical article "Self-Reliance" reveals Emerson's commitment to a masculinist vision of American "brave and manly" individualism, which is contrasted with "feminine," "cultivated classes" and "society...in conspiracy against...manhood."[58] Even though transcendentalism is traditionally represented in opposition to the pioneer tradition of American letters, the tropes it uses to construct the American subject are compatible with the masculinist expansion hero embodied by James Fenimore Cooper's Leatherstocking.

Besides the particular historical echoes of the American Renaissance and the 1916 renascence, the idea of a renaissance in general is interesting from the perspective of masculinity studies. Rites of passage, whose primary goal is rebirth and inclusion into a renewed identity, are acknowledged as ubiquitous to diverse ideologies of masculinity. This phenomenon is explained with a neo-Freudian conception of a man's necessity to symbolically sever the primary gender identification with the mother.[59] The concept of rebirth appears to be central to American masculinity in particular. As D. H. Lawrence claims in his influential analysis of America from the European perspective, *Studies in Classic American Literature*:

> the Leatherstocking novels create the myth of this new relation. And they go backwards, from old age to golden youth. That is the true myth of America. She starts old, old, wrinkled and writhing in an old skin. And there is a gradual sloughing of the old skin, towards a new youth. It is the myth of America.[60]

Since Leatherstocking is recognized as one of the prototypes of American masculinity, Lawrence's insightful thesis can be interpreted as a claim that the dynamic of incessant renaissance is at the very center of American masculine ideology. A preoccupation with rebirth and rejuvenation was also pronouncedly present at the turn of the twentieth century, when intense attempts to redefine hegemonic masculinity took place. Factors such as the suffrage and abolitionist movements, the end of the frontier, the increase in non-Anglo-Saxon immigration, and the evolution of a market economy and new employment patterns led to a "crisis" in American masculinity. Faced with the end of the frontier, the perceived feminization, and overcivilization, American men felt a strong need to revitalize and revalidate their gender identity.[61]

In the light of the above arguments, Locke's extensive preoccupation with the concept of renaissance seems to be a productive trope for a gender analysis. Its significance in Locke's discourse is immense and transcends its use in the name "the New Negro Renaissance." There is a dense net of metaphors and images repeated in his texts on the movement that highlights this trope. The very word "new" is repeated thirty-one times in the ten pages of "The New Negro" and fourteen times in the two-page-long "Foreword." Apart from "the Negro," the noun phrases it qualifies refer to the subjectivity of black people in general, as in "new," "figure," "soul," "psychology," "outlook," "mentality," "temper," "spirit;" the new situation as in a new "dynamic phase," "force," "trend," "vision," "order," or "urge;" as well as the new relationship between the races as in new "relationships," "contacts and centers," "mutual attitudes," or "social understanding." The New Negro finds himself in an unprecedented social situation, which should lead to a redefinition of race relations. The change from the old to the new is represented in dynamic and graphic metaphors. The Negro is compared to a butterfly "shedding the old chrysalis." Other nature-inspired images include "a dramatic *flowering* of a new race-spirit" and "*ripening* forces...culled from the first *fruits* of the Negro Renaissance."[62] The dramatic dynamism of Locke's vision of the renaissance is manifested in figures of speech such as "unusual outburst of creative expression," "new dynamic phase," or "hurdl[ing] several generations of experience at a leap." This rebirth imagery is also enhanced with minor vocabulary items present in the texts, such as "awakening," "nascent," or "resurgence."[63]

Additionally, the concept of renaissance is rhetorically reinforced through Locke's images referring to the East and dawn. He claims that "the actual march of development has simply flanked these positions, necessitating a sudden reorientation of view. We have not been watching in the right direction; set North and South on a sectional axis, we have not noticed the East till the sun has us blinking."[64] In this quote, the East – the destination of the majority of black rural migrants – is a symbol of hope as well as reconciliation with the American nation. The image of dawn appears also in the lyrics of the spiritual that serves as the epigraph for the volume: "O, rise, shine for Thy light is a' coming."[65] In addition, one of the poems by Langston Hughes which Locke quotes in the essay also contains similar imagery: "And *Dawn* today/Broad arch above the road we came/We march!" All the above-listed references allude to the concept of renaissance through a traditional symbolism of the sunrise as hope and enlightenment. Moreover, the trope of the East contains an additional empowering symbolism. Apart from signifying the promise of a new beginning, the East-West axis in American imagination points to the European cultural capital. Analogous to the term renaissance, the East infuses the movement with both revitalizing potential and cultural legitimacy.

The title of the above-quoted poem, "Youth," points to yet another way in which Locke's texts thematize the idea of rebirth. The significance of "the younger generation" in his project is signaled in Locke's letter to Hughes concerning "The Survey Graphic Harlem Number": "My idea is to bring *the younger generation* out in front somewhat, and that means more to me than being out there myself."[66] His intention did not remain private – *The New Negro* is dedicated to "the younger generation" in bold and capital letters.[67] In his essays in the volume, Locke recurrently uses the term "the Young Negro," which, due to the capitalization, seems to be interchangeable with "the New Negro."[68] The most explicit articulation of the central function of the young generation in Locke's project can be found in the *Survey Graphic* essay "Youth Speaks" and its equivalent in *The New Negro*, "Negro Youth Speaks." The latter essay opens with a powerful announcement: "The *Younger Generation* comes, bringing its gifts. They are the first fruits of the Negro Renaissance. *Youth* speaks, and the voice of the *New Negro* is heard... Here we have *Negro Youth*, with arresting visions and vibrant prophesies."[69] The statements clearly identify the New Negro as interchangeable with "the Younger Generation" and "the Negro Youth." In the former version of the essay, Locke additionally criticizes "the chronic tendency to turn to age rather than to youth for the forecast."[70] Thus, even though he gives credit to the older generations, characteristically referring to them in the language of the nineteenth-century western conquest discourse as "the pioneers and path-breakers," being the New Negro implies belonging to "the young generation."

The Young Negro, just as the New Negro, is a gendered concept. Even though Locke mentions Jessie Fauset among the new generation writers in "Youth Speaks," the younger generation is heavily dominated by male authors. Moreover, when constructing the history of the movement in his later texts, he erases Fauset's presence. Thus, even though the essay "The Younger Literary Movement" by Du Bois and Locke introduces two texts that "will mark an epoch" – namely Fauset's *There is Confusion* and Toomer's *Cane* – and it is Locke who devotes his part of the text to her novel, he later refers only to "Jean Toomer's startling and prophetic *Cane*" when he needs a symbol of a "significant opener" of another new generation.[71] This rhetorical erasure of Fauset from the advance guard of the Renaissance to some extent reenacts a controversy concerning the role of *There is Confusion* at the famous Civic Club Dinner. The publication of the novel was the most immediate pretext for the celebration. Yet Charles S. Johnson states in one of the letters discussing this event with Locke that "the matter has never rested in my mind as something exclusively for Miss Fauset or anybody else. The real motive for getting this group together is to present this *newer school of writers*."[72] Locke agreed with Johnson's intention and must have put it faithfully into practice as the Master of Ceremony during the dinner, since in her letters Fauset blamed Locke, not Johnson, for the marginalization of her person at the Civic Club reception.[73] The story of Fauset symbolically exemplifies that the New Negro – in order to "speak as Negro," "see and recognize in the streets of reality tomorrow" – should be both young and male.

Locke's concept of the New Negro as a young man interestingly resonates with the vision of the national character as represented in his early text "The American Temperament" (1914). Having challenged the very concept of an innate national character, Locke states that it is pragmatically useful to forge a "bond between men" provided that, simultaneously, it permits "unhindered exercise of that personal initiative and freedom which an American calls his individuality."[74] Characteristically, he renders the individuality and freedom in metaphors of adolescence – the American character is "Protean and even puerile," like "the healthy child," "youthful, youthful to a fault." "Most of all do we dislike the person who has aged prematurely through contact with older traditions...we contrive to eliminate or ignore him as children do grown-ups." Significantly, the youthfulness of America is gendered in Locke's vision as "superb boyishness."[75] This vision conspicuously echoes Emerson's seminal "Self-Reliance," where the American character is analogously constructed with metaphors of boyhood: "How is a boy the master of society; independent, irresponsible, looking out from his corner on such people and facts as pass by, he tries and sentences them on their merits, in the swift, summary way of boys, as good, bad, interesting, silly, eloquent, troublesome."[76] The reverberation of Emerson's tropes gains further relevance due to the earlier-mentioned parallels between the two American Renaissances, white and black. Locke's vision of the New Negro as young and male complements his vision of the American character as "superbly boyish," which echoes the individualist tradition of transcendentalism. Moreover, since both "the American Temperament" and "the New Negro" position black people as Americans, it seems that the masculinization of the black subject fosters its nationalization; the exclusion of the female sex facilitates the inclusion of the black subject into the American national identity. In order to alleviate the presence of cultural and racial differences and to construct a homogeneous nationality, gender differences are eliminated. The references that conflate youth and "boyishness" can also be read as symptomatic of the desire for rebirth in the ideology of American hegemonic masculinity, which is emblematic of Cooper's novels. The glorification of masculine-gendered youth is analogous to Leatherstocking's desire for eternal adolescence as well as the attempts to revitalize American manhood at the turn of the twentieth century best exemplified by the founding of the Boy Scouts in 1907.

The Midwife and Other Birth Metaphors

In his insistent promotion of the new generation, Locke assumes a peculiar role. His pivotal place in the movement was first publicly acknowledged at the Civic Club Dinner, which indirectly led to the publication of The New Negro. Even though the organizing force behind the dinner was Charles S. Johnson, Locke was selected to chair the event due to his well-established connections with many members of the younger generation. The relationships are recorded in his correspondence with younger artists, including Countee Cullen, Langston Hughes, Claude McKay, and Jean Toomer, which dates back to the early 1920s. Since then, through his letters as well as meetings with the artists, Locke had managed to gain the reputation of the "dean" of the movement, as Johnson refers to him in the letter asking the Howard professor to lead the Civic Club Dinner.[77]

Locke's special relation with the Negro Youth is also acknowledged by many younger artists. Countee Cullen expresses his gratitude to Locke and wishes "more race men were concerned with *younger fellows*." Gwendolyn Bennett states that "we of the younger group somehow feel 'the utter necessity of your presence.'" She also mentions Locke's "unrelenting belief in '*us*' *kids*" and his "faith in the eternal rightness of '*us*.'"[78] Alexander Durnham renders the relationship as parental in an even more elaborate way when he writes to Locke that as a mentor he "will be giving life to men and thoughts again." In another letter he confides that he is "still breathing on the life [Locke's] visit put into" him.[79] Locke's interest in young artists was unrelenting indeed. In the early 1930s, Richmond Barthe, the renowned sculptor of the later days of the Renaissance, states that his stay in Washington with Locke made him "a new person."[80] A decade later, in 1944, Le Roy Foster, a young painter, appreciates Locke's support for "embryo artists."[81] The metaphors found in the letters position Locke not only as a mentor or a parental figure; the use of metaphors connected to childbirth such as "giving life" or "embryo" endows his persona with specifically maternal associations.

Locke himself encouraged if not initiated the rendering of his persona as a maternal figure to the younger generation. Most of the studies of the movement refer to his self-appointed position as the "midwife" of the Renaissance. He allegedly claimed to be "more of a *philosophical midwife* to a generation of younger Negro poets, writers and artists than a professional philosopher."[82] His parental approach to New Negroes is also visible in a line from his letter to Hughes concerning one of the 1925 Civic Club meetings: "We are having a small dinner, largely of contributors to the book,...a sort of *christening party* for the New Negro."[83] The maternal dimension of the relationship is also found in the correspondence between Locke and other artists and intellectuals. In a letter to Carl Van Vechten, thanking him for the publicity he provides for the movement in *Vanity Fair*, Locke refers to himself as a "nurse-maid" to the kids-artists of the Renaissance.[84] In a note to Countee Cullen, he names a number of younger artists – Jean Toomer, Langston Hughes, Cullen, Lewis Alexander, Richard Bruce [Bruce Nugent], Donald Hayes, Albert Durnham – and refers to them as his "spiritual children." This symbolism is elaborated further on in the letter when Locke asks a rhetorical question: "Can a bad tree bring forth good fruit?"[85] Characteristically, many of the artists corresponding with Locke were frequently invited over to spend Easter holidays with him in Washington. The reference to this particular holiday further strengthens the regenerative aspect of the relationships. Thus, Locke not only announced and publicized the rebirth of black culture, but he also positioned himself as the mother of the rebirth.

Moreover, the metaphorical meaning of the Renaissance as rebirth is not limited to the maternal bond between Locke and the younger artists. In many letters, the trope of giving birth refers to literary creativity that is engendered by the relationship between Locke and the artists. In a letter to Hughes, Locke hopes that their "association [will] breed beautiful things, like children, to hallow the relationship."[86] Analogously, in a letter to Johnson, he compares his experience of producing The Negro in Literature to "the travails of pregnancy."[87] Similar ideas are expressed in other letters from and to Locke. Albert Dunham's correspondence is written in a highly elevated and metaphorical style. In one of the letters, Locke's younger academic colleague also writes about their relationship in terms of childbirth: "mayhap your parturition is an echo of the immaculate conception of which I've dreamed a bit. Conceive with me of a volume or two." He reiterates this metaphor when he writes about the spring feeling of being "young and doubtful" and, related to it, being "pregnant in more ways than one."[88] Analogous metaphors are found in the correspondence between Bruce Nugent and Locke. In one of the letters, Nugent devotes two pages to the extended simile between creative writing and childbirth. "Never say a man can not suffer the pangs of child birth. Even more. After the pangs a minute relief in which to gather strength to realize that the offspring is a maimed and cripple[d] incomplete thing." This life-giving process in Nugent's rendering is painful and paradoxical but "most sublime" at the same time. Moreover, he alludes to the godlike quality of artistic life-giving creations.[89] All the above quotes characterize male relationships as life-giving. Images such as "travails of pregnancy" or "pangs of child birth" add a graphic character and grotesquely rejuvenate the concept of male bonding. The grotesque lower-body stratum elements, however, are overshadowed by the emphasis on the spiritual and immaculate character of reproduction, which endows the relationships with a sacred or sublime quality.

Whereas Ross suggests that the black patron was represented as a midwife and the white patron was the parental figure, a more detailed analysis of Locke's correspondence reveals a peculiar conflation of these procreative images in his auto-creation.[90] In the idiosyncratic discourse of Locke's letters with younger artists, artistic creativity and philosophical inspirations are inherently coded as childbirth. These maternal associations do not function, however, to feminize the position of the black artist. Since most of the artists Locke intimately corresponded with were male, the writing-as-birth metaphor enables him to construct a paradigm of birth-giving exclusively for male bonding. The relationship is valued as privileged, since it is defined as "spiritual," bearing a "transcendental" fruit of knowledge and art. On the one hand, the notion of maternity positions Locke as the legitimate initiator of the Renaissance and, on the other, its appropriation represents male relationships as fertile in cultural productions.

The childbearing dimension of Locke's "giving life to men" can be read also as a version of initiation rites. As Elisabeth Badinter claims in the chapter tellingly entitled "It is Man Who Engenders Man," "the objective of all initiation rites is to change the status and identity of the boy so that he may be reborn as a man" after he is "initiated by a mentor or a group of elders."[91] Consequently, Locke's self-fashioning as a maternal figure can be read as a way to position himself as a mentor in a peculiar rite of passage. The appropriation of the rite of passage rhetoric enables Locke to claim female reproductive capabilities and simultaneously, by translating them into the spiritual realm, to position his non-physical reproduction as privileged. Characteristically, since Locke's relation to the younger male generation is inextricably linked to the emergence of the New Negro, the latter can also be interpreted as an initiation ritual. Locke's narrative of the New Negro's birth neatly parallels the structure of the rite: separation from the mother, liminality, and the assumption of a new masculine identity.[92] The feminized Old Negro separates from the equally feminized realm of charity and dependence – the metonymical Southern soil. "In the very process of being transplanted, the Negro is becoming transformed" into the new identity, which is the Young New Negro. The fact that Locke's narrative of the reconstruction of black identity flawlessly fits the pattern of masculine initiation rites further points to the significance of the masculinization of the New Negro and the rebirth rhetoric.

The Renaissance, Greek Antiquity, and Male Bonding

The link between the Renaissance and Locke's mother/mentor relationship with young, predominantly male, artists illuminates the significance of same-sexuality if the term Renaissance is interpreted as a return to the Hellenic roots of Western culture. The European Renaissance is primarily defined by its focus on and revival of classical art, architecture, and literature. Allusions to classical Hellenic culture also frequently recur in Locke's letters. They are most visible in the voluminous correspondence with Cullen and Hughes, especially in the early stages of their relationships.[93] The references gain further significance from the prism of sexuality studies when one focuses on the idea of "the cult of friendship," which is associated by Locke with classical thought. In one of his first letters to Hughes, he explicitly acknowledges the Hellenic influence on his vision of male friendship: "cult [of friendship] I confess is my only religion, and has been ever since my early infatuation with Greek ideals of life. You see I was caught up early in the coils of classicism."[94] The most prominent source of the "Greek friendship" at the time was Plato's *Symposium*. Its key idea of the ladder of beauty, which one can ascend through the erotic relation between the youth, the *eromenos*, and his mentor, the *erastes*, is a useful rhetorical tool for Locke to render his relations with the younger men as an ennobling and transcendental bond. Locke emphasizes the artistic and aesthetic significance of his homosocial relationships, which is analogous to the final stage and goal of the ladder of love – arriving "at the notion of absolute beauty" and the knowledge of "what the essence of beauty is."[95] Plato's dialogue also advances the notion of "spiritual offspring" resulting from a union between two men, which, as I have argued above, is of utmost significance in Locke's rhetoric of friendship:

> He wanders about seeking beauty that he may beget offspring...when he finds a fair and noble and well-nurtured soul,...he tries to educate him...and they are married by a far nearer tie and have a closer friendship than those who beget mortal children, for the children who are their common offspring are fairer and more immortal.[96]

Plato's vision of the relationship between the teacher and the younger beautiful man, as well as the construction of artistic creativity or philosophical ideas as "fair and immortal offspring," is echoed in the discourse of spiritual pregnancy and birth in Locke's letters. This is accurately exemplified by the close parallel between the above-quoted fragment from Plato and the earlier-mentioned sentence from a letter to Hughes: "association [will] *breed beautiful things, like children, to hallow the relationship*."[97] Thus Locke's construction of his relationships with younger male artists in terms of inspiration and philosophical mentoring, which is purer and more transcendental than heterosexual relationships, is deeply rooted in classical philosophical tradition. What further explains Locke's insistent self-fashioning as the male mentor is Ross's claim that "black men attempted to reposition themselves as patrons and 'creators' of culture, prolific progenitors whose sexual identity cannot be reduced to sexual-object status."[98] Locke assumes the position of *erastes*, which grants him agency and empowerment.

Michel Foucault theorizes and problematizes our understanding of the *eromenos-erastes* relationship in the second volume of his *History of Sexuality, The Use of Pleasure*. Foucault warns against imposing contemporary distinctions between heterosexuality and homosexuality onto Greek sexual paradigms and particularly against the simplistic assumption that same-sexuality was regarded as nobler and non-problematic. He states that the Greeks "believed that the same desire attached to anything that was desirable – boy or girl – subject to the condition that the appetite was nobler that inclined toward what was more beautiful and more honourable." Foucault explains that "Urania, the heavenly love – is directed exclusively to boys" because "the more ancient, nobler, and more reasonable love that is drawn to what has the most vigor and intelligence...obviously can only mean the male sex." "The heavenly love" was permeated with the anxiety that the young *eromenos* does not compromise his position of masculine activity. Ideally, this special relationship was supposed to search for "a beautiful form" and later transform into *philia*, a relation of friendship.[99] Foucault claims that the *eromenos-erastes* paradigm was both privileged and problematic in parallel ways to the later romantic courtship with its focus on the heterosexual relationship and the purity of the courted woman.

The link between Greek ideals of love and same-sexuality was not unexplored at the time; in fact, according to scholars of sexuality studies, it was one of the most powerful rhetorical tools that the early gay emancipation drew on.[100] The most influential examinations of this theme can be found in the texts of the prominent British radical thinker Edward Carpenter. In his work, *Iolāus: An Anthology of Friendship* (1906), he constructs the homoerotic male friendship as an important trope, which has been omnipresent in Western culture and was especially celebrated in Ancient Greece. Carpenter summarizes the Greek ideal of friendship in the following way:

> The extent to which the idea of friendship (in a quite romantic sense) penetrated the Greek mind is a thing very difficult for us to realize;...their literature abounds with references to the romantic attachment as the great inspiration of political and individual life...[W]hat we call love, i.e., the love between man and woman...scarcely comes within his consideration – but only the love between men what we should call romantic friendship. His ideal of this latter love is ascetic; it is an absorbing passion, but it is held in strong control. The other love – the love of women – is for him a mere sensuality.[101]

Although Carpenter's description of "Urania" is a gross simplification when compared with Foucault's study, his interpretation of Plato closely parallels Locke's investment in classical ideals of friendship. The parallel is not coincidental, since Locke was familiar with Carpenter's ideas; *Iolāus* was one of the texts he recommended to the younger generation artists such as Cullen and Hughes.

In the light of Carpenter's depiction of friendship in Antiquity and Locke's own thematization of friendship in classical terms, all his allusions to classical ideals and philosophy, being pagan or Hellenic, gain an additional dimension. Thus, even a sentence such as "I do not teach the *classics* – I should like to. I am *pagan* to the core – and how I like the *Hellenic* view," which comes from his letter to Hughes, can be interpreted as loaded with allusions to male bonding and homoerotic desire.[102] This metaphorical thematization of same-sex desire with relation to philosophical ideas enables Locke to construct it as a privileged and ennobling phenomenon. Moreover, due to the impression of subtlety produced through this rhetorical strategy, same-sexuality can be expressed even in letters addressed to men who were not self-declared homosexuals or in letters that might be read by a wider public.

The Rhetoric of Friendship and Locke's Circle of Intimate Comrades

Greek same-sexuality in Locke's correspondence is often conflated with the idea of camaraderie, alluding to the poetry of Walt Whitman. As A. B. Christa Schwarz claims, Locke's "man-loving identity...apparently derived from what appears to be a fusion of the Whitmanesque concept of 'manly,' 'comradely' love with a Greek model of homosexuality."[103] Whitman is an important figure for the New Negro Renaissance, since he was the poet laureate of the American Renaissance, whose significant influence on the rhetoric of the 1920s movement has been mentioned. Additionally, as Foley points out, 1919 marked the centenary of his birth, which contributed to his canonization and popularity.[104] More specifically, he emerges as the role model for the American poet in Locke's reviews and essays. He is the only "literary genius" able to account for the "Protean" and "infinite" American character.[105] The profound influence of Whitman on Locke in particular and on the aesthetics of the Negro Renaissance in general is acknowledged also by George Hutchinson, who claims that "'New Negro' authors enthusiastically embraced Whitman, embraced him with an intimacy that defies the codes typical of interracial relations in the United States, and exceeds that of most white American modernists." Hutchinson goes on to argue that Locke saw Whitman as the only essentially American poet and, consequently, a figure who should be a vital point of reference for all future American writers, black American writers included.[106] According to Hutchinson, an even more significant aspect of Whitman's poetry was revealed to Locke by its new interpretations coming from his European man-loving admirers such as the earlier-mentioned Carpenter.

The link between Carpenter, his interpretation of Whitman, and Locke also brings to light the multifaceted relations between transatlantic intertextualities and sexuality. Carpenter was a friend of Whitman and the author of the first significant attempt to construct him as a poet expressing homoerotic desire. The fact that Locke refers his younger friends to British same-sex desire discourse to explore this at the time controversial reading of the American poet Europeanizes and estranges the homoeroticism of Whitman's poetry. The link between Europe and same-sex desire is further reinforced by Locke's comments on relative tolerance of same-sexuality on the other side of the Atlantic. On the other hand, Locke often refers to Whitman as a significant influence in American literature, whose poetry embodies the spirit of American culture and democracy. Thus the figure of Whitman as used in Locke's letters mediates the dissonance between the seemingly contradictory forces of American democracy and Europeanized homoerotic desire.

The intertextual presence of Plato, Whitman, and Carpenter's *Ioläus* is clearly visible in the references to friendship in Locke's correspondence with his mentees. Allusions to these texts are used by the artists to implicitly and subtly express homoerotic desire or depict same-sex relationships. The tentativeness to express same-sexuality openly is explicitly stated in the letters. Both Cullen and McKay ask Locke to destroy some of the letters after reading since, as Cullen puts it, "sentiments expressed here would be misunderstood by others."[107] In their subtly allusive idiolect, the very word "friend" gains a peculiar meaning in the letters; Richmond Barthe states in one of the letters that he is happy because he found his "friend."[108] The word "friend" is underlined with a double line, which may be read as pointing to the ambiguity of the term. The ambiguous rhetoric of *Ioläus* and the imagery of Whitman provide the artists with a usable, coded language to express their homoerotic desires.

Examples of this homoerotic idiolect are abundantly present in Locke's correspondence with the most notable poets of the Renaissance: Hughes, Cullen, and McKay. In 1922, even before he met Hughes in person, Locke lyrically evokes the spirit of classical friendship: "However we are at least friends – and after all what more can we be – only I hope the gods of friendship, who are ancient not modern gods, will smile on us in an ancient way – and give us the intimacy of pagan happiness." In this sentence the mentor of the young generation manages to stay within the accepted cultural codes of being "at least friends...after all what more can we be" and, at the same time, through the references to "ancient gods" and "pagan" happiness, he lends the text a distinct homoerotic dimension. In fragments such as "perhaps through prosaic hours and days we can keep the gleam of the transcendental thing I believe our friendship was meant to be," Locke alludes to the spiritual quality of classical male friendship.[109] Letters from Hughes do not refer to any particular intimate relationships with men, yet they can also be read as containing certain homoerotic allusions. He refers to Locke as a "sympathetic friend" or "a charming friend for poets." Characteristically, Hughes shares with his mentor his appreciation of Whitman's poetry, focusing especially on the "Calamus" poems from *Leaves of Grass*.[110] That Hughes mentions this particular title is of distinctive significance since, as M. Jimmie Killingsworth argues, the "Calamus" poems mark "the shift from a rhetoric of omnisexuality to a rhetoric of gayness."[111] This reading is also supported by Hughes's biographer, Arnold Rampersad, who claims that the title was most likely used to probe Locke's sexual orientation.[112] Consequently, even a reference to a single title opens up space for homoerotic sentiment in Hughes's letters.

Cullen, in his correspondence with Locke, uses this Greek-Whitmanesque idiolect to render his intimate relationships with men such as Harold Jackman, Ralph Loeb, Donald Duff, and a person called Knapp. He refers to them with elevated figurative expressions such as "*delightful and stimulating comaradie*" [sic], "*friendship beyond understanding*," "greatest fraternal solace" "spiritual sympathy," "the *perfect* fusion of spirits on earth." Interestingly, since the young writers formed a circle of friends, Cullen also writes about the time he spent with Hughes, when they "have been able to see much of each other and to reap a mutual enjoyment of fond days camaraderie." Locke's intimate relationship with a German friend is rendered by Cullen within highly romantic and lyrical terms: "You must be enjoying yourselves, you and Rudolph [Dressler], reveling in the *ecstasies of a perfect friendship*, which is enough to inebriate your senses."[113] Cullen, in contrast to Hughes or McKay, was a poet who did not go for inspiration to the "low-down folk" or the black working class. The discourse of friendship rooted in classical rhetoric perfectly matches his literary inspirations originating in British Romanticism, a movement that was strongly influenced by classical and pagan ideas as well.[114]

McKay, in his correspondence with Locke, writes about male friendship in a manner similar to Hughes and Cullen. In the early stage of their relationship, he refers to his relation with Locke as "comaradie" [sic] which breeds "creative energy." Later, after a dispute between the two over Locke's changes in the title of McKay's poem in The New Negro, McKay only alludes to their past "intellectual and fraternal understanding."[115] Even though McKay was much less influenced by Locke's mentoring, the above-quoted fragments indicate that he was introduced to the classical-Whitmanesque idiolect of male friendship.[116]

Since Locke modeled himself as a mentor to the younger men, his relationships with male artists in the letters allude to the inspirational function of Greek romantic friendship. The erastes-eromenos paradigm is closely connected to the birth-giving tropes discussed earlier in this chapter. Artistic creativity is constructed as a transcendental – hence purer – form of giving birth, which lends a spiritual dimension to male friendships. Not only does it resolve Locke's tension stemming from the objectification of black authors by white patronage politics, the foregrounding of spirituality in the discourse enables the rhetoric to elide the problematic issue of black male sexuality. The scarce images rooted in the lower-body stratum, serving to emphasize the intimate and affective quality of Locke's friendship, are restricted to specifically female and maternal metaphors. Just as Du Bois alludes to the figure of Christ to dignify black illegitimacy and resistance and to dissociate them from the black brute mythology, Locke's representations of spiritual understanding ennoble male bonding to distance it from the pathologized positions of both homosexual desire and black male desire.

Another meaningful feature of male-male intimacy in Locke's correspondence is its transcendence of a simple bipolar relationship. Schwarz confirms the multi-lateral character of his relations when she claims that "with Locke as a pivotal figure, the men involved in the gay network formed an invisible, diverse community which was at the heart of the Harlem Renaissance." Also, George Chauncey and Ross point out the existence of "gay social network" and "a homoerotic coterie."[117] Many correspondents mention each other, their own meetings, and common projects. Barthe confides in Locke about his relationship with another male artist: "You [Locke] are very wise my friend...I shall get a great deal of inspiration from him and I in turn can inspire him to do the good work that I feel so sure that he is capable of doing."[118] Dunham mentions a "spiritual family" into which he urges Locke to include Donald Hayes. He also poetically comments on his relations with other participants of the Renaissance, which gains a new dimension after his conversation with Locke: "what seemed occult takes on the colors of the most vivid reality, to render more crystalline such events as my discovery of Bruce [Nugent] or my almost mystic meeting of [Richmond] Barthe."[119] These chains of inspiration or network images occur also in the letters in which they lack direct homoerotic allusions. Lewis Alexander, a black poet and theater artist from Washington, writes about "the spirit of universal brotherhood" and "brotherly support."[120] In a letter to Scholley Pace, one of the editors of *Harlem*, Locke constructs a poetic vision of the friendship among his male friends: "Strange how things turn out – here are four friends together whom I never dreamed would even come to know one another. As life goes on the threads seem to get tangled and criss-cross – and then suddenly sometimes out of the tangle a pattern looms and it almost looks like *Providence and destiny*."[121] What arises from Locke's correspondence with younger writers is a whole network whose "threads seem to get tangled and criss-cross." The image reveals a deep structural pattern of Locke's "circle" or "coterie," whereas references to providence and destiny endow it with a transcendental dimension. Both the linguistic level of the rhetoric of friendship and the social level of Locke's friendships are communal rather than individual projects. Due to the multilateral character of this male network and its metaphorical life-giving power, it emerges as a male family, which reproduces itself through cultural productions.

Since the rhetoric of "perfect friendship" and "camaraderie" is absent from Locke's personal correspondence with female writers of the Renaissance, it seems that the intimate circle and its idiolect depicted above was restricted to Locke's male friends. Although the famous Niggerati included young women such as Zora Neale Hurston or Gwendolyn Bennett, their correspondence with Locke lacks the tropes of friendship, even in very cordial letters. Hurston, for example, invents and repeatedly uses her own metaphor to depict her relation with Locke. She draws a triangle that symbolizes a "circuit" including Hurston, Locke, and Hughes. The absence of women from the comradely idiolect further strengthens the homoerotic dimension of Locke's rhetoric of friendship.

The Negro Negro and the New Germany

The rhetoric of friendship emerging from Locke's letters abounds in allusions to European discourses of Ancient *philia* and Carpenter's interpretation of Whitman's camaraderie. Apart from these references, there is another European rhetoric that foregrounds masculinity and non-normative sexuality and illuminates the way Locke envisioned his relations with the younger generation. Being a Rhodes Scholar, he spent the years 1907-1911 in Berlin, and in his letters to Hughes he reveals the influence of this time on his conception of friendship. In one of his first letters he states that "the Germans have a perfect genius for friendship, which cult I confess is my only religion." This mysterious sentence becomes clearer after one reads another letter sent to Hughes three months later, when he links German ideas of friendship to Hellenic ones:

the new Germany is more Hellenic and pagan than most people suspect – especially the new Youth movement which intrigues me terribly. My dearest friend is a member of it – this summer, he may succeed in getting me in knickers, sandals and blouse – at any rate we are going to "wandervogel" together for some happy weeks.[122]

Locke refers here to the Wandervogel movement, which was beginning to be an influential youth movement during his stay in Berlin. Even though it emerged approximately at the same time as American Boy Scouts and its founders expressed similar anxieties connected with urbanization, industrialization, and modernization, there was a key difference between the two social phenomena. What was absent from the American movement was the controversial publicity concerning the homoerotic meanings of the Wandervogel movement's activities and rhetoric.

Locke was bound to be more than superficially familiar with the discourse surrounding the movement. We can identify the "dearest friend" whom he mentions to Hughes, with the help of additional information from the correspondence with Cullen, as Rudolf Dressler. Dressler's letters reveal a discourse of intimate friendship analogous to the one from the letters with black artists, but they also point to Locke's preoccupation with the emerging German same-sex institutions and press. For example, Dressler sends Locke issues of *Die Freundschaft, Monatsschrift für den Befreiungskampf andersveranlagter Männer und Frauen* [Friendship, a monthly magazine for the liberation of men and women of different disposition], which contain texts and advertisements for books written by the activists and scholars engaged in the various sections of the German Youth Movement. The magazine, whose very title suggests primary preoccupation with alternative sexuality, covers the activity of organizations and institutions such as the Wandervogel and the Gemeinschaft der Eigenen, which were central to the German man-loving community at the time. Also names such as Hans Blüher, Benedict Friedlaender, Adolf Brand, or Gustav Wyneken recur on the pages of *Die Freundschaft* in the same years that the magazine is discussed by Locke and Dressler, and, as I will demonstrate in the remainder of this chapter, there are many significant parallels between the discourse of their texts and Locke's public and private rhetoric.[123]

The first significant attempt to account for the homoerotic dimension of the German youth movement is found in *Die Deutsche Wandervogelbewegung als ein erotisches Phänomen* [The German Wandervogel Movement as an Erotic Phenomenon] written by the psychologist Hans Blüher (1912). This volume addresses controversies around the alleged homosexuality of one of the leaders of the movement, Wilhelm Jansen. According to Blüher, charismatic male mentors are the "calm center of every youth movement, the actual commanders-in-chief of youth. [They are] often revolutionary figures. Passionately they devote their entire lives to helping youth."[124] Blüher's text constructs the relationship between the older mentor and the younger boys as homoerotic, virilizing, and dependent on the sexual charisma of the mentor. Thus, even though he uses the term "invert" to refer to the mentor, he does not perceive homoerotic desire as a gender inversion, a notion that was popularized at the time by Magnus Hirschfeld in his theory of the third sex; on the contrary, there is a visible influence of another German theorist, Benedict Friedlaender, and his masculinist vision of same-sex relations.

Resonances between Friedlaender's and Locke's writings and preoccupations appear to be a fruitful object for analysis. In 1902, together with Adolf Brand and Wilhelm Jansen, the German sexual theorist founded the man-loving society Gemeinschaft der Eigenen, whose activities also involved scouting and trekking characteristic of the Wandervogel. The word "Eigenen," which means either "special" or "self-owner," is derived from the anarchist philosopher Max Stirner's most influential text Der Einzige und sein Eigentum (translated either as The Individual and His Property or The Ego and Its Own). Brand, the co-founder of the association and the self-proclaimed man-loving magazine of "art and masculine culture," acknowledged that the neologism "Eigene" was a reference to Stirner's influential text. He explicated that "Der Eigene represents the right of personal freedom and sovereignty of the individual to the farthest consequence."[125] Yvonne Ivory analyzes the neologism in a way that further illuminates its homoerotic message. According to her:

Der Eigene proves to be a title with rich layers of meaning: derived from a prefix that encapsulates a whole range of ideas such as idiosyncratic, own, strange, self, and separate, it not only pays homage to the individualist ideology of Max Stirner, it also echoes the nineteenth-century German discourse of sexuality, in which the word "eigen" was generally used to express the idea of sameness in descriptions of "same"-sex desire.[126]

Thus Brand and Friedlaender appropriated the concept and endowed it with a special homoerotic significance.

Stirner's anarchist thought, challenging the ideals of nationalism, church, and socially sanctioned relationships, was useful for the founders of the Gemeinschaft der Eigenen, since within his paradigm of temporary human relations they could construct homoerotic male bonding as a liberating substitute for the limitations of marital relations. This reading is elaborated by Ivory, who convincingly claims that "as increased pressure was exerted on the nineteenth-century man-loving man to identify with new legal and medical models of inversion, the notion of individualist agency and self-culture became more appealing – and even more necessary – for the affirmation of alternative identities."[127] Thus Stirner's discourse of radical individualism provided a rhetorical tool to defy the conventions of social relations as well as the criminalizing and pathologizing discourses of homosexuality at the turn of the century. Stirner's influence on the Eigene movement and writings was also indirectly exercised through Friedlaender's pre-occupation with Friedrich Nietzsche's philosophy, which was profoundly shaped by Stirner. Friedlaender, just as many other *fin-de-siècle* anti-establishment thinkers, strongly relied on the idea of the Nietzschean *Übermensch*, the strong individual not beholden to laws, a notion that the founder of the Eigene appropriated to construct a positive image of same-sex desire.

Both the resonance of Blüher's erotically charismatic mentors, who "devote their entire lives to helping youth," and Der Eigene's investment in German philosophy can be traced in Locke's writings. The former construction is reflected in his self-fashioning as the mentor, which has been explored at length earlier. German individualistic philosophical thought in the rhetoric of Friedlaender and Brand is perhaps less explicit yet also present in Locke's texts, to some extent because he was a philosopher and taught German philosophy to his students. As is manifest in his letters, Locke's preoccupation with the subject goes beyond the walls of academia. German philosophical texts frequently recur as elements in his discourse with the younger Renaissance artists. The name of Nietzsche is frequently repeated in his correspondence with Cullen and Hughes. Locke's admiration for Nietzsche's philosophy is confirmed also by Johnny Washington in *Evolution, History, and Destiny, Letters to Alain Locke (1886-1954) and Others* (2002).[128]

Another interesting parallel between Locke's rhetoric of the New Negro and the German homoerotic discourse is their preoccupation with the period and concept of the Renaissance, whose central position in Locke's writings has been outlined earlier in the chapter. According to Ivory, the notion of the renaissance and revivalism was essential to the formation of European *fin-de-siècle* same-sex rhetoric.[129] This preoccupation with the idea of rebirth can be found even at the level of titles of texts belonging to counter-hegemonic discourse, such as Friedlaender's *Renaissance des Eros Uranios* [Renaissance of the Uranian Eros] or art historian Willy Pastor's "Eine Renaissance der Renaissance" [A Renaissance of the Renaissance]. As Ivory claims, the feature that made the idea of the Renaissance attractive for the Eigene activists was that the period provided great (male) role models to emulate. At the turn of the century, one of the emancipatory tactics of same-sex activism was to reclaim man-loving geniuses of the past, and Renaissance artists such as Michelangelo were especially amply represented in the strategic canons.[130] This reference throws additional light on Locke's application of the term. His preoccupation with this idea might be read as a way to fashion himself as the great Renaissance man-mentor to the younger generation, a concept that gains a homoerotic dimension due to intertextual echoes of Ancient Greek and German same-sex discourses.

This is not the only way in which the Renaissance surfaces in the German man-loving discourse. Characteristically, Ivory opens her discussion of the influence of German individualism on the discourse of the turn of the nineteenth-century same-sexuality with a quote from the influential American Renaissance figure

William E. Channing and his concept of self-culture. The quote is not merely an accidental parallel. The interest in the American Renaissance manifest in the German same-sex discourse goes beyond the generally acknowledged influence of Walt Whitman. In an issue of Der Eigene from 1924, there is a vast section "Die Physiologische Freundschaft in der Auffassung der Grossen Amerikanischen Dichter-Denker" [The Physiological Friendship as Understood by the Great American Thinkers and Poets], which is devoted to Emerson and Thoreau in addition to Whitman. St. Ch. Waldecke, the author of the article, focuses on the ideals of friendship in Emerson's writings and the individualistic lifestyle of Thoreau. Waldecke emphasizes the sublime dimension of male bonding by referring to the friendship of Emerson and Carlyle. Moreover, he points out that neither Thoreau nor Whitman got married, which meaningfully reinforced their individualism as well as the exclusion of heterosexual bonds from their lives. [131]

These references to American literature interestingly resonate within the intertextual network that emerges from the juxtaposition of Locke's ideas, German individualism, and the discourse of Der Eigene. The influences of the American transcendentalist tradition of self-reliance can be traced in German nineteenth-century philosophies of individualism and echoed in the same-sex rhetoric as well as in the New Negro founding texts. Thus, the American Renaissance through its European borrowings becomes a transatlantic intertextual trope that further strengthens the uncanny parallels between the German Youth Movements and Locke's fashioning of the New Negro Renaissance.

Apart from Friedlaender, Brand, the Wandervogel movement, and Der Eigene, yet another significant intertextual connection that is indirectly related to the youth movement is revealed in a publication by the German educator and pedagogical theorist Gustav Wyneken, whose name recurs on the pages of both Die Freundschaft and Der Eigene. Wyneken founded the Wickersdorfer Freie Schulgemeinde [the Wickersdorf Free School Community], which, alluding to the ideal of youth culture (Jugendkultur), was supposed to be the nucleus of future change and reform. Apart from the belief in the transformative and revolutionary potential of the youth, the school system was constructed on the basis of comradeship (Kameradschaften) between the teacher and his pupils. Wyneken, charged with Paragraph 174, Section 1 of the Penal Code (indecent acts with minors), wrote Eros (1921), which was intended to explicate and defend his pedagogical ideas.

Eros to some extent repeats the arguments present in Blüher's Die Deutsche Wandervogelbewegung als ein erotisches Phänomen, yet it is rooted in Greek thought rather than in German individualism. In the book, referring to the Platonic idea of love as represented in The Symposium, Wyneken advances the notion of "pedagogical Eros," which constructs his tutorial practices in terms of "new Hellenism" and in opposition to modern notions of homosexuality. As Thijs Maasen claims in his article "Man-Boy Friendships on Trial: On the Shift in the Discourse on Boy Love in the Early Twentieth Century," intellectuals according to Wyneken were better equipped to initiate the youth into culture than either state or family.[132] Just as in the Greek *eromenos-erastes*, the basis of this relationship was a dynamic between the older and wise lover and the young beloved. In Wyneken's text, this dyad was translated into "leadership" (*Führerschaft*), whose wisdom and spiritual beauty was complemented by the beauty of youth of the "followers" (*Jüngertum, Gefolgschaft*).[133] In order for the bond between the mentor and his follower to be most effective, it needs to be endowed with erotic quality. Yet, since Wyneken wrote the text to clear his name from charges of indecency, he explicitly distinguishes the pedagogical Eros from contemporaneous notions of same-sexuality:

> love for youths, Eros directed at youths...is not the same, however, as that which one today calls same-sex love (Gleich-geschlechtliche Liebe). It involves...a man's erotic ties to youths...and, reciprocally, these youths' erotic ties...to a man."[134]

Wyneken's ideas, as they are rooted in classical sources, are parallel to the rhetoric of mentorship in Locke's writings. Since both men use the term comradeship to depict noble male bonding, another shared intertextual resonance can be found in Whitman's poetry. Wyneken's text seems to be of key interest also because of its contribution to the theory of education. Since Locke was not only a symbolic "dean of the movement" but also an actual academic teacher and a pedagogical theorist, the notion of the pedagogical Eros seems to be especially relevant to his educational practice and ideas.

Uncanny Parallels

There are many parallels between the above-outlined discourses of the German *Jugendkultur* and Locke's writings. As I have mentioned, they construct the male same-sex relationship in a way similar to Locke's rhetoric of friendship, which is consciously rooted in the classical tradition and comradeship of Walt Whitman. Yet one of the most interesting analogies is their shared strong preoccupation with youth. Both the rhetoric of the Wandervogel movement and Wyneken's Eros strongly resonate with Locke's devotion to "the younger generation" and "the Young Negro." Characteristically, the Wandervogel movement, just as the New Negro movement a decade later, refers to the idea of rebirth. As John Alexander Williams argues, the New German Youth was "the code word for a *renaissance*, for the forging of a new, more healthy world."[135] Also the emphasis on the significance of the younger generation and its identification with national identity runs parallel in both movements, which is illustrated by another statement from Williams's text; "Indeed, *the young generation* became interchangeable with the nation in the rhetoric of the many Wilhelmian organizations that were working toward cultural reform."[136] Thus it can be argued that Locke's vision of the New Negro movement, with its excessive emphasis on the youth, was shaped by the ideas of the German youth movement ideology. This reading can be buttressed by Locke's own statement according to which the New Negro needs to be perceived in the context of new European emergent nationalities and avant-garde movements.

Fig. 1, 2, and 3. Der Eigene illustrations: June 1903, June 1903, and March 1903. Schwules Museum, Berlin, Bibliothek.

Moreover, both Wyneken's and Blüher's discourse on youth in Germany are thematized in terms of same-sex desire; the pedagogical Eros as well as the revolutionary potential of the youth in the Wandervogel movement are depicted as inherently homoerotic. This sometimes latent dimension of the Jugendkultur rhetoric is explicitly manifest at the visual level of the earlier-mentioned magazines, Die Freundschaft and Der Eigene. In the years 1900-1925, the discourse of the youth movement in the former magazine was consistently illustrated with pictures predominantly representing young boys against outdoor wildlife backgrounds. This form accurately reflected the central activity of the Wandervogel movement – homosocial hikes in the German wilderness. Such representations of hiking were accompanied by posed nudes modeled on the Ancient Greek sculptures or other classical decorative elements. The pictorial level of Der Eigene was strikingly similar and retained visible continuity in the span of over thirty years between 1896 and 1932, when the magazine was published. It was also dominated by nudes of young males that were frequently represented as sportsmen, such as discus throwers, archers, horse tamers, or rowers, against natural backgrounds (Fig. 1-3, 5). Such poses virilized their representations and distanced the pictures from the traditional female nudes. Apart from the photographs, Der Eigene was illustrated with reproductions of classical and Renaissance sculptures and paintings. The homoerotic dimension of these representations was emphasized and elaborated in articles such as "Die Lieblingsminne in der griechischen Vasenmalerei" [The Preferred Form of Love in the Greek Vase Paintings] from 1922.[137]

UNCANNY PARALLELS

Yet another significant reference present in the visual layer of both *Die Freund-shaft* and *Der Eigene* is the German naturist movement, which emerged in the 1890s and remained influential during Locke's stay in Berlin. One of the emblems of the movement was *Freilichtpark* [Free Light/Open Air Park], a nudist colony founded near Hamburg in 1903. Figure 4 illustrates the similarities in the representation and significance of the male body in the *Jugendkultur*, the man-loving, and the naturist movements. This nude, one from a 100-photograph series by Max Koch, thematizes naturism in terms of the male body represented against a wildlife background. The title of the picture, *Freilicht*, points to the sublime dimension of male homosociality, which is parallel to the noble ideal of Greek Eros and Locke's discourse of friendship. In the context of such visualizations, the focus on the youth in the discourse of the *Jugendkultur* movement is strongly charged with same-sexuality, which, in turn, homoeroticizes Locke's preoccupation with the younger generation.[138]

Fig. 4 and 5. Freilicht by Max Koch, 1897. Der Fahrman by Adolf Brand, March 1921. Schwules Museum, Berlin, Bibliothek.

As I have mentioned, Locke's academic career in philosophy is relevant to the vision of homoerotic bonding in his writings. This link should be emphasized as even more complex and significant, since investment in philosophical discourses is central to all the above-discussed European homoerotic projects: Carpenter's *Ioläus*, *Der Eigene*, the Wandervogel movement, and Wyneken's *Eros*. Their over-lapping visions are a combination of two philosophical strands – German indivi-dualism and the Platonic concept of love – and the same link is established by

Locke. In the earlier-quoted letter to Hughes, he draws attention to a connection between German philosophy and classical philosophy, claiming that especially the new German thought is quite parallel to Hellenic thought. Thus, Locke's academic interests enabled him to refer to and elaborate the philosophical roots of European homoerotic discourse.

As the above analysis has shown, Locke's writing is permeated with latent references to many German same-sex right activists and thinkers, who in turn refer to the towering figures of German and Greek philosophers and American Renaissance writers. The intertextual transnational network is formed of overlapping chains of influence such as the one between Stirner, Nietzsche, and *Der Eigene*; or Plato, Carpenter, and Wyneken. The central importance of intertextuality in Locke's letters is strengthened by the fact that in his correspondence with artists, he devotes ample space to the discussions and recommendations of literary texts. Characteristically, these complex entanglements can be accurately described with a fragment from Locke's letter quoted earlier: "Strange how things turn out – here are four friends together whom I never dreamed would even come to know one another. As life goes on the threads seem to get tangled and criss-cross – and then suddenly sometimes out of the tangle a pattern looms and it almost looks like *Providence and destiny*."

The relevance of this statement to Locke's intertextual endeavors can be read as a meaningful analogy; his complex rhetorical network of references and inspirations parallels the network of his friends, whose function was inspiration as well as the expression of male homoerotic desire. This phenomenon is analogous to the strategy adopted by same-sex activists to create a legitimate history, which is exemplified by the earlier-mentioned practice of forming lists of great man-loving men from the past or canons affirming the tradition of male friendship, with Carpenter's *Iolaus* as the most influential example. German and British activists, just like Locke, established social as well as textual male communities. Characteristically, the German same-sex discourse and Locke's idiolect and coterie transcend Bloom's paradigm of the poetic anxiety of influence. Instead of seeking confrontation with past literary giants, which results from the primal fear that their own ideas have been already expressed, Locke and same-sex activists above all seek legitimization in the texts of their recognized predecessors and hence transform the anxiety of influence into the affirmation of male intertextual bonding. Attempts to construct a patrilineal tradition of black letters as a means to resolve the black anxiety of authorship have already been discussed using the examples of Du Bois and Washington; however, Locke's representations of intertextual homosociality are more complex and multifaceted. Whereas Du Bois and Washington celebrate all-American, both intra- and inter-racial, *arboreal* father-son relationships, Locke forms a multilateral and transatlantic *rhizome*, which combines the vertical *eromenos-erastes* paradigm with the more horizontal brotherly camaraderie, all latent with same-sexual desire.

Transatlantic Intertextualities and Black Interzones

A significant characteristic of Locke's intertextual travels is that, apart from Whitman's vistas, most of the destinations are in Europe and most of the discourses he appropriates do not foreground the race issue. Thus, even though he advocated race solidarity as a pragmatic tool in a world dominated by a racialized conception of identity, male comradeship as constructed in his letters is not restricted to black men and is deeply ingrained in classical (white) European discourses. This strategy is especially interesting in the light of the accounts of the homosexual community in New York in the 1920s in Mumford's *Interzones: Black/White Sex Districts in Chicago and New York in Early Twentieth Century*, Geoffrey Chauncey's *Gay New York*, and Eric Garber's "T'Aint Nobody's Bizness: Homosexuality in 1920s Harlem."[139] Mumford and Garber convincingly argue that due to the Progressive movement's successes in removing red-light districts and bars permitting same-sex relationships from the "white" parts of cities, all such venues found their new location in black districts such as Harlem. The fact that the presence of sexual transgressions was prominent and constituted an inherent element of the black community can be further illustrated also with references to the contemporaneous literary representations. For example, in McKay's *Home to Harlem*, Jake sings a rhyme "And there is two things in Harlem I don't understan'/It is a bulldyking woman and a faggoty man."[140] Even though the main character does not identify with these figures, the lines represent them as structural elements of Harlem culture. A parallel indication of the prominence of transgressive sexualities in Harlem can be found in Hughes's claim that New Negro Renaissance leaders "thought the race problem had at last been solved through Art and Gladys Bentley." Since he devotes almost a page to depict Bentley's "vulgar" and "masculine" performance, the text positions transgressive sexuality at the heart of the Renaissance.[141]

The presence of alternative sexuality in black districts necessarily influenced American same-sexual expression and representations. As Mumford claims:

> because of the racial segregation of vice, African-Americans represented the primary group influencing the fundamental culture of the [homosexual] interzone...In the urban construction of sexuality Freudianism may have supplied the modern theory of homosexuality, but African-American dance and music shaped the practice.[142]

Due to the particular territorialization of the interzones and the influence of Freudianism, which identified black culture with the Id and unrepressed sexuality, the same-sex community's social patterns were culturally blackened.[143] And yet, at a time when American homosexual culture drew on black cultural practices, Locke constructs his vision of homoerotic bonding with references that do not foreground the issue of race, but that are rooted in an exclusively Western philosophy.[144] In this way, he distances himself from the gay community related to black, mainly lower-class social practices of the interzones and chooses to identify with the elitist European philosophical ideals. This distancing from the margins echoes Du Bois's elitism and the *talented tenth* vision. Locke's rejection of the influence of the black proletarian culture marked as sexually transgressive is parallel to his erasure of the New Woman from the New Negro rhetoric. Consequently, even in his construction of same-sex masculinity, Locke remains to a large extent committed to the ethics of respectable middle-class manhood. His omission of criminalized margins and illegitimate sexuality of the interzones as well as the fact that he positions his idiolect on the periphery of the private sphere rather than openly in the public stems from his bourgeois commitment to the separate spheres and the relegation of sexuality to the private realm. His intertextual construction of male coterie and same-sexuality is as an example of "queer" middle-class identity, which, according to Chauncey, fuses hegemonic respectability and same-sexuality, strategically guarding the private-public sphere divide.[145]

Conclusion

This chapter has explored the ways in which Locke's concepts of the New Negro and his Renaissance are charged with various gendered meanings and entangled with European discourses of same-sexuality. The community of New Negroes is symbolically constructed as masculine, whereas the idea of rebirth inherent in the concept of the "Renaissance" enables the representation of this male circle as capable of spiritual reproduction. Locke fashions himself as the maternal, life-giving force behind the fresh young generation and their rite of initiation into the new masculinized identity. His correspondence with the artists from the younger generation reveals that, at the center of the 1920s Niggerati, there was a male circle of intimate friends communicating in an idiolect that affirmed male bonding as a transcendental and inspirational phenomenon and provided positive space for homoerotic desire through allusions to Ancient Greek ideals and Whitman. This rhetoric reveals uncanny parallels with a dense network of texts produced by the early-twentieth-century German Youth Movement and same-sex activists. Their representation of youth as a driving force of change and hope, the homoerotization of the bond between younger and older men, and the investment in individualistic German philosophy as well as classical ideals of friendship constitute a reference that illuminates homoerotic spaces in Locke's writings, both public and private. These allusions are also part of an interesting dynamic of transatlantic intertextual references, which permeate Locke's letters. The Negro Renaissance echoes the American Renaissance, the European Renaissance, the German turn-of-the-century Renaissance of the Renaissance, as well as the intermediate interconnections between them. The network of abundant allusions to both other male writers and their texts providing space for homoerotic desire takes a form of peculiar male homoerotic intertextual bonding.

As a result, both at the level of social relationships in which Locke chose to engage when introducing the New Negro Renaissance as well as at the level of texts chosen as referents for it, the New Negro community emerges as a masculinist circle tinted with latent yet all-pervading homoeroticism. It should be emphasized that the homoerotic dimension of Locke's public writing is revealed only after following a dense network of intertextual references in his correspondence. His commitment to privacy and the bourgeois separate spheres ideal is in stark opposition to Walter Thurman's public violations of respectability, which are discussed in Chapter 4. Whereas Du Bois's and Washington's embrace of middle-class respectability is primarily manifest in their emphasis on traditional family values and "policing of the black woman's body," Locke chooses a path that does not reject respectable manliness yet disregards heterosexual relations. As a result, women are excluded not only from the representative talented tenth but are entirely erased from the discourse. The only significant moments when "the feminine" surfaces is in the feminized land of Harlem conquered by the black migrant-pioneers and in the realm of maternal metaphors, whose appropriation enables Locke to endow his coterie with reproductive capacity and express the affective quality of male bonding. Locke's homosocial vision can also be read as serving the same function as Washington's non-violent manliness and Du Bois's rewriting of the lynch ideology – the consistent exclusion of female subjects prevents the activation of the still influential myth of the black rapist, which necessarily depends on the presence of the pure woman victim. In Jim Crow America, Locke's vision of male camaraderie with its potential homoerotic implications is less threatening to the hegemonic logic than seemingly more normative heterosexual desire.

Chapter 3
Arts, War, and the Brave New Negro: Gendering the Black Aesthetic

We,...soldiers on this particular cultural front, have
a duty of bravely raising our arms against the stereotypes.[1]
Alain Locke, ["On Literary Stereotypes"]

Whether it is evaluated as reactionary or revolutionary, advancement through cultural productivity was unquestionably the fundamental element of Locke's strategy of racial emancipation. Whereas the previous chapter analyzed gender and sexuality constructions in the rhetoric of the movement, this chapter examines these notions in Locke's vision of the black aesthetic. His interest in aesthetic theory is manifest both in his doctoral dissertation on the philosophy of values as well as in his thirty-year-long engagement as a literary and art critic. Between 1928 and 1954, Locke wrote a series of annual retrospective reviews of Negro literature for the *Opportunity* and later *Phylon* as well as a number of individual articles devoted to literature, sociology, and music. The aesthetic that is championed in the texts retains much continuity throughout all the years the reviews span. My analysis scrutinizes the gender implications of Locke's black aesthetic, and it continues the exploration of gender and sexuality tropes in the production of the literary and aesthetic history begun in the previous chapters. Just as the paradigms of the anxiety of influence, the anxiety of authorship, and intertextual homosociality are intimately connected to different ways of asserting black masculinity and sexuality, Locke's aesthetics is inescapably bound to the masculinization of art.

Locke's persistent rhetorical infusion of the black aesthetic with masculine connotations that this chapter explores needs to be read in the context of the contemporaneous gendering of the artist and artistic creativity. Since the mid-nineteenth century, male writers expressed anxiety over the feminization of American authorship, most famously articulated by Nathaniel Hawthorne's resentment towards the "d[amne]d mob of scribbling women."[2] This phenomenon is explored in detail by Ann Douglas, who laments the feminization of Victorian culture and the sentimental dominance established by genteel women and ministers, which paved the way for the emergence of mass culture.[3] Such gendering of artistic output is either resented, as manifest in Hawthorne's remark, or used to assert

American national identity as anti-artistic and hence masculine. The latter strategy is notably executed by Frederick Jackson Turner, who poetically defines the American character as:

> That coarseness and strength combined with acuteness and inquisitiveness; that practical, inventive turn of mind, quick to find expedients; that masterful grasp of material things, lacking in the artistic but powerful to effect great ends; that restless, nervous energy; that dominant individualism, working for good and for evil, and withal that buoyancy and exuberance which comes with freedom – these are traits of the frontier, or traits called out elsewhere because of the existence of the frontier.[4]

The dominance of this representation at the time is illustrated by the fact that it largely parallels Locke's depiction of the American temperament as superb boyishness. The gendered character of Turner's imagery has been noted by Alan Trachtenberg, who argues that this fragment celebrates heroic masculinity and thus genders the American character as male.[5] For the black male artist, the gendering of this powerful image is further complicated by the race dimension. The difficult predicament stemming from this intersection is revealed when Turner's image is juxtaposed with an influential definition of the black race by Robert E. Park, who argues that:

> The temperament of the Negro, as I conceive it, consists in a few elementary but distinctive characteristics, determined by physical organizations and transmitted biologically. These characteristics manifest themselves in a genial, sunny, and social disposition, in an interest and attachment to external, physical things rather than to subjective states and objects of introspection, in a disposition for expression rather than enterprise and action…The Negro is, by natural disposition, neither an intellectual nor an idealist, like the Jew; nor a brooding introspective, like the East Indian; nor a pioneer and frontiersman, like the Anglo-Saxon. He is primarily an artist, loving life for its own sake. His métier is expression rather than action. He is, so to speak, the lady among the races.[6]

Park's definition has been analyzed and criticized by numerous black writers and scholars, from Ralph Ellison to Ross. I quote it here to show how it echoes Turner's depiction and simultaneously redefines what Turner labels American (and explicitly warns not to conflate it with English) into the Anglo-Saxon pioneer. The juxtaposition of these quotes illuminates Du Bois's concept of "two warring ideals," an American and a Negro, and the rhetorical exclusion of African Americans from the national identity. Park represents the black character as an exact opposition of Turner's American temperament, with such symmetrical polarizations as "dominant individualism" versus "social disposition," "restless and nervous" versus "sunny and genial," or "action" versus "expression." The latter binary opposition is especially relevant for an analysis of black authorship and its anxieties. Whereas Turner strategically excludes the feminized realm of the artistic to reinforce the masculine heroism of the American, Park relegates the black race specifically to this sphere. This results in a difficult predicament in which the black male author, already troubled by the anxiety of authorship, faces the anxiety stemming from the imposed feminization of his racial identity and of his artistic endeavors. Such a conflation of blackness, femininity, and the arts sheds light on Locke's relentless insistence to express the black aesthetic as masculine or to render it as production, which is discussed by Summers as a significant element of Locke's assertion of middle-class manhood in the public sphere. Since the gendering of the aesthetics is a part of a continuous struggle of the black writer, parallel anxieties are discussed in Chapter 4, on the example of Thurman's discontents with the unproductivity of the black bohemia, and in Chapter 6, where I explore Wright's attempts to render writing as a weapon.

The context-specific gender dimension of Locke's aesthetic ideology becomes visible in the light of the arguments presented by Ann Douglas in her study *Terrible Honesty: Mongrel Manhattan in the 1920s* (1995), the sequel to *The Feminization of American Culture* (1977). In *Terrible Honesty*, Douglas again evokes the emblematic figure of the Victorian matriarch, this time to claim that the emergence of modernism in the United States was a matricidal project directed against the sentimental culture of the nineteenth century. What makes her study a productive reference in the discussion of Locke's aesthetics is her argument that the death of the matriarch was inherently connected with the emergence of the black man as the figure symbolically central to the modernist breakthrough; feminization was succeeded by "Negroization." The logic of this process becomes more conspicuous when the conflation of the newly emergent Freudian and anthropological discourses at the time is taken into account. The moderns approached race from a peculiar Freudian perspective defined by Douglas as a "quasi-anthropological equation of the 'primitive mind' and the 'savage' with the unconscious and the id." In the light of this identification, sexually-restrained Victorian culture, gendered feminine and raced white, was being displaced by the uninhibited Jazz Age, raced black and gendered as masculine.[7]

The Sentimental Matriarch

This turn from Victorianism to modernism, heavily charged with the notions of race and gender, is visible in Locke's almost obsessive preoccupation with the issue of sentimentalism.[8] The concept recurs as the archenemy of the Negro expression in almost every text devoted to aesthetics. In his writings, sentimentalism is syntactically related to a number of other concepts, which together form a connotative field repeated in a number of texts. It is historicized by Locke as related to the Victorian era, since it recurs together with phrases such as "mid-Victorian" or "prudish Victorian." The sentimental tradition is characterized as the "genteel" culture of "respectability," whose cultural productions are: "melodramatic," "romantic," "romancing," "poeticizing," "subjectively personal," "idealistic," "moralistic," and "apologetic." Descriptions referring to sentimental art, such as "hyper-sensitive," "weak," "squeamish," "mawkish," "prudish," "palliative," "lily-whitist," "pretty-fied," "self-conscious," and "touchy" endow this aesthetic with the gender features of Douglas's Victorian matriarch. The primary forces behind sentimentalism are "race idolaters who at heart were still sentimentalists seeking consolation for inferiority" on the one hand, and "patronizing," "missionary," and "condescending" "interracial sentimentalists" on the other. This echoes Locke's coupling of the passive feminine Old Negro and his white accomplice – white feminine charity. Hence, sentimentalism is the antithesis of self-reliance, which defines the philosophy of the New Negro.[9]

In order to anthropomorphically represent the sentimentalist aesthetic, Locke recurrently evokes the contemporaneously influential figure of Pollyanna. He starkly rejects the "shabby psychology of Pollyanna optimism and sentimentalism" and deplores "placid silence and Pollyanna complacency."[10] According to Douglas, Pollyanna was a "patron saint for a good while" and represented the culture of self-help therapeutics "dominated by feminine practitioners and popularizers."[11] She was a residual trace of "the Victorian matriarch" in the early twentieth century. Locke's persistent repudiation of sentimentalism in his attempt to forge black modernism accurately fits Douglas's thesis about symbolically matricidal tendencies of modernism. However, in the light of the quote from Park, there is additional motivation behind Locke's project; not only must he deal with the Victorian matriarch of the American past, he must also exorcise the present association of the black artist and "the lady of the races." The fact that Park compares the black race specifically to the genteel notion of the "lady" reinforces parallels with Douglas's Victorian femininity.

The rejection of sentimentalism is closely linked in Locke's writings with the issue of propaganda, which was the fundamental bone of contention within the Negro Renaissance discourse. In this dispute, one of the most influential voices was Du Bois's radical position, which is summed up in one of his most often quoted statements that he "do[es] not care a damn for any art that is not used for propaganda."[12] Locke, on the other hand, in his critical articles and reviews, painstakingly repeats his rejection of propaganda as incompatible with the desired racial expression. According to him, propaganda plays into the condescending logic of sentimentalism, and employing it implies assuming a sentimentalist feminized position. Locke's aesthetic dialogue with Du Bois gains a gender dimension in the light of the feminization of sentimentalism and propaganda. Thus, his critique of Du Bois's Dark Princess as "fall[ing] an artistic victim to its own propagandist ambushes" can be read as an attempt to feminize Du Bois's position. Locke challenges the militant masculinity represented by Du Bois's "not caring *a damn*" by associating his text with "mawkish" romanticism, which aptly illustrates the relevance of gender in the production of aesthetic and literary history.[13]

The Brave Modernist

Locke's repudiation of sentimentalism and propaganda is complemented by the affirmation of a contrasting aesthetic, which is defined as modernist. The concept of modernism is particularly useful for Locke, since it structurally parallels the notion of the New Negro. Both are answers to the new modern condition largely determined by urbanization, and both are deeply rooted in the millennial attempts at renewal. As Ross argues, the New Negro "exploite[d] the newness of the century to advocate for a new paradigm of race relations."[14] Analogously, the driving force behind modernism was linked to the often-quoted assumption that "on or about December 1910, human character changed."[15] Locke's modernism clearly emerges as an antithesis to Victorian genteel culture. He assesses the desired literary expression of the New Negro movement as "realistic, rather than sentimental, seriously and scientifically analytic."[16] Just as with sentimentalism, the modernist aesthetic is depicted through a number of associations. In the connotative field of the modernist aesthetic, "mawkish" is replaced with "lusty," and "squeamish" with "penetrating." According to Locke, cultural productions should be "sober," "solid," "searching," "sound and understanding," "brave," "candid and ruthless," "crude," "courageous, frank and objective," "healthy and firm," "boldly racial," and "meaty." His reviews also encompass non-fiction writings, which should be "militant but scientific." In the first of his annual reviews, Locke states that the literature of the new generation constitutes a "hardier richer crop."[17] These connotations strategically masculinize Negro writing, advancing it in opposition to feminized Victorianism. Locke's lexicon begins alluding to even more virile and stronger masculinity when he discovers the talent of Richard Wright. Wright's fiction "sounds like an opener similarly significant to Jean Toomer's startling and prophetic *Cane*. Lusty crude realism though it is, it has its salty peasant tang and poetic glint" and represents "a gusty, lusty, not too clear throated, doubly significant, new strain – proletarian poetry."[18] Locke's rendering of Wright echoes and reinforces his own championing of writing as militant, assertive, and masculine, as discussed in Chapter 6. The black aesthetic advocated by Locke is valid not only for literature but for music and fine arts as well. In an article about African art, Locke agrees that African dance "shows *crude realism*, and for that very reason the dancers...were men exclusively, never women."[19] Here, Locke explicitly forges a connection between "crude realism" and masculine gender.

Apart from masculinist connotations, the modernist aesthetic championed by Locke is based on sincerity and objectivity. In the introduction to the *Exhibition of the Art of the American Negro* in 1940, Locke claims that: "today's beauty must not be pretty with sentiment but solid and dignified with truth," whereas in *Fighting Words* (1940) he calls on the black artists to tell "the truth, and the full truth, about Negro life" and to be "extremely objective."[20] The aesthetic emerging from these statements is intimately related to the modernist principle of "terrible honesty" as outlined by Douglas, who claims that the predominant attitude among the "moderns" was "'being truthful': "opposing every form of 'sentimentality,' they prided themselves on facing facts, the harder the better; 'facts' alone...are the 'acid' test of value."[21] Locke's recurrent praise of realism, which is supposed to be objective and scientific, reveals the same tendency, which Douglas ascribes to the (white) moderns in her chapter "White Manhattan."

Locke's Pragmatic Primitivism

Another characteristic and complexly gendered feature that constitutes a parallel between Locke's aesthetic and modernism is the need to regenerate literature. In many cases, this desire took the shape of primitivist longings for lost vitality and the unrepressed id. This process gains also a gender dimension, as the collective imagination of the day locates the source of the imagined primeval strength in the black male body. Just as Eugene O'Neill resorts to the black idiom in his *Emperor Jones*, a literary epitome of modernist primitivism, Locke also encourages the younger artists to go back or go down; go back to African culture or go down to the black folk culture. Locke's primitivism is necessarily different from that of white modernists, since he has to assume a different position in relation to the otherness of the primitive, which results in what at first sight seem to be apparent contradictions. On the one hand, he claims that black people were "sharply cut off" from their roots and that their relation to Africa did not differ from that of white Americans. Yet he repeatedly encourages young black artists to "recapture a lost artistic heritage."[22] The contradiction is resolved through Locke's commitment to pragmatism, illustrated by his statement that "whatever theory [or] practice [moves] toward [race progress] is sound; whatever opposes and retards it is false," where he explicitly espouses a pragmatic definition of truth value.[23] In his essays on Negro art, he claims that even though "ethnologically" the connection between Africa and black Americans is artificial, "felt brotherhood and kinship is pragmatically a fact."[24] Locke thereby pragmatically reestablishes the connection between Africa and African Americans, which makes them more legitimate appropriators of African idioms than white modernists.

As Michael North argues, the complex dynamic between black and white cultures was one of the central tensions of the modernist revolution. Although he does not analyze the gender dimensions of these racial entanglements, his study illuminates Locke's relation to African culture more accurately than the primitivist paradigm offered by Douglas. North claims that the appropriation of the black idiom in its multifaceted forms, from African American dialect through jazz to African masks, is entangled in a number of contradictions. White moderns rebel against tradition and standardization through the use of idioms perceived as oppositional to the forces of civilization, yet often their appropriations reduce black culture to the natural material, which can be utilized only by the cultured (white) modernists. On the other hand, such ethnographic explorations and racialized borrowings inevitably lead to the relativization of languages and cultures, a process that is in opposition to the simple primitivist desire to return to the authentic primitive natural stability. North credits black modernist texts such as McKay's or Hurston's with the exposure of the main dilemma of black writers and the false dichotomy between the natural black savage and the black imitator of white fascination with the primitive.[25]

North does not elaborate on Locke's project to regenerate black American expression with the transfusion of traditional African aesthetic, yet the black philosopher from Washington envisions Africa in a parallel way to Hurston and McKay. Africa in his texts, even if it is associated with the revitalization of cultural productions, is far from being primitive material. Reversing the dichotomy of white activity and black passivity, inherent in both the scenario of anthropological examination and that of white artistic appropriation, Locke endows the African aesthetic with agency in a statement that "African sculptures have unshackled the modern artist from the tyranny of the camera." However, the evocation of the modern European artist inspired by the Dark Continent, exemplified by Picasso or Cézanne, also serves to legitimize African cultural capital. Locke insists that the representation of cultures such as African as primitive stems from "the desire and suppressed objective in many investigations…to build a social pyramid," whereas, in fact, African art represents highly stylized mastery.[26] Instead of treating African art as the ahistorical cultural unconscious, in Negro Art – Past and Present, he carefully classifies and evaluates different regions of the continent. Hence, Locke's primitivist project problematizes the "primitivism" of African culture; he sees the African mask not as the site of cultural innocence and authenticity but of the stylization and elaboration emblematic of long cultural tradition.

Locke's rhetoric of regeneration and the focus on African cultures, even though it is more complex than Douglas's account of modern primitivism, still resonates with gender connotations analogous to the ones pointed out in Terrible Honesty. These most visibly emerge when African and black American cultures and identities are juxtaposed. Although Locke encourages black artists to explore their privileged connection to African cultures, he repeatedly represents African and American Negro art, especially Negro art of the past, as antithetical concepts:

His taste, skill and artistic interests in America are almost the reverse of his original ones in the African homeland. In Africa the dominant arts were the decorative and the craft arts – sculpture, metal working, weaving. In America, the Negro's main arts have been song, dance, music, and later, poetry. The former, being technical, are rigid, controlled, disciplined; thus characteristic African art expression is sober, heavily conventionalized, restrained. The latter are freely emotional, sentimental and exuberant, so that even the emotional temper of the American Negro represents a reversal of his African temperament...What we have then thought "primitive" in the American Negro, his naïve exuberance, his spontaneity, his sentimentalism are, then, not characteristically African and cannot be explained as an ancestral heritage. They seem the result of his particular experience in America and the emotional upheavals of its hardships and their compensatory reactions.[27]

Ideas expressed in this fragment are an elaboration of Locke's seminal essay from *The New Negro*, "The Legacy of Ancestral Arts" and are also reiterated later in texts such as *The Negro in Art* (1940). The main argument is that slavery and the alienation of black American experience resulted in the loss of "the ancestral skills," which accounts for the disparity between American and African cultural productions. In a stark contrast to Washington's narrative, the contact with white culture through slavery was not a more or less painful way to civilization but, to the contrary, it was a way of cultural decline to what is perceived as "primitive." Locke not only emphasizes the difference in the choice of forms of artistic expression, he also abundantly characterizes the two kinds of artistic temperaments. In the light of the above-discussed gender politics of sentimentalism and its rejection by the moderns, Locke's connotations in the quoted fragment also seem to be loaded with gendered meanings. African art is depicted in terms that bring to mind the ideal of manliness – it is "technical,...rigid, controlled, disciplined,... sober, heavily conventionalized, restrained," whereas black American cultural productions are feminized as "emotional" and "sentimental." African art is depicted as parallel to Locke's masculinist modernist aesthetic, whereas the connotations of traditional black American art uncannily echo the discourse of Victorian sentimentalism. This quote interestingly echoes and complicates the depiction of the Negro temperament as articulated by Park. Locke admits that African Americans are "exuberant," "spontaneous," and "naïve," which neatly parallels Park's Negro who is "genial" and "sunny," yet he claims that these features stem from their American experience rather than constitute "biologically transmitted" racial traits. Moreover, he challenges the assumption that the artistic is necessarily related to the feminine by celebrating masculinist African arts as disciplined and self-controlled. The fact that Locke uses adjectives that are closely related to restrained manliness rather than virile masculinity can be explained as an attempt to challenge the primitivist assumptions about the uncivilized character of African art.

Thus Locke's frequent encouragements to draw inspiration from African art can be read as a desire to remasculinize black American expression. Characteristically, his efforts to regenerate black culture through a reference to African masculinist art parallel the dynamic depicted by Douglas, who argues that the imagined black masculinity was the central symbolic influence on the modernist "terrible honesty." The parallel between modernist primitivism and a need to reclaim an essential masculinity and their dependence on the image of the black body are acknowledged also by Carby in *Race Men*. Carby claims that "the desires of white modernists for an unambiguous, essential masculinity were...located in a black body," which was dehistoricized to fulfill this function.[28] On the example of Paul Robeson's nudes, she argues that Antique stylization erases the raced history from Robeson's body and produces his image as an emblem of "the essential masculine." Analogously, Locke resorts to the image of the African artist from before slavery, whose image is neither contemporaneous nor historicized, to revitalize black cultural productions. He avoids references to contemporary African art, which are necessarily entangled in the history of colonization and hence would not be able either to revirilize black cultural productions or to signify an essential masculinity. His primitivist encouragement to recapture the lost heritage is both opposite and parallel to Theodore Roosevelt's African escapade, whose function, according to Bederman, was to revitalize and virilize his manhood.[29] On the one hand, Locke challenges the notion of Africa as the passive, natural material – the ethnic other gains agency in his narrative. On the other hand, his project is largely motivated by the same urge as Roosevelt's – a desire to regenerate and stabilize masculine identity, in this case that of the black artist. In this African detour and celebration of the pragmatically reclaimed ancestors, the "sentimental," "exuberant," "naïve" "Old Negro" becomes reinvented and revitalized as the active and self-reliant New Negro. The strategy to seek strength and reinvention in African culture, pragmatically hailed as the past adolescence of black Americans, is also analogous to Locke's glorification of the youth as the source of strength and hope for black culture. Just as the reclaimed bond with Africa is supposed to remasculinize and revirilize black expression, Locke's representations of bonding with younger male artists are constructed in masculinist terms of rebirth and revitalization.

The rendering of Africa as the *arche*, the imaginary cultural past, and the land of the ancestors, parallels the way Ancient Greece was used in the logic of the European Renaissance. Just as European Renaissance artists rediscovered Antiquity, black American artists were supposed to "resume lost cultural interests and recapture lapsed skills."[30] By utilizing the logic of the Renaissance and approaching Africa as a site of cultural tradition rather than nature, Locke avoids some of the earlier-mentioned contradictions and false dichotomies that drenched primitivist modernism as discussed by North. On the other hand, in both the European and in the black Renaissance, there emerges a tension between going back to the noble roots of civilization and the fact that both heritages are pre-Christian; Hellenic Greece and pre-slavery Africa thereby simultaneously function as "pagan" and "civilized."[31] Yet this inner tension between artistic heritage and paganism present in the two concepts endows them with additional impetus rather than weakens their potential in the logic of the Renaissance. Locke's appropriation of classical discourse discussed in the previous chapter suggests further analogies between Africa and Greece. Hellenic classicism at the time was represented in European same-sex discourse as the culture of masculine homoerotic expression, which was Spartanly virile rather than "inverted" and effeminate. Analogously, Locke's vision of African art, in contrast to black American art, is distinctively masculinist. Hence, the potential homoerotism of both cultural sources does not clash with the masculinization of artistic productions.

Locke's black primitivism can also be considered a peculiar extension of the white man's burden and civilization ideology, which I discussed as a central issue in the Washington-Du Bois debate. In the debate, the myth was still a potent rhetorical tool that was appropriated by Washington in his missionary activities directed at Native Americans and deconstructed by Du Bois as an exploitation of the underprivileged. With the emergence of modernist primitivism and the popularization of Freudian psychoanalysis, the ideology of civilization gradually began to lose its currency.[32] Whereas for Washington, becoming the burdened civilized man was a path to black manliness, Locke – following the logic of Euro-American primitivism – seeks the revitalization and masculinization of black culture in the lost African heritage. After the crisis of Victorianism, it is the imaginary uncivilized that becomes the site of the masculine. Yet, the power dynamic remains parallel: the white patron uplifting the lower races simply turns into the anthropologist or artist examining primitive cultures and in this process establishing his modern masculine identity as privileged.

Modernism, Decadence, and Sexuality

In the rhetoric of modernism, it is either a stifling sense of standardization or the decadent, degenerate condition that evokes the need for regeneration and the turn to the primitive. The themes of regeneration and primitivism in Locke's writings are also inherently connected with the concept of "decadence." Significantly, he attempts to position the black aesthetic in contrast to (white) Western decadence. Just as he pragmatically forges a special link between African culture and the black American community, he also strategically advances the notion that black Americans are not as culturally decadent as their white compatriots. This attitude is visible, for example, in his article on black art, "To Certain of Our Philistines," where he states that: "we have a right to expect and demand two things of the cultural expression of the Negro, that it should be vital and that it should be contemporary. This is not the creed of being new-fangled for the sake of being so – let others who have more cause to be decadent and blasé than we."[33] In this statement, he conflates decadence with the aesthetic of art for art's sake. At other times, when he is more descriptive than prescriptive, Locke acknowledges that the sense of decadence is determined by class affiliation and living conditions rather than racial identity. Hence, for example, jazz "is an expression of modern hysteria, common to both black and white sophisticates in our hectic, neurotic civilization of today."[34] Analogous to his attitude regarding Africa, the two fragments contain apparent contradictions. Yet what is consistent is that, in both cases, decadence is associated with neurosis and degeneracy. Significantly, phrases such as "the mawkish sentimentality and concocted lascivity of the contemporary cabaret songs and dances" blend the imagery connected with decadence with epithets depicting Victorianism, which rhetorically links the two concepts. Hence, decadence and Victorianism emerge as the two projections against which Locke constructs his vision of strong and vital modernism.

The concept of decadence also interestingly resonates with the European same-sex discourse discussed in the previous chapter. In the collective imagination of the period, nobody embodied the fusion of the two concepts more powerfully than Oscar Wilde. Yet, even though the figure of Wilde was a readily available trope for expressing homoerotic desire and aesthetic vision, it was not used by Locke in his homoerotic rhetoric. Wilde appears in his texts only in connection to Bruce Nugent and his work "Smoke, Lilies, and Jade," which is euphemistically depicted by Hughes as "a green and purple story in the Oscar Wilde tradition."[35] Locke criticizes the "effete echoes of its contemporary decadence," tellingly suggesting that the less flamboyant poet Walt Whitman "would have been a better point of support than a left-wing pivoting on Wilde and Beardsley."[36] Hence Locke's reproachful representation of decadence reveals his rejection of flamboyant homoeroticism together with feminine Victorian sentimentalism, and both are contrasted with the masculinist aesthetic of modernism. This rejection of decadence perceived as degeneracy was also present in the German youth movement discourse, where hiking and natural settings, illustrated in the pictures in the previous chapter, were supposed to be a healthy answer to what was perceived as "a state of advanced decay."[37] Hence, the German intertextual resonances need to be seen as parallel to both Locke's peculiar primitivism and his opposition to decadence.[38] Locke pragmatically positions the New Negro between degenerated decadence and feminized sentimentalism. His vision of the modernist aesthetic regenerated through its inspiration from African cultures perfectly fits the logic of the Renaissance. Moreover, the tropes of renaissance and rebirth enable Locke to further distance himself from the decadent face of modernism.

Art Troops and War Tropes

The masculinization of the black aesthetic in Locke's discourse manifests itself also in his particular use of the war discourse. The rhetoric of militancy and war has been discussed as an element of Du Bois's constructions of black masculinity. The editor of *The Crisis* advanced a vision of black manhood that is militant yet civilized and noble. The preoccupation with militancy has also been mentioned in relation to the roots of the concept of the New Negro. Both *A New Negro for a New Century* and the post-war evocation of the trope were innately linked to combat. As I have indicated, critics argue that Locke's writings seem to elide this issue. His lack of direct political concern was one of the main reasons for the growing gap between his and Du Bois's positions. Nevertheless, war is all-pervasive in the critical texts as a metaphor if not as their subject matter.

The use of war tropes is conspicuous in Locke's contribution to the tellingly entitled text *Fighting Words* (1940), where he states: "And here is where this question of our own front for democracy takes on, I think, a special significance: that we, so to speak, *soldiers* on this particular *cultural front*, have a duty of bravely raising our arms against the stereotypes, of being extremely objective."[39] Locke, at the rhetorical level, repudiates Du Bois's charges about the political uselessness of the arts by positioning artists as soldiers and by fashioning the arts as a battle-front. His appeal to "extreme objectivity" makes this militant position parallel to Douglas's modernist "terrible honesty." Military metaphors are even more elaborate in another text meaningfully entitled "Advance on the Art Front" (1939). In the article, Locke compares "recent advances in contemporary Negro art" to "a courageous cavalry mov[ing] over difficult ground in the face of *obstacles worse than powder and shell* – silence and uncertainty." He adds that "after all, we cannot win on the *art front* with just a thin *advance line* of *pioneering* talent or even the occasional sharp salient of genius; we must have behind this talent and this genius the *backing of solid infantry and artillery support*."[40] Here, artistic endeavors are represented as just as demanding and courageous as war efforts, since they are able to endure "obstacles worse than powder and shell." Characteristically, not only artists are represented as fighters: "the backing of solid infantry and artillery support" refers to the black community's support for arts. Hence, Locke, who throughout his life fashioned himself as the primary supporter of black artists, is included under the labels of infantry and artillery. The editor of *The New Negro* manages to thematize cultural productivity as a struggle also with reference to particular historical events. In the article "Martyrdom to Glad Music: The Irony of Black Patriotism," he refers to the significance of Jim Europe's band for the Hell Fighters Regiment. Locke argues that "there was a *domestic and a foreign enemy*; these men had to fight on a double front – with shot and bayonet on the one, with grit, music, and laughter on the other."[41] The concept of the "enemy" that black artists have to face recurs also in other texts in which Locke discusses artistic expression.

All the metaphors explored above represent the black artist as the militant soldier-fighter and hence masculinize his position. Locke's discourse of the "art front" is in dialogue with Du Bois's rejection of art and culture as politically unproductive. This representation of art as struggle politicizes cultural productions, which also parallels Locke's rejection of decadent art and art for art's sake. Locke's aesthetic philosophy places modernist art as a successful weapon in contrast to propaganda and decadence, a strategy that would be developed by Wright.

In addition, the rhetoric of war, with its inherent exclusion of female subjects, interestingly resonates with Locke's influential article about black soldiers in France "The Black Watch on the Rhine." In the article, he depicts a blissful harmony of a multi-racial and multi-religious community of French soldiers from Africa and the Middle East: "this barracks was a medley of types, costumes, and manners – more like a bazaar than a garrison...and pervading all a good fellowship that was amazing." The logic in the fragment is reminiscent of "The New Negro" gender politics due to its emphasis on diversification and the simultaneous absence of women. The statement echoes the rhetoric of cultural pluralism as advanced by Locke's close friend Kallen, with its characteristic metaphors of the orchestra or mosaic. Additionally, Locke's language uncannily resembles the idiolect of friendship discussed in the previous chapter. The soldiers were "moulded into a more *intimate comradeship* of arms than has ever existed among a foreign mercenary force heretofore." They "are French citizens, *comrades* not only in arms but in all the basic human relationships...leavened with the salt of French *fraternity* and democracy" and "humanly and naturally *brothers* in all the fundamental relations of life."[42] To Locke, this blissful comradeship seems to be "a utopian illusion." In the context of this representation of war as male comradeship, if arts are a battlefield, the community of artists emerges as analogous to masculine fraternity at wartime. Hence, Locke's attempt to create an intimate creative circle of male artists in his private letters is echoed in his public discourse of art and war.

The fragments from "The Black Watch on the Rhine" point to the interconnectedness of several dynamics in Locke's public and private writing. It is deeply divided by the polarity between on the one hand the New Negro, who is metonymically associated with the American character, the African temperament, German and Greek virile same-sexuality, newness, and bravery of the modernist aesthetic, and on the other hand the Old Negro, whose connotations include feminization, inverted same-sexuality, decadent, sentimental, and propagandist aesthetics. The logic of the Renaissance is evoked to call the New Negro into being and to exterminate the Old Negro. The fact that the Old Negro is analogous to "the lady of the races" makes it a matricidal project rather than a patricide, which is parallel to the modernist repudiation of the Victorian matriarch discussed by Douglas. This further confirms that Locke's textual homosociality is less troubled by the anxiety of influence and the death wish towards symbolic fathers than Du Bois's writing. Locke focuses on the celebration of black male authorship at the cost of the exclusion of female artists.

Despite Locke's devotion to the younger generation of the movement, his aesthetic agenda was not embraced by all of its participants. The following chapter explores a competing project of the black aesthetic that was championed by Wallace Thurman. This member of the new *generation*, instead of realizing the vision of a *regeneration* of black American culture, became emblematic of the *degeneration* of the movement.

Part 2

Wallace Thurman
and Niggerati Manor

Chapter 4
Gangsters and Bootblacks, Rent Parties and Railroad Flats:
Wallace Thurman's Challenges to the Black Bourgeoisie

I'm sick of being constantly surrounded by sterile white people,
and of having to associate with Negroes who are also sterile and pseudo white.[1]
Lucille in *Infants of the Spring*

Mulattoes have always been accorded more consideration
by white people than their darker brethren.
They were made to feel superior even during slave days
...made to feel proud...that they were bastards.[2]
Truman Walter in *The Blacker the Berry*

A great proletarian mass...constitutes the most interesting
and important element in Harlem,
for it is this latter class and their institutions
that gives the community its color and fascination.[3]
Wallace Thurman, "Negro Life in New York's Harlem"

Whereas the first part of the book explored the writings of Alain Locke, a mentor of young black artists, the second focuses on a representative of the mentored generation: Wallace Thurman. It examines his embrace of diverse gender and sexuality constructions and their interrelatedness with race and class representations. Thurman's portrayal of the Harlem community and black arts strikingly differs from Locke's vision of the Renaissance. Instead of brave avant-garde, noble mentors, and spiritual comrades, this part will explore much more outrageous figures such as dandies, sweetbacks, and gangsters.

Analogous to Locke, Thurman was recognized as a key participant of the New Negro Renaissance by its participants at the time as well as the literary histories of the movement. Since constructions of gender and sexuality are the main focus of this study, what also makes the juxtaposition of Thurman and Locke interesting is that both made efforts to express non-normative desire in their writings. As Granville Ganter argues, "Thurman's sexual conduct was...*queer* in the sense that he didn't operate by the norms of strictly homosexual or heterosexual culture. Whether Thurman was hetero or homosexual is difficult to say. He was, however, indisputably bisexual."[4] Thurman did not belong to Locke's circle of male friends and did not participate in their homoerotic idiolect. As Ganter convincingly claims, Thurman's constructions and accounts of sexuality cannot be neatly categorized within present-day discourses of homosexuality, which is one of the reasons why he has not attracted much critical attention from contemporary scholars of gay studies in their rewritings of literary history.[5]

Thus his position in the Niggerati circle and his representations of sexuality make an analysis of Thurman's writings and personal correspondence particularly apt to be juxtaposed with Locke's vision of the New Negro. Such a comparison has not been executed in detail, even though there are many structural similarities that encourage it. This most likely stems from the fact that, while Locke's writings have attracted wide scholarly attention, ranging in scope from poststructuralist philosophy to ecocriticism, Thurman's central role in the Niggerati circle has not been reflected by academic interest in his creative output. Many scholars recognize Thurman's pivotal role in the movement without providing a corresponding scrutiny of his writings or life. As a consequence, the scarce evaluation of Thurman's output is fragmented and contradictory.[6] Thurman's leading role in the movement is acknowledged by many participants of the New Negro community. They admit that Thurman both was perceived and fashioned himself as the leader of the younger generation. In one letter to William Jourdan Rapp, he explicitly assumes this role and, referring to his volume of essays *Aunt Hagar's Children*, states that "in it is formulated, rather immaturely I admit, premises for a new philosophy for a new generation of younger Negroes."[7] Moreover, as Eleonore Van Notten claims, on the basis of her analysis of archives and taped interviews with Bruce Nugent, "Locke had...identified Thurman as a potential rival who might interfere with his own plans to monitor, direct, and oversee the production of the entire body of black artistic expression during the 1920s."[8] Thus the two figures, due to their competing ambitions, arise as major opponents in the New Negro Renaissance discourse.

The rivalry between Locke and Thurman for the central position in the New Negro Renaissance stems not only from personal ambition but from the glaring disparity in their visions of the artistic movement, race relations, the black collective subject, and authorship. These differences are metonymically suggested in the dichotomy of Locke's New Negro and Thurman's Niggerati. This polarization is largely predicated on their respective philosophical and political approaches to the black community and culture. Locke adopts a pragmatic stance, which intends to forge a common collective subject position in order to foster group cultural politics and emancipation. He is conscious of the plurality of African Americans and aware that the unity of black Americans and their connection to Africa are grounded more in collective imagination than in any real kinship, be it essential or cultural. The collective subject of the New Negro is supposed to be pragmatically true and politically effective. In contrast, the stance adopted by Thurman is less engaged in politics and less logically integrated. It represents radical individualist cynicism, which undermines the uniting gestures of the Negro Renaissance. Thurman disrupts the unity of the collective subject in his celebration of multiculturalism in Harlem as well as in his representations of intragroup racism illustrated by colorist prejudice or discrimination of immigrants from the Caribbean. Thurman's cynical attitude to the notion of the New Negro and the Negro Renaissance manifests itself when he puts these terms in quotation marks and precedes them with qualifiers such as "so-called" or "well advertised."[9] His vision is deeply committed to radical individualism, which perceives emancipation and enlightenment as possible only for individuals through their individual actions. In terms of art politics and authorship, Thurman advocates the strategy of political non-involvement represented by art for art's sake.

Locke's affirmative pragmatism fosters his choice of the Renaissance as the central metaphor of the black cultural movement, whereas Thurman's skepticism results in his adoption of the discourse of decadence. The choice of these two oppositional tropes is intricately reflected in the themes of production and fertility versus consumption and infertility represented in Locke's and Thurman's writings respectively. This polarized dyad reveals the central significance of gender and sexuality in the two competing projects. Locke's exclusion of female subjects enables him to appropriate the maternal function in relation to male artists. His homoerotic discourse and vision of male intimacy are based on the idea of non-material – and thus more sublime – reproduction, primarily in the form of cultural productions. In contrast, Thurman's decadent vision is saturated with miscellaneous images of infertility. He responds to Locke's dedication of The New Negro to the younger generation by entitling his novel on the movement Infants of the Spring. The book openly challenges Locke's optimistic celebration of youth, since Thurman's New Negro does not produce any lasting offspring, be it biological or artistic. This is signaled already in the epigraph: "The canker galls the infants of the spring/Too oft before their buttons be disclosed/And in the morn and liquid dew of youth/ Contagious blastments are most imminent."[10] Thurman's reference to the warning addressed to Ophelia by Laertes in Hamlet cautions against the premature expression of youthful desires.[11] The youth depicted in the fragment is eroded with "canker" before it reaches maturity, which undermines the optimism embedded in the concept of the Negro Renaissance. Significantly, the novel's motto is echoed by the main character's claim that: "the average Negro intellectual and artist had no goal, no standards, no elasticity, no pregnant germ plasm."[12] When Raymond, who is acknowledged as one of Thurman's alter egos, links artistic production to biological reproduction, it challenges Locke's celebrations of artistic fertility. "The effort to formulate a new attitude toward life had become a seeking for a badge of courage. That which might have emerged normally, if given time, had been forcibly and prematurely exposed to the light. It now seemed as if *the Caesarian operation was going to prove fatal both to the parent and to the child.*"[13] Thus Thurman clearly undermines the affirmation of black male artistic childbirth omnipresent in Locke's renderings of the Renaissance and black authorship liberated from the anxiety of influence. Characteristically, if Locke figuratively appropriates female biological fertility in his vision of cultural rebirth, Thurman's vision of artistic decadence is reinforced by his choice not to depict reproduction in his texts despite his abundant representations of sexually active young women. The only two children represented in his two seminal novels, *The Blacker the Berry* and *The Infants*, are, respectively, aborted without guilt and left without proper care, physically deformed, and bound for certain death. Although Thurman's project is less optimistic and drenched with cynicism, it provides more space for the emergence of liberated black femininity. Although he undermines the existence of the New Negro, he entertains the vision of the New Negro Woman.

Another set of contrasts between the two projects emerges at the level of their rhetoric and the group identity they foster. As his emancipatory strategy, Locke forges a *homogeneous* racial and national identity at the cost of exclusion of black females. This strategic projection of cultural *sameness* is mirrored in his *same*-sex idiolect, which relegates sexual innuendoes to the private sphere. In contrast, Thurman defiantly assaults two of the most powerful hegemonic boundaries of the day: the separate spheres divide and the color line. His trespasses produce liminal and liberated moments of *heterotopia*. These pluralistic and democratic spaces harbor racial and sexual *otherness* as well as class and cultural *difference*. They are intimately related to Thurman's poetics, which will be analyzed with Bakhtin's notion of *heteroglossia*.

These strikingly symmetrical differences suggest that Thurman's project was constructed as a strategic assault on Locke's Renaissance. His most conspicuous attempt to challenge Locke's leading position can be found in *The Infants of the Spring*, where he masquerades the Howard professor as Dr. Parkes. He mocks Locke's elaborate self-fashioning as the maternal figure of the New Negro movement by referring to him throughout the novel as a "clucking mother hen."[14] This metaphor cleverly parodies Locke's attempts to become the midwife-*erastes*-mother-mentor of the artistic network. Thurman's recurrent references to the domestic bird rhetorically disempower Locke's self-positioning at the center of the movement. The metaphor is even more demeaning for Locke and relevant in the polemic between the two figures when it is juxtaposed with the phrase "the cock o' the walk" which is used in *The Blacker the Berry* to depict Walter Truman – Thurman's thinly veiled alter-ego.[15] The heavily gender-marked contrast between

Locke as a "hen" and Thurman as a "cock" reveals the relevance of masculinity in the debate between the editor of *Fire!!* and the editor of *The New Negro*.

As Part 1, this will analyze both published and unpublished texts. In the case of Thurman, the motivation behind such an approach slightly differs from the logic according to which Locke's texts were examined. One of the reasons for the focus on his unpublished writings is that, before the publication of *The Collected Writings of Wallace Thurman: A Harlem Renaissance Reader*, a vast part of Thurman's texts remained unpublished, available only in archival collections. The contemporaneous audience for these texts consisted of Thurman's literary friends, most notably Langston Hughes, Claude McKay, and Rapp. Consequently, their correspondence is of central significance in any analysis of Thurman's literary output, being the only space in which some of his texts existed in the discourse of the New Negro Renaissance.[16] Moreover, the boundary between the letters and Thurman's texts is often blurred. Many of his testimonies are reminiscent of his fiction, and this ambiguity is acknowledged by the author himself. For example, in a letter written to McKay in 1929, Thurman ends a brief autobiographical sketch with a statement that "the rest you can read in my autobiography, ready for fall publication, 1930," which playfully indicates that the letter is a fragment of a book intended for publishing.[17] The sentence, however, does not refer to any particular publication that was being prepared, which even further manifests that Thurman's writings interrogate the boundaries among letters, biography, and fiction. Moreover, this strategic conflation of fact and fantasy will gain additional significance in the context of decadence, the main theme of the following chapter, which, as many critics point out, is informed by the tension between life and art, history and fiction.[18] Since they constitute playful artistic self-creations, Thurman's letters will not be approached as privileged and more authentic texts than his works intended for publishing.

Decadence and dandyism constitute the central framework of analysis in Chapter 5, which focuses on the European connection in Thurman's writing. Before this transatlantic route is followed, however, Chapter 4 examines his entanglement in various contemporaneous American ideologies. It explores his commitment to residual discourses of respectable manliness and roughened new masculinity, especially as represented by the figures of the gangster and the proletarian. This investigation is followed by an analysis of Thurman's counter-bourgeois attempts to challenge hegemonic gender, race, and class politics in Jim Crow America.

Manliness and Roughing It: Residual Discourses of Hegemonic Masculinity

The few critical essays on Thurman written from a gender and sexuality-studies perspective focus on the role of queer sexuality in Thurman's writings and life.[19]

For example, Ganter's fundamental claim is that Thurman's ambiguous representations and self-expressions of sexuality function as a systemic element of his artistic project, which is informed by resistance to the existing social and ontological boundaries.[20] Even though Ganter's arguments are persuasive – and his study will be elaborated on and developed later in the following chapter – his approach misses Thurman's entanglement in the dominant contemporaneous ideologies of masculinity and the ways in which they influence and complicate his representations of gender and sexuality.

As illustrated in his depiction of the New Negro as the cultural producer, Locke largely subscribes to the notions of respectability and productivity, which are central to the ideology of Marketplace Manhood. In Thurman's gender constructions, productive manliness can be traced as an influential although residual rather than dominant factor. Thurman's role in the shifts in ideologies of black masculinity is acknowledged by Summers. Although he does not analyze Thurman's output in detail, he suggests that the author of The Infants was at the center of the transformation of respectable producerist manhood into modern virile consumerist masculinity. According to Summers, this liminal position is illustrated by the paradox that he was a member of the black bourgeoisie, and simultaneously, most of his artistic endeavors were intended to challenge bourgeois respectability.[21] Consequently, although Thurman openly rebelled against bourgeois gender relations and productive marketplace masculinity, there are a number of ways in which his texts remain invested in these concepts.

The fact that Thurman constructs his identity in terms of his intellectual and artistic productions is manifest in his first letter to McKay.

> I am a 25 year old, American born Negro. Salt Lake City, Utah knew me first. I came to New York two and a half years ago from Los Angeles, California to start my career as a writer. Meanwhile I had lived in Chicago, and Omaha, attended the University of Utah and the University of Southern California, edited and published a magazine in Los Angeles, known as The Outlet...I have become a poet, because I once wrote a poem which gained honorable mention in an Opportunity contest and was used by the honorable Mr. Braithwaite in one of his anthologies. I have also become a critic, because I wrote two articles, one for the New Republic and one for The Independent...I have become an actor too, because I was a member of the mob in the Theatre Guild's production of Porgy, until just a few weeks ago. I have become a novelist also, because I am about to have one published by Boni-Liveright. But most important of all and probably the most thrilling, at least it is to me, I have become a playwright, really, having just had my first play.[22]

The tone of this fragment is marked by an ironic distance resulting mainly from the contrast between the diversity of Thurman's productions and the scarcity of output in each of the fields: he is a one-poem poet, a two-review critic, and a one-play walk-on actor. Characteristically, his description focuses less on the details of his cultural productions and more on the ways in which they are publicly acknowledged – published or even anthologized. He hardly mentions any titles, themes, parts, and yet he lists the names of publishers and editors. Consequently, even though the fragment is ironic, Thurman's choice of self-representation through the sphere of publicly recognized productions indicates that his self-image is influenced by marketplace masculinity, which is defined by its productive achievements in the public sphere. This residual trait in Thurman's gender assertion can account for his self-contradictory and ambivalent attitude to bohemianism, which is explored in the next chapter.

Other reflections of hegemonic masculinity traceable in Thurman's letters and essays include the sense of crisis of respectable producerist manhood and, resulting from it, the attempt to refashion American masculinity at the time. These efforts were intimately connected with primitivist longings and fascinations with cultures imagined as less civilized. White men appropriated African or Native American cultures in their touristic, artistic, and anthropological endeavors. Similarly, Locke encouraged young black artists to revitalize their cultural identity through the rediscovery of virile, masculinist African heritage. Thurman is less interested in cultural excavations. In *Infants of the Spring*, he misrepresents and openly mocks Locke's pragmatic efforts to forge a link between black Americans and African heritage. The literary convention of the *roman-à-clef* satire enables Thurman to distort and thus further caricature Locke's ideas. When Locke's alter-ego in the novel, Dr. Parkes, enthusiastically calls on the black artists to "go back to [their] pagan heritage for inspiration," Thurman's and Nugent's alteregos, Raymond Taylor and Paul Arbian, respond with skepticism. They question the connection with Africa celebrated by Locke: "How can I go back to African ancestors when *their blood is so diluted* and their country and times so far away? I have no conscious affinity for them at all...I ain't got no African spirit...*I'm an American and a perfect product of the melting pot*."[23] Taylor and Arbian argue that Africa is neither the dominant genetic nor cultural influence on black Americans; thus, Locke's genealogy is represented as fallacious from both the essentialist and the constructivist points of view. The final pinch of irony is produced by the juxtaposition of Locke's call for "healthy paganism" and his "cluck[ing] for civilized behavior" at the end of the heated discussion. From the point of view of Thurman's individualism, Locke's pragmatic project of reclaiming "lost" ancestry and African heritage appears as hypocritical, genealogically erroneous, and prescriptive, and consequently, dangerously limiting the artistic self-expression of black artists.

Nevertheless, there is a way in which Thurman's letters and essays echo the contemporaneous sense of crisis in hegemonic masculinity. As historians argue, the remaking of masculinity – apart from seeking revitalization through the appropriation of cultures perceived as civilizationally less advanced – took the form of the athletic craze and fad for predominantly homosocial outdoor pastimes for men.[24] These efforts were intended to save men from overcivilized weakness, frequently discussed in medical terms charged with feminine connotations, such as neurosis, neurasthenia, and hysteria. Thurman's personal letters, especially the ones from his retreats to Utah and California, indicate his embrace of these notions. Unlike Locke, who focused on Africa, or many New Negroes such as Hughes or Hurston, who turned to the South as a source of revitalization of black American expression and identity, Thurman chose to go West. This gesture plays into the mainstream myth of the American West and its role in the remaking of American masculinity. The earlier-mentioned outdoor male homosocial activities were often thematized in the metaphors of the West, which was most influentially exemplified by Theodore Roosevelt and his regiment of Rough Riders. In the national consciousness, the revitalizing function of the West was memorably expressed by Frederick Jackson Turner, who metaphorically referred to the frontier experience as the source of "eternal youth."[25]

Thurman's flights to the West were so sudden and frequent that they earned a phrase in the Niggerati idiolect; as Van Notten states, the expression "Doing a Wallie" stood for disappearing like Thurman to Salt Lake City.[26] There are at least two ways in which his escapades can be read within the hegemonic paradigm of American masculinity. First of all, he flees to the West after his marriage fails. This gesture repeats the scenario analyzed by Nina Baym as a male flight from society in search of imaginary freedom in the West. According to her, in the American myth as constructed by literary theories, women are "agents of permanent socialization and domestication," "entrappers and domesticators."[27] Thus, Thurman's flight from his marriage to Louise Thompson to the West can be read with reference to this founding myth of American masculinity. More specifically and significantly, the motivation behind other retreats to his hometown and to California is largely analogous to the anxieties that pushed white men at the time to pursue sports and celebrate the mythology of the West. In his letters, he expresses a sense of exhaustion with the urban life of Harlem and its "erotic bohemian life."[28] In the summer of 1928, he confides in Hughes that "I have disappeared! Yes I have. Once more. Had to do it. Harlem was too hectic for me. You really don't know. So here I am in the wilds of somewhere no one knows."[29] Six months later the ritual repeats itself and another letter opens: "Dear Lank-y-yank-yank: Forgive me my informal salutation. 'Tis merely the result of having spent two weeks out here in the wild west."[30] The letters explicitly juxtapose New York and the North East with a place of refuge that is represented with references to the American West. In a 1926 letter to Hughes, Thurman states that he is "still here [in New York] though weak," which indicates that the retreats from Harlem aimed at helping him to deal with his weakness, a condition which is elaborated in other letters in terms of health problems and neurasthenic tendencies.[31] In a 1929 letter to Rapp, Thurman expresses a sense of both mental and bodily weakness: "the curse of being the *neurotic son of neurotic* parents is that one is such a *weakling* and succumbs so easily to mental ills which soon become manifest in one's body."[32] In a letter to Hughes from the same period, he describes the lifestyle he leads in the West as based on "Good meals, plenty of sleep, cod liver oil to put *flesh on my bones and build up my nervous system*, meditation and quiet."[33] Since the retreats are meant to help Thurman counterbalance the turmoil of his New York life, whereas his health weakness is depicted in terms echoing the turn-of-the-century discourse of neurasthenia, the city becomes associated with physical enfeeblement. Moreover, this bodily weakness is linked to intellectual activities, which parallels the link between neurasthenia and overcivilization. In another 1929 letter to Rapp, Thurman claims that: "I have been reading far too much: Proust, Joyce, Dostoyevski, Shakespeare's tragedies, Ibsen, Moliere, Hardy and Swift. Is it any wonder I'm depressed and *enfeebled both mentally and physically?*"[34] The trips to the West are supposed to restore and virilize Thurman from the sense of weakness, which is rhetorically linked to intellectual effort and urban lifestyle.

The fact that Thurman's revitalizing retreats follow the discourse of revirilization of American masculinity is clearly manifest in the description of his outdoor activities in the West. In his letter to Rapp from July 1929, Thurman states that "I feel like a million dollars this morning. Spent Sunday, Monday and Tuesday in the canyon, hiking, chopping wood, fishing, *roughing it* in general...I had planned a hiking and camping trip into a nearby canyon with a group of former school chums this week but the doctor advised against it. I shall however go next week."[35] The activities are supposed to enhance Thurman's bodily strength, which parallels the contemporaneous athletic craze. Their relation to the myth of the West and masculine retreats is emphasized by the phrase "roughing it," which alludes to the semi-autobiographical novel of the same title by Mark Twain, narrating adventures during a stagecoach journey across the Wild West. The intertextual link between Thurman's and Twain's "roughing it" is further reinforced by the fact that Twain also depicts his pseudo-autobiographical adventures in Salt Lake City. Significantly, Thurman makes a rhetorical attempt to "roughen" his intellectual activities. "I am sleeping and writing *in the open*...I finished the first draft of my novel about five A.M., yesterday morning. Writing it has been *an adventure.*"[36] In this fragment, writing – a potentially enfeebling cerebral endeavor – is represented within the mythology of the West, which can be read as Thurman's attempt to reinvent himself as a masculinist artist. This gesture is parallel to Locke's repudiation of the "lady-artist of the races" and celebration of the brave New Negro "winning his artistic spurs."

The turn-of-the-century "cult of muscularity" manifested itself also through its rewritings of historical and mythical figures into virile superheroes, illustrated by the figure of Du Bois's black Jesus and its connection to the muscular Christ discussed in Chapter 1. This tendency to emphasize physical prowess can be found in Thurman's account of one of "his favorite Negro characters...Fred Douglass."[37] In his unpublished anthology of essays, one of the three biographical texts is devoted to Douglass. His representation strikingly differs from Washington's appropriation of this figure as a paragon of manliness and exceeds the militancy of Du Bois's depictions of the defiant abolitionist. Thurman's Douglass:

> was possessed of unusual physical strength, his labors on the plantation fields and in shipyards of Baltimore had hardened his body and steeled his muscles. He was equal to resisting any mob and seldom suffered a more severe beating than he was able to inflict upon others. Fists failing, he would not hesitate to avail himself of a club or some other bludgeon and proceed to fight his way to safety, leaving behind him many cracked skulls as mementoes of the encounter.[38]

This excerpt extensively focuses on Douglass's physical strength and, in the context of the whole text, it is represented as one of the features that made him "The Black Emancipator." Interestingly, the reference to physical labor and shipyards apotheosizes him as a workingman, which parallels white middle-class nostalgia for the imagined virility of working-class masculinity. This interest in the lower classes was visible in the appropriation of sports such as boxing and prizefighting, which are echoed here in the praise of Douglass's impressive ability to fight. Through the inclusion of details such as "cracked skulls," Thurman reinforces the rough character of his hero. The choice of an abbreviated name – Fred – instead of the commonly used Frederick further positions this portrait against traditional depictions that stress Douglass's respectability. The text's celebration of virile masculinity and its challenge to Victorian manliness reaches its climax when Thurman refers to Douglass as "a dangerous nigger."

The motif of "a dangerous nigger" constructed with lower-class references and an emphasis on bodily prowess also appears in the representations of characters from *Infants of the Spring* and the play *Harlem*. One of the members of the Niggerati Manor community, Bull, clearly falls into this category. Just as the animalistic connotations of his name suggest, he is "a personification of what the newspaper headlines are pleased to call a "burly Negro" with a "bulky body," "virile, scarred face," and a physique "exud[ing] strength and vitality," which "made everyone else in the room appear to be puny, inferior." In his representation of Bull, Thurman utilizes contemporaneous movie images: "He was every inch the tough, every inch the cinema conception of a gangster."[39] Bull's virile masculinity is also manifest in a violent attempt to police the relations between white men and black women. He gets into a fight with Stephen, a white intellectual, and curses his black lover Aline in a way that clearly flouts the conventions of respectable manliness: "You goddam bitch, I'll kill you." Even more revealing than the fight itself is the way in which Bull explains his aggressive behavior on the next day: "I'm a man," he claims, "An' I expect to be a man among men...The bastards lynch every nigger that has a white woman and I kinda thinks darkies ought to do the same." According to this argumentation, his aggression is a way to reassert his endangered masculinity. The scenario outlined by Bull identifies the Southern lynch ideology as the source of his gender anxiety, which is further exacerbated by his lack of control over black female sexuality. Moreover, Bull's assertion of masculinity strategically embraces white mainstream assumptions: "we ought to do the same." The text tactically stages black male aggression rather than representing it as uncontrollable violence. Thurman further problematizes this scene through Paul's account of Bull's behavior. This controversy-loving bohemian, referring to the ideology of respectability, claims that the fight just proves that Bull is "a good Negro" "trying to protect the chastity of his womenfolk."[40] Thus black male aggression in this incident is first introduced through the stereotypical white representations of "the burly Negro" and "a gangster," but these appearances are complicated through Bull's testimony appropriating the white Southern lynch logic and Paul's explanation alluding to middle-class respectability.[41]

Another significant twist in Thurman's representation of Bull is produced through references to his artistic activities. Even though he is not as talented as Paul, his paintings are assessed in the novel as considerably better than the art of Pelham Gaylord, an acknowledged member of the Niggerati community. Bull is characterized as a gangster-artist and the only difference between his image and that of a thug is that "instead of being fortified with a blackjack or a gun, his left arm was burdened with a mysterious packet of medium sized sheets of cardboard." This depiction of the creative effort, which conflates artistic and physical prowess, is reminiscent of Thurman's rendering of his writing as "adventure...in the open." Moreover, Bull's paintings are depicted as "vigorous and clean cut" – images that represent "huge amazons with pugilistic biceps, prominent muscular bulges, and broad shoulders."[42] His art is masculinized through its form and content. Significantly, the figures in his paintings allude to the lower-class muscular boxers and prizefighters.

Thurman's discontent with rough masculinity represented by Bull is not revealed until his affair with Lucille, the alter-ego of Louise Thompson, Thurman's ex-wife. Lucille's desire for the gangster-artist is explained with the hegemonic logic of overcivilization and its fetishistic hypermasculinization of the lower classes and ethnically-marked masculinities. Lucille explicates her actions in the following way: "I'm sick of being constantly surrounded by *sterile* white people, and of having to associate with Negroes who are also *sterile and pseudo white*. I suppose I find the same thing in Bull that white women claim to find in a man like *Jack Johnson*. That's the price I pay, evidently, for becoming *civilized*."[43] The allusion to Jack Johnson places her account within the mainstream masculine fascination with and anxiety over black virile masculinity. Johnson was the first black Heavyweight Champion of the World (1908-1915), which resulted in nationwide panic among whites over black physical superiority. According to Ken Burns, "For more than thirteen years, Jack Johnson was the most famous and the most notorious African-American on Earth."[44] Johnson was prosecuted under the Mann Act, intended to prevent traffic in women, for his affairs with white lovers. Thus Lucille juxtaposes white sterility, conflated with the secondary overcivilization of herself and the rest of the black bourgeoisie, with the virile non-white masculinity that is meant to revitalize it. Thurman exposes the myopic and fatal character of this logic by making Lucille pregnant with Bull. She is mistreated by her lover and decides to have an abortion. Although Bull's character loses the narrative's sympathy as the plot progresses, he is not furnished with a tragic destiny unlike the rest of the bohemian circle. Contradictions in the depiction of Bull illustrate Thurman's ambivalent attitude to rough black masculinity.

Another representation of such a model of masculinity can be found in Thurman's first and most successful play *Harlem: A Melodrama of Negro Life in Harlem* (1928). Since it is addressed to the mainstream Broadway audience, the image of manly roughness is necessarily less elaborate and ambiguous than the one from *The Infants*. The main character, Delia, who will be discussed in detail in the following chapter, longs for "a real man." Near the end of the play she plans to escape from her family home with "a leader of the Harlem underworld," who happens to be an ex-pugilist and describes himself as "a hard guy." The Kid fits "the cinema conception of a gangster" even more accurately than Bull. His name also alludes to the legendary cowboy outlaw of the Old West, Billy the Kid. He is depicted as a "large, well-built, handsome brown fellow" and the plot exposes his ability to act in cold blood. Having just killed another gangster, he hears that "the doorbell rings. The Kid quickly drags the body into the alcove and draws the curtains. The bell rings again. He calmly goes to the door and opens it."[45] These laconic stage directions indicate that Kid's actions are devoid of emotions and unnecessary meditations. As one critic notes, Thurman's portrayal of the Kid arouses respect for his bravado, especially when he decides to come over to Delia's house and risk his freedom.[46]

The sympathetic representation of gangsters can be read as rooted in the historical context of Prohibition. As Thomas H. Pauly claims, "neat definitions of legal and illegal, acceptable and unacceptable, good and bad" were blurred as "the public's thirst for illegal alcohol liberated criminals" from the obvious thug image. Moreover, according to Pauly, as far as the transformations of gender are concerned, identification with the gangster image in movies also played into anxieties of corporate masculinity and counterbalanced the need to "situate oneself within a promising professional or corporate bureaucracy."[47] Consequently, Thurman's engagement with criminal rough masculinities as exemplified by the Kid and, to some extent, also by Bull can be read as a desire for a more transgressive, potentially aggressive masculinity marked by criminal bravado, which was strongly present in the mainstream cultural discourse.[48] This longing for underworld experience and vigorous manhood also surfaces in accounts of Thurman's life from his letters and from Bruce Nugent's autobiographical novel *Jigger*. These texts indicate that Thurman was engaged in a relationship with a Harlem pickpocket, Otto, who was his guide to the black underworld. As Van Notten argues, "Thurman exploited this friendship to his financial and sexual advantage, and, of course, to find material for his articles on Harlem life."[49] Significantly, this account conflates the fascination with the criminal milieu and the eroticization of lower-class masculinity, which is parallel to the contemporaneous sexualization of the working class within the discourse of the crisis of hegemonic masculinity.

Thurman's play, however, necessarily differs from white gangster productions, since the fetishization of the lower classes in *Harlem* is also intricately entangled in racialized primitivist discourse. Characteristically, even though in *The Infants* Thurman clearly distinguishes between the imaginary African primitiveness of black Americans and the non-mainstream lifestyles of the lower classes, the two notions are conflated in the advertising campaign for *Harlem*. The elements of the working-class and criminal world of Harlem, such as "Rent Parties" or "Number Runners," are rendered in terms of primitivist mythology, according to which Harlem is "a strange exotic island" and its inhabitants are characterized by "primitive passion." This marketing strategy is also reflected in the reception of the play, which was depicted by reviewers as representing "unself-counscious and barbaric" people, "sensuous, Ethiopian savagery," and "uncerebral directness." Harlem, where "the bucks are snarling jungle beasts," strikes "an authentic jungle note." This primitivist reading of the play's lower-class characters is also intertwined with a projection of brutality: "Men and women who dance like that have the strength for violence." Thus *Harlem*'s marketing and reviews participate in the hegemonic primitivist logic, projecting imaginary savage behavior onto racialized lower-class subjects. The result of this cultural maneuver is the costless appropriation of the imaginary vitality. As one of the reviewers puts it: "I can recommend it [*Harlem*] to those who might be going to Harlem for a frolic, and would thereby save taxi fare."[50]

Such publicity was one of the reasons critics such as Locke or Du Bois accused *Harlem* of exhibitionism and race treason. Similar disclosures are also abundant in Thurman's publication "Negro Life in New York's Harlem: A Lively Picture of a Popular and Interesting Section," where he acknowledges that in the Harlem collective imagination, "hot stuff" signifies clothes "stolen by shoplifters or by store employees or by organized gangs who raid warehouses and freight yards."[51] Even though Thurman denies these rumors, possibly having in mind the white audience of this pamphlet, identifying bankruptcy sales as the main source of "hot stuff," he recognizes that the criminal element increases the attractiveness of such shopping. "There is certain glamour about buying stolen goods...People like to feel that they are breaking the law."[52] Thurman's espousal of this law-breaking aspect of "hot stuff" trade and "hot men" can be read as one of the ways in which he rebels against the bourgeois respectability of the emergent black middle class.

Yet the extensive presence of the criminal world in Thurman's writings, including fiction, drama, as well as his numerous accounts of Harlem life, goes beyond teasing the "dicties" and cashing in on cheap sensationalism. Thurman's fascination with the underworld is translated into his non-judgmental depictions of black criminal activities. He positions the black criminal world as a natural result of the economic conditions of black people in the North. This structural materialist approach is best exemplified by Thurman's depiction of the "hot men" phenomenon. He reads the phenomenon of "hot stuff" as a way to challenge the oppressive economic and race system. Because "a mass of people working for small wages...make good use of the 'hot man,'...low salaried folk in Harlem dress well, and Seventh Avenue is a fashionable street crowded with expensively dressed people."[53] The consumption of fashionable attires from an illegal source enables black people to resolve their anxieties resulting from the tension between their economic deprivation and the emergent advertising culture as well as to challenge the capitalistic conspicuous consumption by endowing law-breaking with a sense of "glamour."[54] Significantly, "hot stuff" refers only to elements of attire, which indicates that consumption patterns in Harlem focus on the performance of the self. This aesthetic self-performance will be explored in more detail with the examples of black dandies and sweetbacks in the next chapter.

As the above-analyzed excerpts illustrate, Thurman's representations of criminal culture, and in particular the rough masculinities associated with it, are multifaceted. They can be read as part of the contemporaneous mainstream fascination with criminality and rough lower-class masculinities; in this case, black lower classes function in the same way as white lower classes in the hegemonic discourse of remaking masculinities. This parallel is problematized by the fact that, in some texts, the black underworld is depicted in racialized primitivist terms, which fetishize the black criminal milieu as exotic and barbaric. Both primitivism and the fascination with lower classes project virility and prowess onto the groups perceived as less civilized and set in motion a dynamic of hegemonic compensatory appropriations. This dialectic attempts to appropriate the desired virility and yet retain the distanced position of hegemony, which criminalizes and disempowers the groups functioning as screens. What distinguishes Thurman's representations of Harlem's lower classes from this logic, however, is his non-judgmental approach to criminality, visible primarily in his sympathetic depictions of gangsters in *Harlem* and hot stuff in *Negro Life in New York's Harlem* and in his Marxist perspective highlighting the economic deprivation of the black community. The glamorized, socially justified criminality is a challenge and alternative to producerist Marketplace Manhood and middle-class respectability.

Private-Public Divide and Romantic Class Alliances

The rough masculine models are not the only example in which working-class representations contribute to Thurman's counter-bourgeois attitude. The remaining part of this chapter examines the ways in which working-class cultures and their alternative space arrangements are utilized to transgress the bourgeois private and public sphere divide. As Elaine Showalter claims, "the nineteenth century had cherished a belief in the separate spheres of femininity and masculinity that amounted almost to religious faith." This gendered division reveals a particular obsession with the impenetrable character of the sacred private sphere, which is inextricably linked with the protection of respectable domestic femininity and heteronormative marriage. Showalter elaborates on this well-acknowledged fact, arguing that the boundary between the female domestic/private and male marketplace/public spheres was closely intertwined and often conflated with race and class boundaries.[55] This assumption can be further developed in the light of the fact that the safety of white womanhood in the American imagination of the day was inseparable from the racialized discourses of rape and lynching, which positions the issue of race at the center of this ideology. Consequently, an investigation of Thurman's assaults on the private/public borderline constitutes an important element of an examination of his works focusing on the intersections of gender, sexuality, race, and class.[56]

The most significant challenge to the private-public boundary is manifested in the trope of the Niggerati Manor represented in The Infants. This house, whose tenants are young black artists, transcends a simple function of the novel's setting. Its existence determines the action in the novel, which is best exemplified by the coincidence between the end of patronage for this housing project and the ending of the plot. Moreover, the Manor and its final fall have become the leading trope signifying the New Negro community in the literary histories of the movement.[57] Apart from its central significance in the novel as well as its metonymical representation of the generation, the place is a fictionalized rendering of the real quarters shared by Thurman and Nugent at 267 West 136th Street. The very principle on which the house is based defies the bourgeois separate spheres doctrine. The owner, Euphoria Blake, "reasoned that by turning this house over to Negroes engaged in creative work, she would make money, achieve prestige as a patron, and at the same time profit artistically from the resultant contacts."[58] Thus the Niggerati Manor is the locus of both the domestic sphere as lodging and the marketplace sphere of "creative work" and "artistic profit." During a talk with Raymond on the way to "her own private home," Euphoria repeats that the project of the manor is to be "a monument to the New Negro," where artists would be able to devote themselves to creative activities. She is disappointed that none of the tenants "seem to be doing much work" and all she "run[s] into are gin parties."[59] Euphoria's concerns reveal that her attitude to art is deeply invested in the marketplace logic of productivity. As the tenants of the house flout this logic by indulging in "gin parties," Euphoria's expectations of publicly acclaimed productivity clash with the private revelries of the artists.

The anxiety over non-productivity, caused to a large extent by the blurring of the boundaries between the public and the private, is also expressed by the bohemian characters in the novel. Raymond is not free from the marketplace attitude to art represented by Euphoria. Characteristically, the moment when the blurring of the boundaries between productive and private activities begins to bother Ray and distracts him from work is framed with two episodes focused on female characters, Euphoria and Janet. Ray's crisis follows one of the central chapters in the narrative – the story of Euphoria's life. Structurally, it is one of the most significant scenes because it represents a fractal element of the narrative as a whole.[60] It parallels the trajectory of the Manor, with its hopeful beginnings, disillusionments with all available black emancipatory discourses, and its ending with a successful black female presence in the American marketplace. This positioning within the narrative gains further significance, since Euphoria's story is also rendered as an artistic performance. Her interlocutors are referred to as "the audience" throughout the chapter and some of them question the verity of her account, which places it on the level of fiction. The suspicion of fictitiousness is upheld by the narrative when at the end of her story Euphoria's interior monologue suggests conscious artistic manipulation of memory: "she was very pleased with herself, and with her story, her story which she had told many times, and which she had *embellished with gestures and rhetorical ornamentation.*"[61]

Her performance stands for female artistic productivity and, by contrast, emphasizes the ineffectiveness of the Manor's tenants. It logically follows that Ray, at the beginning of the next chapter, is frustrated by writer's block, which he ascribes to private interruptions undermining his studio's productive function. He is "trying to write a book review, which was already three days overdue" when "a tap on the door" intrudes his working space. Significantly, the reviewed author is a female novelist, modeled on Jessie Fauset, who is criticized in terms that conflate her gender and class identification. Her "silly" and "sophomoric" novel's only function is to "apprise white humanity of the better classes among the Negro humanity." Ray's scathing critique of black feminine creativity can be read as compensation for the anxiety of authorship caused by Euphoria's masterful performance. What is most relevant in the light of the separate spheres and the violation of the boundary between them, however, is that Ray is disturbed by Janet, a satellite of the Niggerati Manor bohemia. After the visit, Raymond comes to the conclusion that Janet and another black girl "were *decorative* and did *liven up the parties*, but there was no reason why they should make this house their second home."[62] Thus they are positioned as elements of decoration belonging to the non-productive sphere of enjoyment, which parallels Thorstein Veblen's assessment of domestic feminine duties as "decorative and mundificatory."[63] Janet represents the threat of changing a potentially productive place into the realm of domesticity suggested by the phrase "second home." These associations are further reinforced when it turns out that she came to confide in Ray about her personal problems. Ray's sphere of masculine creativity is threatened on the one hand by the mastery of Euphoria's artistic performance in the preceding scene and the intrusion of domesticity and private intimacy represented by Janet, which together reinforce his anxiety of black male authorship.

Whereas bourgeois ideology was predominantly obsessed with the impene-trability of the private sphere, the Manor artists' anxiety results from the lack of an inviolable productive sphere, "a studio of one's own." This is one of the rea-sons why the Manor, in the course of the narrative, changes from an idyllic trans-gressive space into a "damn house...getting on [the] nerves" of Ray, who in turn feels he "must escape from Niggerati Manor and from all it had come to stand for."[64] Also Steve, Ray's white friend, claims towards the end of the novel that "this house has been bad for us," suggesting that the experimental nature of its space was "insane" and the setting led to the decline of their interracial friend-ship. The sense of disillusionment is gradually growing in the attitude of Euphor-ia, who refers to the Manor as "a miscegenated bawdy house."[65]

Despite the discontent with the Manor experiment in terms of artistic produc-tivity, the alternative organization of space in the novel challenges the hegemonic bourgeois ideology of separate spheres, class divisions, Jim Crow segregation, and hetero-normative sexuality. The scene that epitomizes all of these transgres-sions is the donation party organized by the artists. Through the conflation of these various trespassings into one space, Thurman's text reveals the interdepen-dencies existing among them. The very idea of the donation party or the rent party constitutes a challenge to the separation of the domestic sphere and the market-place. This custom, according to Thurman, originated in the rural South and was transmuted by the black working classes in the North into a private party with a cover, which enabled many hosts to make ends meet. As he states in "Negro Life in New York's Harlem," such parties constitute the "commercialization of spon-taneous pleasure," hence they sacrifice the bourgeois sanctity of the domestic sphere for marketplace profit. Moreover, sometimes this emergency solution be-comes a regular source of income: "[the rent party] in order to pay the landlord has been abused, and now there are folk who make their living altogether by giving alleged House Rent Parties." Thurman also points to the fact that this phe-nomenon blurs the public/private boundary by characterizing it as "a joyful and intimate party, open to the public yet held in a private home." He also acknowledges its compensatory or escapist function for the underprivileged classes, since such parties enable one to forget "problems of color, civilization and economics."[66]

Thurman's fascination with this phenomenon is manifest in depictions of such parties in all of his major works: Harlem, The Blacker the Berry, and The Infants. I will focus on the party described in The Infants, where it is linked with decadence unlike the original lower-class revelry in *Harlem*, and where it is more elaborately described and better incorporated into the narrative than in *The Blacker the Berry*. From the very opening of the event, it is clear that the socializing patterns of the donation party not only challenge the private/public sphere ideology, they also blatantly flout race and gender boundaries. The first glimpse of the guests is focalized from Ray's perspective:

> The room was crowded with people. Black people, white people, and all the in-between shades. Ladies in evening gowns. Ladies in smocks. Ladies in tailored suits. Ladies in ordinary dresses of every description interspersed and surrounded by all types of men in all types of conventional clothing.[67]

The color line is challenged not only by the intermingling of black and white race but also due to the presence of "all the in-between shades," which represent race as a continuum rather than a polarity. The representation of racial fluidity is an assault on the hegemonic discourse of Jim Crow America, which was rooted in the polarization of races resulting from the adoption of the one-drop rule. Significantly, the challenge to the race boundary is immediately followed by a transgression of normative gender identities. The last four sentences in the fragment are structured in a Whitmanesque catalogue, which positions the ladies dressed in typical feminine attire – "evening gowns" and "ordinary dresses" as equal to the ones following masculine fashion of "smocks" and "tailored suits." The fact that each of the two respective groups, the femininely dressed women and women in drag, is represented by two types of attire reinforces the democratic character of this vision. The democratic potential of the inclusion of diverse, both privileged and marginalized, groups within the space of one paragraph can be further elucidated with a reference to Bakhtin's novelistic imperative, according to which "the novel must represent all the social and ideological voices of its era...It must be a microcosm of heteroglossia."[68] The textual space of the quoted paragraph and the represented space of the rent party constitute a heteroglot microcosm, where diverse ideologies coexist, enter a dialogue, and hence relativize and illuminate one another.

It is more than a formalist pun to move from Bakhtin's *hetoroglossia* to Foucault's conception of *heterotopia*. As Foucault claims, the twentieth-century construction of space retains many boundaries whose origins date back to the Medieval notion of the sacred:

> These are oppositions that we regard as simple givens: for example between private space and public space, between family space and social space, between cultural space and useful space, between the space of leisure and that of work. All these are still nurtured by the hidden presence of the sacred.[69]

Against these normative boundaries, Foucault constructs his vision of heterotopias – liminal spaces that are real and yet charged with utopian possibilities – "a kind of effectively enacted utopia in which the real sites, all the other real sites that can be found within the culture, are simultaneously represented, contested, and inverted."[70] Especially relevant in the reading of Thurman's rent party is the heterotopia of the festival, reminiscent of Bakhtin's carnivalesque, which is enacted in a liminal space between the private and the public. It is manifested in a coexistence of "heteroclite" subjects and their diverse interactions. Foucault's notion further illuminates the function of the Niggerati party as a liminal space that challenges the abiding spatial segregations.[71]

Diversity, inter-group intimacy, and its heterotopian potential increase as the party continues and reach the climax with the introduction of flamboyant male inverts. "Raymond made a tour of the house, surprised many amorous couples in the darkened rooms upstairs by turning on the light, disturbed the fanciful aggregation of Greenwich Village Uranians Paul had gathered in Raymond's studio to admire his bootblack's touted body."[72] This fragment indicates the close relation between the black bohemia from Harlem and the white bohemia from the Village; moreover, the "Uranians" and the homoerotic representation of the bootblack's male body charge this relation with transgressive sexuality. The term "Uranians" refers to Karl Heinrich Urlichs's concept of the "Urning," the third sex or "the invert," originally referring to subjects whose female psyche was trapped in a male body. The "inverted" identity was mentioned in the second chapter as one of the available emancipatory discourses of same-sex identities, which nevertheless was not adopted by Locke in his idiolect due to its feminized image. The fact that the effeminate homosexuals are focusing on the black body of a member of the lower classes fits contemporary notions of sexual attractiveness among the gay community of New York as depicted by Chauncey. According to Chauncey, the effeminate homosexual masculinity, represented by "the pansy," often perceived the rough masculinities of the working class as the model of sexual attractiveness. This argument is also articulated by Showalter, who points to "the late-nineteenth-century upper-middle-class eroticization of working-class men as the ideal homosexual objects."[73] Thus the socialization at the party simultaneously transcends and eroticizes class boundaries.

Since the scenes are focalized by a dark-complexioned Ray, who, unlike Paul, is represented in the text as a normative heterosexual, the main emphasis in narration falls on the trespassings of the color line. A scene that follows offers a promise of more democratic intimacy than the erotic gaze pointed at the black working-class body of Bud:

The party had reached new heights. The lights in the basement had been dimmed, and the reveling dancers cast grotesque shadows on the heavily tapestried walls. Color lines had been completely eradicated. Whites and blacks clung passionately together as if trying to effect a permanent merger. Liquor, jazz, and close physical contact had achieved what decades of propaganda had advocated with little success.[74]

Due to the dim lights, "color lines had been completely eradicated" in a literal way – it is difficult to distinguish between different bodies. More significantly, on the level of socialization, the dancing and drinking result in interracial intimacy, the nightmare of Jim Crow ideology. The erasure of the boundaries is further reinforced by the way the images are framed and focalized in this scene. What is depicted are only the shadows of dancers, not the dancers themselves. This results in the image of moving shadows, where neither the skin colors nor the boundaries between bodies are visible. The fact that the shadows are "grotesque" implies the movement of the dancers and Ray's intoxication with alcohol, but it can also be read in terms of the grotesque aesthetics as defined by Bakhtin. Bakhtin claims that the grotesque body is characterized by its fluidity, boundarylessness, and being in the process of becoming. It is closely associated with bodily processes such as digestion, procreation, or childbirth.[75] Thus the grotesque distortion of shadows further contributes to the erasure of boundaries and strengthens interracial intimacy.

This fragment, depicting shadows projected on the walls of the basement, can also be read as a peculiar rewriting of the classic scopic scenario from Plato's *Cave* into the context of urban space. The subject in Plato's hyperbole is able to see only the shadows of true ideas projected onto the walls of the cave. Shadows, darkness, and the lower space implied by the cave are valued as artificial, illusory, and secondary, in contrast to the true ideas, light, and outdoor space. Thurman seems to invert this organization – here what is represented by the shadows is a utopian interracial merger. Due to their erasure of the color line, the shadows rather than the reality that projects them embody the idealistic level. The privileging of the secondary, artificial level of representation mirrors Thurman's fascination with decadence and its celebration of artifice, which are the main focus of the following chapter. The intertextual reference to Plato, which endows the Manor basement with a cave-like quality, leads back to Bakhtin's grotesque aesthetics, which privileges the lower level, and where the cave is an essential element signifying fluidity and openness of boundaries.[76]

The space of the donation party also includes the interrelations between different classes, which are signaled already in the intelligentsia's appropriation of the working-class custom. The presence of different classes is indicated in the earlier-quoted differences between the women's dresses – ranging from "evening" to "ordinary." Moreover, individual guests at the party represent many social strata from the black and white bohemia to the black middle class, intelligentsia, and proletariat. The fact that the party is an inter-class fraternization is explicitly emphasized, since it becomes a source of controversy particularly among the black bourgeoisie. This perspective is represented by Dr. Parkes who warns about the detrimental effects of "drinking and carousing with a low class of whites from downtown," since "the white press should take up this business of whites and Negroes mingling so indiscriminately and drunkenly together."[77]

Parkes's remarks point to the central significance of class intermingling and appropriation of proletarian behavior by the bohemian community as a strategy of rebellion against the bourgeois classes. As Showalter claims, "The decadent... celebrated *romantic alliances between the classes...turning to working class lovers for passion and tenderness* missing in their own class surroundings."[78] These "romantic alliances" are represented in *The Infants* by the relation between Paul and the boot-black boy. A closer scrutiny of this relationship reveals the parasitic and appropriative nature of the relation between the decadent bohemians and the lower classes. Although his name, Bud, is mentioned once, the narrative, focalized by Ray, represents him in the chapter as "a bootblack," or even more tellingly "his bootblack," "Paul's Spartan bootblack."[79] The hierarchical nature of this relationship is even more explicit when Bud is openly announced to be the sexual object of the bohemian gaze. Paul's introduction is devoid of prudence: "Bud...has the most beautiful body I've ever seen. I will get him to strip for the gang soon"; the promise is fulfilled six pages later when Ray finds in his studio the earlier mentioned "fanciful aggregation of Greenwich Village Uranians" "admir[ing Paul's] bootblack's touted body."[80] Thus the celebration of "romantic alliances" is based on the romanticization of the lower classes and the fetishistic projection of eroticism onto the proletarian black body.

The trespassing of the class boundary is only one of the ways in which the donation party challenges established social boundaries. Yet, in the context of Thurman's counter-bourgeois project as represented in his other texts, it arises as omnipresent and especially significant. In "Negro Artists and the Negro," Thurman claims that a focus on the lower classes to oppose the respectable middle-class ethic is a salient element of the editorial policy of the new generation magazine. "*Fire!!*," he declares, "was experimental. It was purely artistic in intent and conception. Its contributors went to the proletariat rather than to the bourgeoisie for characters and material. They were interested in people who still retained some individual race qualities and who were not totally white American in every respect save color of skin."[81] He comes back later in the text to the class issue, this time summarizing the attitude of the black bourgeoisie, who "are in the process of being assimilated, and those elements within the race which are still too potent for easy assimilation must be hidden until they no longer exist."[82] In the literary salon depicted in *The Infants*, Cedric alias Eric Walrond, voices a strikingly similar opinion: "The lower orders of any race have more vim and vitality than the illuminated tenth."[83] Such an attitude can also be traced in Thurman's socio-journalistic writings, where what fascinates him most about Harlem are the lower classes and the fact that, in this "cosmopolitan" and "democratic district," social barriers are not as strict as in other parts of American society: "people associate with all types should chance happen to throw them together."[84] In "Negro Life in New York's Harlem," he admits that "a great proletarian mass... constitutes the most interesting and important element in Harlem, for it is this latter class and their institutions that gives the community its color and fascination."[85] Thus Thurman's counter-bourgeois project is constructed through his romanticization of the lower classes as non-standardized, "potent," and full of "vim and vitality." Moreover, the lower classes are also racialized in this approach. In contrast to the bourgeoisie, they still manifest "color" and "individual race qualities." Whereas Du Bois and Locke are anxious that Jim Crow segregation, which forces the proximity of the lower and upper class, endangers and compromises the respectability of the black bourgeoisie, Thurman welcomes the democratic cosmopolitanism of Harlem's residential structure.[86]

Yet these celebrations of democracy and the romanticization of the lower strata reveal their inherently parasitical character, which is symbolically represented by the Paul-Bud relationship discussed above. Thurman's fascination with the lower classes becomes even more ambivalent in the light of his elitist contempt for the masses. These tensions are openly expressed in his hospital letter to Hughes, where he remarks that "being bedded among the proletariat is enough to make me or anybody become a rabid lover of the aristocrats."[87] Thurman, often referred to as the most introspective of the New Negro Renaissance artists, is aware of the dubiousness in the relationship between the intelligentsia and the lower classes. He critically examines both white and black Negrotarian fascinations. This self-awareness is manifest in The Blacker the Berry, when he puts on the narrative masks of Emma Lou and Walter Truman. The black bohemia represented in the novel also turns to the lower classes for inspiration; their escapade to the working-class rent party is cynically depicted by Truman as a "pilgrimage to the proletariat's parlor social." Emma Lou, who cannot decide if the members of the bohemia are "intellectuals or respectable people," is equally cynical about their working-class fascinations: "Looking for material, they had said. More than likely they were looking for liquor and a chance to be licentious."[88] On the other hand, in The Infants, Thurman's alter-ego Ray is "disgusted with the way everyone sought to romanticize Harlem and Harlem Negroes."[89] Thus Thurman's texts simultaneously perform a gesture of romantic appropriation of lower-class imagery and comment on the parasitical nature of the relation between the intelligentsia and the proletariat.

Thurman's fascinations with the working class defiantly challenge the bourgeois ethic, whereas his appropriation of lower-class customs offers an alternative structuring of the public and private space. The above-discussed notion of the rent party is probably the most explicit example but not the only one. The most detailed depictions of working-class life and its spatial organization come from "Negro Life in New York's Harlem," the play Harlem, and numerous articles on black New York. Apart from the rent party, the two elements represented in these texts that conspicuously violate the bourgeois sanctity of the private sphere are "tenants" and "railroad flats." The institution of tenants is discussed by D'Emilio as a popular way of increasing income among the lower classes in the North in the early twentieth century. He claims that the fact of letting a (male) stranger into the household was perceived by the middle class as immoral and dangerous to the protection of the domestic sphere. On the other hand, he argues that, from the working-class perspective, it enabled many women to remain at home instead of working in factories and made it possible to educate their children. Moreover, since the tenants were very often treated as family members, they were protectors rather than violators of the domestic sphere and its women.[90]

Thurman's cynical representation of the tenant institution does not support D'Emilio's findings. In *Harlem*, the Williams family sublet rooms in their flat to two young men and a couple. The young men, Jenks and Basil, enter into intimate relationships with the daughters of the family rather than protect them, whereas the couple violates the ethic of respectability by living together without being married. Effie and Jimmie are characterized as "a pair of youngsters who are happy-go-lucky and full of pep and joy. Tired of drifting around from room to room singly, they have decided to live together without the benefit of the clergy...They are not immoral, but practical...They get quite a kick out of life and out of themselves. Everything is food for their fun mill."[91] The couple also actively participates in the rent parties in the flat and encourages Delia, the main character of the play, to adopt a similar sexually liberated lifestyle. Consequently, from the perspective of bourgeois ideology, the institution of tenants as represented in *Harlem* violates the sacred private sphere of the family, which is invaded by strangers whose lifestyles menace the Williams family's respectability. The play does not offer an alternative working-class ethic that would reflect the logic of working-class self-representations discussed by D'Emilio. Yet Thurman's text does not adopt a judgmental attitude to this situation. As is emphasized in the stage directions, the couple is not "immoral."

Thurman's empathy for the tenant institution manifests itself also in his analysis of its economic roots in "Negro Life in New York's Harlem." In this publication, Thurman stresses the overcrowded living conditions in black Manhattan, which is inhabited by "two hundred thousand Negroes living, loving, laughing, crying, procreating, and dying." The long string of gerunds produces the effect of dynamic mobility and adds to the unbearable crowdedness signified with numbers. Due to the overpopulation, "living conditions are ribald and ridiculous." "There are as many as 5,000 persons living in some single blocks; living in dark, mephitic tenements, jammed together, brownstone fronts, dingy elevator flats and modern apartment houses." The impossibility of maintaining strict boundaries because of the sheer number of people is further exacerbated by the spatial organization of tenements into "railroad flats, so called because each room opens into the other like coaches on a train." Such a structure forces people to pass other bedrooms on their way to a shared bathroom situated in an alcove in the kitchen. Thurman makes this picture even more shocking to a middle-class reader by adding that children and adolescents sleep with parents and different people use one bed in shifts. He concludes that "there is still little privacy, little unused space." The living conditions as represented in the above-quoted fragments evidently violate the sanctity of the bourgeois private sphere. The violation is reinforced by the evocation of the grotesque merger of life and death, "procreation and dying." Thurman's rendering of overpopulation in Harlem is characterized by the general ambivalence with which he depicts the lower class. He points to the economic causes of such a situation – high rents and corrupted landlords – and represents it in a non-judgmental descriptive fashion. In other places, he assesses it as "mad" and "disconcerting." On the other hand, he is clearly fascinated with the boundary-blurring environment, which is visible in expressions such as the alliterative "ribald and ridiculous" or the figurative "magic melting pot, a modern Babel mocking the gods with its cosmopolitan uniqueness."[92]

The organization of living conditions among the lower classes in Harlem is in many respects parallel to the representation of the bohemian life in the Manor. The fact that Ray, for the better part of the novel, lives in his studio together with Paul and Steve can be interpreted as a peculiar form of subletting rooms to tenants. The details of this living arrangement explicitly violate the heteronormative bourgeois space. A typical morning in the Manor is depicted in the following way: "It was noon before Raymond awoke. Stephen was still asleep beside him. Paul stretched on the floor indolently smoking a cigarette. He smiled as Raymond sat up in bed. 'Good morning.'"[93] Just as in a railroad flat, there is just one bed available for three adult men. Furthermore, instead of a private bedroom shared by a heterosexual couple, there is one bed shared by two men and another man sleeping on the floor underneath. This configuration also challenges Jim Crow ideology, since the men sharing the bed are of different races. The counter-hegemonic character of this living arrangement is further emphasized by a challenge to daytime productivity – the artists wake up in the afternoon and "indolently" smoke cigarettes. The lack of privacy in the house, which lends it a railroad-flat-like character, has been already discussed with reference to the scene where Ray feels constantly disturbed and cannot focus on his work.

On the whole, Thurman's transgressions of the separate spheres ideology are both multifaceted and contradictory. On the one hand, the organization of space in the Manor characterized by the lack of impenetrable productive space results in the tenants' anxieties over creative infertility, which reveals Thurman's residual investment in hegemonic producerist masculinity. On the other hand, he rebels against the bourgeois ethic by celebrating lower-class culture epitomized by his violations of the sacred private sphere. As a result, the texts long for the exclusiveness of a masculine-gendered productive sphere and experiment with the transgressions of a feminine-gendered domestic sphere, often resorting to working-class cultural codes to achieve the latter.[94] Thurman's romantic fetishization of working-class institutions is in many respects parallel to white fascination with black culture at the time; just as the whites go slumming to Harlem, "inspectin' like Van Vechten," the black bohemia sets out on "pilgrimages to proletarian parlor social." This analogy is further strengthened by the racialization of the lower class in the texts and its construction as racially more authentic than the upper classes. Furthermore, as is revealed in the relationship between Paul and Bud, the bohemian perception eroticizes working-class bodies. The erotic gaze is emblematic of more general narrative focalization and other forms of artistic scrutiny of the lower class by the black literati. The working class represents "material" used by the intelligentsia in their decadent experimentations, whereas its institutions such as the rent party or the railroad flat community constitute idioms appropriated to rebel against the bourgeois respectability. Yet, between these bourgeois anxieties and bohemian appropriations, Thurman's texts provide a liminal space, a heterotopia, which challenges the established borderlines and enables the representation of figures such as "ladies in frocks" or interracial male intimacy. Ray's studio in the Niggerati Manor defies both the heteronormativeness of the private sphere and the Jim Crow racial segregation. The carnivalesque and grotesque represented by the atmosphere of the rent parties retain the original democratic potential ascribed to them by Bakhtin.[95] This aesthetic is reinforced by the very co-existence and dialogization of different languages, social groups, and ideologies, which is a vivid example of Bakhtin's novelistic heteroglossia.

The fact that this transgressive space can lead to transformations is represented in the way a rent party affects the respectable Emma Lou. "The music augmented by the general atmosphere of the room and the liquor she had drunk had presumably *created another person* in her stead. She felt like flying into an emotional frenzy – felt like flinging her arms and legs in *insane unison*. She had become very *fluid*, very *elastic*."[96] The adjectives used to depict Emma's state of mind indicate that the type of socialization offered by rent parties can lead to at least a temporary transformation and bending of the strict social norms. In the context of Bakhtin's claim that heteroglossia consists of "an ideological translation of another's language, and an overcoming of its otherness – an otherness that is only contingent, external, illusory," "another person" in Emma's head can be read as a metaphor for relativization and embrace of otherness within her consciousness.[97] Such a change leads to Emma's grotesque longing for "insane unison" at the party peopled with different races and classes. The passionate integration enabled in the heterotopia of the rent party proves that Thurman's textual romantic alliances with the lower classes transcend a simple anti-bourgeois rebellion, and they open spaces alternative to Jim Crow America, which was strictly divided along the lines of race, class, gender, and sexuality. As Ray ironically comments on the bohemian party in *The Infants*, "Liquor, jazz music, and close physical contact had achieved what decades of propaganda had advocated with little success."[98]

Other Assaults on the Bourgeoisie

Thurman's focus on criminal and lower-class cultures aroused severe criticism from the emergent Negro middle class, who, basing their identity on the notions of bourgeois respectability, strongly opposed any cultural images that could reinforce the negative stereotypes of black people in the American collective imagination. Thurman's upbringing in a well-to-do blue-vein family in Utah could have made him a loyal follower of the black middle-class ethic, the residue of which is visible in my earlier analysis of his self-narration in terms of publicly acknowledged productivity and anxieties over artistic non-productivity. Yet both his fascination with rough masculinities and the violations of the separate spheres ideology show that if any permanent attitude can be found in Thurman's contradictory cynical project, it is his rebellion against the bourgeoisie and its ideologies. Therefore the remainder of this chapter will focus on Thurman's explicit attack on the black middle class and his deconstruction of the bourgeois ethic of respectability. What makes it even more interesting is that his rhetorical assaults are inextricably entangled with notions of gender and sexuality.

Thurman's criticism of the bourgeois ethic is pronouncedly present in his works, beginning with the publication of *Fire!!* (1926), where he launches an attack on the hypocritical critics of Van Vechten's *Nigger Heaven*. In "Negro Life in New York's Harlem," he acknowledges the existence of the "dicties" – the emerging middle class – yet he dismisses this section of society as:

> successful mulattoes...absorbing all the social mannerisms of the white American middle class...they are both stupid and snobbish as is their class in any race...They are also good illustrations, mentally, sartorially and socially, of what the American standardizing machine can do to susceptible material.[99]

At first it seems that Thurman's criticism of the black middle class transcends the notions of race and is a part of his more general contempt for "several million begging, cringing, moaning nonentities" who represent mediocrity. Yet the emphasis on skin color – "successful mulattoes" – in this excerpt is of special significance to Thurman's representation of the black bourgeoisie and its intra-racial color discrimination, which is painstakingly depicted in the history of Emma Lou in *The Blacker the Berry*.

This semi-autobiographical novel about Emma Lou's struggle with internalized racism directed at her dark complexion also represents Thurman's in-depth criticism of hypocrisy and colorism inherent in black bourgeois ideology. He attacks the middle class with their own ethic of respectability. The echoes of Emma Lou's family wisdom reveal that the blue-vein longings of the black bourgeoisie are not only a thinly-veiled desire for whiteness and a manifestation of intra-racial discrimination, but, most importantly, they necessarily depend on the past miscegenation between white masters and black slave women. The essence of the blue-vein propaganda is summarized as "whiter and whiter every generation. The nearer white you are the more white people will respect you...eventually people will accept this racially bastard aristocracy."[100] The narrator in this fragment distorts the ideology that Emma Lou still espouses at this point in the novel, which results in an ironic tension between her actions and the narration. A character whose attitude is closer to that of the narrator – Walter Truman, a lightly-disguised representation of Thurman himself – delivers a speech where he argues that "mulattoes have always been accorded more consideration by white people than their darker brethren. They were made to feel superior even during slave days...made to feel proud...that they were bastards."[101] Thus the novel shows the paradox intrinsic to the black bourgeois ideology. The "dicties" embrace the white decorum and associate light skin color with privilege, which clashes with the fact that the mixed racial heritage of mulattoes stands for transgressive, non-normative sexuality and the lack of control over black female sexual activity. In a similarly perverse way, Thurman rewrites the representation of blackness: "he [Emma's dark father] had come from one of the few families originally from Africa, who could not boast of having been seduced by some member of southern aristocracy, or befriended by some member of a strolling band of Indians."[102] Here, blackness, which in the social perception depicted in the novel is strongly collocated with lower-class or rural Southern Negroes, is constructed in the metaphors of virginal femininity – not euphemistically "befriended" or "seduced" by other races. Thurman deconstructs bourgeois respectability as dependent on non-normative sexuality and contrasts it with the proletariat, whose blackness is represented in terms of sexual restraint and racial purity.

Still another rhetorical assault on the black bourgeoisie can be found in Thurman's literary criticism. Just as in the case of Locke's aesthetics, Thurman's evaluation of black bourgeois literature is gender-marked. He consistently deplores texts addressed to an audience that consists of the black bourgeois public and sentimental whites. In the light of the discussion of sentimentalism in the previous chapter, the fact that Thurman categorizes it together with "the black bourgeoisie" charges this group with feminine quality. Yet, what is more telling, Thurman's favorite objects of anti-bourgeois and anti-sentimental criticism are two black female novelists – Jessie Fauset and Nella Larsen. Both in his texts intended for publication such as *Aunt Hagar's Children* and in his personal correspondence, Thurman conflates and dismisses the two novelists as "untalented Fausets and Larsens." In "Negro Artists and the Negro" – a text that significantly exacerbated the hostility between Thurman and the black bourgeoisie existing since his editorship of the *Fire!!* – he claims that "Miss Fauset's work [*There is Confusion*] was an ill-starred attempt to popularize the pleasing news that there were cultured Negroes."[103] He also uses her as the pet novelist of the black middle class in "Fire Burns: A Department of Comment" and contrasts her with Van Vechten and his *Nigger Heaven*.[104] As I have mentioned earlier, when Raymond is writing a review of a black novel, his criticism clearly echoes Thurman's assessment of Fauset and alludes to her commitment to the black bourgeois ethic. The fictional novelist is represented as "a woman who, had she been white and unknown, would never have been able to get her book published." Ray "was tired of Negro writers who had nothing to say, and who only wrote because they were literate and felt they should apprise white humanity of the better classes among the Negro humanity."[105] In a private letter to Hughes, Thurman is even more explicit: "Jessie Fauset should be taken to Philadelphia and cremated."[106] A similar, if less intense, criticism is directed at Larsen. Just as in *Fire!!*, Fauset is juxtaposed with Van Vechten, in *Harlem: A Forum of Negro Life*, the two figures occupying analogous positions are respectively Rudolph Fisher, who is accused by Du Bois of not writing "of better class Negroes," and Larsen, the author who "pleases Du Bois for she stays in her own sphere and writes about the sort of people one can invite to one's home without losing one's social prestige."[107] In both cases, gentile respectability embodied by the female author is contrasted with the male novelist who dares to challenge the bourgeois ethic. Through his rendering of Fauset and Larsen as the poets laureate of the black middle class, Thurman genders the black bourgeois aesthetic as feminine.[108] Just as in Locke's reviews, Du Bois represents here the feminized side of the black aesthetic. Whereas in Locke's texts, it stems from his conflation of sentimentalism and propaganda, in Thurman's texts, Du Bois is the patron of the feminized conservative black bourgeoisie.

In the light of the persistent counter-bourgeois attitude in Thurman's writings, it seems productive to scrutinize the contemporaneous discourses that represented such an approach. The most obvious of the available rhetorics that would enable Thurman to express his resistance to bourgeois ideology is Marxism. His left-wing allegiance is most conspicuously present in Thurman's personal vita in his collaboration with *The Messenger*, the most prominent black socialist magazine. Although the most radical years, when the publication was under the control of A. Phillip Randolph and Chandler Owen, predated Thurman's "hegira to Harlem" in 1925, it was still perceived as "opposed to the old guard ideology and leadership... and actively courted a younger readership of educated liberals and socialists."[109] Thurman's alliance with left-wing ideology is visible in his consciousness of economic privilege and discrimination in his works, which, as I have argued, are present in his depictions of criminal activities in Harlem. Yet, as is explicitly illustrated by the literary salon scene in *The Infants of the Spring*, Thurman dismisses a "wholesale allegiance" to left-wing rhetoric along with Du Bois's militant propagandism and Locke's primitivism as "futile and unintelligent."[110] When communist Glenn Madison calls on the intellectuals to "join hands with the workers of the world and overthrow the present capitalistic regime," he is opposed by Thurman's alter ego, Ray, who agrees to "let each young hopeful choose his own path" and claims that "individuality is what we should strive for. Let each seek his own salvation."[111] Even though Ray does not unequivocally espouse Marxism, this scene confirms the presence of left-wing rhetoric at the center of the New Negro Renaissance, which is pointed out by Foley and Maxwell.

As is indicated in the quote above, the only rhetoric that Thurman openly embraces is cynical individualism. In the preface to *Aunt Hagar's Children*, he summarizes his philosophy, which is concurrent with the criticism expressed three years later in *The Infants*:

> He [the author, Thurman] believes it to be the duty of those who have the will to power in artistic and intellectual fields to shake off psychological shackles, deliberately formulate an egoistic philosophy, develop a cosmopolitan perspective, and soar where they may, blaming only themselves if they fail to reach their goal. Individual salvation may prove a more efficacious emancipating agent for his generation and those following than self sacrifice or morbid resentment.[112]

References to the philosophical ideas of Nietzsche and Stirner are clearly manifest in this excerpt; its first sentence alludes to the Nietzschean concept of "the will to power" and the Stirnerian concept of "the egoist." Yet these intertextual allusions are filtered through American texts on the European individualistic philosophers. Thurman himself admits that "through Huneker he learned of Max Stirner and became an egoist, worshipping at the shrine of the superman," referring to a 1909 publication of *Egoists: A Book of Supermen*.[113] Similarly, according to Van Notten, his espousal of Nietzscheanism is to a large extent informed by *The Philosophy of Friedrich Nietzsche* by H.L. Mencken. Referring to W.H.A. Williams's study of Mencken, she names a set of polarities from this text that were particularly attractive for Thurman: "the elite in opposition to the mob, the individual to the mass, the artist to the society, rebellion to conformity, excellence to mediocrity, and skepticism to mindless assent."[114] Although this individualistic, anti-democratic approach is to an extent in conflict with Thurman's flirtations with the proletariat, communism, and democracy, the quote is the most adequate outline of Thurman's project for the new black aesthetic and the new generation of the New Negroes as expressed in his writings.

Thurman's self-fashioning as a leader is haunted by the tension between his radical individualism and his identification with the black community, which is analogous to Du Bois's predicament of being a privileged leader of the unprivileged. Interestingly, even though Thurman rejects any "wholesale allegiance" to collective emancipatory projects as represented by Du Bois, Locke, or communism, his characterization of individualism as "an efficacious emancipating agent" reveals that freedom of artistic expression is the basis of his own collective project – "a new philosophy for a new generation of younger Negroes."[115] Artistic freedom, art for art's sake, according to Thurman, will enhance the quality of black arts and hence contribute to emancipation through cultural productions, a position that is largely compatible with Locke's endeavors.

Thurman's "new philosophy for a new generation" is entwined in a number of American cultural dynamics, which also shape his representations of race and gender relations. What emerges from such a mixture is a contradictory project that combines residual investments in producerist masculinity with celebrations of black rough criminals. Thurman's predominantly counter-bourgeois attitude and his assaults on respectability, the separate spheres ethic, and blue-vein ideology are closely entangled with his vision of individualism. His insistence on radical independence and individuality, however, should not be read as an expression of American traditional individualism and exceptionalism, which are at the foundation of the capitalistic entrepreneurship, but as the "cosmopolitan" allusion to Nietzsche and Stirner manifests, they are indebted to European philosophical discourses. The following chapter aims to show that this European connection is as significant as Thurman's entanglements in American ideologies of class, race, and gender.

Chapter 5
Discontents of the Black Dandy

A strange kind of fellow...,
who liked being a Negro but thought it a great handicap;
who adored bohemianism but
thought it wrong to be a bohemian.[1]
Langston Hughes, *The Big Sea*

Interestingly, the European connection in Thurman's project is produced through the same intertextual references that are central to Locke's rhetoric of friendship. On Thurman's self-declared reading list, one can find authors fundamental for Locke's homoerotic idiolect, such as Plato or Nietzsche. Both writers forge a network of cosmopolitan textual influences. These intertextual bonds are articulated on a number of levels: in Hughes's literary recollections of Thurman, in Thurman's own correspondence, and in the declarations of his textual alter-egos such as Raymond Taylor or Paul Arbian. Such celebrations of literary predecessors signify that in Thurman's writing just as in Locke's, in the dialectic of the anxiety of influence and the anxiety of authorship, the latter clearly dominates. Yet Locke and Thurman interpret the same philosophical texts in different ways. As Van Notten persuasively argues, Thurman lacked the in-depth academic knowledge of the philosophies he refers to, which is in stark contrast to Locke's scholarly investment in philosophy. Moreover, although Thurman's individualist philosophy is concurrent with representations of transgressive sexualities, he does not use these philosophical texts as emancipatory tools for same-sex desire. European intertextual reverberations mediated through American monographs in Thurman's texts might be shallower than Locke's, but they also are more inclusive. This chapter examines multifaceted representations of non-normative sexualities, including "Spartan" same-sexuality, effeminate Uranians, dandies indebted to the aesthetic of female performers, and androgynous bodies illustrated in Aubrey Vincent Beardsley and Oscar Wilde's *Salome*.

The difference between Locke's and Thurman's representations of alternative sexualities can be aptly illustrated with a juxtaposition of two European visual discourses of alternative sexualities. The contrast between *Salome* illustrations alluded to by Thurman and male nudes against natural background from German same-sex press echoed in Locke's idiolect perfectly pinpoints the gap between their divergent projects. Thurman's dandyist celebration of artifice and theatricality challenges Locke's naturalized same-sex masculinity. If Locke forges a unified masculinist race consciousness in the figure of the New Negro, Thurman's narratives explode such uniform identity in their experimentations with cross-dressing, homoerotic self-display, and racial passing. Yet, despite these symmetrical differences between Locke's *idioglossia* and Thurman's *heteroglossia*, in both cases it is transatlantic intertextual travels that engender their rhetorical transgressions.

"Bohemianism...was alternately fascinating and repellant, more the former than the latter, but sufficiently both to unbalance him," as Thurman confesses in his own review of *The Infants*.[2] Even though in this review Thurman misrepresents his relation to the bohemian lifestyle by dating it six years too early, the fact that it was both contradictory and intimate is adequately reflected in this third-person testimony. Due to the residual ideology of producerist masculinity in Thurman's writings, he is never able to wholeheartedly embrace the bohemian and decadent lifestyle. On the other hand, his life-long opposition to the middle-class ethic and his allegiance to artistic individualism made decadence the most attractive of the available counter-hegemonic discourses. This chapter focuses on Thurman's appropriation of European decadence and dandyism, which are seminal for representations of gender and sexuality in his writings. It also scrutinizes the way (white) European decadence intersects with (black) American cultural phenomena such as passing or "sweetbacks."

Thurman's investment in the discourse of decadence and dandyism is visible in a number of intertextual allusions in his writings. Several works and authors that he openly names as constitutive of his intellectual mind-frame belong to the canon of decadence, including Huysmans, Gustave Flaubert's *Madame Bovary*, and Charles Baudelaire. In *The Infants*, the discourse of decadence is most explicitly referenced through the figure of Paul, Bruce Nugent's *roman-à-clef* alter-ego, who claims that "Oscar Wilde is the greatest man that ever lived. Huysmans's Des Esseintes is the greatest character in literature, and Baudelaire is the greatest poet."[3] Strong parallels between his and Thurman's own declared reading lists make Paul a medium for the expression of the decadent longings of Thurman's autobiographical persona. Such indirect yet multiple allusions and literary references in his private and published writings evoke the figure of the dandy. Thurman avoids the term itself, which can be explained as an attempt to prevent any associations between his bohemian characters and the minstrel stereotype of the black urban dandy embodied by Zip Coon. This latent resonance problematizes Thurman's passionate espousal of dandyism.

Decadence is the main prism through which Thurman's project is perceived by its most severe critics such as Locke and Du Bois. This connection is first made in Locke's review of *Fire!!*, in which he states that the magazine is a "hectic imitation of the 'naughty nineties' and effete echoes of contemporary decadence" and advises against seeking inspiration in "Wilde and Beardsley."[4] In the light of the analysis of decadence, modernism, and sentimentalism in Chapter 3, through this criticism Locke engages in a debate which concerns not only aesthetics but also gender and sexuality. The accusation of decadence also implies effeminate male same-sex desire and feminization. The simultaneous allusion to Wilde and Beardsley refers to Wilde's controversial play *Salome*, which was illustrated by Beardsley. Since Beardsley's illustrations of androgynous bodies and male nudity illuminate the same-sexual and transgressive desires in the play, this intertextual reference, further reinforced by the adjective "naughty," is a coded accusation of overtly explicit homosexual expression. In the context of my analysis of Locke's homoerotic idiolect, his critique of *Fire!!* is not simply a homophobic rejection of homosexual expression, but a rejection of a particular effeminate articulation of male same-sex desire and its insistence on public display intended to shock. Locke's interpretation of decadence reflects also the contemporaneous meaning of the term, which, as Showalter claims, was "the pejorative label applied by the bourgeoisie to everything that seemed unnatural, artificial, and perverse, from Art Nouveau to *homosexuality*, a sickness with symptoms associated with cultural degeneration and decay."[5] Thus the fact that Thurman's project was rendered as decadent not only criticizes its art-for-art's-sake lack of engagement in race politics but also suggests that it embraces transgressive sexualities and effeminate masculinity.

Dandyism and Aesthetics of the Self: "One should either be a work of art, or wear a work of art."

The analysis of dandyism in this chapter will primarily focus on the collapse of the boundary between life and art and its implications for the representations of gender and sexualities. It will complement the analysis of Thurman's assaults on the private-public divide analyzed in the previous chapter. Before discussing the ways in which dandyism is preoccupied with the periphery of life and art, it is necessary to point to the gendered character of the dandy. Showalter names the New Woman and the dandy as respectively the feminine and masculine embodiments of decadence, which implies that dandyism is a bohemian counter-bourgeois ideology of masculinity.[6] Dandyist rebellion against bourgeois masculinity is manifest in the very fact that it depends on a carefully designed public image displayed to be admired, which positions the masculine body as the object of potentially erotic desire. Additionally, the stylistics of dandyism used in this spectacular self-fashioning is indebted to the female *fin-de-siècle* performers and performances, which further challenges the normative masculinity.

On the other hand, the dandy persona was in many ways fashioned as inherently masculinist in character by *fin-de-siècle* writers. One of the most influential champions of dandyism, Baudelaire, states that "Woman is the opposite of the Dandy. Therefore she inspires horror...Woman is natural, which is to say abominable."[7] This brief yet explicit statement is elaborated in other manifestoes of decadent dandyism such as Wilde's "The Critic as an Artist: With Some Remarks upon the Importance of Discussing Everything" or Huysmans's *Against Nature*. As one of Wilde's characters claims, "to be natural is to be obvious, and to be obvious is to be inartistic."[8] Metonymically, the woman becomes the epitome of the natural realm, since her actions and social existence are completely determined by biology. As Showalter comments on the figure of the woman in decadent discourse, referring to Jean Pierrot's *The Decadent Imagination*, "Antinaturalism...inevitably leads to antifeminism."[9] This logic is further explained by Rhonda K. Garelick, who argues that "by virtue of their association with the human life cycle and reproduction, women threaten the dandy's eternal present with temporality, and hence become objects of fear and disdain in decadent literature."[10] Thus, even though the dandy challenges hegemonic notions of masculinity and appropriates the stylistics of the feminine lifestyle or performance, it remains a gender exclusive and masculinist category. Hence dandyist tropes in Thurman's writings will be analyzed as elements of a peculiarly counter-bourgeois masculinity.

Dandyism is primarily defined by its focus on the aesthetics of life. As Garelick claims, "to be a dandy is to turn one's life into a work of art." This rule is exemplified by Wilde, whose "entire *oeuvre* is dedicated precisely to collapsing distinction between private and public, life and work, artist and celebrity." The collapse of the boundary between life and art is manifested in two ways. First of all, it is evident in the aesthetic lifestyle, where life becomes "a performance, the performance of a highly stylized, painstakingly constructed self, a solipsistic social icon." This dimension is clearly visible in the close relation between fashion stylistics and dandyism. The other important implication of this paradigm is "the classic dandyist confusion of reality and literature," which is manifested in biographical and autobiographical trends of decadent literature. Interestingly, it can be interpreted as related to the fact that "dandies long to establish a nonsanguinary, nonbiological parallel genealogy, a family tree without women," which is pointed out by Garelick. According to her, biographical literature establishes patterns of dandyist stylistics, which can be imitated and hence reproduces dandies. Characteristically, decadent biographical literature does not make pretences to authenticity and historical verity – "the real and the imaginary are closely joined."[11] As I will demonstrate, both characteristics – the aesthetic dimension of life and the playfully biographical aspect of art – are central to Thurman's writings.

It is important to point out that the decadent concept of an "aesthetic lifestyle" is charged with gender implications. Just as the dandyist celebration of culture is often constructed as misogynist antinaturalism, the desire to make one's life into a work of art and to live in the Baudelairian "eternal present" clashes with matrimony and the burdens of reproduction. The link between aesthetics, lifestyle, and masculine privilege is also mentioned by Foucault in his discussion of "the arts of existence" in classical Greece. He defines this notion as "those intentional and voluntary actions by which men not only set themselves rules of conduct, but also seek to transform themselves, to change themselves in their singular being, and to make their life into an *oeuvre* that carries certain aesthetic values and meets certain stylistic criteria." However, it was "an ethics for men,...in which women figured only as objects." These aesthetic self-transformations were available only to free men and served as "the elaboration and stylization of an activity in the exercise of its power and the practice of its liberty."[12] Hence the aesthetization of life is predicated on male authority and freedom, which leads to the exclusion of women from the decadent circle.

The Niggerati Manor's artistic core consists of four artists: Ray, Paul, Eustace, and the untalented Pelham. The women they associate with, Janet and Aline, function only as decorations and are not admitted to the circle. This exclusion is even more visible when the newcomer Steve, neither an artist nor a Negro, is automatically included into the Niggerati Manor community almost upon his arrival in Harlem because he becomes the best friend of Raymond. The expulsion of female subjects is also manifest in the way Ray's close friend Lucille is introduced. She is the only non-decorative woman – "she personified what he was wont to call an intelligent woman. And there were few such women, in his opinion, to be found among the Negroes he knew."[13] Yet, despite her friendship with Ray, her intelligence, and her emancipated beliefs, not only does she not become a part of the Manor, but it is emphasized that their meetings take place outside of the house. Hence, the woman who is the most likely threat to "the eternal present" in Ray's life is positioned outside of the dandyist space of the Manor. Also, the fall of the Manor and its aesthetic project are intricately connected with the feminine presence in the house. Steve moves out largely because of the conflict resulting from Aline's and Janet's erotic desires; Gaylord Pelham is sent to prison for the alleged rape of the girl living in the house; Paul moves out because of his conflict with the landlady Euphoria, who in the end decides to exchange the male artistic tenants of the house for young working black women. Hence, female characters are both positioned on the periphery of the Manor and metonymically stand for its ending.

Before it falls, however, the Niggerati Manor and the lifestyle of its tenants are the tropes that signify the dandyist collapse of the life and art boundary. One of the most visible ways in which this private sphere is aestheticized is the interior decor of Ray's studio. It is highly significant for the novel's structure because it constitutes the opening of the novel. The studio is positioned from the very beginning as an aesthetic object to be looked at rather than a utilitarian living or working space. It is evident in the theatrical way it is introduced – "Raymond opened the door *with a flourish*, pushed the electric switch and preceded his two guests into the dimly illuminated room." The room is made visible by a single gesture, which adds a dramatic character to the scene. Its ornamental performativity is also highlighted by the "flourish" in Ray's movements. Ray proudly displays his interior to the guests, pointing to the "red and black draperies, the red and black bed cover, the crimson wicker chair, the riotous hook rugs."[14] Both the colors and types of furniture point to Orientalist influences, which were one of the most popular stylistics adopted by fin-de-siècle dandyism.[15] The drawings on the walls form the most controversial element of Ray's apartment and at the same time the most central to the collapse of the life and art boundary. Being simultaneously works of art and inseparable elements of the living space, they transform the whole studio into an artistic object. The artifice of the place is further reinforced by smaller details such as "the false fireplace." Also its very name "Niggerati Manor" invented by the inhabitants in the fourth chapter parallels the function of the title in an artwork. Finally, it is positioned as a work of art in the metaphor Euphoria uses to depict its function as "a monument to the New Negro."[16]

Also, the inhabitants of the place seem to operate on the level of art rather than life, which manifests itself in expressions such as a "rare collection," used twice to refer to the Manor tenants. In addition, they are first introduced in a theatrical way as "strange beings who...unceremoniously...forced themselves into the spotlight."[17] The Manor artists have carefully crafted public personas accurately fitting the ideal of the dandyist "stylized, painstakingly constructed self."[18] Raymond is a cynically decadent and wittily debonair Nietzschean. Although only briefly present in the narrative, a more dandyist incarnation of his character can be found in Walter Truman in The Blacker the Berry, depicted as "cock o' the walk" and characterized by a consciously performative use of witticisms and limericks. Eustace Savoy's very name appears to be an almost pretentious stylization. "The word elegant described him perfectly. His every movement was ornate and graceful." The way he dresses and does his hair is depicted as "bizarre." Also his inclination towards extravagantly aesthetic or snobbish objects is emphasized in the quote listing his passions: "cloisonné bric-a-brac, misty etchings, antique silver pieces, caviar, and rococo jewelry."[19] Eustace's aesthetically playful persona also manifests itself in his use of spoonerisms throughout the novel.

The most prototypical dandy in the novel, however, is represented by Paul Arbian. Apart from his frequent references to decadent writers and his declaration that "Oscar Wilde is the greatest man that ever lived," his own self is carefully designed for aesthetic display. "It was his habit not to wear a necktie because he knew that his neck was too well modeled to be hidden from the public gaze."[20] His performative attitude to life is most explicitly revealed in the inherently decadent ending of the book. Paul, who is the most talented of the Manor artists, commits suicide in a way that is clearly intended for the public:

> On arriving, he had locked himself in the bathroom, donned a crimson mandarin robe, wrapped his head in a batik scarf of his own designing, hung a group of his spirit portraits on the dingy calcimined wall, and carpeted the floor with sheets of paper detached from the notebook in which he had been

writing his novel. He had then, it seemed, placed scented joss-sticks in the four corners of the room, lit them, climbed into the bathtub, turned on the water, then slashed his wrists with a highly ornamented Chinese dirk. When they found him, the bathtub had overflowed, and Paul lay crumpled at the bottom, a colorful, inanimate corpse in a crimson streaked tub.

In the narrative, the scene of Paul's death is referred to as "a gruesome yet fascinating spectacle."[21] The elements used in this peculiar *tableau vivant* include Paul's artistic productions: the novel and the drawings as well as the highly stylized *décor* props: the decorative dirk, crimson robe, batik scarf, and scented joss-sticks, which clash with the typical downtown Manhattan bathroom characteristics, such as the dingy calcimined walls. Paul's dead body itself is transformed into a work of art, as it constitutes the central element of the composition. The color of his blood merges with the crimson of the robe. Bloody water also overflows, merges with Paul's novel, and destroys the sole artistic production to come from the Manor. What survives is only the title page decorated with a drawing of "a distorted, inky black skyscraper, modeled after the Niggerati Manor."[22] This frame also frames the novel's structure, which begins and ends with the theatrical image of the Manor. The fact that the ending explicitly positions the house on the level of artistic production exposed to the public gaze emphasizes its function as an aesthetic object throughout the text.

What makes the ending especially significant from the race perspective are the Orientalist components of the scene, since borrowings from the Far East are both exoticized and racialized in the white bohemian discourse. Paul, a black bohemian, appropriates a haphazard selection of elements from Asian cultures – a robe, a dirk, and incense sticks – into his final performance. These props are supposed to allude to the title of his book – *Wu Sing: The Geisha Man.* Hence, Paul indiscriminately mixes Chinese, Indian, and Japanese cultural references. The random character of his Orientalist fascinations is further manifested by the fact that before his death, Paul writes a letter to the Shah of Persia in Paris, in which he declares that he wants to be his "most priceless jewel."[23] Since Paul's Orientalist novel is dedicated to the European decadents Huysmans and Wilde, whereas the Persian Shah is in exile in Paris, his textual itinerary places occidental Europe on the way to the Orient. All these intertextual allusions manifest that Paul adopts an aesthetic lifestyle by reinventing himself with the use of racialized Orientalist imagery, which was characteristic of *fin-de-siècle* dandyism.[24] The omnipresence of Asian images in *The Infants* makes Locke's erasure of them in his revision of "The Survey Graphic Harlem Number" into *The New Negro* even more conspicuous and significant.

The aesthetic project of the Niggerati Manor neatly fits into the dandyist aesthetic of the self. It is concerned with the aesthetization of life and a creative approach to identity, which results in the conscious performance of the self. The

exclusion of female subjects erases the natural destiny and reproductive consequences from the plot, which distances the dandyist spectacle from femininity
and prevents the ultimate feminization of dandyist masculinity. Both factors result in the purposeful display of male personas to the (male) public gaze, which
opens space for homoerotic desire into the Niggerati Manor.

Another integral connection between the dandyist aesthetic approach to life
and gender relations is the way Thurman refers to marriage in his writings. In
his letters to Hughes he formulates a rule that "artists should never marry,"[25]
which follows the dandyist repudiation of matrimony and its consequences. Yet,
to the surprise of his friends and acquaintances, which is abundantly recorded in
his correspondence, he breaks this rule by getting married to Louise Thompson
in 1928. He reconciles his individualistic and dandyist approach to life with marriage by creating a peculiar narrative of his marital experiences. As David Mazella
claims with reference to a character from Wilde's *Picture of Dorian Gray*, "even marriage can be seen as a source of Art rather than Life" when approached in the
right way.[26] Following this logic, Thurman writes about his marriage just as he
writes about the publication of *Fire!!* – both are rendered as modern experiments.
He depicts his vision of marriage to Thompson in a letter to McKay in a way that
clearly challenges the separate spheres paradigm of the middle-class family. "My
only point of extenuation is that I happen to have married a very intelligent woman who has he[r] own career and who also does not believe in marriage...Ours
is a most modern expe[r]iment, a reflection of our own rather curious personal-
ities."[27] Thurman narrates this event as a curiosity, an experimentation, and a
paradox – tropes central to decadent and modernist aesthetics, hence he positions
it on the level of art rather than life.

The real-life experiment of Thurman and Thompson as recorded in his correspondence did not succeed in the long term – Thurman escaped to the West after
a couple of months only, and later attempts to repair their relationship apparently
failed. Yet, Thurman rewrites their marital experimentation in *Infants of the Spring*
in the relation of Ray and Lucille. As I have mentioned, Lucille is represented
predominantly outside of the bohemian space of the Manor; her extratextual relation to Thurman's real-life wife makes this exclusion even more understandable
from the dandyist point of view. Another device that reconciles the dandyist lifestyle and the female romantic presence in the novel is Lucille's approach to maternity. When it turns out that she is pregnant, she immediately decides to have
an abortion. The narrative represents this event in a detached and unemotional
way. "Lucille was introduced to the lady, arrangements were completed, and in
almost no time, and with little ill-effect, her body had been rid of Bull's seed once
and for all. 'Well, old dear, I'm a free woman.'"[28] Not only does Ray focalize the
abortion in a detached manner as the completion of the arrangements with no ill-
effect, without any reference to the fetus, only the "seed," but Lucille's unambiguous reaction also fully embraces such an unemotional attitude.[29] To further

make Ray and Lucille's relation compatible with the decadent ethic, they do not believe in marriage and decide not to get married in the text.

The stories of Taylor/Thurman and Lucille/Louise are symptomatic of the multifaceted interrelations between historical figures and Thurman's fictions. He is not the only author of the milieu to resort to the crypto-biographical narrative strategies of the *roman-à-clef*. Such narration is also exemplified by probably the most notorious of New Negro Renaissance publications – Carl Van Vechten's *Nigger Heaven*. Characteristically, this is a feature that is pointed out by Thurman in his review of the novel:

> Nigger Heaven will also provide high Harlem with a new indoor sport, namely, the ascertaining which persons in real life the various characters were drawn from. Speculations are already rampant even before a general circulation of the book, and I have heard from various persons whom each character represents with far more assurance than the author himself could muster.[30]

The last comment of the paragraph indicates that Thurman perceives the relations between fictional characters and real people as less unambiguously equivalent than some of the interpretations of Thurman's own writings suggest. The fact that the readers' interpretations are more confident than the author's further challenges the idea of authorial intention and authenticity in fiction, even in a genre as entangled in reality as the *roman-à-clef*.

It is widely acknowledged that Thurman's fiction is highly autobiographical and almost all of the characters from *The Infants* have been matched with their real-life models. Van Notten devotes more than one-third of her *Wallace Thurman's Harlem Renaissance* to trace the parallels between life and fiction both in *The Infants* and in *The Blacker the Berry*. The aim of this study, however, is neither to read the texts from an autobiographical perspective nor to provide insight into Thurman's life through a reading of his fiction. The intricate and complex relations between stories narrated in his correspondence and his fiction will be approached as an element of the dandyist fusion of life and art. Hence this analysis will be interested in the multifaceted and playful tensions between historical narratives and fiction rather than the one-to-one equivalent relations on which Van Notten's analysis focuses.

As Van Notten convincingly argues, Paul's character is based on Thurman's friend and roommate – Nugent. His narrative presence in both *The Infants* and *The Blacker the Berry* is complex and involves many levels of representation. His persona is constructed like a Chinese box – the authentic artist Nugent is mirrored as Paul Arbian, who, in the novel's finale, is transformed into the geisha man from his own novel.[31] Significantly, Nugent had indeed written a novel under such a title, yet it was not published at the time. The interrelations between Thurman's and Nugent's fictions are very close and complex, including suggestions of plagiarism voiced by the latter. Van Notten carefully traces the parallels between Thurman's *Infants* and Nugent's unpublished autobiographical novel *Gentleman Jigger* and supports Nugent's accusations. Such claims shed further light on the fact that Thurman's narrative strategically destroys Paul alias Nugent's text. Within *The Infants*, apart from the above-mentioned allusions to *The Geisha Man*, there is a fragment in which Paul tells his dream, which, as many critics point out, bears noticeable resemblance to the short story – scandalous for its expression of bisexual desire – that Nugent published in *Fire!!*. Paul's presence in the novel illustrates the way in which Thurman intertextually juggles with texts and plays with authentic personas, combining allusions to real-life persons, their texts, and the characters in their texts. Ironically, in the case of Thurman's fictionalization of Nugent, "nature avenged art;"[32] instead of dying as the first of the Niggerati, Nugent outlived them all.

An even more elaborate play on the periphery of the real and imaginary is represented by Thurman's own alter-egos in his fictions. Before I analyze his novels, however, it should be mentioned that, as Ganter points out, a comparative analysis of Thurman's letters and prose "suggests the close relationship between Thurman's life and fiction."[33] He refers to probably the most often analyzed of Thurman's letters, a message to his friend Rapp from 1929, where Thurman relates incidents in the course of which he was incarcerated for prostitution. Most of the critics interpret the letter's narrative as Thurman's refusal to identify himself as a homosexual simply because he was involved in sexual intercourse with another man. Ganter complicates this reading and claims that Thurman in general refuses to have his sexuality defined in binary oppositions.

What is most relevant, however, from the point of view of the relations between Thurman's personal and fictional writings is that the letter is narrated in a parallel way to the short story "Cordelia the Crude" (1926), which Thurman published in *Fire!!*. In the middle of the letter, which is written in the first person, Thurman switches to the third-person narration: "Now for the scandal. In 1929 a young colored lad anxious to enter a literary career came to New York."[34] Then, the narration switches back to the first person, revealing his personal involvement in the story. In "Cordelia," the narrative structure is parallel – it begins with the third-person narration, introducing Cordelia as a "potential prostitute" because of her "blasé and bountiful" manner "of bestowing sexual favors," and switches to the first-person narration of her male companion. In the short story, Thurman splits his narrative identity into the male observer and the female signaling her sexual availability. Even though Thurman's persona in the letter to Rapp significantly differs from the "half-literate product of rustic South Carolina" from "Cordelia the Crude," both figures become "potential prostitutes" as a result of their migration to New York.[35] What is more, both narratives depict the event of initiation into prostitution and in each case the pecuniary reward for this is exactly the same sum of money, two dollars.

The story of Cordelia is the first but not the last of Thurman's attempts to experiment with narrative cross-dressing. As is generally acknowledged by critics, "Thurman initially wrote the autobiographical fictions from a woman's viewpoint."[36] Two other narratives include the play *Harlem* and his first novel *The Blacker the Berry*. The play is a Broadway adaptation of the above-discussed short story.[37] The half-literate prostitute Cordelia Jones is transformed into sexually liberated Delia Williams, who changes her men three times in the span of one Saturday night. The main character from Thurman's first novel, the respectable and intelligent Emma Lou Morgan, significantly differs from the Delias. Here the most significant parallel stems from the fact that Emma Lou's story largely follows Thurman's own peculiar itinerary from Utah, through Los Angeles, to Harlem. Other important similarities include their family and educational background, which is discussed in detail by Van Notten.[38] Many critics also point out that both Thurman and Emma Lou suffer from intraracial prejudice because of their dark complexions. Yet, reading the story of Emma as a simple autobiography greatly oversimplifies Thurman's narrative. Not only does he gender-bend his personal history in the figure of Emma but in the middle of the narrative, he introduces the character of Truman Walter, who turns out to be her friend from college, and hence necessarily follows a similar itinerary to Harlem. Walter, whose very name positions him as Thurman's conspicuous alter-ego, is a self-confident witty bohemian, who revels in delivering philosophical speeches and ornamental utterances such as "the bawdy bowels of Beale street!"[39] The introduction of Truman challenges the univocality of reading Emma Lou as Thurman's alter-ego. Thurman's playful attitude to his autobiographical personas is visible in the names he gives them. "Tru-man" suggests an intended close relation between the author and the character, yet it simultaneously indicates that the character is truer than the real-life persona. Such an approach to autobiography accurately follows the dandyist philosophy of Wilde, whose aphorism "Nature imitates art" is quoted by Paul in *The Infants*.[40]

Thurman's female autobiographical personas have been interpreted by critics in a number of ways: as a way to achieve dramatic distance and to detach himself from his personal insecurities; as artistic experimentation in identifying with another person's point of view; as a dialogical response to Jessie Fauset's middle-class protagonist, Joanna Marshall from *There Is Confusion*; and as an attempt to produce a black *Sister Carrie* or *Madame Bovary*, novels that were highly praised in Thurman's letters.[41] From the perspective of this study, Thurman's appropriation of a female persona plays into the self-conscious artificiality of the decadent aesthetic. The obvious contravention of the authenticity of autobiographical accounts by narrative sex-change points to the artifice of all autobiographical accounts. Moreover, as Garelick claims, "the decadent dandy...exhibits great interest in the spectacle of the woman,...since dandyism attempts to incorporate into the male persona something of the highly social performance usually expected only of women."[42] Hence, Thurman's feminine masks can be read as the integration of the spectacular and performative into his plural autobiographical personas. This reading can be supported further by the fact that both Delias as well as Emma Lou spend a considerable amount of the narratives on fashioning their looks and are conscious (or in the case of Emma Lou even hyper-conscious) of their exposure to the public gaze. Moreover, Emma Lou and Cordelia from Harlem entertain similar wishes of becoming performers and "standin' in de lights above deir heads, makin' de whole world look up."[43] Hence, Thurman's feminine masks can be read as a peculiar version of dandyist investment in female spectacle as discussed by Garelick.

The link between Thurman's feminine masks and dandyism also has peculiar implications for the constructions of sexuality in the texts. Namely, female focalization enables Thurman to express desire for the male body within the normative romantic framework. Since they are to a large extent modeled on the sexually liberated New Woman, Thurman's autobiographically-charged female characters perceive men in terms of their bodily attractiveness. Moreover, in the case of Emma Lou, this kind of perception is motivated by the fact that she perceives people through the prism of her desire for light-toned complexion; hence she necessarily focuses on their physical characteristics. The focalization of her first love, Weldon Taylor, is constructed primarily in corporeal terms, when she admires his "tall, slender body."[44] Later in the text, the perception of the male body continues to be narrated in a similar way. After coming to Harlem, Emma Lou is fascinated by the spectacle of anonymous males in the streets. "She began to admire their well formed bodies and gloried in the way their trousers fit their shapely limbs...she...loved to watch them."[45] Here Emma is not emotionally attached to the men she looks at. The absence of a romantic dimension further emphasizes the physical and erotic character of the gaze.

Both Delia and Cordelia refer to the men they find attractive as "sheiks." In the short story, the male narrator is depicted as "different from mos' of des' sheiks," whereas in the play, Roy – the object of Delia's desire and her fiancé's jealousy – is repeatedly referred to as "that sheik."[46] This expression, assimilated by the Harlem vernacular in phrases such as "that sheik cousin of Ippy," comes from the mainstream discourse and refers to the figure of Rudolph Valentino, who was one of the first sex symbols of the silent cinema, most famous for his role in The Sheik and The Son of the Sheik. The link between the Harlemese concept of the sheik and the actor is made explicit in The Blacker the Berry, where the light-skinned sexually attractive Braxton strongly identifies with the Italian-American actor, fashioning himself as "a golden brown replica of Rudolph Valentino...the late lamented cinema sheik."[47] This interracial identification is perceived by his friend Alva as a "flapperish ritual," which, through the reference to the female "flapper," alludes to the popular female fascination with Valentino and positions the Valentino-sheik persona as the object of the New Woman's desire. Characteristically, Valen-

DANDYISM AND AESTHETICS OF THE SELF

tino's persona was complexly racialized in the popular discourse – his racial ambiguity conflated his Italian-American origins, his image as a "Latin lover," and
his screen embodiments of Middle Eastern characters. The fact that, as the above-
analyzed fragments reveal, his "sheik" image was essentially based on sexual attractiveness racializes also the position of the sex object of the female gaze, in
contrast to the hegemonic paradigm of the white male gaze/female object. The
racial ambiguities exploited in Braxton's identification with Valentino as well as
Paul's dressing up as a geisha will be explored later in the chapter.

As the above examples suggest, Thurman's fictions abound in the representations of female desire for the male body. The use of female focalization enables
the representation of men as objects of sexual desire, which simultaneously plays
into heterosexual normativity and flouts it. Since the male body in the text is positioned as the object of the gaze, which is traditionally coded as male, the gaze
gains a homoerotic character. The homoerotic element is further strengthened
when the published texts are read in the context of Thurman's personal narratives
from the letters, which reveal a close relation between his self-fashioned persona
and his female characters; the women explicitly express the desire which remains
unspoken in his male characters.

The analysis of Thurman's literary alter-egos – Emma Lou, the Cordelias, Truman, and Taylor – shows that his peculiar autobiographical fiction should not be
read in terms of a purely mimetic expression. It is neither a record of authentic
historical events, places, and persons, nor a strategically tailored biographical text
constructed in a way that produces the illusion of authenticity. Just as Paul dedi-
cates his novel to Oscar Wilde's Oscar Wilde, both Thurman's letters and fictions
construct Wallace Thurman's Wallace Thurman, a second-order representation
rather than an unambiguously transparent sign referencing reality. Especially
when read together, which is encouraged by the fact that some characters transgress the limits of single texts, his writings constitute an attempt to merge the
boundary between the real and the fictitious. This liminal space between life and
art is produced by the insertion of a number of representative levels into the novels and narrative experiments with multiple pseudo-autobiographical personas.
Significantly, the blurring of the boundary between autobiography and fiction is
also produced by Thurman's bending of his autobiographical identity by narrative
gender cross-dressing. Moreover, since Thurman's personal writings assert his
aesthetic approach to life, which is manifest in his attitude to his marriage, the
relation between his fiction and his auto-representations becomes intertextual
rather than purely autobiographical. Such a creative approach to life is also manifest in the inclination to produce fictitious rumors about himself to which Thurman admits in his letters.

The phenomenon of dandyist creative self-reinvention and its emancipatory
potential has been discussed by Foucault with reference to "dandysme" as represented by Baudelaire. Foucault claims that modern consciousness, ideally illu-

strated by the dandy, is "a mode of relationship...with oneself." He acknowledges that the dandy is a person "who makes of his body, his behavior, his feelings and passions, his very existence, a work of art." Yet he focuses on "the ascetic elaboration of the self," which is essential in this process, and points out that "modernity...compels [the dandy/modern man] to face the task of producing himself." The dandyist creative approach to identity and the aesthetic reinvention of the self are part of "work carried out by ourselves upon ourselves as free beings," and hence it interrogates the social norms imposed on the individual subject and may lead to enlightenment and social transformation.[48] Nonetheless, as Anita Seppä convincingly claims, both in Foucault's and Baudelaire's writings, this liberating aesthetic stylization is constructed primarily from the free-white-male perspective, and there are "various *practical* limitations individuals might face, depending on their gender, ethnicity, class and sexual identity." As I mentioned before, Foucault himself recognizes such constraints in the case of Greek "arts of existence." What makes Seppä's comments on Foucault's text interesting is her elaboration of the issue of the modern subject. She discusses Baudelaire's project in terms of lower modernity, which attempts to "turn the life and body of an individual into a transgressive site of a living artwork." It transcends the limitation of the Kantian subject, which is based on reason and independence, by "including in the notion of aesthetic subjectivity the 'lower' dimensions of human existence such as sexuality, affectiveness, desire, and the body."[49] The inclusion of and focus on the level of the body, according to Seppä, make it possible to transcend the constraints of universal and autonomous subjectivity. Yet simultaneously, it can be an obstacle in the pursuit of the aesthetics of the self for the groups marked with a biological difference. Significantly, biological unchangeability in the case of skin color can be seen as parallel to the natural determinism associated in the dandyist imagination with femininity and hence in opposition to the aesthetic recreation of the self.

These biological constraints on creative reinventions of the self are acknowledged in Thurman's texts. As Thurman complains in one of his letters to Rapp, "I was told at M.G.M. that were it possible for me to pass for white, i.e. should I have happened to be a mulatto, I could possibly have become connected with their staff...They did not mind my being a Negro, oh no, it was just that I was too obviously one."[50] The problem of unambiguous blackness is also at the center of *The Blacker the Berry*, whose main character, Emma Lou, desires to change both her sex and her skin color. Her desire for whiteness results in her engagement in various whitening practices, which although they can be read within the framework of reinventing one's body, clearly accept rather than challenge the imposed social norms of beauty and feminine identity. Her "pyrrhic victory," that is final enlightenment, in the text is precisely to "accept her black skin as being real and unchangeable" and her desire for whiteness as the internalization of prejudice.[51] This approach is articulated earlier by another autobiographical character in the text, Walter Truman, who states that the desire for whiteness and intraracial discrimination stem from consent to the hegemonic standards set by the white majority.[52] Truman's narratives show that the arts of existence are limited not only by the abstract privilege of "free men" but even more intensely by the corporeal unchangeability of race and sex.

Since both Emma Lou's and Thurman's personas are constrained in their exercise of the aesthetics of the self, the most prototypical dandy figures in Thurman's texts are light-skinned. Paul, for example, seems to be more successful in his decadent performance than Ray, mainly due to his racially ambiguous identity. He can easily move from Harlem to Greenwich Village, or from black society in Washington to South America and back to the Spanish Legation in DC. The ability to transgress Jim Crow boundaries is largely predicated on Paul's light skin color. This freedom to travel also enables him to reinvent himself as the *flâneur*, the wandering observer in the urban spaces, a decadent foil to the dandy engaged in self-display. As Griselda Pollock argues, "The *flâneur* symbolizes the privilege or freedom to move about the public arenas of the city observing but never interacting, consuming the sights through a controlling but rarely acknowledged gaze, directed as much at other people as at the goods for sale."[53] In her account, the *flâneur*'s "freedom to move about the public arenas" is contrasted with female immobility. In the context of Jim Crow America, this freedom is also restricted by skin color. Paul's poetic adventurous wanderings are in stark contrast to the walk across Manhattan taken by his black-complexioned foil, Ray. Feeling stifled by the Manor, he visits Pelham in jail, wanders through the city, collapses in the street, and ends his *flâneur* endeavor in Bellevue, where he overhears being referred to as "the coon."[54] These divergent experiences prove that unambiguously racialized subjects are limited in their adoption of the *flâneur* position and aesthetic reinventions of the self.

Since Thurman's project of individual artistic freedom is deeply indebted to dandyism, the correlation between skin tone and the aesthetics of the self explains the omnipresence of racially ambiguous characters in his texts. Whereas evident blackness can be an obstacle to the dandyist performance of the self or *flâneur* explorations of the city, racial ambiguity seems to be a privileged position even in comparison with white identity, since it implicates a greater number of self-inventing possibilities and inclusion into more than one community.

Decadence, Sexual Liberation, and Superwomen

Apart from dandyism, another aspect of the decadent project that is centrally relevant for this analysis is the bohemian embrace of sexual liberation. This attitude is manifested primarily in Thurman's rebellion against Victorian respectability and, in particular, against its gender and sexuality norms.[55] His authorial persona in "Notes on a Stepchild," refers to the two most influential European figures in the American sexual liberation rhetoric, claiming that "he learned...the mysteries of sex from Havelock Ellis and Freud."[56] His interpretation of their writings as advocating a lack of sexual repressions is visible in his later letter to Dorothy West, where he gives her friendly advice to "get rid of the puritan notion that to have casual sexual intercourse is a sin. It is a biological necessity." "Don't repress yourself," he adds, because "more tragedies result from girls clinging to their virginity than you would imagine."[57] In the story of her life, Euphoria Blake states that "I believed in free love, too...it was all in the game."[58] "The game" refers to Euphoria's allegiance to socialism and her participation in the white bohemian life in Greenwich Village, which indicates the extent to which sexual liberation was interconnected with other counter-hegemonic discourses of the day.[59]

Thurman's assertion of a sexually liberated attitude parallels the way in which he represents the destinies of his autobiographically-charged female characters. As mentioned in the analysis of Thurman's narrative cross-dressing, both Cordelia and Delia represent an attitude to sexuality which is definitely not rooted in the puritan view of sex as sin. Significantly, neither of the narratives judges such demeanor in moral terms. Thurman insisted that the ending of his Broadway play does not moralize about the main character's liberated sexuality.[60] Not only is the play not explicitly judgmental, the narrative does not punish the uninhibited behavior in any way. In the end, Cordelia leaves her family with the piano player in order to become a stage celebrity. Her determinate and consistent attitude throughout the three acts makes it possible for the audience to believe that "when you hears from me again, I'm gonna be livin' high, standin' in de lights above deir heads, makin' de whole world look up at me."[61]

An analogous representation of female sexuality can be found in *The Blacker the Berry*. Even though Emma Lou internalized black bourgeois blue-vein ideology, her approach to sex is far from subscribing to respectable Victorian purity. Her extramarital sexual initiation is depicted in terms of "surging ecstasy," "magnetic force," and the discovery of "a new and incomparably satisfying paradise," whereas her body is compared with "a kennel for clashing, screaming, compelling urges and desires." The narrative explicitly denies that Emma experienced any moral doubts concerning her illicit sexual relations: "Not for one moment did Emma Lou consider regretting the loss of her virtue." The right to sexual desire is also granted to Emma in her sexualized perception of male bodies, which has been mentioned earlier. Emma's libidinal urges, explicitly depicted when she is "lying in bed late every morning, semi-conscious, body burning, mind disturbed by thoughts of sex," lead her to look for men in the ballrooms. Furthermore, her sexual escapades seem to be acceptable in the context of Harlem's social codes. "She did feel foolish, going there without an escort, but the doorman didn't seem to notice. Perhaps it was alright. Perhaps it was customary for Harlem girls to go about unaccompanied."[62] In this scene, Emma's sexually liberated demeanor is explained with the general espousal of sexual liberation in

Thurman's Harlem. As he states in his critique of Van Vechten's *Nigger Heaven* and its representation of the virtuous Mary Love, "show me any girl in Mary's milieu [Harlem intelligentsia] who is as simple as Mary in the matters of an *affair du coeur*."[63] Hence, Thurman's fiction embraces or even celebrates liberated black female sexuality without moral judgment and links it with the cultural context of Harlem.

This fascination with liberated female sexuality can also be found in one of Thurman's letters, where he openly asserts that Norah Holt Ray is "one of Negro America's most interesting characters."[64] This black woman is remembered in literary history primarily as the model for Van Vechten's notorious Lasca Sartoris in *Nigger Heaven*. Thurman, arguing that Van Vechten's prudish account did not give justice to the power of her transgressions, expresses a desire to write his own text based on Ray's life story. Even though such a novel has not been produced, what can be analyzed is the way Thurman outlines his vision in the letter:

> Should one give a faithful depiction of the lady the censors would all die of apoplexy so astounding and a-moral are her escapades. She has figured in innumerable divorce and alienation of affection suits, all with prominent and wealthy Negro men, and she has a whole slew of white suitors. While in New York she resides at the Ritz or Plaza and makes all the first nights with Carl Van Vechten!![65]

Thurman uses Holt Ray's persona as a symbol of rebellion against bourgeois respectability and the purity of womanhood; he enjoys the thought of shocking his audience to the point of apoplexy. The events he focuses on in his depiction of Norah flout the taboo of miscegenation as well as the sanctity of marriage. That it is precisely the bourgeois idea of marriage that is the target of Norah's "a-moral" transgressions is evident in Thurman's emphasis that men who divorce because of her are "prominent and wealthy." It seems that such an attitude, liberated from the restraints of social norms, and her ability to afford "resid[ing] at the Ritz or Plaza," fit Thurman's model of racial liberation. His sympathy for Norah Holt Ray is also visible in the fact that he names his alter-ego in *The Infants* and his white lover's persona in *The Blacker the Berry* Ray. Both male Rays from fiction and Nora Holt Ray from Thurman's letters violate the taboos of intimate interracial relations as well as extramarital sex. One could also speculate on the semantic charge of the word "ray" and its associations with sun and light, suggesting hope and enlightenment just as it is in the case of Locke's tropes. Yet, whereas Locke used the imagery of the East, birth, and dawn publicly to point to the abstract sublime, in Thurman's fiction, liberation is intertwined with the lower corporeal level of sexuality.

The fact that Thurman reads Van Vechten's black female characters against the grain of the narrative of *Nigger Heaven* is also significant from the perspective of contemporary re-readings of this text. Carby claims that Van Vechten's narrative punishes the main character, Byron, for his choice of Lasca – "whose behavior is absolutely outside of all moral boundaries" and who represents "overt and degenerate sexuality" – over Mary Love, an epitome of virginal purity.[66] Thurman's scathing critique of Mary's authenticity and his celebration of Lasca's real-life model prove that his texts do not embrace the respectable bourgeois attempts to police black female sexuality intended to secure and confirm respectable black masculinity.

Another way in which Thurman's writings celebrate, or at least refrain from punishing, liberated black female sexuality, is the lack of undesirable reproductive consequences in most of the narratives. The narratives save both Cordelias from pregnancy, whose likelihood, in the context of the narratives, would be quite realistic. As I have signaled before, the character that gets pregnant, Lucille, decides to have an abortion and is spared any post-abortion trauma. Emma Lou engages in a number of sexual relationships, which include the earlier mentioned Weldon, a theater porter called John, accidental men she meets in Harlem such as a sweetback Jasper Carne or the respectable striver Benson Brown, and her tragic love, Alva, yet she does not get pregnant in the course of a several-year-long storyline. Temporarily, she adopts the function of "the mammy" of Alva's child; however, her conscious recognition and rejection of this slave stereotype marks the enlightening moment in her life. Hence, the deliberate rejection of motherhood is narratively conflated with the moment of epiphany and liberation. Ross argues that "through the Alva-Geraldine subplot, Thurman is able to redirect the tendency of urban folk fiction to repress the question of children and child raising... [T]he heroine-based novels at least raise the specter of children as a complicating factor for urban mobility, sexual independence, and race uplift."[67] Nonetheless, when it is acknowledged that Emma's rejection of the baby signifies enlightenment, Geraldine successfully abandons the burden of motherhood, the whole event takes up only a few pages of the novel, and any affirmative representations of maternity are absent from his "heroine-based" texts, Ross's claim seems to be an exaggeration. Thurman's narratives liberate his black female characters from the possibly negative consequences of sexual freedom. His representation of sexually liberated "superwomen" can be read as an attempt to construct the New Negro Woman. As I have argued, one of the possible reasons behind Locke's exclusion of the New Woman from his vision of the New Negro was his commitment to the ideology of respectable producerist masculinity. In contrast, Thurman's rebellion against gentility provides ample space for the New Negro Woman.[68]

Interestingly, the case of the sexually liberated male New Negro is more problematic in Thurman's writings. The new black masculinity which, according to Summers, challenged the respectable producerist manhood and was rooted in "bodily virtuoso and sexual virility" had its own discontents.[69] This is most tellingly exemplified by the tragic destiny of Pelham, one of the characters from *The Infants*. It is repeatedly emphasized in the narrative that he is the "natural born menial with all a menial's respect for his superiors." His subservient tendencies developed under the influence of his Grandma Mack, who "had never forgiven Abraham Lincoln for freeing the slaves."[70] Pelham's grandma, with her strong personality and dominating position over the male offspring, a concern that her ex-master's children do not "suffer for want of care," and a vehement embrace of the Southern slave system, perfectly fits the stereotypical mammy. Pelham, on the other hand, accurately embodies the submissive but happy slave, the harmless Sambo, another powerful image from plantation mythology. His tragic ending results from the clash between his allegiance to the slavery ideologies and his artistic inclinations, which result from the desire to emulate his white master's career as a portrait painter. Artistic ambitions lead Pelham to socialize with the black bohemia represented by Paul, Ray, and Eustace. His attempts to imitate their artistic endeavors also lead to his peculiar adoption of a sexually liberated bohemian lifestyle. The first attempt to change his persona from the Sambo to the bohemian dandy is his name change – from George Jones to Pelham Gaylord. The name contains many intertextual references, including Gaylord Ravenal, the leading male character from the musical *Show Boat* (1927) and, even more significantly from the point of view of decadent aesthetics, Pelham from Edward Bulwer-Lytton's *Pelham: or The Adventures of a Gentleman* (1826).[71] Bulwer-Lytton's novel contains a fictionalized portrait of Beau Brummell né George Bryan Brummell, a persona credited with being the first dandy. Moreover, in the text, another character – the title-giving Henry Pelham – represents an adventurous cynical dandy hero. The black artist-to-be reinvents himself in a truly dandyist manner, shedding the name of George Jones, which emanates with mediocrity, and taking a name that suggests both decadent and erotic refinement. Yet, Pelham's autocreation is reminiscent of the caricatured minstrel figure of the black dandy, which served to resolve the anxieties of urbanization and working-class resentment against the upper classes, rather than of Foucault's modern man enlightening himself through self-reinvention.[72]

The ironic clash between Pelham's subservient persona and his fancy name gains a tragic dimension after he is introduced to Paul and Ray's version of Freudian thought. "When he [Pelham] declared himself to be an uninitiated[,] 'You are repressed,' they cried. 'A man of your age with no sexual experience is liable to develop all sorts of neuroses and complexes. You're inhibited and should let yourself go.'"[73] As a result of this conversation, Pelham engages in an affair with a black girl Gladys, who, despite being a minor, is sexually more experienced than the black would-be artist. Yet, in Jim Crow America permeated with the lynch logic and an obsession with predatory black male sexuality, this affair ends in Pelham being tried for rape and "found guilty of being sexually intimate with a minor under the age of consent."[74] Thus the narrative outcome of an attempt to sexually liberate a black man ends in him being publicly stigmatized as the stereo-typical brute.

Pelham's story shows the powerful double bind formed by the coexistence of the pervasive lynch ideology and Freudian thought. As a result, Thurman's text reveals a lynching anxiety linked to the expression of black male (hetero)sexuality. Even though he fashioned his public persona as nonchalantly detached from the problem of lynching and "those hapless blackamoors who happened to be lynched or burned in the backwoods of Dixie," *Infants of the Spring*, contains two other references to lynching apart from Pelham's case.[75] Euphoria Blake, having seen a lynched black man, cannot forget this haunting image, and decides to join the NAACP cause and "to be a black Joan of Arc."[76] Witnessing a lynching is also the driving force behind Bull's attack on Steve, who is involved in an interracial affair with a black woman.[77] Hence, such a significant, if implicit, presence of the lynch theme shows that it was a deeply lingering anxiety in the black bohemian appropriations of Freudianism and sexual liberation discourse. To "let oneself go" might have easily led to public stigmatization or even lynching. The position of black male (hetero)sexuality in the American imagination dramatically re-strains the vision of individualism and decadent sexual liberation in Thurman's writings.

Dandyism and Homosexuality

Whereas black heterosexual desire is drenched with lynching anxiety, the black homosexual subject, just like the New Negro Woman's liberated sexuality, consti-tutes a libidinal position which is not threatening within the lynch ideology, since it does not endanger the purity of white womanhood. As I have mentioned, in the collective imagination of the day, the decadent project is also directly connected with a particular version of homosexual identity, epitomized by Wilde. According to Showalter, the link between the two notions is so close that "'decadence' was also a *fin-de-siècle* euphemism for homosexuality."[78] Same-sex discourses recog-nize a liberating potential in the earlier-discussed antinaturalism of dandyism; dandyist glorification of things perverse, artificial, and against nature fosters its acceptance of homosexuality, which has been traditionally attacked as a violation of the natural laws.

The homosexual masculinity represented by Wilde was perceived as effeminate by the black bourgeoisie and hence leading to the degeneration of black male identity. It is fundamentally distinct from the wholesome, sublime, masculinist rhetoric that is constructed by Locke for the closed circle of his male friends and which alludes to the male nudes in an outdoor context. Whereas representations of German men against natural backgrounds forge a metonymical link between nature and male same-sexuality, which makes such homoeroticism seem utterly natural, the Wildean attitude celebrates the artifice, cross-dressing, performance, and androgyny. The contrast between the two competing visions of alternative sexuality is further increased by the fact that Locke's rhetoric is to a large extent implicit and conducted on the periphery of the private sphere, whereas dandyist engagements with sexual transgressions are meant as shocking public exhibitions. Dandyist homoerotic masculinity depends precisely on the blurring of the boundaries between the public and the private, art and life.

Some ways in which Thurman's writings provide space for homoerotic expression have already been discussed in my analyses of the function of the female focalization of male bodies and the depictions of transgressive sexualities at the Niggerati Manor rent party. In order to further explore the issue of transgressive sexuality in Thurman's texts, it seems fruitful to compare two characters who explicitly represent sexual experimentation and are in many ways parallel – Paul from *The Infants* and Alva from *The Blacker the Berry*. Even though Van Notten argues that it is Braxton, Alva's roommate and a foil character, who is Nugent's fictional alter-ego, as far as the construction of desire is concerned, there is a stronger parallel between Paul/Nugent and Alva.[79] Because of this striking similarity to Paul, even though Alva is not represented as a member of the bohemian milieu but rather as its satellite, he will be discussed in reference to dandyism.

Paul's character functions as the main channel for transgressive sexuality in *Infants of the Spring*. From the very beginning, his persona is characterized by an inclination towards exhibitionist sexual experimentation. Not only does he challenge the sexual norms, but he does this either in the public sphere or in his art. He constitutes the link between Harlem and Village bohemias, and the latter, as has been mentioned, is represented mainly by the "Uranians." For Paul, the rent party becomes a space for the exhibition of non-normative sexuality, where he advertises and organizes a homoerotic spectacle of Bud's body. Paul's sexual transgressions are also represented in his drawings decorating Ray's flat, which are referred to by the respectable Sam as "nothing but highly colored phalli" and according to the white Canadian Steve they are "all Greek."[80]

Interestingly, the complex and contradictory readings of the pictures in the text racialize their homoerotic content in different or even contradictory ways. Ray offers a reading, which he attributes to Sam's hypocritical racist perspective according to which the colors in the sexual drawings point to "inferior race heritage" of black people who "must go for loud colors." A more complex explanation for why the "flamboyant and vulgar" character makes them typically black is provided by the historical accounts according to which, in the white imagination, black neighborhoods constituted "the interzones" where vice districts as well as the exhibition of non-normative sexuality was both more acceptable and more visible.[81] In contrast to this interpretation, Paul explains the drawings by naming a list of white artists, famous both for their sexual and artistic experimentation: Wilde, Huysmans, and Baudelaire lead the catalogue and are followed by Blake, Dowson, Verlaine, Rimbaud, Poe, and Whitman. As Ganter insightfully comments on this group, "although several of the artists that Paul cites are well known for their nonconformist sexuality, he is also declaring that he prefers artists who question the boundaries of the acceptable."[82] Yet, if we read the list from the point of view of race, it clearly points to white, predominantly European influences. Even Poe and Whitman are intertextually Europeanized in the context of other Thurman's writings, where he refers to them as exemplifying the phenomenon of American artists appreciated in Europe and disregarded in America. Hence, the homoeroticism of the drawings is read by Paul in terms of white European decadence. Finally, Steve's comment points to the rhetoric analyzed in the second chapter, positioning the homoerotic content in the context of European Antiquity and its subsequent revivals. The echoes of Greek same-sexuality resurface also in Ray's depiction of "Paul's Spartan bootblack." The fact that Thurman's text thematizes homoeroticism with reference to different racially-coded discourses resonates with the conflation of transgressive sexuality and racial passing, which will be explored later in the chapter. The intertextual presence of so many different discourses indicates that Thurman's representations of alternative sexuality are more inclusive, ambiguous, and intricate than Locke's.

Paul's sexuality is most openly foregrounded in his monologue depicting the dream, which in many ways parallels Nugent's "Smoke, Lilies and Jade." As I have mentioned earlier, this text was infamous at the time due to its explicit expression of male-male and male-female desire. Sam, a white hypocritical philanthropist, expresses deep concern about the sexual intimacy represented in the dream. He interrogates Paul's sexual orientation to make him admit that he is homosexual. Paul wittily maneuvers Sam's questions, which results in the expression of an ultimately liberated attitude to sexuality: "After all there are no sexes, only sex majorities, and the primary function of the sex act is enjoyment. Therefore I enjoyed one experience [sexual intercourse with a woman] as the other [sexual intercourse with a man]."[83] The reasons for Sam's discontent with Paul's dream, however, might not be purely homophobic. In the light of other comments in the novel that reveal his fear of miscegenation, his concern may stem from the fact that the dream lover is depicted as "an ivory body," which indicates an interracial relationship. This dialogue has significant implications for Thurman's construction of the sexuality. It liberates sexuality from reproduction, since "the primary function of the sex act is enjoyment," a statement that is reinforced by the predominant lack of parental burdens in Thurman's texts. Paul refutes being defined by his acts, hence he resists the modern ideology of the homosexual as a species as defined by Foucault in his *History of Sexuality*, where sexual activity or desire determines one's identity.[84] The rejection of strict identity boundaries is also expressed in Paul's repudiation of imposed binary gender identities. The sexual ambiguity of the attractive "ivory body" is reminiscent of Beardsley's androgynous figures in *Salome*. Additionally, since the dialogue refers to the dream where Paul depicts "supreme ecstasy" resulting from "a complete merging" with the "ivory presence," racial boundaries are also challenged. The juxta-position of these three transgressions in the text indicates an integral correlation between them. This conflation is also revoked in Paul's self-creation in the final suicide scene. By reinventing himself as the Geisha Man, he disrupts both his racial identity and his gender identity, since he cross-dresses as a fundamentally feminine character of the oriental Geisha. Moreover, the very adoption of Orien-talist elements in the scene can be read as expressing transgressive homoeroti-cism. As Eve Kosofsky Sedwick claims, due to the "commodity-based oriental-ism" and its entanglement in the Opium traffic discourse, Wilde's *Dorian Gray* "accomplished for its period the performative work of enabling a European com-munity of gay mutual recognition and self-constitution."[85] Hence, within the decadent male same-sex desire discourse, Paul's Orientalist props point to a par-ticular version of homosexual identity represented by Wilde.

Sedgwick's reference to Wilde, or even more importantly the dedication of *Wu Sing: The Geisha Man* to this influential dandy, encourages yet another intertextual reading of Paul's suicide. Wilde's notorious play *Salome*, whose homoerotic con-tent has already been mentioned as stemming from both the text and Beardsley's illustrations, was banned in England until 1931. The notoriety of this controversial text explains the central significance of Salome's myth in the decadent imagina-tion, which has been acknowledged by a number of critics.[86] Importantly, the title character was identified with Wilde, which is accurately illustrated by the debate surrounding a picture that most likely represents a Hungarian opera singer, Alice Guszalewicz. Until 1994, Wilde's biographers mistakenly claimed that it was a picture of Wilde himself posing as Salome.[87] The juxtaposition of Wilde's narra-tive or alleged visual performance as Salome and Paul's finale reveals a number of significant parallels. The most obvious common structural element is that both spectacles represent male cross-dressing that is meant for public display. The similarities, however, are also visible in the details. Salome is remembered as a "damsel," who "danced, and pleased Herod," and thus, due to her Orientalist character brings to mind the Turkish Odalisque or the Arabic Samira.[88] Salome's performance for Herod neatly parallels the function of the Geisha as a female performer. Moreover, since *fin-de-siècle* fascination with the East randomly con-flated various geographical and cultural realities, in decadent collective imagina-tion both the geisha and Salome embody the myth of the mysterious oriental female entertainer. Hence, just like Paul's dream, the bathtub suicide scene can be read as an expression of transgressive sexuality, which in this case is addition-ally performed through racial cross-dressing.

Paul's resistance to being defined by bourgeois social norms represented by Sam's viewpoint parallels Thurman's stance in his autobiographical testimony about his experience as a male prostitute in a letter to Rapp. I have discussed the similarities between this letter and the narration of the short story "Cordelia the Crude." However, the attention it has attracted among critics mostly stems from its concern with homosexuality. The letter narrates the incident in which Thurman was arrested for male prostitution. It begins by contextualizing the event primarily as a result of his economic situation – "he [Thurman] owed room rent and was hungry."[89] What follows is a narration that is objective and emotionally detached. The distance is further strengthened by the earlier-mentioned use of the third person. The reason for the testimony and the result of the incident is that it is used in Thurman's divorce process by his wife Louise – "they threatened to make charges t[h]at I was homosexual, and knowing this and that I was incapable of keeping up my marital relationship [and] had no business marrying. All of which Louise knew was a lie. The incident was true, but there was certainly no evidence therein I was a homosexual."[90] Thurman's response to these charges and to the incident has been read by most critics as evidence of his closeted homosexuality. Yet as Ganter rightly argues, "Thurman refuses to have his sexuality defined by someone else. Thurman confesses to engaging in an act of homosexual prostitution but denies that it is 'evidence therein' of his homosexuality."[91] He also refuses to be defined within the binary logic of homosexual/heterosexual. Hence Thurman's testimony about his same-sex experience, even though it conspicuously differs from Paul's exhibitionist performance of transgressive sexuality, parallels it in its refusal to be defined and confined by existing social categories.

Paul's sexual relations can also be contrasted with the narration from the letter in yet another way. His utopian decadent vision of "no sexes" ignores social context and economic relations, whereas the persona of young poor Thurman clearly indicates a connection between the underprivileged classes and transgressive interzones. The relationship between the young writer who turns to prostitution and his sexual "aggressor" personified by a wealthy Fifth Avenue hairdresser is a mirror reflection of Paul's relation with Spartan Bud the bootblack. With regard to the issue of prostitution or the objectification of sexual pleasure, the contrast between Thurman's authorial persona and Paul is problematized by the fact that Paul cross-dresses as a geisha and hence becomes himself the embodiment of objectified sexual pleasure. Yet, there is a distinctive difference between being economically impelled to become a prostitute in a Harlem public restroom and entertaining a creative fantasy of reinventing oneself as a character from a novel in a Village bathtub. Hence, whereas the black bohemian in *The Infants* entertains a dream of sexual utopia, Thurman's personal narration is aware of the decisive connection between economic exploitation and non-normative sexual behaviors.

In the context of black decadence, the link between the liberation of desire from gender, sexuality, and race boundaries forged in Paul's statements is also present in the intertextual parallels between Paul and Alva. The first noticeable similarity between the two is their racially ambiguous physical appearance. This indeterminate skin color is of particular significance for both narratives, since their centers of consciousness, Raymond and Emma Lou respectively, are very

DANDYISM AND HOMOSEXUALITY

dark-skinned and not able to transcend their biological racial identity. Paul and Alva function as foils to Ray and Emma, and this emphasizes their racial dubiousness. Paul's racial indeterminacy has already been discussed in relation to his Orientalist fascinations and his ability to cross the Jim Crow color line. The issue of racial ambiguity has also been mentioned in the context of "the sheik" and the intertextual presence of Valentino in Thurman's writings. As Van Notten argues, Nugent has been known for his fascination with the actor; since Paul's character is clearly modeled on Nugent's persona, this connection can be extended onto the bohemian character, which additionally highlights his racial indefiniteness. The text further foregrounds the fluidity of Paul's race identification when he claims towards the end of the novel that he is going to "quit being a nigger" and that he "can pass for Spanish."[92] Analogously, Alva is constructed as racially equivocal. He is first introduced when Emma catches a glimpse of his "smiling oriental-like face, neither brown nor yellow in color."[93] The description both highlights Alva's "neither brown nor yellow" liminal racial character and links it to Orientalist imagery. Hence, both characters whose desires transgress heteronormative codes also challenge the idea of unambiguous race differentiation; they represent both bisexuality and biracialism. The correlation between the notion of racial ambiguity and sexual transgressions is illuminated by the figure of the mulatto represented by Alva and Paul. The mulatto traditionally stands for past interracial hence transgressive intimate relations. This association is explicitly manifest in Thurman's texts, which mock bourgeois blue-vein ideology precisely by pointing out the connection between mixed racial heritage and bastardy. Such non-normative sexual behavior evidently differs from Alva's and Paul's voluntary bisexual relations, yet it corresponds to the sexually transgressive aspect of their figures.

Despite a number of relevant similarities between the two characters, Alva's alternative sexuality is constructed in a different way from Paul's. Narratively, it is not put on display until the very end of the text. Whereas Paul uses his sexually transgressive gestures as essential props of his dandyist performance, Alva's sexuality is more closeted. The first time same-sexuality is openly represented in the text is in the figure of Alva's friend Marie, "the creole Lesbian."[94] The "creole" attribute can be read as referring to various ethnic mixtures, including French, Spanish, Native American, and West Indian ancestry. Such a diverse ethnic potential of the term indicates that the only unequivocal meaning of "creole" is precisely racial ambiguity. Thus the juxtaposition of the two indicators of Marie's identity – Creole and lesbian – again conflates racial indefiniteness and sexual transgression. Characteristically, Marie is mentioned only once in the novel, and does not have any relevance for its plot. Hence, if her narrative function is not purely decorative, it serves to foreshadow Alva's sexual and racial transgressions.

Alva's bisexuality is not explicitly revealed until the final scene, when Emma Lou sees him in a "vile embrace" with the "effeminate" Bobby. This graphic image, however, forces one to re-read the earlier glimpses of Alva's intimate relationships. For example, the narrative insistently refers to his partners in a way that does not reveal their sex, as in the fragment depicting Geraldine, "who of all the *people* he [Alva] pretended to love, really inspired him emotionally as well as physically, the one *person* he conquested without the thought of monetary gain." Instead of the heteronormative "women," Alva's lovers are referred to as "people" and "persons." This strategy of ambiguation or inclusion is also visible in many other moments when his partners are referred to with gender-undefined phrases such as "contacts" or "others."[95] What further contributes to the symbolic dislocation of gender identities in Alva's relationships is his gender-ambiguous first name. This representation of sexual desire without defining the genders of its subject and object parallels Paul's decadent vision of sexual enjoyment with "no sexes;" the difference between the two rhetorical strategies is between implicit innuendo and explicit bohemian performance.

Thurman, in his writings, opens up space for non-normative sexualities, primarily for male bisexual and same-sexual desires. They are thematized primarily in terms of dandyist masculinity, the homoeroticization of the male body by positioning it as the object of the gaze, and bohemian free-love utopia. A comparison of the sexually transgressive characters from The Infants and The Blacker the Berry reveals also an integral connection between non-normative sexualities and racial ambiguity, an issue that is a peculiar result of the intersection of white European decadent discourse and Jim Crow cultural codes.

Blurring Boundaries in Harlemese: Bisexuality, Cross-dressing, and Passing

As hitherto discussed, Thurman's incorporations of decadence and dandyism produce tensions and frictions stemming from the racialized positions of both Thurman's authorial persona and his fictional characters. These are primarily visible in the constraints imposed on the aesthetics of the self and sexual liberation. The unchangeable fact of race limits the freedom of creative self-invention, whereas Jim Crow lynch logic restrains representations of black male (hetero) sexuality. Another implication resulting from the intersection of white European decadence and American racialized cultural codes is a peculiar link between passing and dandyist self-reinventions.[96] If the decadent project is based on a challenge to the established boundaries, Thurman's black bohemianism extends this transgressive desire to include racial boundaries. As discussed before, his texts are conscious of the biological limitations of the dandyist aesthetics of the self, yet they also exhibit a preoccupation with the possibilities to transcend them textually by representing racially ambiguous characters such as Paul and Alva. These two characters embody the intersection of decadent acceptance of same-sexuality, gender cross-dressing, and racial ambiguity with the possibility of passing implied in it. The interconnection between racial passing and sexual defiance is central to Thurman's texts in general, since, as Ganter rightly argues, "for Thurman, writers' imaginative *queerness* lay in their cosmopolitan ability to *pass comfortably into another identity*, be it sexual, racial, or cultural. Thurman sought to materialize this transgressive imaginative sensibility in both his fiction and non-fiction."[97] The desire to experiment with fluid identities manifests itself in the inclusion of Paul's and Alva's bisexuality and their biracial appearance. Although it may limit his ability to exercise the aesthetics of the self, the biological fact of Thurman's unambiguous skin color is transcended on the textual level, where he can "pass comfortably into another identity." Thurman's attempts to write through a woman's consciousness are just one example of his narrative reinventions of the self. As far as his textual racial passing is concerned, it is exemplified on the level of characters such as Paul and Alva. Additionally, it is manifest on the level of overall design in Thurman's writings that represent white characters only, such as *The Interne* or *Tomorrow's Children*. Before exploring the relation between racial passing and sexuality, the issue of desire for fluidity of Jim Crow social boundaries will be discussed by considering a text where it constitutes a leitmotif – *The Blacker the Berry*.

Thurman's choice of Emma Lou as the center of consciousness in the novel is a doubly-layered exercise in gender cross-dressing. On the one hand, as has been stated earlier, Emma's character functions as a female persona for the expression of Thurman's autobiographical experiences, hence it illustrates Thurman's narrative's attempt to "pass comfortably into another identity." On the other hand, the text is saturated with Emma Lou's own desire to change her gender identity because "should she have been a boy, then the color of skin wouldn't have mattered so much,...a black boy could get along, but...a black girl would never know anything but sorrow and disappointment."[98] Thus, in the intertextual perspective of Thurman's personal writings, which position Emma Lou as his alter-ego, the text represents a two-way desire – the one of the male authorial voice to express itself through the female character and the female character's desire to change her sex.

Emma Lou's sex-change desires clearly stem from her attempts to improve her social status and gain privilege. The narrative, through her disadvantaged perspective, reveals multifaceted interconnections between different aspects of her social identity. Her experiences reveal that privilege is constructed at the dynamic intersection of skin color, gender, and class, which results in her desire to "pass" in each of these identity categories. As she observes in college, there are girls who are as black as she is but come from more affluent and more respectable families, which results in their being socially accepted. A black girl called Verne is included into bourgeois mulatto sororities because she is "a bishop's daughter with plenty of coin and a big Buick."[99] Similarly, it is frequently emphasized that men who are as black as Emma can do well, which is most visible in the figure of the socially successful Truman Walter. On the other hand, the fact that feminine sexual appeal is reversely proportional to blackness is revealed in the words of Braxton, who claims that "when they comes blacker than me, they ain't got no go."[100] This quote, uttered by the heterosexual Braxton, implicates that blackness masculinizes women, because it deprives them of sexual allure. Hence, Emma's experiences prove that her social standing would improve if any of her identity categories were changed – her sex to male, her skin color to lighter, and her social background to more respectable through education or money. More significantly, these categories are powerfully interconnected – changing her skin color would result in her becoming more feminine and would enhance her employment opportunities.

Emma's desire to transcend the identity imposed on her is manifest in her dream to pass into other identities as well as in her whitening practices. Thurman's text accurately depicts how her self-perception is distorted by the internalized bias against blackness. Her use of whitening formulas and make-up is perceived by others as grotesque, exaggerated, and vulgar. Emma Lou's normalizing attempt to transform her body in accordance with the hegemonic standards can be seen as parallel to more general female beauty practices, which are diagnosed by Foucauldian feminists as symptoms of "individual docility...manifested through *aestheticized* practices of the self, in other words, through aesthetic practices of appearance that are meant to shape the individual's body to better meet stereotypical gender ideals."[101] Hence, Emma Lou's desire to transform through corporal practices, in the context of the narrative, is represented as submission to the hegemonic discourses and can be defined with reference to the Foucauldian notion of bodily docility.

On the other hand, Thurman's texts openly accept the possibility of actual racial passing in the case of mulatto subjects. His representations of and experimentations with passing and the desire to pass can be interpreted as a peculiar version of the decadent assault on social norms and boundaries. Just as the earlier-discussed moments of collapse of the private/public and life/art divides, passing is based on the transgression of the socially constructed color line. Moreover, all these transgressions are inherently connected to gender and sexual representations. Thurman's writings deny that the denunciation of one's racial background leads to later regrets. *Infants of the Spring* represents the light-skinned Aline, who successfully manages to "cross the line." Raymond supports her decision: "May it prove profitable, and may all your children escape the tarbrush." Furthermore, he mocks essentialist racial longings as a part of propaganda literature. To Aline's fears of "getting homesick" and "coming back," Ray answers that "thousands of Negroes in real life cross the line every year and I assure you that few, if any, ever feel that fictional urge to rejoin their own kind. That sort of nostalgia is confined to novels."[102] Ray's words echo the views on passing as articulated by Thurman in his "The Negro Literary Renaissance," where he states that "there is in real life none of that ubiquitous and magnetic primitive urge which in fiction draws them [passing black people] back to their own kind. This romantic reaction is purely an invention of the fictioneers and like sheep, they all make a use of it, following the leader over the cliff of improbability."[103] This parallel emphasizes the autobiographical aspect of Ray's character and further reinforces the acceptance of passing in the novel. Thus, both on the level of the views expressed by the novel's center of consciousness and Thurman's alter-ego as well as on the level of the plot that represents Aline's success in passing, the text approves of crossing the color line.

Ray's dialogue with Aline is in stark contrast to the final scene, which follows the conversation. Set in the white bohemian bathroom, Paul's suicide also represents a peculiar attempt at passing. As I have pointed out earlier, Paul's spectacular death is characterized by experimentation with both racial identity and gender cross-dressing. The fact that he dresses up as the Geisha Man by putting on his "Mandarin robe" and a batik scarf can be interpreted as a performance of racial passing.[104] This reading is also suggested by the preceding scene, in which Paul declares that he is going to pass, and he moves to white bohemian Greenwich Village. Paul's passing is conceptually more complex than Aline's venture. His performed suicide constitutes a peculiar *tableau vivant*, which turns into a *still life*. He tries to recreate the geisha image from his novel, yet the *performance*, through his death, is transformed into a *nature morte*.[105] Here, to further follow the playfulness of the two terms, the level of *nature* follows the level of *tableau*, i.e. art is succeeded by nature, just as in Wilde's aphorism "nature imitates art," which Paul quotes earlier in the text. It also forcefully resonates with Thurman's claim that "nature avenges art," which refers to his being hospitalized in the same hospital he had depicted in his last novel.[106] The art level of Paul's staging of his death as a performance is followed by his natural death as a character in the novel, just as Thurman's death took place in the hospital whose decay he had chosen to represent in The Interne.

The investment of the final scene in visual representations encourages reading Paul's suicide with reference to contemporaneous phenomena in fine arts. This connection is reinforced by the fact that he is a painter and engages in debates concerning art in the novel. It is commonly acknowledged that the decadent imagination thrived on the fascination with the East, which is visible in the *fin-de-siècle* fine arts. These appropriations can be illustrated with a number of paintings by James Abbott McNeill Whistler, an American painter who spent most of his life in Europe. Whistler is explicitly mentioned by Paul as an influence on his drawings, which adds further relevance to this reference.[107] His Orientalist paintings, such as Caprice in Purple and Gold or Harmony in Flesh Color and Red, represent white occidental women dressed in kimonos in interiors decorated with oriental props. Hence Paul's final performance can be read as a *tableau vivant* representing Whistlerian images of ethnic cross-dressing. This intertextuality further complicates Paul's masquerade; he puts an Orientalist mask on a white female mask over his racially ambiguous dandy face.

Exemplifying Thurman's general tendency towards ambivalence, passing is represented in a twofold manner in his texts. The first type, illustrated by Paul and Alva, is based on a fascination with racial ambiguity and a desire to create a utopian sphere where the boundaries of sexuality, gender, and race collapse. The donation party discussed in the context of the public/private division is a textual space, a heterotopia, which illustrates this dynamic. Furthermore, social experimentation with boundaries represented by a sexually liberated attitude or a liberal attitude to passing is represented by Thurman's artistic experimentations with female narrations. On the level of fictitious plots, such experiments are paralleled by Paul's artistic and sexual transgressions. These passing endeavors attempt to challenge and transform the existing boundaries, yet most often they occur either on the level of authorial textual plays or in the utopian dreams of his characters. On the other hand, there is a desire to pass that acknowledges the boundaries even though it seeks to cross them. It is represented by Emma Lou's desires for a sex-change or lighter skin and Aline's passing. Both characters accept the social boundaries as they are and the privilege determined by them. Hence, their passing attempts lack a transformative aspect. As I have already mentioned in the context of Emma Lou's corporal practices, not all reinvents of the self are emancipatory in their character. Especially if the subjects in question represent the subaltern positions, their bodies tend to be more docile in their reinvents of the self.

The Dandy Meets Jim Crow: Superwomen and Sweetbacks

The contrast between Aline's success and Paul's death can be read as the failure of the artist in contrast to the social striver's success. If this difference is read in the context of Ray's claim that the most liberated figures in the black community are "the artist and the Babbitt," Paul (the artist) fails and Aline (the Babbitt) succeeds.[108] Significantly, social success is attributed to the woman, whereas failure is attributed to the man. An analogous conclusion can be drawn from the way the Manor project ends. The artists' destinies end in places such as prison (Pelham), a mental asylum (Eustace), and a suicidal bathtub (Paul), whereas the Manor is given over to young working black women. Hence, the text creates a clear-cut opposition between unproductive black male artists and productive black professional women. Since this opposition informs many other writings by Thurman, such gender divergences appear to be the central anxiety permeating his project of black decadence. Thurman's texts abound in representations of strong successful women, whose liberated sexuality is celebrated. Nora Ray Holt and Euphoria Blake signify both sexual liberation and socio-economic success. Moreover, Euphoria's story is, in fact, the only successful artistic performance represented in the novel, since Paul's text is destroyed.

Another significant place in which Thurman foregrounds a strong female figure at the cost of a male figure is the title of his unpublished collection of essays concerning black politics and aesthetics, *Aunt Hagar's Children*. This title, especially in juxtaposition to Richard Wright's *Uncle Tom's Children* released in the year Thurman died, substitutes the masculine persona of "uncle Tom" from Stowe's novel with a black woman. A peculiar strength signified by the concept of "aunt" becomes visible, especially if this persona is read as embodied by Grandma Mack, Pelham's dominating foster mother. Hence, Thurman positions black dominating femininity at the center of the black collective imagination. The name that Thurman gives to his title patron is also significant, since the biblical roots of the name Hagar refer to Abraham's Egyptian concubine, who bore his first child. She was expelled from the house after his legitimate son, Isaac, was born, yet was spared death in the desert by God who showed her a well. This interethnic union represents American interracial intimacies and historical exploitations. In the title, Thurman positions the young generation as (male) descendants of the perseverant black mother and absent white father. Moreover, the name Hagar is etymologically related to the term "hegira" or "hijra," which stands for the migration from Mecca to Medina, a starting point of Islam. It was appropriated by Thurman and Hurston to refer to the Great Migration to Harlem, in particular to their personal migrant experiences. Hurston creates her persona of "Zora of Eatonville before the Hegira," and Thurman, in a parallel way, confides in McKay that he "must make a hasty hegira to Harlem."[109] This link emphasizes the significance of Orientalist tropes in Thurman's writings and contrasts it with the erasure of the oriental connection from Locke's *New Negro*. It also marks the Great Migration with feminine connotations, which is in contrast to Locke's masculinist list of migrants. Thus, the title phrase "Aunt Hagar's Children" foregrounds strong femininity in a number of ways.

Thurman's empowerment of womanhood is also revealed in his review of *Heloise and Abelard* by George Moore (1926), in which he praises "Heloise [as] a more interesting character." She is depicted as practical and "super-realistic" to the extent that she is perceived as a "*super-woman* while the gestures of Abelard are for the most part purely masculine and purely normal."[110] Characteristically, she defies the norms of traditional femininity by her "heroic acceptance of the loss of her child" and her intimate relationship with Abelard "without the benefit of clergy because she felt passion's urge."[111] Hence Thurman's writings repeatedly contrast black female "super-women," such as Heloise, Euphoria, or Nora, and women who succeed in the end of the narratives, such as Emma Lou, Geraldine, Aline, or Janet, with black male impotence. These masculine failures are represented most conspicuously by the bohemian men from the Manor. *The Blacker the Berry* is parallel in this respect, since it ends with Alva sinking into alcoholism and sickness after Emma leaves him, which most likely leads to his death and that of his male child. In the play *Harlem*, an analogous polarization is represented by the determined Cordelia on the one hand and her two dead lovers and arrested fiancé Basil on the other.

Significantly, this gendered contrast is also articulated in Thurman's essayistic writings, where he explicitly comments on the asymmetrical relation between black men and women in 1920s Harlem. The two fragments that depict the problem in the most explicit way come from Thurman's "Negro Life in New York's Harlem" and from an article which, although published by Rapp, reveals many structural similarities to Thurman's account. Besides, it is acknowledged that Rapp's knowledge of Harlem comes from Thurman. Additionally, the issue of authorship is complicated between the two writers due to their cooperation in two Broadway plays, which is explicitly expressed in Rapp's use of the first-person plural form "authors" in his text. Thurman, in his publication, argues that:

> there are 110 Negro women in Harlem for every 100 Negro men...This, according to social service reports, makes women cheap, and conversely I suppose makes men expensive. Anyway there are a great number of youths and men who are either wholly or partially supported by single or married women. These male parasites, known as sweetbacks, dress well and spend their days standing on street corners, playing pool, gambling and looking for some other "fish" to aid in their support. Many immigrant youths...think that it is smart and citified to be a parasite and do almost anything in order to live without working.[112]

The account explains the asymmetry with the fact that women outnumber men in Harlem, which is repeated in Rapp's article as "the large preponderance of women over men." The latter text additionally indicates that the existence of a socio-economic situation in which "colored women of the lower middle class find it easy to secure work at good salaries as maids, cooks, seamstresses and nurse girls, and that colored men of the same class find it difficult to obtain work even at low salaries as porters and elevator boys, has resulted more and more in men being supported by women."[113] The difficulty in obtaining a job even as "porters and elevator boys" is illustrated by Thurman's problems with finding work as an elevator boy, which is followed by his act of male prostitution as depicted in the letter to Rapp. This particular organization of gender relations in Harlem, just as it was in the case of sexual liberation or certain criminal behaviors, is explained in a non-judgmental tone, indicated by phrasings such as "according to social service reports" or "I suppose." Thurman's texts are free from resentment against strong black femininity, which were, for example, visible in Du Bois's representation of slavery as the mammy. They do not express assumptions as the one ascribed by Hurston to the black community of the day: "you know what dey say 'uh white man and uh nigger woman is de freest thing on earth.' Dey do as dey please."[114]

The social phenomenon named in both texts as a result of the material conditions in Harlem is "the sweetback." The relation between the sweetback and the male prostitute is close yet marked by significant differences. Even though he is defined in the glossary to Thurman's play *Harlem* as "a colored gigolo, or man who lives off women," the description does not give justice to the colorful depiction of this persona in his texts. Sweetbacks are represented as one of the fascinating elements of Harlem's life; due to their colorful appearance and tendency to display it in public, they contribute to the spectacular character of Harlem streets.

Yet both in the fragment from "Negro Life in New York's Harlem" and in Rapp's text, despite their non-judgmental tone, sweetbacks are referred to as "parasites." As it is expressed in the article, "the men dress up, strut, talk, loaf, smoke, gamble and fight, while the women do all the work."[115] Characteristically, this situation is associated with a non-white ethnic background. In Rapp's article it is compared to the culture of "Old Indian tribes," whereas Thurman claims that a similar phenomenon takes place among new immigrants, who at the time were predominantly non-Anglo-Saxon Europeans, and perceived as not completely white. These ethnic connotations emphasize the exotic and racialized character of the sweetback. What makes these ethnic allusions even more significant is that Thurman juxtaposes black and new European immigrant experiences. For both groups, migration entailed moving to Northern American cities from originally rural backgrounds – both blacks and non-Anglo-Saxon Europeans are "citified." This "citification" can be perceived as negative in its consequences in the context of Thurman's insistent critique of the myopic optimism with which many black leaders such as Du Bois and Locke approach black urbanization. Such an implicit critique of migration is explicitly reinforced in Thurman's tongue-in-cheek yet open support for Washington's anti-migration policy. Analogously, Thurman's *Harlem* represents the family tragedy resulting from migration of an uneducated rural family to the North, where especially the older generation finds a "City of Refuse" instead of a "City of Refuge." A similar message can be deduced from Emma Lou's disillusionment with the North, where she expected "life [to be] more cosmopolitan and people...more civilized."[116] Thurman's use of the sweetback, however, assaults Locke's project not only in regard to migration. Whereas the editor of the famous anthology identified urbanization with the emergence of the independent black male subject embodied by the New Negro, in Thurman's texts, it produces the sweetback, who is dependent on black productive femininity – "it is smart and citified to be a parasite." As Summers contends, "the sweetback represented a sharp divergence from the bourgeois ideal of manliness; his manhood was defined through the presentation of his body and his immersion in consumer culture much more than his commitment to respectability, character, producer values, or traditional notions of patriarchy and separate spheres."[117] Thurman's representations of consumerist sweetbacks challenge Locke's producerist masculine ethics.

The fact that Thurman was deeply preoccupied with the sweetback phenomenon is visible not only in his foregrounding of such personas in the marketing of Harlem.[118] *The Blacker the Berry* is densely peopled with more and less explicitly visible sweetbacks. The black male bodies at one of Harlem's corners, which have been mentioned earlier as objects of Emma Lou's desire, accurately fit the depiction of the sweetback: "They seemed to congregate in certain places, and stand there all the day. She found herself wondering when and where they worked, and how could they afford to dress so well."[119] Emma's naïve eyes do not see through the appearance of respectability signified by their being "well-dressed." In another fragment, narrated by an omniscient narrator rather than focalized through Emma, "a crowd of well dressed young men and boys" is depicted in front of a theater. This time, they are explicitly referred to as sweetbacks by the narrator. Their presence decorates the narrative with local color focalized by the outsider-observer – "It costs nothing to obstruct the entrance way, and it adds much to *one's* prestige. Why, *no one* knows."[120] The flow of these two sentences reveals the narrator's ambivalent attitude to sweetbacks. The first sentence, through the use of "one," makes an attempt to identify with the perspective of the men at the corners. What follows is a gesture of distancing and disidentification signified by "no one knows." This structure reflects the hesitant approach of Thurman's narratives to this Harlem phenomenon.

The sweetbacks' presence in the novel, however, transcends a decorative function. They seem to signify a systemic feature of the narrative's gender relations, since after a closer analysis of the plot, it turns out that many main characters are in fact undisclosed yet more or less successful "sweetbacks." The character of Braxton embraces sweetbacks' philosophy, claiming that "the only thing a black woman is good for is to make money for a brown-skin papa." Also Emma Lou's lovers Alva and Jasper Crane take money from the women they are in intimate relationships with. Alva avoids the exhibitionist dimension of the sweetback's profession: "His means of remaining master of all situations were both tactful and sophisticated; for example, Emma Lou never realized just how she had first begun giving him money."[121] Yet the narrative indicates that he makes being a sweetback his main source of income after he quits his job in the summer because it gets too hot to work. The position of women in this arrangement is ambivalent. It is stated that "they pride themselves on the degree of splendor they can bestow upon their men. And, be it well remembered, many a woman prefers a half interest in a handsome man to a full interest in an ugly one" and "there's a gal ready to pay to have a man, and there are lots more like her."[122] On the other hand, the case of Emma Lou and her parasitical lover Alva proves that not all such relations are so harmonious and mutually satisfying.

The relation between the sweetback and his "contacts" is the exact opposite of Victorian bourgeois gender relations since it positions the woman as the provider and the producer and the man as the object of sexual desire. Even though Thurman's texts represent it without explicit moralizing, there is an underlying dis-content embedded in this scenario. Narratively, it is revealed in Emma Lou's abu-sive relationships with her sweetback-like lovers. Also the fact that sweetbacks are depicted as parasites reflects Thurman's commitment to the logic of masculine productivity. Thus the sweetback's embodiment of passive male sexuality consist-ing of being the object of the gaze and the providee rather than the provider is depicted both with fascination and disapproval. This ambivalence is the predomi-nant factor shaping the general contradictory attitude to decadence that informs Thurman's writings. Since sweetbacks are represented as a systemic element of Harlem's gender relations, their presence is centrally relevant in the process of Thurman's transplantation and rewritings of the decadent project into the context of 1920s black New York. Hence, the discontent with decadent masculinity in Thurman's writings can be read as stemming from its peculiarly intimate relation to the sweetback.

There are many striking parallels between the dandy and the sweetback. First of all, both consciously perform their gender identity in a way that violates bour-geois ideology. The dandy carefully designs his public image so that it is "worthy to be looked at and admired by others," following the philosophy of Beau Brum-mel, who was both the founding dandy and an influential arbiter of taste. Further-more, as Mazella argues, this performance was organized as a "selective violation of certain social conventions of masculine dress and conduct."[123] Analogously, the earlier-quoted fragments emphasize the utmost significance of being "well-dressed" for the sweetback. Rapp, in his article, depicts sweetbacks as "dressed in flashy clothes," which further emphasizes the to-be-looked-at-ness of their mas-culine code.[124] In consequence, both the dandy and the sweetback share the posi-tion of the object of the gaze. As I have argued before, this positioning produces a homoerotic dimension which is celebrated by dandyism. Yet, when the dandy is juxtaposed with the sweetback, liberated non-normative sexuality becomes bur-dened with the implications of economically determined male prostitution.[125]

Another parallel discontent that arises from the pairing of the dandy and the sweetback is the above-mentioned issue of being "a parasite." According to scho-lars, one of the defining features of dandyism is its open resistance to the ideol-ogy of productivity. It is aptly illustrated in the title of one of Wilde's dialogues, "The Critic As Artist: With Some Remarks upon the Importance of Doing Noth-ing," which conflates art, aesthetics, and non-productivity. As Garelick argues, referring to Balzac's text on Brummel, if humanity is divided into "those who work, those who think, and those who do nothing – the dandy belongs to the third group, the only one that matters."[126] This is read as a resistance to bour-geois ideology by Christopher Lane, who argues that "the dandy expressed his class dissent by disdaining labor and affecting an indifference to economic advan-tage."[127] Finally, Mazella points out that there is a close correlation between the eschewal of labor and the focus on public self-display. He also briefly comments on the gender significance of this strategy, which "demonstrated that a man need not be useful or productive to be a man."[128] Thus the prototypical European dandy shamelessly and explicitly articulates the gospel of unproductiveness, which is read as a public performance of class resistance. The Manor artists' adoption of the unproductive attitude of dandyism is also intricately entangled in gender relations. Just as sweetbacks, depicted as parasitical on the women who support them, the male artists from the Niggerati Manor are unproductive and subsidized by Euphoria's (female) charity. She criticizes the Niggerati community for being "unproductive": "None of you seem to be doing much work. All I run into are gin parties." The avoidance of work is established as the characteristic feature of the Niggerati community at the very beginning of the novel. After Steve declares that "if I stop going to school, I'll have to work...I don't want to do that," Paul accepts him into the milieu with a performative speech act of "He is one of us [Niggerati]." The desire to evade the productive position seems to be constitutive of the Niggerati community. Significantly, in one of her dialogues with Ray, Euphoria refers to Paul, the most prototypical dandy in the text, as "nothing but a parasite." In this scene, Ray justifies him, claiming that this "most charming parasite" is the most talented person in the house, and it is such artists that will enable the New Negro Renaissance to "live up to its name and reputation."[129] Yet the narrative proves Euphoria right – Paul dies as an artist without any output due to his decadent fascinations. The anxiety over productivity insistently recurs in Thurman's texts and was discussed in the previous chapter in connection to the reorganization of the public/private divide in his counter-bourgeois project and was partially explained with his residual investment in the ideology of productive manliness. It seems, however, that a factor that is even more significant in these discontents is the presence of the unproductive sweetback, in many ways uncannily similar to the dandy. Thurman's texts are concerned that the black dandy might be no more than a slightly changed incarnation of the black sweetback. The adoption of leisure by his male characters, apart from resisting the bourgeois ideology, also repeats the dominant relations of black society, which significantly reduces its radical potential.[130]

Furthermore, European dandyist resistance to the bourgeoisie is often read as a mourning of the decline of aristocracy. Hence, the class associations in the original discourse of dandyism refer to the culture of the court with its unproductiveness and preoccupation with public display.[131] In Thurman's writings, the name of the house – "Manor" – might be read as a gesture representing the aristocratic ambitions of dandyism. However, all other class associations primarily lead in the opposite direction – to lower classes and particularly to the self-display and idleness of male gigolos. It must be admitted that the European decadent discourse includes also the *flâneur* position, a passive observer of the lower classes with the "covetous and erotic" gaze.[132] Yet the fetishization inherent in this gaze implies distance and hence disidentification from its objects. For black artists in Harlem,

the distanced position to the lower classes represented by the *flâneur* is more problematic to assume due to their close structural resemblance to sweetbacks and
the volatility of class boundaries in Harlem, where "people associate with all types
should chance happen to throw them together." This systemically imposed proximity to the lower classes results in a lesser distance from the objects of the *flâneur*'s gaze and the dandy's stylistic borrowings, and hence deprives the black
male bohemian of the ultimate control over the objects of his desire.

Conclusion

As many critics rightly agree, Hughes's depiction of Thurman, which serves as
the epigraph for this chapter, aptly illustrates the internal contradictions that
permeate Thurman's writings. My analysis of Thurman's involvements with decadent rebellion shows that his espousal of the bohemian project was not without
reservations. These contradictions can be read as resulting from his residual investments in the discourses of Victorian manliness and hegemonic revitalized
masculinity discussed in Chapter 4. Thurman partially subscribes to the notions
of manly productivity and masculine physical vitality, which are at odds with the
bohemian masculinity as represented by the dandy. Nevertheless, the anxiety in
Thurman's representations of the bohemian project primarily stems from the tensions produced by the transplantation of European dandyism and decadence into
1920s black New York. The racialized position of Thurman's subjects clashes with
the dandyist aesthetics of the self, since unambiguous blackness constrains the
possibilities of creative self-reinvention. Jim Crow reality restricts the freedom of
movement, which is essential for the decadent figure of the *flâneur*. Moreover,
lynch mythology, an omnipresent element of American imagination at the time,
limits the freedom of expression and the celebration of black male heterosexual
desire in Thurman's texts. Paradoxically, due to this restraint, Thurman manages
to challenge the original masculinism of dandyism. He is more at ease with the
expression of female libidinality and transgressive sexualities such as same-sexuality and bisexuality, especially where interracial unions are concerned.[133] Finally,
the prevailing discontent with dandyist masculinity stems from its uncanny resemblance to the masculine ideology represented by the sweetback. The fact that
the bohemian man closely mirrors the Harlem sweetback is disturbing, since
Thurman's texts represent the sweetback as primarily determined by material
conditions. The materially imposed character of the sweetback undermines the
freedom of bohemian reinvention.

The implications of the transplantation of European discourse onto the differently racialized American context, however, are not only negative and constraining. The representations of racial ambiguity endow the character of the dandy
with additional possibilities of self-reinvention. Paul's self-creations are even
more intricate and multifaceted precisely due to his racially mixed identity. More-

over, since dandyism celebrates artifice, the fact that the figure of the black dandy as epitomized by Paul's cross-dressing as the Geisha Man wears more than one mask, reinforces his dandyist character. One could even speculate that due to this fact the black American appropriative transplantations of dandyism are essentially truer to the dandyist ideology of artificiality and celebrations of appearances than its original European embodiments. Furthermore, the American racialized discourse and the Jim Crow boundaries imposed on subjectivity and space provide additional room for decadent transgressive experimentation. The omnipresence of race in the American imagination enables Thurman's writings to thematize trespassings in racial terms, which is primarily visible in the theme of passing and its intricate connections to sexual transgressions. Passing provides Thurman with additional metaphoric possibilities to express non-normative sexuality and gender cross-dressing, which is best illustrated by Paul's dandyist performances. On the whole, Thurman's Harlem of sweetbacks and superwomen, dandies and Delias, androgyny, passing and cross-dressing, heterotopias and Jim Crow divides, constitutes a complex inclusive space, which contains considerable emancipatory potential despite its contradictions and discontents.

Chapter 6
Epilogue: Richard Wright's Interrogations of the New Negro

> Negro writing in the past has been confined to humble novels, poems, and plays, decorous ambassadors who go a-begging to white America.[1]
> Richard Wright, "Blueprint for Negro Writing"

> [The] mode of isolated writing ha[s] bred
> a whole generation of embittered and defeated literati.[2]
> Richard Wright, "Blueprint for Negro Writing"

> I discovered that their ideas were but excuses for sex, leads to sex, hints at sex, substitutes for sex. In speech and action they strove to act as un-Negro as possible...
> Swearing love for art, they hovered on the edge of Bohemian life.[3]
> Richard Wright, Black Boy

According to traditional African-American literary histories, the turn of the twentieth century was dominated by the Washington-Du Bois debate, the 1920s and early 1930s by the New Negro movement, and the following years by the unquestionable hegemony of a single figure: Richard Wright. Since my study is interested in the dialogic relationships in literary history, the concluding chapter examines the ways in which the rhetorical tropes and ideological dynamics hitherto introduced and analyzed are employed in Wright's early writings. It focuses on the way Wright forges collective black subjectivity in response to the earlier concepts of the Talented Tenth, different New Negroes, and Niggerati. This analysis will develop the argument about the significance of gender and sexuality in black literary identity politics, which constitutes the main thread of reasoning in The Making of the New Negro.

The most significant difference between Wright's revisions and the earlier emancipatory constructs arises from the way he recapitulates the relationship among the masses, the bourgeoisie, and black agency, unanimously privileging the working-class identity. This in turn influences the dialectic between the anxiety of authorship and the anxiety of influence in his texts. Whereas the anxiety of authorship and the attempts to build a patrilineal interracial lineage or even network of influences characterized both Locke's and Thurman's writings, Wright militantly enters the battle with his well-established predecessors and challenges their fortified positions with his proletarian rhetoric. He attacks their elitism and bohemianism through gendered and sexualized tropes. Consequently, both on the level of aesthetic theory and the aesthetics of his texts, he entertains a much rougher and more assertive vision of black masculinity than the preceding black leaders and authors. The construction of femininity in his depiction of black gender relations shifts accordingly. Whereas the analysis of Locke's texts focused on his appropriations of maternal imagery for self-empowerment and the part devoted to Thurman examined his affirmation of strong black femininity, this chapter will explore Wright's repudiation of black female – especially maternal – dominance. Such a construction of gender ideologies results in a particular depiction of sexuality and communality. I will analyze the way Wright's writings oscillate between representations of problematic male homosociality and pathological heterosexual relations, both haunted with the underlying threat of lynching.

Canonizing New Negroes

Before the main analysis, this chapter briefly examines the position occupied by the Renaissance in a selection of publications analyzing black literature: The Negro in American Fiction (1937), The Negro Caravan (1941), and Negro Voices in American Fiction (1948) and in the seminal sociological text An American Dilemma (1944). These texts provide a relevant context for the subsequent analysis because, similar to Wright's fiction, they were published immediately after the announcements of the ending of the New Negro Movement.[4] They constitute the first critical accounts of the movement and thus shed light on how it was later perceived, anthologized, and canonized. An examination of how these texts evaluate the Renaissance will provide insight into the sentiments surrounding the movement in the late 1930s and early 1940s as well as the relation between Wright's texts and the New Negroes. An exploration of these literary histories also illustrates the thesis about the critical relevance of gender and sexuality in the process of writing literary history, developed throughout this book. My analysis will demonstrate how sexually charged arguments about dependence on white sponsorships and decadent licentiousness are used to criticize the New Negro Movement. Subsequently, I will show how such representations of the movement are in turn used as a contrast to advance a radically masculinist vision of black authorship exemplified by Wright's courageous proletarian realism.

Sterling Brown's The Negro in American Fiction (1937) is a Federal Writers' Project publication introducing literature written by both black and white writers about the black community. Assuming a left-wing stance, Brown represents the black author of the Jazz Age as the epitome of bohemianism and challenges the ideology of masculinity it carries. The New Negro Renaissance is presented as "The

Harlem School." The change in the name of the movement is highly significant – the term "school" lacks the power and transformatory potential of the term "renaissance." In addition, the qualifier "Harlem" furthermore limits the influence of the movement, implying that it was confined to a group of upper-Manhattan writers. Moreover, scholars suggest that Brown identifies the label "Harlem Renaissance" with commercialism and the exploitation of the black vernacular.[5] The movement is evaluated from a left-wing perspective; the novels are judged by the level of their social engagement and protest. Brown concludes that:

> The Harlem School neglected the servitude...the drama of the workday life, the struggles, the conflicts are missing. And such definite features of Harlem as the lines of the unemployed, the overcrowded schools, the delinquent children headed straight to petty crime, the surly resentment – all of these seeds that bore such bitter fruit in the Harlem riot – are conspicuously absent.[6]

Hence, New Negro writers are dismissed because of their lack of left-wing engagement and preoccupation with the "black masses" and their everyday lives. He clearly echoes Hughes's famous statement that "the ordinary Negroes hadn't heard of the Negro Renaissance. And if they had, it hadn't raised their wages any."[7] Interestingly, Brown transfers the reproductive potential from the term "the Negro Renaissance" and from "the Younger Generation" – which in Locke's project both produces and is identified with "the first fruits of the Negro Renaissance" – onto the "seeds" of working-class poverty and crime, which bear the "bitter fruit" of political and economic protest. The accusation that "drama of the workday life" is missing from the New Negro narratives can be read as an attack on Thurman's Niggerati and the consumerist, non-productive, dandyist masculinity they represent.

The Negro Caravan (1941) judges the New Negro movement less politically and less harshly; however, it also employs gendered tropes to criticize the Niggerati. The authors claim that "ideas that were cardinal in the New Negro movement" can be summarized as "a sort of literary Garveyism more romantic than convincing;" "Africa was looked upon atavistically" and "race pride was sponsored by celebrating brown beauty and by recounting Negro history."[8] Texts such as Thurman's Harlem "capitalized on the Harlem-mania." The Negro Caravan acknowledges that Locke attempted to resolve the anxiety of black authorship, since The New Negro is praised for "plac[ing] creative writing among Negroes in a position of self-respect" and "giv[ing] something of a unifying bond to struggling Negro artists." Nonetheless, the movement in general is evaluated as a failure. It is essentially perceived in terms of decline rather than a renaissance: "For a moment the New Negro movement thrived in Harlem...A semiorganized group, the 'New Negroes,' declined into ineffectual Bohemianism caricatured in Thurman's Infants of the Spring."[9] Locke's strategy to resolve the anxiety of authorship proves unsuccessful and the movement is rendered as non-productive, a conclusion analogous to Brown's critique of decadence and dandyist masculinity.

A more detailed, yet largely parallel, examination of the New Negroes can be found in Hugh Gloster's *Negro Voices in American Fiction* (1948). It continues the political critique of its predecessors and articulates it in a gendered manner. Furthermore, it uses sexually charged implications to condemn dependence on white funding. Gloster devotes one-third of his text, spanning from Chesnutt to Wright, to the 1920s movement. Just like Brown, Gloster is not faithful to the self-naming of the New Negro writers, referring to the movement as "the Negro Renascence." The seemingly small change from "renaissance" to "renascence" voids the original name of its references to the European and American Renaissances, which functioned as a validation of the movement's historical significance. It perceives the movement only as a part of an American "renascent" period announced by Young America. Again, just as in Brown's text, the literature of the movement is negatively evaluated for its political message – or rather its absence – and for its "libertinism." Especially the works of writers labeled as belonging to the Van Vechten Vogue – McKay and Thurman – are dismissed as decadent and lacking political significance. Thurman's self-portrayal in *The Infants* is characterized as "morbid in outlook, diffuse in thinking, and destructive in purpose." This fad, according to Gloster, "spent itself in excess and exaggerations." His analysis of the decline of the movement clearly points to these decadent exaggerations as the reason for its premature ending. "The great failure of the Renascence...was to make a fetish out of the cabaret and not to produce consummate studies of Harlem life."[10] Thus, similar to the previous chroniclers of the movement, he criticizes the unproductive and individualist character of the black bohemia and implicitly attacks the masculine ideology of the black dandy. Apart from the decadent indulgence of the Niggerati, another major factor contributing to the movement's lack of long-lasting influence is found in the predominantly white sponsorship and its distance from ordinary black people. Gloster represents "the Renascence" as an affair between the "excessive," "fetishist," "self-destructive", hence effeminate black writer and predatory white sponsor. Such criticism can be read as charged with erotic overtones in the light of Ross's claim that the relationship between the white patron and the black protégé was deeply sexualized in the discourse of the movement. The bond was likened to prostitution and, more specifically, to a male same-sexual liaison, where the black male occupied the stigmatized passive position. Potentially, this link is reinforced with the adjective "morbid," which, as scholars claim, "was also sometimes adopted as a provocative euphemism for homosexuality."[11] Gloster thereby criticizes the Renaissance through the implications of submissive same-sexuality.

White patronage is also named as one of the defining features of the movement by Gunnar Myrdal in his *An American Dilemma* (1944). Even though he admits that the Renaissance left a lasting influence and strengthened the black intellectual community, on the whole, his evaluation is not enthusiastic. Myrdal states that:

> Although it was somewhat chauvinistically Negro and although it was nurtured by Negro intellectual leaders,...it was primarily a white-sponsored movement...This white patronage...brought money and fame to a relatively small number of Negroes...it was primarily a fad to most whites...With the decline of white support, the movement largely broke up among Negroes.[12]

Interestingly, Myrdal echoes Locke's attempt to position himself as a mother figure of the movement, since he claims that black intellectuals "nurtured" the movement. However, this positive nurturing is overshadowed and enfeebled by white financial sponsorship. Myrdal ascribes the failure of the movement to its excessive dependence on the white sponsors, who approached black literature as parallel to exotic "jazz bands and burlesque shows."[13] The erotic innuendos of these statements are parallel to Gloster's.

As these studies illustrate, the criticism immediately following the Renaissance defines it primarily by two features: dependence on white sponsorship and decadent tendencies. Even though Gloster and the authors of *The Negro Caravan* mention Locke as a continuously influential figure and refer to his reviews in the *Opportunity*, his success in constructing the New Negro primarily through self-reliance is undermined in their narratives of the movement. Moreover, their accounts parallel to a large extent his own criticism of "white charity" and "decadence" in black literature that was supposed to be antithetical to the New Negro project. These criticisms are gender-charged and contain an emasculating attack, this time directed against the New Negro movement. Within the paradigm according to which Locke's literary guidance was analyzed in the texts from the 1930s and 1940s, dependence on charity renders the New Negroes effeminate, whereas decadence correlates them with sexual non-normativity. Ross's analysis of patronage politics provides an additional link through which black artistic activity sponsored by white patrons acquires connotations of prostitution and sexual exploitation. Interestingly, the literary histories immediately following the Renaissance chose to exclude the writer most explicitly demonstrating his sexual difference, Bruce Nugent, who is also entirely absent from the anthologies of the movement published at the time.

In all of the above-discussed critical texts and literary histories, such emasculating depictions of the New Negroes and the connotations of passive same-sexuality serve as a contrast for the new voice in black American literature – Richard Wright. Their unanimous critique of the New Negro Movement and praise of the radically left-wing author manifests the powerful character of the shifts occurring in black letters at the time. Wright's literary emergence is perceived as simultaneous with the end of the Renaissance. Symbolically, this radical change falls on the year 1938, which marks Wright's literary debut, *Uncle Tom's Children*, and the death of the central figure of the previous part of this study, Wallace Thurman. On the other hand, the main actor of the first part, Locke, decisively contributed to Wright's hegemony. Locke actively promoted his writings in the *Opportunity* and *Phylon* reviews. Yet, in contrast to the above-analyzed studies, he narrates the shift from the New Negro Renaissance to Wright's writing not as a break but as continuity. In the 1939 literary overview, Locke refers to Wright as "either a newer Negro or a maturer 'New Negro.'"[14] Hence, the author of *Uncle Tom's Children* represents a newer incarnation of Locke's masculine New Negro.

Referring to Locke's praise, as early as in 1937, Brown eulogizes Wright's short story "Big Boy Leaves Home" for its "robust understanding" and "well informed realism, rendered with power and originality."[15] The authors of *The Negro Caravan* also position Wright as the dominant voice in American literature. *Native Son* is evaluated as "the best example of the new social realism," which "pleads a burning case." Wright is praised for his courage and insight. Characters from his short stories are referred to as belonging to "the heroic stock of Denmark Vesey and Nat Turner; their development may have been stunted by their environment, but the stuff of heroism is there."[16] Gloster joins the other critics in their enthusiastic evaluation of Wright when he assesses *Native Son* as "the most perdurable and influential novel yet written by an American Negro," which "is at the same time one of the masterpieces of modern proletarian fiction." Referring to the famous comment by Wright that never again will he write "lachrymatory fiction," "which even bankers' daughters could read and weep over and feel good," Gloster admits that *Native Son* lives up to Wright's promise that his next text will "be so hard and deep that they would have to face it without the consolation of tears."[17] Gender and sexuality are highly significant in the way Wright's fiction is contrasted with the New Negro movement. In contrast to the femininely dependant and sexually decadent Niggerati, Wright is characterized by "power," "originality," "courage," and "insight." His "hard and deep" fiction represents the "heroic stock." Not only do the reviewers praise Wright as a better writer, but his fiction is evaluated in gender-marked terms as more masculinist than the Renaissance writings.[18] This shift suggests that the 1930s and 1940s introduced and celebrated new constructions of black masculinity, sexuality, and black gender relations; they are examined in the remainder of the chapter on the examples from Wright's essays and fiction.

Too Much Slumming, Too Few Slums: Wright's Narrative of the Renaissance

Wright positions himself against the Renaissance heritage and militantly enters into a battle with the strong predecessors from the 1920s, exhibiting strong anxiety of influence. The most explicit evaluation of the movement can be found in

"Blueprint for Negro Writing" (1938), which Wright wrote from a Marxist perspective for the left-wing magazine *New Challenge*. His criticism is significantly harsher and more graphic than the one found in the earlier-mentioned literary histories:

> Negro writing in the past has been confined to humble novels, poems, and plays, decorous ambassadors who go a-begging to white America. They entered the Court of American Public Opinion dressed in the knee-pants of servility...These were received as poodle dogs who have learned clever tricks.[19]

This fragment expressively elaborates the earlier-mentioned objections concerning the degree of dependence on the part of black writers. They are reduced to humble, servile "Uncle Toms," received as childish curiosities and not as cultural producers by whites. The lack of autonomy and independence of the New Negro writers positions them in the servile group of the "poodle dogs." When juxtaposed with another poodle from Wright's texts, the canine metaphor can be read as feminizing. In his autobiography, young Richard owns Betsy, a female dog of that breed.

In his account of post-war black American history, Wright does not regard the Renaissance as an important event. It is referred to with Brown's term "the Harlem school," which is even further weakened by the qualifier "so-called":

> To depict this new reality, to address this new audience, requires a great discipline and consciousness than was necessary for the so-called Harlem school of expression...The Negro writers' new position calls for a sharper definition of the status of craft, and a sharper emphasis upon its functional autonomy.[20]

In an earlier, longer version of the text, Wright erases the movement from the historical narrative of black emancipation: "Since the World War a great many disturbances *have broken the slumber* of the Negro people. The period of migration, the boom, the Depression, the struggle for unionism, all these have created conditions which should complement the rise of a school of expression."[21] This absence is rhetorically surprising, since the sentence metaphorically refers to an awakening or rebirth. Similar to Brown, Wright relocates the reproductive and regenerative potential into social and political class struggles.

Another way in which Wright attacks his literary predecessors can be found in his critique of white charity. Such a message is suggested by the turn of events in the narrative of *Native Son*. In the novel, a white family, who cooperates with the NAACP and is known for its charity towards black people, hires Bigger, an underprivileged black boy. This charitable gesture leads to their daughter's death and is inevitably followed by Bigger's imprisonment and death sentence. Hence, Wright's seminal narrative positions white charity as lethally dangerous to the emancipation of the black community. An analogous implication can also be deduced from the attitude of Wright's autobiographical persona. When he is offered support from an influential Communist party member, Wright's answer is short and univocal: "I'm not looking for a patron."[22] Here, he clearly refers to and rejects the patronage politics of the 1920s.

Wright diagnoses that the lack of independence and social consciousness "have bred a whole generation of *embittered and defeated literati*."[23] The choice of the word "literati" can be read as specifically referring to the younger generation of "Niggerati." Their dependence on white sponsorship is criticized in sexualized terms as "*that foul soil which was the result of a liaison between inferiority-complexed Negro 'geniuses' and burnt-out white Bohemians with money*."[24] Another place in Wright's writing where the epithet "foul" is found is his autobiography, where the phrase "foul practices" functions as a euphemism referring to sinful sexual activities and sexual discourse, the knowledge of which, supposedly, young Richard acquired from fiction. Hence, the "foul" relationship between the white and black bohemia is charged with a sexual dimension. This innuendo confirms Ross's thesis that in the discourse of white patronage, "leading black men must necessarily become sexual objects to more powerful white arbiters of culture."[25] The decadent "liaison" and simultaneous isolation from the black masses resulted in literature produced "for the sons and daughters of a rising Negro bourgeoisie," which is defined as "a sort of conspicuous ornamentation," characterized as "bloodless, petulant, mannered, and neurotic" and, in the unpublished 1937 version of the text, summarized as "parasitic and mannered."[26] All these epithets have effeminate connotations and rhetorically emasculate the texts of the New Negro Renaissance. Interestingly, in contrast to Locke and Thurman who constructed the middle class against the bohemia even though they valued each group in an opposite way, Wright conflates the bourgeoisie with the bohemia, effeminizes them, and contrasts them with the masculine masses. According to the "Blueprint," the new, socially and nationalistically conscious black writer should "help to weed out these choking growths of reactionary nationalism and replace them with *hardier and sturdier* types."[27] This gendering of the proletariat is especially revealing when juxtaposed with Du Bois's strategic feminization of the "masses" and "people" discussed in Chapter 1.

Wright's perception of bohemian Renaissance artists can be further illuminated with a reference to his memories of the Chicagoan black bohemia recorded in *Black Boy* (1945). According to the narrative, Richard meets the black writers when he is in a stage of deep cynicism, doubting that organized protest can bring any change. This attitude is strikingly similar to the one represented by Thurman's alter-egos in *Infants of the Spring*, especially Ray and his friend Paul. Hence, there is a high likelihood that the young cynical Wright should find the black bohemia a suitable environment. In the narrative, however, he passionately rejects their attitude to life:

[The Negro literary group] was composed of a dozen or more boys and girls, all of whom possessed academic learning, economic freedom, and vague ambitions to write. I found them more formal in manner than their white counterparts; they wore stylish clothes and were finicky about their personal appearance. I had naively supposed I would have much in common with them, but I found them preoccupied with twisted sex problems...I was encountering for the first time the full-fledged Negro Puritan invert – the emotionally sick – and I discovered that their ideas were but excuses for sex, leads to sex, hints at sex, substitutes for sex. In speech and action they strove to act as un-Negro as possible...Swearing love for art, they hovered on the edge of Bohemian life. Always...reading, they could never really learn; always boasting of their passions, they could never really feel and were afraid to live.[28]

This lengthy quote provides additional insights into Wright's attitude to the Renaissance literati and in particular to figures such as Thurman.[29] This detailed depiction perfectly fits the earlier-quoted qualifiers such as "bloodless" or "mannered." One of Wright's main points of objection is the bohemian excessive care about looks, which can be read as an attack on the dandyist attitude to life. What in Thurman's fiction can be read as a liberating aesthetic of the self, in Wright's narrative is regarded as a mannerism and an artificial striving to be as "un-Negro" as possible. Even more fervent criticism is directed at the bohemian preoccupation with sexual issues. This objection is quite surprising, since Richard frequently finds it interesting or even inspiring when groups of black boys raise such subjects. When he encourages black writers to draw inspiration from folklore, one of the inspirational examples are "the swapping of sex experiences on street corners from boy to boy in the deepest vernacular."[30] Examples of such boy-talk found in Wright's fictional texts concern mostly episodic affairs with women and the related issue of sexually transmitted diseases. The difference between these two black sexual discourses can be observed after a closer analysis of the above excerpt depicting the bohemia. Constructions such as "*twisted* sexual problems" and "emotionally *sick*" can be read as pointing to same-sexual behaviors. This is even more manifest in the phrase "Puritan *invert*," which contains a strong allusion to homosexuality represented as gender inversion. Hence, Wright's objection to the uselessness of the "bloodless" and "mannered" bohemians and their dependence on white patrons is constructed in homophobic terms.

Wright's attitude to the black bohemia can also be interpreted as representative of contemporaneous shifts in the ideologies of the artist. As Michael Denning claims in his analysis of the transformations in the structure of intellectual activities, in the 1930s, "the older notions of the bohemian artist and freelance intellectual were no longer adequate to the new armies of white-collar and professional workers in cultural bureaucracies." The influence of left-wing thought popularized by the Popular Front resulted in the "laboring" of artistic creativity manifest in the emergent concept of "mental labor."[31] This transformation of authorship is in stark contrast to the dandy posture, which was defined by a contempt for productivity. Although I have read it as a gesture of resistance to the bourgeois work ethic and hence as potentially anti-capitalist, it is also in conflict with the Marxist and working-class discourses espoused by Wright. In the emergent paradigm, black artists should identify with the black working class and hence should reinvent themselves as workers, the very antithesis of the aristocratic non-productive dandy. Thus, Wright repudiates both Locke's bourgeois producerist masculinity and Thurman's consumerist dandyism. In opposition to the New Negro and Niggerati, he "labors" artistic productivity and realigns it with working-class identity. Overall, Wright criticizes Renaissance writers more fervently than the literary critics in the earlier-analyzed histories of black literature, which illustrates his strong anxiety of influence. The 1920s writers are emasculated as servile "poodle dogs," whereas their texts are feminized as "petulant" and "neurotic." The critique of their financial and stylistic dependence on the white community, especially on the "burnt-out white Bohemians with money," contains multiple sexual innuendoes and is deeply charged with homophobia.

Aesthetic Gangsters and Literary Knock-Outs: Metaphors of Reading and Authorship

By rejecting the mannered comportment of the bourgeois bohemia, Wright, in his texts, represents a vision of black masculinity that diverges both from Thurman's dandyist personas and Locke's producerist comrades. Wright's rejection of "art for art's sake" or, as he puts it, "conspicuous ornamentation," is a repudiation of experimental models of masculinity – particularly the dandy, who proudly positions himself as the object of a sexual gaze. In opposition to these constructions, Wright proposes a markedly different attitude to literacy and literature and, hence, a different image of the black author. In his vision, literature becomes a mode of resistance, and Wright resorts to militant imagery in order to emphasize it. Similar to Locke, Wright uses combat metaphors to render the black artist, yet his depiction markedly varies from Locke's noble avant-garde on the art front.

Before scrutinizing the metaphors of war and conflict in Wright's vision of literature, it is important to introduce the anxieties regarding writing and masculinity present in his texts. As Stephen Michael Best claims, Wright struggled with the influential assumption according to which "a tradition of letters [is] 'not manly enough'" and "writing...[is] an inadequate site of cultural resistance."[32] Although Best does not refer to Park, in the case of any black author, this anxiety is inextricably linked to the image of the Negro as the lady-artist of the races discussed in Chapter 3. Additionally, Wright's texts point to the link between literature and a lack of mental strength or virility, which echoes the residual link between reading and mental neurasthenia examined in Thurman's correspondence and interpreted as loaded with gender implications. This connection appears in several comments regarding books. For example, young Richard in Black Boy is warned that too much reading will "addle [his] brain" and make him "weak-minded."[33] Almost the same phrases are echoed in the interior monologue of the narrow-minded main character of Lawd Today, who remembers that "a schoolmate of his...had become queer from trying to memorize the Bible." This makes him convinced that "too much reading's bad. It addles your brains, and if you addle your brains you will sure have bookworms in the brain."[34] The danger depicted in the above quotes is that of mental weakness, which can be associated with the discourse of neurasthenia and hence feminization. Moreover, the adjective "queer" can be read as pointing to a particular model of same-sexual masculinity. The bookworms that threaten to destroy black mental health are also uncannily parallel to "white lice crawling on black bodies," a term used by McKay to refer to white patrons' Negrophilia. In both cases, the authors juxtapose the healthy peasant or working-class black body with a graphic parasite representing white culture and civilization. Yet although Wright's narratives acknowledge these sentiments, they distance themselves from them by ascribing them to ignorant people and politically reactive characters.

The anxiety over black masculinity and authorship provides an additional motivation behind Wright's construction of reading and writing as revolutionary. Best convincingly claims that Wright strategically positions reading and literacy as a form of resistance and as activities that produce black male agency.[35] This argument can be further supported with the example of Richard's early attempts at reading in Black Boy. Reading is positioned as rebellious in the text because his grandmother perceives fiction as "Devil stuff" and "Devil's work" and strongly objects to his literary activities.[36] Given that from his early childhood, his Grandma is established as the main figure of authority, the secret act of reading feels like a significant rebellion against (female) domination. Significantly, Richard reads Zane Grey – the popular western dime-novel author, whose fiction was of central relevance to the debates on American masculinity at the time.[37] He remembers that: "to me, with my roundhouse, saloon-door, and river-levee background, they were revolutionary, my gateway to the world."[38] In this narrative, reading literature in general, and the western genre in particular, is presented as an element of manly self-assertion against female authority.[39]

In the autobiographical narrative, the child rebellion against his grandmother is transformed into a more mature protest as Richard's reading list expands. Characteristically, just like in the case of Thurman, the pivotal role in this process is ascribed to the figure of H.L. Mencken.[40] Richard becomes interested in Mencken for a reason that is political rather than aesthetic, namely because the controversial critic is attacked in a Southern newspaper.[41] Having read Prejudices and A Book of Prefaces, Richard experiences an epiphany:

Yes, this man was fighting, fighting with words. He was using words as a weapon, using them as one would use a club. Could words be weapons? Well, yes, for here they were. Then, perhaps, I could use them as a weapon? ... how on earth anybody had the courage to say it.[42]

At this moment he discovers that writing can be a militant act, which answers his problem of finding forms of resistance and emancipation that would not be self-destructive in the Southern context. "Outright black rebellion could never win. If I fought openly I would die and I did not want to die. News of lynchings were frequent."[43] Since literal militancy is not feasible, Wright militarizes literature and black male authorship.

An analogous vision of the fighting black writer is repeated in Wright's literary manifesto "Blueprint for Negro Writing."[44] This is visible in the very quantity of confrontational terms used to depict black history and authorship. The word "struggle" appears thirteen times in this twelve-page essay. Other recurrent lexical items that produce the air of militancy and political engagement include "strength," appearing three times, "oppressed" and "suffering," recurring five times each. This violent lexis is further reinforced by dynamic vocabulary including recurrent items such as "action" or "progress." That violence is an inherent and founding feature of Wright's black cultural paradigm is clearly visible in claims such as "this special existence was forced upon them from without by lunch [sic] rope, bayonet, and mob legislation" or "the whole special way of life which has been rammed down their throats."[45] According to Wright, black writers should assume a pivotal position in this struggle. They are compared to fighters who should choose their artillery wisely – "Negro folklore remains the Negro writer's most powerful weapon, a weapon which he must sharpen for the hard battles looming ahead."[46] Wright graphically constructs a particular and explicit image of sharpened weapons to militarize black authorship.

The influential character of this vision is manifested in the correspondence between Wright and Ralph Ellison. In the early 1940s, when Ellison still remained a faithful student of Wright, having read 12 Million Black Voices, he states that "we people of emotion shall land the most telling strokes, the destructive-creative blows in the struggle. And we shall do it with books like this!" Later in the letter, Ellison's use of metaphors becomes even more expressive. He argues that "after the brutalization, starvation, and suffering, we have begun to embrace the experience and master it. And we shall make of it a weapon more subtle than a machinegun, more effective than a fighter plane! It's like seeing Joe Louis knock their best men silly in his precise, impassively alert Negro way."[47] In these private conversations between the writers, the elements of combat are even more explicit than in Wright's published manifesto. Instead of an abstract "weapon," Ellison evokes images of machine guns and fighter planes, which increases the graphic and dynamic character of his rhetoric. Moreover, in his use of terms such as "stroke," "blow," and "knock out," Ellison compares writing to the ultimate physical struggle – boxing. The link to boxing is reinforced by the figure of Joe Louis, a black boxing champion whom Wright celebrated as a working-class hero in one of his first and most influential reportages, "Joe Louis Uncovers Dynamite" (1935), and later in the lyrics to "King Joe," a blues song sung by Paul Robeson. In his published review of *Black Boy*, Ellison expresses similar sentiments about the militant character of Wright's fiction. The imagery used to depict Wright's writing alludes to *corrida*, Ellison's Hemingway-inspired hobby: "Western culture must be won, confronted like the animal in a Spanish bullfight, dominated by the red shawl of codified experience and brought heaving to its knees."[48] Ellison renders literary history in terms of a struggle between black and white writers, which aims to emasculate the pretensions of the "Western civilization" to the status of the masculinist "bull." On the whole, in the 1940s, Ellison's private and public metaphors referring to Wright's texts comprise a coherent imagery of boxing, bullfighting, and mechanized combat, and they accurately echo Wright's own notion of black militant authorship.

Wright's vision of literature is deeply rooted in Marxist discourse, which dominated American intellectual community at the time.[49] The Marxist aesthetic is represented as both attractive and defiant in *Black Boy*, when young Wright encounters "passionate" left-wing magazines. They lack "the lame lispings of the missionary," which most likely refers to the NAACP, entangled in white patronage politics. The narrator paraphrases the message of the magazines into a challenging declaration: "If you possess enough courage to speak out what you are, you will find that you are not alone."[50] Similarly, the way Wright represents Marxism considerably adds to the revolutionary mood of "Blueprint for Negro Writing." "Dramatic Marxist vision," which "has laid bare the skeleton of society," motivates "the writer to plant flesh upon those bones out of the plenitude of his will to live."[51] Instead of a maternal and natural procreation appropriated by Locke, Wright renders creativity in terms that combine medical allusions to surgery or x-ray and the peasant activity of "planting." The rural echoes, however, are far from the pastoral idyll – the image of "planting flesh" is grotesquely dramatic. Another important empowering element in Wright's representation of Marxism is the image of the working class. Unlike "the Harlem School," which according to him did not try to bridge the gap between the "mannered" elite and the masses, he calls on the black writer to realign with the group that is the source of political resistance. According to Wright, the "[black] working class is pushing militantly forward" and "the militant Negro workers" "strive to forge organizational forms of struggle to better their lot and they manifest the same restlessness"; hence he encourages "Negro writers to stand shoulder to shoulder with Negro workers."[52] Just as Thurman in his rent-party expeditions to lower-class homes seeks to revitalize physical strength, masculine virility, and creative possibilities, here Wright also projects the spirit of powerful militancy onto the black worker. Yet, in Thurman's texts, the bohemian relationship with the lower classes is to a large extent parasitical, whereas here black writers are positioned on a par with the workers. Still, similar to Thurman's texts, this inter-class friendship serves to virilize the black writer. "He may, with disgust and revulsion, say *no* and depict the horrors of capitalism encroaching upon the human being."[53] His identification with the lower classes enables the black writer to assume an assertive position, "say no," and depict the struggle with "the horrors of capitalisms."

Also in later texts regarding literature, Wright represents a defiant vision of the writer. Frequently, this effect is achieved through naturalistic imagery. For example, in a publication whose very title "I Bite the Hand That Feeds Me" is telling, Wright assertively admits that he "reveal[s] rot, pus, filth, hate, fear, guilt, and degenerate forms of life."[54] This assertive catalogue of subject matter for literature endows writing with audacity and defiance. The unpublished version of this text ends on a challenging note of "That's biting the hand that feeds one, isn't it? Well, I hope I bit hard enough."[55] Here, the process of "biting" refers to the textual response to a negative review of *Native Son* by David Cohn, hence it positions writing as a physical struggle. By transforming the phrase "biting the hand that feeds one" into "biting hard enough," Wright defamiliarizes the fixed expression and adds graphic and violent impact to the image. Wright's challenge to a white critic and white culture that "feeds him" is also yet another violent rejection of the patronage politics.

The revolutionary and violent rhetoric remains pronounced even when Wright's initial infatuation with Marxism recedes. In the essay "On Literature," Wright criticizes the current "bulk of the left and social novels" and regrets that:

> literature has been roped off and policed; no aesthetic gangsters sneak in and pull off quick raids, no stylistic air alarms are sounded, no bombs are planted under the critics, no daring technical hold-ups take place, no structural absconding with plots occurs, no sudden beams of light are thrown upon the familiar to make it seem strange,...no insurrections against form, no dynamiting of content.[56]

Here the metaphors predominantly point to crime and terrorism: "raids," "bombs," "hold-ups," "absconding," "beams of light," and "dynamite" evoke images of a gangster movie from the 1930s. Hence, the struggle moves from the battlefield to the city, whereas terrorists or gangsters replace soldiers or boxers. What is more important, however, is that Wright does not compare black or Marxist writing in general to these violent activities, but only innovative, daring, and technically experimental fiction. The struggle is relocated from the level of the act of writing, which is directed against racial or economic oppression, on to the level of technical experimentation, which struggles against the "flat" and "dead" form of the socialist novel.

Wright's militant vision of writing is constructed in opposition to the New Negro project, even though it echoes Locke's strategic comparisons between war and literature. The differences between Locke's and Wright's militant discourses on literature illuminate Wright's criticism of the Negro Renaissance, the discrepancy between their projects, and the gender constructions implicated in them. Locke's references to the war rhetoric in the texts on the New Negro art endow the black artist with a political and militant character, which otherwise was played low in the movement. He compares young black artists to the "advance line" of the front. The elitism of his vision undermines Locke's performative declaration in "The New Negro" that "it is the rank and file who are leading, and the leaders who are following."[57] Rather than representing "the rank and file," Locke's New Negro reincarnates Du Bois's "talented tenth" paradigm, in which the artists and intellectuals fight for the uplift of the rest of the black community. Locke's elitism is further strengthened through the allusions to the advance line or avant-garde – terms that ascribe artistic and military progress to a small troop of highly skilled soldiers or artists. The black author serves as an elite guardian and fighter for the remaining strata of black people. This structural relation is reversed in Wright's rhetoric. In his texts, artists are not alone on the advance line; on the contrary, they rely on the workers in terms of militancy, courage, and willpower to engage in organized struggle. Significantly, there are also considerable differences as far as the sources of combat metaphors are concerned. Locke admits that his rhetoric was inspired by "one book on military strategy," which is reflected in references to "courageous cavalry," "pioneering," "advance line," "solid infantry," and "artillery support."[58] The metaphors that construct the vision of writing in Wright's essays and his correspondence with Ellison come from newspaper war and crime reports rather than from theoretical treaties. They evoke particular weapons ranging from "clubs," "machine guns," and "fighter planes" to "bombs." The graphic fierceness of these tropes is additionally reinforced with suggestions of direct physical violence indicated by "biting," "strokes," "blows," or "knock-outs." Instead of the "courageous cavalry," which suggests associations with romanticized warriors fighting mounted on horseback, in Wright's Marxist paradigm, it is the workers who lead and empower the intellectual elite. Instead of Locke's avant-garde or Du Bois's muscular black Christ, Wright utilizes the working-class icons of rough masculinity – the boxer and the gangster – to charge his vision with militancy. The contrast between Wright's working-class fighter and Locke's courageous cavalryman illustrates not only the difference between their class affiliations but also the difference in the ideology of black masculinity that they espouse in their writings. Locke's vision of cavalry evokes manly camaraderie, noble manhood, whose sexuality is closeted in the private sphere, whereas Wright's militant metaphors advance the ideology of a much tougher, lower-class, more physically virile masculinity.

Wright's military rhetoric also contains an interesting reference to Thurman's embrace of dandyism. Wright's critique of the black bohemia focuses on its preoccupation with appearance, embodied by the iconic fashionable dandy. In *Lawd Today*, one of the initial scenes interestingly merges the military discourse and narcissistic self-reinvention. The main character, Jake Jackson, devotes as much as a page of the novel to "the big job of the morning," which turns out to consist in combing his hair. Jake imagines himself to be "a veteran field marshal" fighting against "an alien army" of "the unruly strands." The scene is densely interwoven with complex military metaphors. Apart from the above-mentioned images, his hair is compared to "foe," "fortifications and wire-entanglements," "enemy lines," "trenches," "brave fellows [breaking] at their knees," and "troops in shell holes under bombardment." This formidable enemy is encountered with "many devices of strategy," including using a comb "like a Colt .45" and hair pomade like "mustard gas in Flanders." The latter is referred to as "the most powerful weapon at his command" and depicted in detail as a "deadly contraption" in "a pink jar...labeled LAY 'EM LOW." Jake's "assault" on the "warweary strands" conquers "the enemy." After his military victory, Jake has to resort to political influence because "failing to get his hair under [a] peace treaty immediately, it would soon flounce back into a thousand triumphant kinks." Ironically, what is referred to on the metaphorical level as a "peace treaty," an "ingenious implement of exploitation," and a "standing army which conquering nation leaves to guard the conquered one," on the literal level of the narrative, is a cap "made of a woman's stocking." The irony is reinforced by the detailed description of this object: "it is elastic, about four inches long, tied securely at the top, and when stretched tightly over the cranium resembles the gleaming skin of a huge onion."[59]

In the above-described scene, the military discourse is used to mock Jake's narcissistic efforts in front of the mirror. Jake, in the course of the novel, entertains infantile dreams of omnipotence signified by such audacious careers as a soldier because "a soljer gets a chance to do a lot of things"; a gangster since "it takes nerve to be a gangster! But they have plenty of fun. Always got a flock of gals hanging on their arms. Dress well in sporty clothes. Drive them long, sleek automobiles"; and a war pilot because "*being an aviator must be fun, 'specially when you on top of another plane and can send it spinning down like that.*"[60] Yet, these tabloid- and film-inspired narcissistic scenarios are enacted only in the morning mirror ritual. Apart from the ironic distance between Jake's mass-cultural fantasies and his real-life everyday battle of combing his hair, the irony is primarily produced by the clash between the culturally masculine-gendered combat rhetoric and a strongly feminine-gendered ritual of personal care. This is further reinforced by the above-mentioned elements of "a pink jar of hair pomade" and "the top of a woman's stocking," which makes Jake's skull look like "a gleaming skin of a huge onion." Moreover, even though, after all the effort put into his looks, Jake, in his interior monologue, perceives himself to look like "a big time football player" and a "Maltese kitten," his self-image dramatically contrasts with the image of his body that is represented in the external narrative. Jake is repeatedly represented as fat and far from muscular or attractive: "A *soft* roll of fat seeped out of his neck, buttressing his chin," "a broad nose squatted *fat* and *soft*," and his "lips were full, *moist*, and *drooped loosely*, *trembling* when he walked."[61] Adjectives such as "soft," "moist," "fat," "trembling," and "loose" clash with the desired firmness of the male body associated with the "big time football player." The contrast between Jake's excessively flamboyant accessories and his financial standing, symbolically depicted by the titles "Squirrel Cage" and "Rats' Alley," further adds to the ridiculousness of his aesthetic self-reinvention. Hence, the disparity between his imaginary self-image and the way he is represented in the third-person narration, paralleling the contrast between his professional fantasies of omnipotence and social reality, renders Jake grotesquely emasculated and stylistically ridiculous. Also, since Wright primarily focuses on Jake's battle with his "kinks," the battle can be read as an attempt to defeat his blackness. This is supported by other moments when Jake's inferiority complex regarding his "kinky" hair is revealed.[62] Just as the bohemians depicted in Black Boy, Jake attempts to look as "un-Negro" as possible. Such a reading points to the danger of docility specifically in the self-reinvention of subaltern subjects, to which Emma Lou fell victim. Jake's efforts to look less black are analogous to Emma Lou's attempts to comply with the hegemonic white standards of beauty. Such transformations, far from being liberating self-creations, follow the desire to conform to the dominant norms.

The narrative ironically, and yet not without some sympathy, represents Jake's ritual as well as the audacious fantasies of omnipotence and reactively nationalistic political outlook as his ways of managing his everyday sense of economic emasculation in the depression era.[63] Yet, apart from the personal story of Jake, who feels trapped in a "Squirrel Cage" and fenced in the dead-end "Rats' Alley," the hair routine gains additional significance when confronted with Wright's remarks about the black bohemia, who "wore stylish clothes and were finicky about their personal appearance." When read in this intertextual way, the scene mocks not only Jake but the extensive preoccupation of blacks with their self-image in general, epitomized by the figure of the black dandy. Significantly, the accessories carefully selected by Jake after his hair battle are uncannily reminiscent of the props that decorated and defined Thurman's dandyist characters in The Infants. Jake's "huge imitation ruby that burned like a smear of fresh blood" is a cheap equivalent of Eustace Savoy's "most treasured possession": "an onyx ring, the size of a robin's egg," whereas the extravagant "purple embroidered orange handkerchief" brings to mind Paul's colorful handmade oriental "batik scarf." Even though he is a postal worker and not a bohemian artist, Jake's persona serves to mock dandyist aesthetic reinventions of the self.[64] The contrast between Jake's flamboyance and his depression-induced economic plight mirrors the disparity between the "neurotic" and "twisted" narcissistic preoccupations of the bohemia and the working-class struggle with political and economic obstacles. The representation of Jake complements Wright's depiction of the black bohemia as feminized and sexually non-normative.

An intertextual examination of Wright's military metaphors in the light of Locke's analogously combat-inspired imagery and Thurman's dandyist aesthetics of the self provides further insight into Wright's critique of both the older leaders of the movement and the young bohemian generation of New Negroes. Wright's critique proliferates in gendered and sexualized images. The older generation's militant assertions represented by Locke, when confronted with Wright's radical working-class imageries, seem elitist and lacking in virility. Wright's texts rhetorically emasculate Thurman's bohemian life and black dandyism, which are criticized for their lack of political engagement, narcissistic childishness, and effeminate preoccupation with appearance.

Big Boys, Black Boys, and Native Sons: Constructing the Black Subject

The confrontation of Wright's texts with the New Negro discourse brings to light his construction of the black subject characterized by militant masculinity and tinted with a shade of homophobia. This construct is worth studying in more detail in the text that usurps the right to represent black collective identity in the very title – 12 Million Black Voices. Wright's representation of black agency in this publication is echoed in his other seminal texts such as Uncle Tom's Children, Native Son, Lawd Today, and Black Boy. That masculinity is of central relevance in Wright's assertions of black subjectivity is visible in the very titles of his early texts. He shifts the origins of the black community from Aunt Hagar, of Thurman's eponymous text, to "Uncle Tom" in Uncle Tom's Children. Later, the names become even more masculinist – "Uncle Tom" is transformed into "Bigger Thomas" in Native Son. The masculinist tone recurs also in other titles such as "Big Boy Leaves Home," Black Boy, and "Man in the Making." The content of the texts is predominantly faithful to the titles; both Wright's fiction and non-fiction are interested in and preoccupied with black men. Significantly, the above-listed texts share the common paradigm of the black (male) migration from the rural South to the urban North. This theme is of central significance in Locke's and Thurman's texts and their gender constructions, hence its relevance in Wright's works encourages an intertextual analysis. In his peculiar scenario of the Great Migration, Wright positions black female domination in the South as a push factor and the opportunity for black men to become the head of the family as one of the critical pull factors.

12 Million Black Voices is a publication commissioned by the Farm Security Administration, and it portrays the black community's transformation from the rural

to the urban. To a large extent, it is faithful to the FSA mission, which was to depict the underprivileged strata of American society – predominantly sharecroppers and migrant workers – who were to be relieved through New Deal programs. The FSA, directed by Roy Stryker, was intended to empathically represent "'one third of a nation ill-housed, ill-clad, ill-nourished,' burdened but not bowed."[65] The major part of the pictorial layer of 12 Million Black Voices was supplied by the venture undertaken by Russell Lee and Edwin Rosskam in Chicago in the early 1940s. According to Nicholas Natanson, their photographic project was partly inspired by the popularity of Wright's Native Son, which focused nationwide attention on the race issue.[66] The published volume is the result of the cooperation between Rosskam and Wright, who together textually represent the story of the black community. The text is an intersection of an allegorical folk tale and sociological data coming from scholars such as E. Franklin Frazier, Horace R. Cayton, and George S. Mitchell. The combination of the vernacular aesthetic and statistics results in a peculiar construction of the collective black subject.

In the text, Wright executes his prescriptive theory that the function of literature is to communicate a "collective sense of man's struggle on earth."[67] The communal aspect is conspicuously visible on the level of pronouns. The text is narrated in the first-person plural, hence the pronouns "we," "our," and "us" are repeated hundreds of times in the span of this 150-page publication. In order to make his story coherent and his narrator integrated, Wright states in the "Foreword" to the text that he will exclude "the so-called 'talented tenth,'" "the isolated islands of mulatto leadership," and "the growing and influential Negro middle-class professional and business men." With this gesture, Wright attempts to give the voice back to the subaltern, the "debased feudal folk," "the countless black millions," and "legions of nameless blacks."[68]

Wright's sweeping use of "we" is found problematic by scholars such as Natanson, who claims that "in the course of his narrative, Wright shifted, without acknowledging the implications of the shift, between all-encompassing and an obviously male voice, between a cross-generational voice and an obviously paternal voice."[69] Such critique misses the political significance of organizing the black community and providing it with a unified position, reclaiming the voice for the hitherto silenced subaltern strata; it also overlooks left-wing literature's aim to communicate social consciousness in contrast to bourgeois individualism. Nonetheless, Natanson's brief references to the gendering of the collective subject as "male" and "paternal" are highly convincing.[70] This is primarily visible when phrases such as "we men" or "we black men" interrupt Wright's communal identity of "we millions of black folk," "we black slaves," "we captives," "we blacks," or "we black folk." Such masculinist interventions are also reinforced with distanced representations of black women preceded by a possessive pronoun: "our sisters and wives" or "our wives." This split in the construction of an otherwise relatively seamless black identity is dramatized in a fragment devoted to the issue of black womanhood. Not only does Wright not identify with black women, in the sentence "*our women* fared easier *than we men*," he clearly constructs their identity in opposition to the first-person narrative voice. Thus the collective pronoun excludes women as subjects, just as the inclusive "he" used by Locke to refer to the New Negro. As this gender conflict shows, it is easier for Wright to integrate past and present than male and female black identities into a coherent subject position. The strategy to resolve the tensions inherent in Wright's first-person narrative voice exemplifies the reactive centrifugal forces defined by Bakhtin as opposite to the centripetal forces of heteroglossia. Wright tries to find a unitary language for a diverse community rather than represent diverse voices within a unified artistic structure.

The main focus of *12 Million Black Voices* is black migration and urbanization, which decisively influence black gender relations. The trajectory of black migration in the text starts with the Middle Passage and continues through slavery and Reconstruction in the Southern context to finally end with the Great Migration to the Northern city. At the beginning, Wright erects an almost idyllic image of pre-slavery Africa, where:

We had our own civilization...before we were captured and carried off to this land...We had our own literature, our own systems of law, religion, medicine, science, and education; we painted in color upon rocks; we raised cattle, sheep, and goats; we planted and harvested grain – in short, centuries before the Romans ruled, we *lived as men*.[71]

As the final summary suggests, Wright identifies cultural empowerment and freedom with masculine identity. The fact that enslavement and the Middle Passage are constructed also in gendered terms is visible in Wright's long and graphic passage about "floating brothels." He narrates a dramatic scene, in which "bound by heavy chains, we gazed impassively upon the lecherous crew members as they vented the pent-up bestiality of their starved sex lives upon our sisters and wives."[72] Apart from exemplifying Wright's shift from the gender-neutral to a manifestly male narrative voice, the excerpt links slavery with the black man's lack of control over female sexuality. This vivid image communicates a sense of absolute disempowerment of black men "bound by heavy chains" and forced to witness their "sisters and wives" being raped. The narration from the men's point of view encourages identification with the male trauma rather than with the female victims. Characteristically, the women are positioned exclusively in respectable, either marital or kin, relation to men, which fosters empathy and adds even more drama to the situation of male slaves. Enslavement is identified not only with black men's loss of control over their own bodies but also "their women's" bodies. Wright's representation of African origins echoes both Du Bois's images of pre-slavery African chastity as well as Locke's masculinist vision of African cultures.

The experience of the Middle Passage generates black male disempowerment, which intensifies in the Southern context, where the black woman assumes the privileged position. Wright expresses resentment on the part of black men because black females "did not always belong to us" and "enjoyed the status denied us men." This feeling of bitterness results from the fact that black women exercised "supreme authority" and "reign[ed] as arbiters in our domestic affairs." Significantly, Wright links this special status of black women to the above-mentioned lack of black male control over the black female body. The privileged status of the black female results from the "enforced intimacy" between black women and white men.[73] The black woman is positioned as a traitor who gains privileges because of her sexual availability to white men. Importantly, Wright conflates the times of slavery with Reconstruction and Jim Crow reality into a single extratemporal vision of the South. The feminine-gendered domination in this part of the narrative is reinforced with a dramatic vision of the cotton plantation:

> From now on the laws of Queen Cotton rule our lives. (Contrary to popular assumption, cotton is a queen, not a king. Kings are dictatorial; cotton is not only dictatorial but self-destructive, an imperious woman in the throes of constant childbirth, a woman who is driven by her greedy passion to bear endless bales of cotton, though she well knows that she will die if she continues to give birth to her fleecy children![74]

This fragment further illuminates the resented representation of female authority in the text – it is characterized as "greedy" and "self-destructive." This kind of domination of "an imperious woman" results in the "brutal and bloody" "ritual of Queen Cotton." The reference to ritual, rather than production or work, positions female domination in the non-rational sphere of religion. Female authority seems to be driven primarily by biological necessities that are irrational, and hence the results of her reign are crueler than the ones of the "dictatorial kings." The feminine character of Southern dominance also resurfaces in the allegorical representation of the South as "the Land." The gendering of the image is even more clearly visible when contrasted with the allegory of the Northern white hegemony, "the Bosses of the Buildings." Significantly, Queen Cotton in Wright's text bears strong resemblance to the image of the "awful black face[d]" mammy from The Souls of Black Folk, which also coded Southern slavery as a woman defined by her biological functions. Images conflating emasculation and the Southern context appear also in other texts by Wright. In Lawd Today, one learns from Jake Jackson's interior monologue that "anything which smacked of farms, chain gangs, lynchings, hunger, or the South in general was repugnant to him."[75] The

South here is identified with images of deprivation and specifically male disempowerment signified by lynchings and chain gangs. This reading is supported by
Anthony Dawahare, who convincingly claims that in Wright's narratives, migration to the North constitutes a "flight not only from oppression…but also from
the psychological pain resulting from the stronger social controls of black men in
the South."[76]

Another text that dramatizes the sense of black emasculation in the South is
Wright's autobiography, Black Boy. It follows the narrative itinerary of 12 Million
Black Voices, being divided into "Southern Nights," devoted to his childhood and
youth in the South, and "The Horror and the Glory," covering his life in Chicago
in the 1930s. The first part is densely interpolated with images of female authority
represented by Richard's mother, grandmother, and aunts. This gender dominance is introduced on the very first page of the text, when Richard remembers
that "all morning my mother had been scolding me" and "I was dreaming of
running and playing and shouting, but the vivid image of Granny's old, white,
wrinkled, grim face, framed by a halo of tumbling black hair, lying upon a huge
feather pillow, made me afraid."[77] In contrast to the absent father and grandfather living in the distant past of the Civil War, Richard's female relatives are
figures of authority in the family. The fear that they evoke in the young boy is
graphically represented in the scene in which Richard, having set the house on
fire, is punished and put to bed. To relieve his fever, packs of ice are put on his
forehead. The boy is "lost in a fog of fear" because, as he narrates:

> Whenever I tried to sleep I would see huge wobbly white bags, like the full
> udders of cows, suspended from the ceiling above me…I could see the bags in
> the daytime with my eyes open and I was gripped by the fear that they were
> going to fall and drench me with some horrible liquid…Time finally bore me
> away from the dangerous bags…I remembered my mother had come close to
> killing me.[78]

This vision of being almost killed with breast-like images of "the full udders of
cows" and "dangerous bags" "full of liquid" represents overpowering black matriarchy and, as Claudia Tate puts it, this "malevolent breast fantasy" signifies
black male helplessness and passive victimhood.[79] Another violent image that
depicts female domination and a threat to the integrity of the black male body
features Richard's grandmother. The scene begins innocently – his grandma tells
him to take a bath. Yet in Black Boy, the activity typically associated with nurturing
is narrated as violent and disturbing. "She snatched the towel from my hand and
began to scrub my ears, my face, my neck. 'Bend over,' she ordered. I stooped
and she scrubbed my anus."[80] What follows is Richard's disrespectful response
and a beating he gets for it, while he is still naked. The peculiar depiction of the
incident can be read as a homophobically tinted fear of penetration combined

with a repudiation of maternal dominance. Also, if juxtaposed with Washington's "gospel of the toothbrush," Richard's rebellion against cleanliness can also be read as a repudiation of the strategy of uplift and assertion of masculinity in the domestic sphere depicted in Up from Slavery. As is also manifest in Wright's other texts, Washington's politics and black female privilege are the obstacles on the way to black manhood. Wright's narrative does not easily give in to matriarchal domination. Throughout the first part of the text, young Richard narrates his more or less successful, very often violent, attempts to stand up to female authority in his family. Nonetheless, his struggle to defy this matriarchal control does not end until his migration first to Memphis, and then finally to the North, to Chicago.

Significantly, the first images of the Northern city in Black Boy, strongly echo the Freudian contrast between the feminine "Land" and the masculine "Buildings" from 12 Million Black Voices: "I looked northward at towering buildings of steel and stone. There were no curves here, no trees; only angles, lines, squares, bricks and copper wires."[81] The fact that Richard looks northward underlines the link between this particular image and the direction of black migration in general. The city is represented in psychoanalytically masculinist terms of phallic "towering buildings" and "angles, lines, squares, bricks and copper wires." The masculine character of the imagery is strengthened by the absence of feminine "curves." If this psychoanalytical reading is enriched with a more historicist approach, even the absence of "trees" can be interpreted as the lack of emasculating danger, since the tree in the context of Southern race relations at the time is unequivocally associated with lynching. This link, most memorably recorded in "Strange Fruit" performed by Billy Holiday, is established in another of Wright's texts, Lawd Today, when, in response to the presence of a desirable white woman, black male characters sing that "whenever there's trees there's rope."[82] Hence, the Northern city is metaphorically depicted in terms of phallic omnipotence and a lack of castration threat.

As these strongly gendered images of the rural and the urban suggest, migration to the city offers a chance for masculine empowerment. The causal link between the end of black matriarchy and Northern migration is explicitly recognized in 12 Million Black Voices. Wright's narrative voice shifts from the general to the specifically masculine and states that: "we men were freed and had moved to cities where cash-paying jobs enabled us to become the heads of our own families."[83] Here, Wright espouses the hegemonic ideology of "Marketplace Masculinity" as defined by Kimmel, analogous to the producerist black masculinity introduced by Summers. After the industrial revolution and the emergence of the capitalist marketplace, masculine gender identity was defined by success in the labor market, by holding a "cash-paying job."[84] Black male performance in the public sphere of the Northern city is in stark contrast to the new position of black women. Whereas they were figures of authority in the rural South:

In the Black Belts of the northern cities, our women are the most circum-scribed and tragic objects to be found in our lives...Because their orbit of life is narrow – from their kitchenette to the white folk's kitchen and back home again – they love the church more than do our men, who find a large measure of the expression of their lives in the mills and factories.[85]

Not only are the women referred to as "objects," they also seem to be excluded from the public sphere. They live in a "narrow orbit" between the kitchen and the kitchenette – a residential symbol of black poverty in Chicago, a cramped studio apartment. The conflation of the kitchen and the kitchenette reinforces the op-pressive relegation of all black female activity to the private sphere. Such render-ing of women's work in the kitchen is in stark contrast to the way in which Wright's fellow Marxist Andy Razaf challenges the low status of menial jobs by using the term "kitchen mechanics" in the musical *A Kitchen Mechanic's Revue*. In-stead of such affirmative and empowering tropes, 12 Million Black Voices focuses on the oppression of black women. Since the narrative voice is male, such depictions serve to privilege the position of the black men by comparison rather than to protest against and change the situation of the women. Black women's lifestyles result in their self-exclusion from Western civilization – "more than even that of the American Indian, the consciousness of vast sections of our black women lies beyond the boundaries of the modern world." Just as Washington uses the Native American identity to gain privilege, Wright asserts male civilizational advantage at the expense of both black women and American Indians. In this fragment, Wright further increases the difference between "we men" and "our black wo-men." Since 12 Million Black Voices constitutes a "folk history of black people," by identifying women with Indians, Wright distances them from the subject matter of the text. The fate of women in the North seems to be restricted to the kitchen and the church on the one hand, and prostitution on the other. "Outside of the church, many of our black women drift to ruin and death on the pavement of the city; they are sold, by white men as well as by black, for sex purposes...As moder-nity and complexity spread through the cities, our black women find that their jobs grow fewer."[86] Black women appear to be unfit for the complexity of the modern world, which parallels the fact that their authority is linked in the text to the extratemporal South and the pre-modern conditions of plantation life. By con-structing a vision of black matriarchy rooted in the rural context, Wright is able to account for women's failure in the urban environment and to justify male domi-nation as an inevitable and irreversible result of urbanization. In addition, Wright's text contains an implicit threat of "ruin and death" to those black wo-men who decide to leave the sanctity of the private sphere and defiantly enter the public realm of "the pavement."

Overall, the migration North is represented as a process which is not without obstacles, but which nevertheless constitutes a necessary step towards emancipation and provides black men with opportunities to perform their masculinity in the marketplace. Black women are excluded from this empowerment and destined either for the kitchen or the brothel. This gender gap is also visible in the promising title of the last part of the text: "Men in the Making." The text ends with an image of resurgence and organizing: "We are with the new tide. We stand at the crossroads. We watch each new procession. The hot wires carry urgent appeals. Print compels us. Voices are speaking. Men are moving! And we shall be with them."[87] Again, Wright's inclusive "we" in this fragment is clearly gendered as masculine.[88]

When Wright's black subject is confronted with Locke's New Negro project, significant parallels arise. First of all, both projects strategically attempt to forge a common identity for the black community as a whole. More importantly, Wright, just as Locke, perceives migration and urbanization as an opportunity for emancipation. Wright's naturalistic urban protest fiction is far from the promising image of the New Negro in Harlem, yet when compared with his depictions of the South in Black Boy, Uncle Tom's Children, or 12 Million Black Voices, the Northern city offers far more freedom and economic opportunities. Also, the author of Native Son, just as the editor of The New Negro, perceives the South as a metonymy of feminization and enslavement, whereas the black subject in the North is represented in masculinist terms. Both authors, at least partially, ascribe to the ideology of Marketplace Masculinity, which is defined in terms of success in the public sphere and is contrasted with the domestic mythology of femininity. On the other hand, Wright's construction of the black subject profoundly differs from Thurman's representations of the black community. Even though both choose to portray lower-class locales rather than dicty brownstones, and Wright's Chicago kitchenettes are in many respects similar to Thurman's New York railroad flats, the urban narratives in their texts are almost opposite. First of all, Thurman, never having experienced Southern race relations, repeatedly claimed that the exodus to the North was far too optimistic and resulted in confusion for many rural families, who were unable to function in the modern city. The difference between the two black writers in this respect is aptly illustrated by their representation of Booker T. Washington and his race politics. Thurman ascribes some wisdom to Washington's advocacy of living in the South, whereas Wright quotes his "let down your buckets where you are" as treason against the black community, treason sponsored by white men.[89]

The difference between the two visions is clearly manifest also in the way they depict black gender relations in the context of urbanization. Characteristically, whereas in 12 Million Black Voices, women are the victims in the migration scenario, in Thurman's Harlem, the most modern, liberated, and successful character in the text is young Delia, a daughter of a migrant family. Thurman stresses that black women are easily employable in the city, which often results in their sponsorship of black "sweetbacks." This is the exact opposite of Wright's claim that black women suffer from unemployment and turn to prostitution. Thurman's superwomen are superseded by Wright's "circumscribed and tragic objects," arrested in their pre-modern condition, and confined to the kitchen and kitchenettes. Thurman's texts provide ample space for black female sexual assertiveness, which, on the other hand, in Wright's writings is policed and constitutes a source of male anxiety. Such a disparity cannot be satisfactorily explained with the structural differences between New York in the 1920s and 1930s and Chicago a decade later. The level of disempowerment and unemployment of black women envisioned in 12 Million Black Voices is not supported by the statistical data as presented in one of the most sweeping accounts of the social standing of the black community at the time, Black Metropolis by St. Clair Drake and Horace R. Cayton, a publication that includes an introduction by Wright. Although the statistics for the black female labor market show widespread deprivation in relation to white women, this disproportion is comparable with the disparity between black and white men.[90]

The polarization between Wright's and Thurman's representations of the black community can be explained by the fundamental difference between their approaches to black literature. In contrast to Thurman's texts, which celebrate bohemian individuality, Wright attempts to forge a collective black identity. In this respect, the collective "we" of 12 Million Black Voices is analogous to the inclusive "he" of Locke's New Negro and the exceptional "men" of Du Bois's talented tenth. In order to unify the black community, all these projects employ centrifugal forces that obliterate the gender difference. They illustrate that building a collective identity as a way to group emancipation is dangerously predicated on the exclusion of women as subjects and the representation of enslavement and racial oppression as feminization.[91]

Communality, Homosociality, and Sexuality

The radical masculinization of collective identity as represented in 12 Million Black Voices is translated in Wright's fictional texts into recurrent representations of black male homosociality. His narratives are much more at ease with representations of male bonding than of heterosexual relations. In this section, I will analyze the way in which female presence either threatens black male authority or triggers lynching anxiety. Since, unlike Locke, Wright is not able to erase female presence from his representations of the black community, it frequently disturbs and troubles male homosocial intimacy, which results in reactive frustration and violence.

The most accomplished portrayal of black men's communality can be found in Lawd Today. As Denning rightly claims, the passages depicting Jake socializing with his friends offer a "promise of community."[92] The significance of this theme to the novel is primarily manifested in quantitative terms – three-quarters of the narrative follows Jake and his three friends, Slim, Al, and Bob. Their fraternity starts hours before work, when they play bridge and drink, and their playful dialogue continues through their work time late into the evening entertainment in a buffet flat.

The most interesting parts of their dialogue consist either in the ritual of insult performed in the form of banter battles or in continuous storytelling dialogically structured as call-and-response.[93] An elaborate example of a bantering conversation begins as a talk about shirts and fashion between Jake and Al. The motivation behind the verbal challenge is Jake's desire to disturb the assertive calm of Al: "Jake wanted to...make some of that strength of that repose his own."[94] The men challenge and criticize each other's fashion tastes, but as the tension increases, the dialogue shifts to very complex offenses directed at the opponent's family. These insults are dominated by sexualized images of their female relatives. Thus, men in the dialogue strive to draw strength and self-confidence from attacks on the other's female family members, who in this case appear to be the only valuables in a black man's life. It seems that what is threatening to the black male ego are willful sexual relations between women in his family and white men, which parallels the image of slaves "bound" and made to watch their "sisters and wives" raped by white men in 12 Million Black Voices. As the men's reactions suggest, a masturbating black woman is even more offensive an image for them to entertain. Their conversation features two such representations, which, analogous to other bantering utterances, are detailed and graphic: "your old grandma was out in the privy crying 'cause she couldn't find a corncob" and, more explicit, "your old aunt Mary...watching with her finger stuck in her puss." Surprisingly, the dialogue's climax is not directly sexualized but ends with images of black women eating – "pork chops" in Heaven and "missionary chitterlings" in Africa.[95] All the images suggest that for a black man, the most offensive insults represent corporeal agency of his female relatives – through eating, masturbation, or sexual relations with white men. Consequently, the strength and calm of black men depend on the control of their female relatives' libidinal and alimentary needs.

Even though in form and content this dialogue expresses animosity, it is a social ritual that in fact strengthens the bonds between Jake and Al. Despite Jake's failure to match Al's last utterance, "they all laughed so they felt weak in the joints of their bones."[96] In a similar scene, a quarrel about a game of bridge also ends in communal laughter:

Jake and Bob laughed so long that Al and Slim began laughing. And when Jake and Bob saw that they had made their opponents laugh at their own defeat, they laughed harder. Presently they stopped laughing at the joke Jake had made, and began laughing because they were all laughing. And they laughed because they had laughed. They paused for breath, and then they laughed at how they had laughed; and because they had laughed at how they had laughed, they laughed and laughed and laughed.[97]

This long excerpt accurately depicts black male homosociality in the novel and rhetorically reflects Wright's use of the vernacular in the dialogue. Just as the dialogues between the characters, the fragment is very repetitive – the verb "to laugh" recurs sixteen times in the span of six lines. This reiterative collective activity both binds the men together and serves as the release of their tensions, which do not find any other outlet outside of male homosociality in the novel. This representation of laughter can also be productively read with reference to Bakhtin's theory of communal laughter, which is characterized by "exceptional radicalism, freedom, and ruthlessness." Analyzing medieval laughter rooted in folk humor, Bakhtin claims that "the truth of laughter embraced and carried away everyone; nobody could resist it" and "folk laughter presents an element of victory...over all that oppresses and restricts." In contrast to "the [modern] satirist whose laughter is negative" and who "places himself above the object of his mockery," in the case of ambivalent laughter, "he who is laughing also belongs to it."[98] The repeated scenes of communal laughter in Lawd Today do not belong to the modern subjective, individual, satirical, distancing humor but retain the communal potential of folk laughter, which challenges hegemony and blurs social boundaries. The men are laughing not at something, but they "began laughing because they were all laughing." Moreover, the themes from the men's dialogues primarily belong to what Bakhtin defines as the lower body stratum, the realm that includes bodily processes such as eating, metabolism, and procreation and is privileged in the folk humor. Thus their laughter can be read as a counterhegemonic intervention in the novel. The only important difference between these scenes and Bakhtin's notion of ambivalent laughter is the relative homogeneity of the laughing group. Unlike the grotesque boundary-blurring rent party in Thurman's novel, which is defined by the diversity of the guests, Lawd Today imagines a utopian unity consisting of black men only.

The fragment depicting laughter is also a peculiar combination of the black vernacular and modernist experimentation with the narrative. The link between the two linguistic modes is established in Wright's favorable review of Gertrude Stein's Wars I Have Seen, where he claims that "semi-literate Negro stockyard workers" – "basic proletarians with the instinct for revolution" – find Stein's texts such as "Melanctha" familiar and comprehensible.[99] This connection is further strengthened, since Stein's fiction is mentioned in the male dialogue from Lawd Today when one of them states that "some old white woman over in Paris said a rose is a rose is a rose is a rose."[100] This iconic Steinian sentence is criticized by the folk common sense, and yet its repetitiveness and superfluousness parallel both the flow of dialogues and the narration of the novel. Importantly, despite her being "some old white women," Stein is masculinized through the allusion to black revolutionary industrial workers in Wright's review. This is further manifest when her fiction is described as "defiant" and she is quoted saying that "I so naturally had my part in killing the 19th century and killing it dead, quite like a gangster with...a tommy gun." Hence, modernist experimentation is represented as politically revolutionary and militantly masculine. The reference to Stein corresponds to Wright's construction of experimental writing as guerilla combat, and the militant tropes highlight the masculinist character of the black vernacular.[101]

The second type of homosocial dialogue in the novel is based on the call-and-response paradigm and consists of four voices interweaving a single intelligible narrative. There are many dialogues that follow such a pattern, and their length ranges from a few lines to a few pages. For example, the second part of the text, devoted to work at the post office, ends with a conversation about women:

'And that feeling a woman gives you!'
'Jeeesus!'
'Boy, it's terrible thing!'
'It's like fire!'
'Like ice!'
'Like a 'lectric shock!'
'It knocks you out!'
'It gets you all over ...'
'... in your head ...'
'... and legs ...'
'... and thighs ...'
'... like somebody pouring water over you ...'
'It's a funny feeling.'
'It's the greatest feeling in the world.'
'Yeah, but a man couldn't stand that feeling for long.'
'Naw, he just couldn't bear it.'
'It'd kill 'im.'[102]

First of all, this multivocal narrative is unified through the use of anaphora. Rhythmic repetitions of the same syntactic structures such as "It's" or "like" introduce consecutive new elements. Additionally, one sentence is uttered in parts by a few interlocutors and is unified by the use of punctuation, especially the three-dot or even four-dot ellipsis, and the lack of capitalization of the first words in each of the utterances. All these elements contribute to an effect which can be described as a collective monologue. Analogous to the collective laughter, the call-and-response dialogue seems to be an example of Bakhtin's novelistic heteroglossia, a dialogic yet structurally unified presence of many voices and languages in the text. Nonetheless, just as in the case of laughter, its democratic potential is limited by the lack of diversity among the voices.

Black male homosociality performed in a vernacular dialogue recurs also in *Black Boy* and *Native Son*. In *Black Boy*, Wright acknowledges this ritualistic talk to be an important element of growing up as a black man. Young Richard remembers that:

> I now associated with older boys and I had to pay for my admittance into their company by subscribing to certain racial sentiments...None of this was premeditated, but sprang spontaneously out of the talk of black boys who met at the crossroads. It was degrading to play with girls and in our talk we relegated them to a remote island of life. We had somehow caught the spirit of the role of our sex and we flocked together for common moral schooling...And the talk would weave, roll, surge, spurt, veer, swell, having no specific direction, touching vast areas of life...Money, God, race, sex, color, war, planes, machines, trains, swimming, boxing, anything...Folk tradition was handed from group to group.[103]

This fragment establishes a link among "the talk," its main content of "racial sentiments," and the exclusion of black women. Black male identity – "the spirit of the role of our sex" – is predicated on the animosity towards white men and the repudiation of black women. Wright repeatedly emphasizes male homosociality – "we flocked together," "our talk," "admittance into their company." The masculinist character of the talk is manifest also in the content of the dialogues. Even though Wright claims that they refer to "vast areas of life," these areas, apart from the very abstract "Money, sex, race, God," are culturally gendered as specifically masculine: "war, planes, machines, trains, swimming, boxing." In addition, the verbal performance of the vernacular talk is depicted in terms that appear pronouncedly masculine from a psychoanalytical perspective: the dialogues "surge," "spurt," and "swell." Finally, male talk is again celebrated as an expression and communication of black folk wisdom in general.

Similar remarks about black male speech frequently recur throughout Wright's autobiography. These homosocial talks seem to be the only moments when young Richard "could talk, joke, laugh, sing, say what [he] pleased" because "all the boys were Negroes," and he "was happy."[104] Such boy talk constituted a powerful inspiration for Wright as a writer. In *Black Boy*, he remembers his work in the South Side Boy's Club, where the Bigger-Thomases-to-be provided Richard with rich vernacular material. "For hours I listened to their talk of planes, women, guns, politics and crime. Their figures of speech were as forceful and colorful as any ever used by English-speaking people."[105] Again, the content of the talks is gendered as masculine, which is furthermore emphasized by the militant character of the figures of speech described as "forceful."

Both *12 Million Black Voices* and *Lawd Today* represent a black communality that is masculinized through its homosociality as well as through the themes and tropes that construct it in the texts. The "promise of communality," however, is much more convincing in the fictional form than in the FSA publication. In Lawd Today, the collective aspect is manifest in the plurality of voices in unison rather than in the forced grammatical plurality of the narrative voice. The call-and-response narrative of Lawd Today sounds more credible and compelling largely because it does not pretend to represent anything more diverse than a homosocial community. Hence, the authentically communal moments in Wright's texts are masculinist intra-racial utopias, where idyll is necessarily predicated that all the members are "boys" and "Negroes."

In Native Son, which focuses on the alienation of the black man in the urban context, the homosocial communality is downplayed in comparison with Black Boy and Lawd Today. Yet Bigger also has a group of close friends from a male street gang. They play pool, rob shops, and go to the movies. The relationships among the boys are structurally similar to the ones represented in other texts; however, sexually charged homosocial activities are more visible here than in Lawd Today or Black Boy. Whereas Jake and his friends leave the buffet flat early and the sexual encounters they plan together never take place, in Native Son, a homosocial enactment of sexuality is explicitly manifest at the very beginning of the novel, when Bigger and Jack masturbate together in the cinema. The fact that they simultaneously weave their call-and-response talk makes this scene a sexualized example of Wright's communal monologues and dialogues. In Native Son, the "promise of communality," however, is not fulfilled mainly because of the fear-induced violence that drenches the lives of Bigger and his friends. The verbal challenges that serve to perform self-assertive masculinity in Lawd Today here are transformed into physical assaults.

Almost quoting sociologists such as Myrdal, Wright explains such intra-racial violence in the following way: "Many Negroes solve the problem of being black by transferring their hatred of themselves to others with a black skin and fighting them." Additionally, the issue of violence between black men in Wright's texts can be interestingly illuminated by a fragment from Black Boy depicting young Richard's predicament when he works in a hotel. Two white men spread untrue gossip about Richard and another black man, Harrison, which is supposed to make them want to fight each other. Both are given weapons. Finally, when they refuse to settle the conflict in a violent way, they are offered a financial reward for boxing against each other. Richard initially declines the offer, acknowledging that it makes him equal to a "dog or rooster" – he does not want to become Thurman's "cock o' the walk." Nonetheless, he finally surrenders to the white men's insistence. The scene of the fight is depicted in a very telling way: "only white men were allowed in the basement; no women or Negroes were admitted. Harrison and I were stripped to the waist. A bright electric bulb glowed above our heads."[106] The black fighters are exposed to the exclusively white male gaze, since "no women or Negroes" are admitted. Their visibility is emphasized with the bright light, which, according to Wiegman's claims, necessarily highlights the corporeality of their figures.[107] The gaze here can be read as not only corporealizing but also sexualizing, since the black men are forced to "strip to the waist." This sexualization can further explain why Richard narrates that "I felt that I had done something *unclean*, something for which I could never properly atone."[108] This scene sexualizes black male violence and represents it as a performance for the potentially desiring white male gaze. This reading interestingly resonates with James Baldwin's famous statement about Wright's fiction that "there is a great space where sex ought to be; and what usually fills in this space is violence."[109]

Baldwin's claim accurately illuminates many more scenes and themes in Wright's fiction. For example, it also sheds light on the dynamic of prohibited black male desire, in which Wright's texts abound. In his narratives, signals of male desire are followed by images of lynching rather than romantic scenarios. In *Lawd Today*, Jake and his friends sing a song about lynching just after they have watched how "obliquely across the aisle a white woman propped her feet upon a vacant seat, exposing the curved ascent of white thighs." Black men's desire for the female passenger is visible in their movements – "Slim looked and his mouth dropped open...They moved in their seats as though on pins, looking alternately at the woman and out of the window." Significantly, their desire seems to be performed as a homosocial ritual analogous to the scene of masturbation in the cinema in *Native Son*. The men start singing a call-and-response song, where each of them sings a consecutive line: "'Oh, Lawd, can I ever, can I ever?...'/...'Naw, nigger, you can never, you can never...'/...'But wherever there's life there's hope...'/...'And wherever there's trees there's rope.'" This communal singing, which ends with laughter, is a way to manage the tension connected with the haunting images of lynching. The lynching anxiety is one of the subjects repeatedly recurring in the long communal dialogues among the four men. One of their talks ends in a memory of a particular lynching witnessed by Jake's friend. All of them agree that "there ain't no trouble with black men bothering white women. Hell, they scared." The power of the fear of lynching is vividly illustrated in *Black Boy* in a scene in which a waitress "came forward with a tray of food and squeezed against [Richard] to draw a cup of coffee." Young Wright perceives this innocent gesture as "an incident charged with a memory of dread."[110]

A similar pattern of desire followed with a reference to lynching can be found on the level of narrative structure. Jake, in the course of the narrative, has repeated, although fragmented, erotic fantasies and moments of desire. All of them are suddenly interrupted and one in particular is broken with an explicit image of lynching:

A plump, brown-skinned girl passed; unconsciously, he pulled his hat to a rakish angle and jingled his silver louder. He looked up at the wide sweep of blue sky and felt how good it was merely to be alive. As he passed a newsstand his eyes caught for a fleeting moment a black and white picture of a nude, half-charred body of a Negro swinging from the end of a rope. At the top of the picture ran a caption: DEATH TO LYNCHERS. Jake grunted and whistled louder.[111]

Here, even desire for a black woman is punished by a reference to a lynching. The same picture recurs towards the end of the text in a copy of the paper bought by Jake's friend. Significantly, they comment on the photograph on their way to a "joint" with "red-hot mamas," which is to end without any engagement in sexual activities.[112]

In Wright's fiction, black male desire in general and desire for the white woman in particular are inescapably interconnected with fear and violence. Nowhere, however, are black male desire, white femininity, and lynching as dramatically entangled as in Native Son. This link is first introduced in the cinema scene when Mary Dalton is shown in the newsreel. Jack expresses his desire for the girl, and Bigger responds with a comment that echoes lynching practices: "you'd be hanging from a tree like a bunch of bananas."[113] This signal of black male desire for a white woman and a lynching image foreshadows the dramatic plot of the novel: the killing of Mary is publicly perceived as rape. When Bigger tells his girlfriend Bessie how he had accidentally killed Mary Dalton, her immediate response is "'They'll say you raped her.'...So deeply he had pushed it all back down into him that it was not until now that its real meaning came back. They would say he had raped her and there would be no way to prove that he had not."[114] Unsurprisingly, this is the line of reasoning chosen by the prosecution.

Apart from lynching, there is another element that recurs in both Black Boy and Lawd Today that links male sexual activity with bodily injury, namely gonorrhea. One of Jake's friends, Bob, suffers from this medical condition. His pain and the advanced stage of the illness are repeatedly signaled in the text. This is contrasted with Jake's comment, which treats it as an essential and natural part of being a black man: "A man ain't a man unless he's done had it."[115] This assumption is echoed in Black Boy by a coworker of Richard, who claims that: "you ain't a man 'less you done had it three times...'Tain't nothing worse'n a bad cold."[116] The castration anxiety connected with gonorrhea is visible when Bob is compared by Al to a woman in the end of the novel because of his condition of being unfit for drinking and carousing with prostitutes. Black masculinity hence is defined by risky, extra-marital sexual activity, which as both narratives show ends in pain and suffering of the black body and a threat of castration.

All the above-discussed scenes represent a common dynamic of black male desire followed with an image of lynching or other bodily injury underlain with a castration anxiety. Even though Wright's urban fiction does not narrate any incidents of lynching, its memory haunts black male sexuality and produces a dynamic where desire is causatively linked to the threat of violence. Significantly, this in turn results in a peculiar conflation of fear and desire in the narrative, which is visible in the most climactic scenes of *Native Son*. When Bigger puts drunken Mary to bed, he takes advantage of the situation to feel around her body. "He was aware only of her body now; his lips trembled. Then he stiffened. The door behind him had creaked."[117] Since the ambiguous phrase "he stiffened" is inserted in the narrative between an image of desire and fear, it can refer to either of them. This ambiguity is repeated in the next paragraph: when he is still holding Mary, "Mrs. Dalton was moving slowly toward him and *he grew tight and full, as though about to explode*."[118] It also surfaces in Bigger's memories of the scene in Mary's bedroom: "He really did not know just where *that fear and shame* had come from; it had just been there, that was all. Each time he had come in contact with her it *had risen hot and hard*."[119] Here the ambiguity is produced by the pronoun "it," which in the flow of the text can be read either as referring to "fear and shame" or Bigger's penis. Rather than privilege one of the interpretations – fear or desire – the text encourages the reader to interpret the "stiffness" as a sign of a pathological conflation of the two. Since in the cultural imagination, black male desire is so closely related to fear and violence, in *Native Son*, fear is a factor stimulating black male excitement. As James Baldwin puts it, Wright's texts are drenched with images of "gratuitous and compulsive violence," which stems from "the rage, almost literarily the howl, of a man who is being castrated."[120] The castration mentioned by Baldwin accurately describes the haunting lynching anxiety that both limits black male heterosexual desire and pathologically connects it with fear and violence.

Yet even though black male sexual desire is haunted by destructive images of violence in *Black Boy*, *Lawd Today*, and *Native Son*, none of the plots narrates any incidents of violence actually punishing male desire.[121] Instead, the "compulsive" violence is transferred from imaginary images of lynching onto female bodies in the narratives. In *Lawd Today*, although it is Jake's desire that is repeatedly interrupted with a destructive lynching anxiety, it is his wife's body that is beaten. Jake beats her before leaving for work and after he comes back, robbed and almost fired from his job. Lil fights back and cuts him with a fragment of window glass. The novel ends with their both being cut and bleeding, laying in a cold room, with a broken window letting in wind and snow: "Outside an icy wind swept around the corner of the building, whining and moaning like an idiot in a deep black pit."[122] Interestingly, an almost identical sentence – "Outside in the cold night the wind moaned and died down, like an idiot in an icy black pit" – is introduced between the rape of Bessie and her being brutally murdered with a brick by Bigger.[123] The verb "to moan" is used earlier in the text to refer to the coital sounds. Analogous to the logic of substitution described by Baldwin, sexual activity is replaced with a sense of meaninglessness and dead-end symbolized by the deep/icy black pit. The sentences can be read as referring to modernist masterpieces focused on the decline of Western civilization – Eliot's "The Hollow

Men" and Faulkner's *The Sound and the Fury*.[124] These allusions serve to thematize the condition of black relationships in the texts. Wright's works seem to suggest that the real decline of human relationships can be found in the tragic and pathological lives of the oppressed groups, rather than among the decadent bourgeois modernists.

Apart from the violence that engulfs black male sexuality, the denial of black female desire is another factor that perverts black romantic relations. This combination – a violent black man and a frigid black woman – recurs in the relationship of Jake and Lil as well as Bigger and Bessie. Lil is not able to engage in sexual relations after an abortion she is persuaded to have by her husband. Jake's sexual life in the novel is limited to the earlier-mentioned masturbatory fantasies. A parallel situation is illustrated by Bigger's relationship with his girlfriend. Bessie is not a willing sexual partner. Both times they have sexual intercourse it is Bigger who desires it, the second time being a blatant case of rape. His sexual life is even more parallel to Jake's in the light of Dawahare's interpretation of Bigger's sexual relationships with Bessie as masturbatory in character.[125] The gendered representation of sexual assertiveness in the narratives parallels the representation of black subjectivity in 12 *Million Voices*; both positions are denied to black women.

When a heterosexual intercourse between black people is finally represented, it is one of the series of pathological images Bigger sees during his flight from the police, when he reflects on the Jim Crow oppression of the South Side. Hence, it is metonymically positioned on a par with "big black rats leaping over the snow" and black people "bottled up like animals." Hiding in a deserted building,

> Through a window without shades, he saw a room in which were two small iron beds with sheets dirty and crumpled. In one bed sat three naked black children looking across the room to the other bed on which lay a man and woman, both naked and black in the sunlight. There were quick, jerky movements on the bed where the man and woman lay, and the three children were watching. It was familiar; he had seen things like that when he was a little boy sleeping five in a room. Many mornings he had awakened and watched his father and mother. He tinned away, thinking: Five of 'em sleeping in one room...He crawled back to the chimney, seeing before his eyes an image of the room of five people, all of them blackly naked in the strong sunlight, seen through a sweaty pane: the man and woman moving jerkily in tight embrace, and the three children watching.[126]

The pathology of the image primarily stems from the lack of private boundaries inside the flat and any screens sheltering it from the public gaze. The theme of looking and watching, which is enabled by the lack of boundaries, is obsessively repeated throughout the excerpt. The children's gaze, repeated three times, is mirrored by Bigger's gaze at the children as well as his own visual memory from childhood. This compulsive repetition suggests that the image triggers one of Bigger's deepest traumas. What emphasizes the visibility and perhaps also reinforces the pathology of the scene is the strong light mentioned twice in the short excerpt. Because of the intensely lit corporeality and the presence of the gaze, this scene seems parallel to the fight between young Richard and his colleague staged by white men. A similar vulnerability of private boundaries is illustrated in Black Boy, when "thin walls" and "cracks at the top of the door" enable young Richard to see an intercourse with a prostitute in a flat next door. The proximity between the brothel and Wright's family home makes his mother decide to move house, but before it happens, Richard repeats Bigger's specular scenario. The link between the pathology of the black family and the lack of proper private boundaries appears also in the scene when Jake and Lil fight and break a window, which lets in wind "whining and moaning like an idiot in a deep black pit." All these scenes illustrate Wright's Marxist approach, since they point to structural conditions as the main source of pathology in the black community.

Conclusion

Wright's vision of black social and sexual relationships is structurally different from those represented in Locke's and Thurman's writings. Locke avoids the problem of lynching and fear by the celebration of male homosocial bonding and the exclusion of heterosocial images. He also evades explicit sexuality as such and, ascribing to the separate spheres ethic, closets it in the private sphere. Instead of using explicit sexual metaphors, he constructs male bonding primarily on the level of textuality, inspiration, and creativity. The male family in his writing reproduces through texts, whereas cultural productions are supposed to form its sublime offspring. Wright to some extent retains this scheme in the friendship of the four men in Lawd Today, though his vision is far bleaker than Locke's. Since he does not exclude women from the narrative, the constant fear related to lynching surfaces in the men's call-and-response dialogues. In addition, the ending of the novel is hardly promising for any of them: Jake, penniless and badly cut, is bleeding in a cold room; Bob suffers from a bad case of gonorrhea; whereas Slim's TB cough steadily intensifies in the course of the novel. Their relationship does not offer any promise for the future. Moreover, black male continuity, in Wright's texts in general, is endangered by the lack of a father-son relationship. This absence is dramatically visible in Black Boy, when Richard remembers that "the image of my father became associated with my pangs of hunger, and whenever I felt hunger I thought of him with a deep biological bitterness."[127] The significance of this sensation to the text is emphasized by the title of the initially unpublished parts of the autobiography – American Hunger. Whereas Locke assumes the maternal reproductive position, Wright's texts represent the absence of the father and repudiate maternal images as domineering and emasculating.

As a result, black boys, in his texts, are completely alienated from their families. The lack of a father figure can be read as a symptom of Wright's deep and unresolved anxiety of authorship, which is dramatically interlocked with the anxiety of influence manifest in his challenges to the past giants of black letters.

Wright's focus on the obscene and naturalistic elements of black life echoes Thurman's exhibitionism. Both abundantly depict violence, drunken revelries, the lack of separate spheres, and non-normative sexuality. But whereas Thurman's fiction explores alternative sexualities and rent parties with fascination and endows them with democratic potential, in Wright's vision, the focus is clearly on violence and pathology. Whereas Thurman celebrates the trespassing of the separate spheres divide, Wright causally links it to pathological sexuality, which is open to the potentially predatory gaze. Although the issue of lynching is present in Thurman's writings as a factor constraining black male sexuality, it is not transformed into violence against (black) women. Whereas Thurman's most influential novel, Infants of the Spring, represents a relationship between the white man Steve and Aline, a black woman desiring him, Wright's iconic text deals with the tension between black male desire and white womanhood, represented by Bigger and Mary. This difference leads to probably the most significant divergence in their visions of black sexuality. Whereas Wright's textual answer to lynching and emasculation anxiety is compensatory violence against the woman, Thurman chooses to represent female sexual desire, which is not threatened by lynching in the American cultural imagination.

Another emblematic difference in the representation of gender and sexual relations by the two authors concerns the issue of abortion. Both Thurman and Wright represent this phenomenon as a significant element of their seminal novels, Infants of the Spring and Lawd Today respectively. Yet the two narratives strikingly differ. Whereas for Thurman's Lucille, abortion is an independent decision and a sign of her (sexual) emancipation, in Wright's text, Jake tricks Lil into the procedure, which is to ruin her health. The disparity between the ways in which this theme functions in the two novels closely parallels their divergent representations of female subjectivity. In Thurman's text, abortion signifies an independent decision of the woman and the beginning of her more mature existence, whereas in Wright's novel, the same incident signifies female oppression and lack of subjectivity, which leads to sexual passivity.

Accordingly, the two writers represent a different range of black masculinities. Due to their celebration of female heterosexual desire and sexual bohemian experimentation, Thurman's texts position the black male body as an object of sexual gaze. To an extent, this liberates black masculinity from the traumas of sexual violence and provides an affirmative homoerotic space in the novels. Wright's texts, although they represent sexualized activities between men, do not celebrate homoerotic desire. Homophobia underlies his evaluation of the black bohemia and its white sponsorship. It can also be discerned in Wright's repudiation of female domination and sexual assertiveness, which trigger fears of male (sexual) passivity. Thus, in contrast to both Locke's and Thurman's writings, Wright's fiction is devoid of affirmative homoerotic spaces. If it explores non-normative sexualities, they are represented as pathological rather than liberating. They serve to dramatize the trauma of American Jim Crow race relations rather than look for liberation in alternative narratives of desire.

Wright's texts graphically illustrate the shifts in ideologies of gender and sexuality that followed the New Negro Movement. His intense political engagement in the 1930s and 1940s was representative of the writers of these decades, who were influenced by the growing impact of left-wing ideologies and the Popular Front. Despite several continuities, Wright primarily uses the New Negro Renaissance as a springboard to assert his black male agency and authorship. Symbolically, in this dialogical literary history narrative, the Native Son, armed with his working-class virility, interrogates the elitist hope of the New Negro and conducts a full-blown literary assault on the bohemian explorations and dandyist reinventions of the Niggerati.

Conclusion
Black Male Authorship, Sexuality, and the Transatlantic Connection

The Epilogue, like the Prologue, expanded the scope of this study's main focus to demonstrate the work of dialogical relationships in the process of constructing literary history with the tropes of gender and sexuality. What emerges as the most relevant dynamic in the history of African American literature in the Jim Crow era is the double bind of the anxiety of influence and the anxiety of authorship, both resolved through different masculinity politics, which either challenge the father figures or celebrate male filial relationships. Whereas their need to resolve the anxiety of influence varies, none of the authors discussed here is free from the anxiety of authorship, and all pay tribute to a chosen – black or white – male predecessor. Interestingly, it is not the choice of the particular forefather that is significant but the way he is represented, which is most aptly illustrated by the disparate reincarnations of Frederick Douglass, ranging from Washington's self-sacrificing gentleman to Thurman's muscular pugilist. African-American attempts to assert male authorship are also complexly entangled in hegemonic ideologies of American masculinity and the social constructs directly connected with them, such as race, class, and sexuality. Washington's writing evades conflict, images of black aggression, the lynch logic, and the anxiety of influence, and it appropriates Victorian ideologies of respectable manliness, the Genteel Patriarch, and the white man's burden, positioning them in the domestic and rural contexts. In this way he avoids the anxieties that drench Du Bois's appropriation of the emergent ideology of modern masculinity for the elite of the talented tenth, which is located in the urban and public realms. Locke, similar to Du Bois, constructs a black group identity based on producerist masculinity in the urban context, yet because he consistently erases women from his narratives of black identity, he circumvents the lynch logic as well as the anxiety over the purity of black womanhood haunting Du Bois. Locke's writings resolve the anxiety of authorship by celebrating different black male writers positioned within a network of multiple textual influences. The anxiety of male authorship also dominates the writings of Thurman, who openly celebrates textual influences on his fiction to resolve it. His cultural references appropriate European counterhegemonic dandyist masculinity positioned in the urban context, which, unlike producerist manhood, violates the private-public divide along with other central Jim Crow boundaries. The affirmative position of Locke and the bohemian attitude of Thurman are strategically used by Wright, who attacks them to assert his own virile masculinity rooted in working-class mythology and to construct black male authorship as a militant struggle.

Locke's and Thurman's multiple textual influences, much more abundant and celebratory than in the case of the other writers discussed here, are correlated with the profusion of spaces for alternative male sexuality. Thus the presence of non-normative sexuality emerges as a significant element of the New Negro Renaissance discourse in contrast to the rhetorics preceding and following it. In their explanations of this phenomenon, scholars refer to the biographical data, which indicates that many of the central male artists and intellectuals of the Renaissance were either actively gay or bisexual.[1] What is more important from the historicist perspective that this study adopts is that at the beginning of the twentieth century, due to the successes of the Progressive movement, unlawful and non-normative sexual activities were structurally forced out of white downtown areas to black urban districts such as Harlem or the South Side. The prominent presence of alternative sexualities in the black community of the day is confirmed both by historical accounts and by contemporaneous narratives such as McKay's *Home to Harlem* or Hughes's *The Big Sea*. Hence, the social context that was characterized by the visible presence of transgressive sexualities can be read as fostering the expression of alternative desires in the texts of the New Negro Renaissance.

Nonetheless, Thurman's and Locke's texts represent two divergent constructions of non-normative sexuality and the differences between them should not be neglected. Locke draws on the masculinist vision of male intimacy and camaraderie, which is championed as more sublime and transcendental in character than heterosexual relationships. His embrace of the hegemonic boundary between the public and the private renders the erotic dimension tacitly implicit in his public writings; however, when they are analyzed in the context of his private correspondence, his aesthetic valorization of the male patrilineal canon turns out to correspond to his ideal of erotic male friendship and textual bonding. Additionally, because of his commitment to the public-private divide and bourgeois respectability, he does not resort to the imagery from unlawful and non-normative sex institutions that were driven out of white districts to Harlem. Instead, his main cultural references are drawn from a complex network of European discourses. Thurman's texts, on the other hand, manifest a deep fascination with the counter-bourgeois and illegal institutions of Harlem. His representation of sexuality allows for more fluidity and does not exclude female desire. He challenges rather than embraces the public-private divide and the ideal of bourgeois respectability. In consequence, in Thurman's texts, the black male body is put on public display for the desiring homoerotic gaze. His textual explorations of alternative sexualities are correlated with other experimentations, including textual sex-change and racial passing.

What is parallel between Locke's and Thurman's representations of transgressive sexuality is their intertextual debt to European discourses. In the case of Locke, these references notably include Greek and German philosophy, German and British early gay liberation discourse, and the German youth movement. Thurman, on the other hand, draws on the discourse of decadence and modernist European literature. This transatlantic connection suggests that there is a strong correlation between European intertextual appropriations and the potential to express non-normative desire. The authors whose projects are national rather than cosmopolitan in their scope and predominantly focus on American race relations and the lynch ideology either silence non-normative sexuality or apply heteronormativity as a way to empower the masculine black subject. On the other hand, the presence of transatlantic hybridity seems to foster the expression of alternative sexualities. This is not to suggest that European discourses are simply less heteronormative, although the assumptions about European culture as less Puritan and more sexually liberated recur in the discourse of the movement, but rather to indicate that there exists a particular inclusive potential in American appropriations of European discourses. This potential partly stems from the fact that in a variety of traditional American attempts at self-definition such as Emerson's "Self-Reliance" or Turner's "The Significance of the Frontier in American History," the image of Europe is projected as America's other and is marked by characteristics such as aristocratic, decadent, overcivilized, which in turn are easily associated with effeminacy and, at least since the Wilde trials, with homosexuality. Moreover, the mediation of alternative sexualities through European codes distances them from the core of American identity, and this strategy possibly relieves anxieties inherent in any representation of non-normativity. In the 1920s, transatlantic appropriations were more productive than today, since European cultural capital was still widely acknowledged as dominant and hence such mediation legitimized marginalized desires.

The fact that Locke's writings received far more critical attention and acknowledgement than Thurman's rhetoric can be read as stemming not only directly from the difference between their representations of alternative sexuality but also from the way they fuse European and American discourses. Locke's notions of the New Negro and the Renaissance are hybrids comprising on the one hand traditional American ideas of regeneration and redefinition as embodied by the rhetoric of the American Renaissance, and European emancipatory and philosophical discourses on the other. His use of the figure of Whitman as both exceptionally American and tinted with European same-sexual discourse is most emblematic of these hybrid constructions. In contrast, Thurman's writings merge European discourses of decadence with American discourses that are highly critical of the traditional American ideology of exceptionalism, which is exemplified by his celebration of Mencken or Huneker. The heteroglot structure of Thurman's writings does not embrace American pragmatism or narratives of progress, and in turn, his black dandies and superwomen are not warmly embraced by traditional histories of American literature. The New Negro and the Renaissance were seamlessly assimilated into the narrative of American exceptionalism, whereas until recently, decadent Niggerati and their heterotopian Manor remained excluded from the core of the literary canon and scholarly scrutiny.

Notes

Introduction

1. J. Saunders Redding, *To Make a Poet Black* (Chapel Hill, NC: University of North Carolina Press, 1939), 95-96; emphasis added.

2. Leroi Jones (Amiri Baraka), "The Myth of a 'Negro Literature,'" in *Within the Circle: An Anthology of African American Literary Criticism from the Harlem Renaissance to the Present*, ed. Angelyn Mitchell (Durham, NC: Duke University Press, 1994), 171; emphasis added.

3. The term "Harlem Renaissance" was popularized by the literary histories of the movement published from the 1960s onward, which strategically avoided the term "Negro," whereas the most prevalent self-name for the variety of black cultural, predominantly literary, activities in the 1920, was the (New) Negro Renaissance. This renaming can be accurately illustrated by the fact that the seminal publication of *The New Negro: An Interpretation* (1925) was reprinted as *The New Negro: Voices of the Harlem Renaissance* (1968). In this study, the term "New Negro Renaissance" will be preferred, since it does not limit the movement's activity to the geographical and cultural limits of Upper Manhattan, and, even more significantly, it emphasizes the attempt to remake black identity, which will be of considerable relevance in the analysis. The term "New Negro" is approached as a particular textual construction, reflecting the cultural and linguistic codes of the 1920s rather than regarded as derogatory from the perspective of contemporary standards.

4. Harold Bloom, *The Anxiety of Influence: A Theory of Poetry* (New York: Oxford University Press, 1997). Sandra M. Gilbert and Susan Gubar, *The Madwoman in the Attic: The Woman Writer and the Nineteenth-Century Literary Imagination*, 2nd ed. (New Haven, CT: Yale University Press, 2000), 45-93. An analogous claim that the anxiety of influence is not an appropriate paradigm to analyze black literature is made by Henry Louis Gates in *The Signifying Monkey: A Theory of Afro-American Literary Criticism* (New York: Oxford University Press, 1988), 83. Yet, whereas Gates searches for the sources of this phenomenon in African roots or the black vernacular, I rather see it as a strategy for the legitimization of black tradition. This lack of desire to confront and defeat literary father figures also could be productively juxtaposed with Franz Fanon's controversial claim about the absence of the Oedipus complex among black men from colonized Martinique.

5. For a more detailed theoretical introduction of hegemonic masculinity, see Robert W. Connell, *Masculinities* (Cambridge: Polity Press, 2005), 37. For my discussion of hegemonic masculinity, see Anna Pochmara, "Are You a 'Real Man'?: the Construction of Hegemonic Masculinity in American Culture," *Polish Journal for American Studies* 2 (2009): 127-140.

6. Gail Bederman, *Manliness and Civilization: A Cultural History of Gender and Race in the United States, 1880-1917* (Chicago: University of Chicago Press, 1995). Michael S. Kimmel, "Consuming Manhood: The Feminization of American Culture and the Recreation of the Male Body, 1832-1920," in *The Male Body: Features, Destinies, Exposures*, ed. Leo Goldstein (Ann Arbor, MI: Michigan University Press, 1998) and "The Contemporary 'Cri-

sis' of Masculinity in Historical Perspective," in *The Making of Masculinities*, ed. Harry Brod (New York: Routlege, 1987). See also Michael S. Kimmel, *The History of Men: Essays in the History of American and British Masculinities* (Albany, NY: SUNY Press, 2005).

7. The focus on the working class is central, especially in the sociologist strand of black masculinities, among which *Cool Pose: The Dilemmas of Black Manhood in America* by Richard Majors and Janet Mancini Billson is the most influential (New York: Lexington Books, 1992). The working class and especially Marxist residue in the New Negro discourse is also the central interest of two New Negro Renaissance studies: William J. Maxwell, *New Negro Old Left: African-American Writing and Communism between the Wars* (New York: Columbia University Press, 1999) and Barbara Foley, *Spectres of 1919: Class and Nation in the Making of the New Negro* (Chicago: University of Illinois Press, 2003).

8. Marlon Bryan Ross, *Manning the Race: Reforming Black Men in the Jim Crow Era* (New York: NYU Press, 2004), 3, 7.

9. Kobena Mercer and Isaac Julien, "True Confessions," in *Black Male: Representations of Masculinity in Contemporary Art*, ed. Thelma Golden (New York: Whitney Museum of Art, 1994), 196.

10. For an analysis of the pitfalls inherent in the concept of racial authenticity in black and white discourse, see Cornel West, *Race Matters* (New York: Vintage Books, 1994), especially 37-39.

11. Despite the recent popularity of the New Negro movement, it did not attract much scholarly attention until the 1970s, when Nathan Huggins's *Harlem Renaissance* (1971) generated interest in 1920s Harlem. It was followed by the publication of David Levering Lewis's *When Harlem Was in Vogue* (1981). These two classic studies are primarily preoccupied with the success and failure of black aesthetics as an emancipatory strategy. To some extent, the earlier absence of scholarly interest can be explained by the critical evaluations from the 1930s and 1940s, discussed in Chapter 6, which represented the movement as lacking significance. A later strand of scholarship on the 1920s movement focused on its relation to mainstream American modernism and contemporaneous philosophical thought. The first scholarly work representing this approach was Houston A. Baker's *Modernism and the Harlem Renaissance* (1989). This angle of research was notably developed by Michael North in *The Dialect of Modernism: Race, Language, and Twentieth-Century Literature* (1994), by Ann Douglas in *Terrible Honesty: Mongrel Manhattan in the 1920s* (1995), by Sieglinde Lemke in *Primitivist Modernism: Black Culture and the Origins of Transatlantic Modernism* (1998), and by George Hutchinson in *The Harlem Renaissance in Black and White* (1997). Only relatively recently did we witness an outburst of scholarly interest in the gender politics of the movement. This perspective was initiated by the publication of Gloria T. Hull's *Color, Sex, and Poetry: Three Women Writers of the Harlem Renaissance* (1987) and continued by Cheryl A. Wall in *Women of the Harlem Renaissance* (1995). One of the latest approaches to the discourse of the movement focuses on the relationship between the New Negro movement, Marxist rhetoric, and the communist party, and it is represented by James Smethurst's *The New Red Negro: The Literary Left and African American Poetry, 1930-1946* (1999), William J. Maxwell's *New Negro, Old Left* (1999), and Barbara Foley's *Spectres of 1919: Class and Nation in the Making of the New Negro* (2003).

12. Ross, 193.

13. Richard Wright, *Black Boy (American Hunger)* (New York: Harper Collins, 1993), 83-84.

Chapter 1

1. W. E. B. Du Bois, "The Negro Race in the United States of America," in *On Sociology and the Black Community*, ed. Dan S. Green and Edwin D. Driver (Chicago: University of Chicago Press, 1978), 111.
2. Booker T. Washington, "The American Negro and His Economic Value," in *Negro Social and Political Thought, 1850-1920*, ed. Howard Brotz (New York: Basic Books, 1966), 423.
3. Dudley Randall, "Booker T. and W. E. B." in *Modern and Contemporary Afro-American Poetry*, ed. Bernard W. Bell (Boston: Allyn and Bacon, 1972), 69.
4. Alain Locke, "A Decade of Negro Self-Expression," in *The Critical Temper of Alain Locke*, ed. Jeffrey Stewart (New York: Garland, 1983), 7. Contemporary scholars share this view: for example, Houston A. Baker claims that these two rhetorical compositions principally contributed to the development of the mature art of the Harlem Renaissance (*Modernism and the Harlem Renaissance*, 71-72).
5. Histories of American literature introduce the debate as canonical; there are also many studies devoted to it specifically: Hae Sung Hwang, *Booker T. Washington and W. E. B. Du Bois: A Study in Race Leadership, 1895-1915* (Seoul: American Studies Institute, Seoul National University, 1992); Thomas E. Harris, *Analysis of the Clash over Issues between Booker T. Washington and W. E. B. Du Bois* (New York: Garland, 1993); Jacqueline M. Moore, *Booker T. Washington, W. E. B. Du Bois, and the Struggle for Racial Uplift* (Wilmington, DE: Scholarly Resources, 2003).
6. Harris, 60, 70-71.
7. Ross, 2.
8. Quoted in Eric J. Sundquist, *To Wake the Nations: Race in the Making of American Literature* (Cambridge, MA: Belknap Press, 1993), 238; emphasis added.
9. Herbert Shapiro, *White Violence and Black Response: From Reconstruction to Montgomery* (Amherst, MA: University of Massachusetts Press, 1988), 9-10, 32.
10. Bederman, 51; Shapiro, 30.
11. Richard M. Perloff, "The Press and Lynchings of African Americans," *Journal of Black Studies* 30, no. 3 (January 2000): 318.
12. Shapiro, 37.
13. Robyn Wiegman, *American Anatomies: Theorizing Race and Gender* (Durham, NC: Duke University Press, 1995), 82-89.
14. August Meier and Elliot Rudwick, *From Plantation to Ghetto* (New York: Hill and Wang, 1970), 213.
15. Benjamin Quarles, *The Negro in the Making of America* (New York: Collier Books, 1969), 193.
16. Bederman, 49.
17. Ibid., 18, 28.
18. Ibid., 19.
19. *Webster's New International Dictionary of the English Language*, 2nd ed., s.vv. "manly," "masculine."
20. Bederman, 17, 21.
21. Donald Gibson, "Chapter One of Booker T. Washington's *Up From Slavery* and the Feminization of the African American Male," in *Representing Black Men*, ed. Marcellus Blount and George Philbert Cunningham (New York: Routledge, 1996), 95; Louis Lomax, introduction to *Up from Slavery*, by Booker T. Washington (New York: Dell Publishing, 1965), 13.

22. Maurice O. Wallace, *Constructing the Black Masculine: Identity and Ideality in African American Men's Literature, 1775-1995* (Durham, NC: Duke University Press, 2002).
23. Gibson, 95.
24. Shapiro, 137.
25. Booker T. Washington, *Up from Slavery* (New York: Dell Publishing, 1965), 22, 23, 27, 49.
26. Shapiro, 6.
27. *Up from Slavery*, 63.
28. Ibid., 64; emphasis added, 155.
29. Ibid., 120, 121, 223.
30. Shapiro, 137-138.
31. Ibid.
32. *Up from Slavery*, 22.
33. When juxtaposed with Douglass's narrative, this choice seems even more meaningful, since Douglass, in his act of self-naming, changes his original name "Frederick Augustus *Washington* Bailey" into Frederick Douglass under the accidental influence of Walter Scott's "The Lady of the Lake," whose characters are among others James Douglass and Ellen Douglass.
34. *Up from Slavery*, 79.
35. Ibid., 48-50.
36. Ibid., 130-131; emphasis added.
37. Ibid., 183, 117-118, 95.
38. Ibid., 78.
39. Ibid., 186.
40. Ibid., 18, 20.
41. Ibid., 223-224.
42. Zora Neale Hurston, *Their Eyes Were Watching God* (New York: HarperCollins, 1990), 73.
43. *Up from Slavery*, 72.
44. Bederman, 50.
45. Ibid., 24-25.
46. It should be noted, however, that despite Washington's embrace of the imposed cultural hierarchy, the introduction of ethnic and cultural differences embodied by Native Americans destabilizes the hegemonic ideology of the white man's burden. Intercultural exchange makes Washington realize that "no white American ever thinks that any other race is wholly civilized until he wears the white man's clothes, eats the white man's food, speaks the white man's language, and professes the white man's religion" (77). The passage suggests that the standards of white civilization are arbitrary and are coercively imposed on "other races." The fact that Washington admits a possibility of different cultural standards and yet follows the hegemonic route illuminates the pragmatism of his emancipatory strategy.
47. Ibid., 76.
48. Frederick Douglass, *The Life and Times of Frederick Douglass: His Early Life as a Slave, His Escape from Bondage, and His Complete History*, ed. Rayford Whittingham Logan (Mineola, NY: Courier Dover Publications, 2003), 205.
49. *Up from Slavery*, 77, 108.
50. Ross, 59.
51. *Up from Slavery*, 77.
52. Ibid., 42; 47-48; 51, 95, 126.
53. Ibid., 95, 126, 127; emphasis added.
54. Ibid., 42.

55. Such a choice of predecessors illustrates Hortense J. Spillers's thesis about the African American subject being "twice-fathered," by the biological black father and symbolically by the white slave master. Since Spillers's concept refers to chattel slavery, if read from this perspective, Washington's choice of father figures seems even more accommodationist and conservative. "'The Permanent Obliquity of an In(pha)llibly Straight': In the Time of the Daughters and the Fathers," in *Changing Our Own Words: Essays on Criticism, Theory, and Writing by Black Women*, ed. Cheryl A. Wall (New Brunswick, NJ: Rutgers University Press, 1989), 127-149.

56. *Up from Slavery*, 169-170.

57. W. E. B. Du Bois, *Writings: The Suppression of the African Slave-Trade, The Souls of Black Folk, Dusk of Dawn, Essays and Articles*, ed. Nathan Huggins (New York: Viking Press, 1986), 1286.

58. Harris, 37; W. E. B. Du Bois, *The Autobiography of W. E. B. Du Bois: A Soliloquy on Viewing My Life from the Last Decade of Its First Century* (New York: International Publishers, 1968), 222.

59. Baker, 51.

60. Cornel West, *The Cornel West Reader* (New York: Basic Civitas Books, 1999), 88.

61. Hazel V. Carby, *Race Men: The W. E. B. Du Bois Lectures* (Cambridge, MA: Harvard University Press, 1998), 10.

62. W. E. B. Du Bois, *Darkwater: Voices from Within the Veil* (New York: Schocken Books, 1972).

63. Stuart Hall, "The Rediscovery of 'Ideology': Return of the Repressed in Media Studies," in *Culture, Society and the Media*, ed. M. Gurevitch, T. Bennett, J. Curran, and J. Woollacott (London: Methuen, 1982), 79-80.

64. W. E. B. Du Bois, *The Souls of Black Folk* (New York: Vintage Books, 1990), 9, 74, 10, 11, 42, 44, 65, 70, 126, 128, 142, 159.

65. Ibid., 135, 104.

66. Ibid., 18, 12, 23, 28, 29, 29, 30, 31, 37, 43, 47, 60, 100, 119, 126, 162.

67. W. E. B. Du Bois, "The Talented Tenth," in *Writings*, 842; emphasis added.

68. Ibid., 851-852, 845, 842-852, 848.

69. *Autobiography*, 236-237; emphasis added.

70. "The Talented Tenth," 842, 855.

71. *The Souls of Black Folk*, 4.

72. *The Souls of Black Folk*, 50-51.

73. *Darkwater*, 5.

74. Ibid., 147.

75. "The Negro Race in the United States of America," 91-92; "A Question of Policy," in *Writings*, 1156; "Harding and Social Equality," in *Writings*, 1192; "An Open Letter to Woodrow Wilson," in *Writings*, 1144.

76. *The Souls of Black Folk*, 110; emphasis added.

77. Ibid., 36-48.

78. David D. Gilmore, *Manhood in the Making: Cultural Concepts of Masculinity* (New Haven, CT: Yale University Press, 1990), 11.

79. Bederman, 10.

80. *Darkwater*, 8, 110.

81. W. E. B. Du Bois, "The Religion of the American Negro," in *On Sociology and the Black Community*, 223-224.

82. Ibid., 48; emphasis added.

83. W. E. B. Du Bois, "I Am Resolved," in *Writings*, 1137; emphasis added.

84. "The Negro Race in the United States of America," 111.

85. W. E. B. Du Bois, "The Niagara Movement Statement," in *Writings*, 184, 186; emphasis added.
86. W. E. B. Du Bois, "The Conservation of Races," in *Writings*, 826.
87. *Darkwater*, 141.
88. Arnold Rampersad claims that the main difference between Du Bois and Washington lies precisely in their rendering of slavery – according to Washington, cruel and immoral yet to some extent beneficial for black people; according to Du Bois, a key pathological influence on the contemporary black social position, family relations, economic and political attitudes. "The Founding Fathers: Frederick Douglass, W. E. B. Du Bois, Washington," in *Slavery and the Literary Imagination*, ed. Deborah E. McDowell and Arnold Rampersad (Baltimore, MD: Johns Hopkins University Press, 1989), 1-25.
89. *The Souls of Black Folk*, 12; emphasis added.
90. *Race Men*, 33.
91. "The Negro Race in the United States of America," 86.
92. "The Conservation of Races," 826; emphasis added.
93. W. E. B. Du Bois, "The Problem of Amusement," in *On Sociology and the Black Community*, 237.
94. W. E. B. Du Bois, "The Philadelphia Negro," in *On Sociology and the Black Community*, 126, "The Black North in 1901: New York," in *On Sociology and the Black Community*, 143.
95. W. E. B. Du Bois, "Negroes of Farmville, Virginia," in *On Sociology and the Black Community*, 171.
96. *The Souls of Black Folk*, 27.
97. *Race Men*, 38.
98. "The Damnation of Women," in *Darkwater*, 180-181.
99. Ibid., 184, 186.
100. Ibid., 177.
101. *Race Men*, 19.
102. "Consuming Manhood: The Feminization of American Culture and the Recreation of the Male Body, 1832-1920," 23.
103. W. E. B. Du Bois, "The Negroes of Dougherty County, Georgia," in *On Sociology and the Black Community*, 162-163.
104. Ross, 153, 159.
105. W. E. B. Du Bois, "The Negro American Family," in *On Sociology and the Black Community*, 208-209.
106. George L. Mosse, *Nationalism and Sexuality: Respectability and Abnormal Sexuality in Modern Europe* (New York: Howard Fertig, 1985).
107. *The Souls of Black Folk*, 175.
108. Ibid., 179.
109. *Darkwater*, 53. The poem was first published in 1914 in the *Crisis* as "The Burden of Black Women."
110. Ibid., 54.
111. Jacquelyn Dowd Hall, "'The Mind that Burns in Each Body': Women, Rape, and Racial Violence," in *Powers of Desire: The Politics of Sexuality*, ed. Anne Snitow, Christine Stansell, and Sharon Thompson (New York: Monthly Review Press, 1983), 337.
112. In "Litany of Atlanta" we learn that "God cannot be white," and in the following text "the black Christ" is called on to be born (27, 54). The prayer is answered in "The Second Coming," where, at Christmas, three bishops, each of a different race, witness the birth of a black child to a mulatto girl in a shed in the South. The figure returns explicitly in the title of "Jesus Christ in Texas," where he remains recognizable only to

black people and witnesses the lynching of a black thief. The two figures – that of the black man unjustly accused of an assault on a white woman and that of the black Christ – merge into one, as the lynched and burned body changes into "heaven-tall and earth-wide" "crimson cross" (133). This fusion is later repeated in "The Prayers of God" from the perspective of the white man. He confesses to God that "in Thy name, I lynched a Nigger" (251). God's answer is missing but it is repeated in the next line of the white man's monologue: "Thou? /Thee?/I lynched Thee?/...That black and riven thing was it Thee?" (251). The volume ends with a more positive scenario of the black man as both Jesus Christ and Adam of the human race on a post-disaster earth.

113. "The Religion of the American Negro," 221.

114. Sundquist, 596.

115. Ibid., 592-626.

116. Clifford Putney, *Muscular Christianity: Manhood and Sports in Protestant America, 1880-1920* (Cambridge, MA: Harvard University Press, 2003), 42, 92-98.

117. The link between biracial heritage, the implicit violation of black womanhood, and the figure of Christ is interestingly echoed in one of Langston Hughes's mulatto texts, the poem "Cross." The title refers to both the black and white heritage of the speaker and Christ imagery, yet the Christ persona here is far from being a militant avenger and he only tries to deal with his liminal mulatto identity.

118. *Darkwater*, 269.

119. W. E. B. Du Bois, "Returning Soldiers," in *The Portable Harlem Renaissance*, ed. David Levering Lewis (New York: Viking, 1994), 4, 5; emphasis added.

120. W. E. B. Du Bois, "The Negro College," in *Writings*, 1018, 1019, 1019; emphasis added.

121. Quoted in Harris, 52.

122. W. E. B. Du Bois, "Propaganda and World War," in *Writings*, 731-732.

Chapter 2

1. Alain Locke, "Negro Youth Speaks," *The New Negro: An Interpretation*, ed. Alain Locke (New York: Albert and Charles Boni, 1925), 47.

2. Quoted in Horace Kallen, "Alain Locke and Cultural Pluralism," *The Journal of Philosophy* 54, no. 5 (February 1957): 122.

3. Plato, "The Symposium," in *The Dialogues of Plato*, trans. Benjamin Jowett (Oxford: Clarendon Press, 1875), 62.

4. Countee Cullen to Alain Locke, box 164-13, folder 30, Alain Locke Papers, Moorland-Spingarn Research Center, Howard University.

5. Eugene C. Holmes, "Alain Leroy Locke: A Sketch," *The Phylon Quarterly* 20, no. 1 (1959), 84.

6. Ross, 264.

7. Ibid., 6.

8. Ibid., 234-237, 281-284.

9. Martin Summers, *Manliness and Its Discontents: The Black Middle Class and the Transformation of Masculinity, 1900-1930* (Chapel Hill, NC: University of North Carolina Press, 2004), 206, 244.

10. Countee Cullen to Alain Locke, box 164-13, folder 30, Alain Locke Papers, Moorland-Spingarn Research Center, Howard University.

11. Carl Van Vechten to Alain Locke, box LO-MJ, Carl Van Vechten Correspondence JWJ, Beinecke Rare Book and Manuscript Library, Yale University.

12. Arnold Rampersad, "The Book That Launched the Harlem Renaissance," *The Journal of Blacks in Higher Education* 38 (winter 2002-2003): 87.

13. For a detailed examination of this issue, see Henry Louis Gates, "The Trope of a New Negro and the Reconstruction of the Image of the Black," *Representations* 24, no. 1 (autumn 1988): 129-155. For a detailed analysis of the connections between the black and white American Renaissance's rhetoric, see Gregory Holmes Singleton, "Birth, Rebirth, and the 'New Negro' of the 1920s," *Phylon* 43, no. 1 (1982): 29-45.

14. "The Trope of a New Negro and the Reconstruction of the Image of the Black," 131.

15. J. E. MacBrady, introduction to *A New Negro for a New Century: An Accurate and Up-to-Date Record of the Upward Struggles of the Negro Race*, by Booker T. Washington, Fannie Barrier Williams, and N. B. Wood (Chicago: American Publishing House, 1900), 4 (emphasis added), 28, 47.

16. Bederman, 44.

17. Ross, 63.

18. "African American Regulars in Cuba (Continued)," in *A New Negro for a New Century: An Accurate and Up-to-Date Record of the Upward Struggles of the Negro Race*, 51-52.

19. "The Trope of a New Negro and the Reconstruction of the Image of the Black," 141.

20. Walter White, *Fire in the Flint* (New York: Alfred A. Knopf, 1924), 167.

21. Fannie B. Williams, "Club Movement Among Colored Women," in *A New Negro for a New Century: An Accurate and Up-to-Date Record of the Upward Struggles of the Negro Race* (Chicago: American Publishing House, 1900), 424; emphasis added.

22. Alain Locke, "Enter the New Negro," *Survey Graphic* 6, no. 6 (March 1925): 631.

23. "The Trope of a New Negro and the Reconstruction of the Image of the Black," 147.

24. William J. Maxwell, *New Negro, Old Left*; Barbara Foley, *Spectres of 1919: Class and Nation in the Making of the New Negro*, 14.

25. Henry Louis Gates Jr. and Gene Andrew Jarrett, eds. *The New Negro: Readings on Race, Representation, and African American Culture, 1892-1938* (Princeton, NJ: Princeton University Press, 2007), 13.

26. Foley, 71.

27. Alain Locke, "The New Negro," in Locke, *The New Negro: An Interpretation*, 3-16.

28. "The New Negro," 3.

29. *The Souls of Black Folk*, 24. This association plays into the sentiment of the feminization of boyhood due to the feminization of teaching at the time. For analyses of this phenomenon, see Joe L. Dubbert, "Progressivism and the Masculinity Crisis," in *The American Man*, eds. Elizabeth Pleck and Joseph H. Pleck (Englewood Cliffs, NJ: Prentice-Hall, 1980), 303-320; Jeffrey P. Hantover, "The Boy Scouts and the Validation of Masculinity," in *The American Man*, eds. Elizabeth Pleck and Joseph H. Pleck (Englewood Cliffs, NJ: Prentice-Hall, 1980), 285-301.

30. For a detailed discussion of the concept of Americanness in the Harlem Renaissance, see Gregory Holmes Singleton, "Birth, Rebirth, and the 'New Negro' of the 1920s."

31. Foley, 221.

32. Alain Locke, "Harlem," *Survey Graphic* 6, no. 6 (March 1925): 629-630.

33. Foley, 175-182, emphasis added; Hutchinson, 78-93.

34. "The New Negro," 6.

35. Ibid.; emphasis added.

36. "The Contemporary 'Crisis' of Masculinity in Historical Perspective," 121-53.

37. For example, he claims that "if it ever was warrantable to regard and treat the Negro en masse, it is becoming with every day less possible, more unjust and more ridiculous" ("Enter the New Negro" 631), and in a later text he even concludes that "there

is...no 'The Negro'" ("Who and What is 'Negro'?" *Opportunity* 20, no. 2 (February 1942): 19-37).

38. "The New Negro," 14; emphasis added.
39. Annette Kolodny, *The Land Before Her: Fantasy and Experience of the American Frontiers, 1630-1860* (Chapel Hill, NC: University of North Carolina Press, 1984); Nina Baym, "Melodramas of Beset Manhood: How Theories of American Fiction Exclude Women Authors," *American Quarterly* 33, no. 2 (summer 1981): 123-139.
40. Alain Locke, *Negro in Art: A Pictorial Record of the Negro Artist and of the Negro Theme in Art* (Washington, DC: Associates in Negro Folk Education, 1940), 22; emphasis added.
41. For the connections between American masculinity and the Western expansion, see Alan Trachtenberg, *The Incorporation of America: Culture and Society in the Gilded Age* (New York: Hill and Wang, 1982); "Consuming Manhood: The Feminization of American Culture and the Recreation of the Male Body, 1832-1920;" and Bederman.
42. "Harlem," 629.
43. *Women of the Harlem Renaissance*, 4. This argument is also supported by Summers, who agrees that Locke's choice of examples of the New Negro reinforces the "conscious gendering of the cultural movement" (202), and by Foley who contends that "neither version of Locke's anthology paid much attention to the New Negro who was not male" (228).
44. "The New Negro," 6; emphasis added.
45. Elise Johnson McDougald, "The Task of Negro Womanhood," in Locke, *The New Negro: An Interpretation*, 376, 381. Interestingly, McDougald is silent about black gender inequalities, yet she notices the parasitical relationship between black women's labor and white upper-class women's liberation from the domestic sphere obligations: "Through her drudgery, the women of other groups find leisure time for progress" (379).
46. The only instance where a New Woman is alluded to is in an article on the new black art, "To Certain of Our Philistines," where she surfaces as "the parasitic, society-loving 'flapper.'" The "parasitic" and "society-loving" qualities suggest the white shallow primitivist interest in black culture primarily represented at the time by the practice of slumming, which is condemned by Locke in the article. It is significant that he chooses emancipated (white) femininity to represent white exploitation of the black community and arts. In this indirect way, the New Woman is represented as being at war with the emancipatory project of the Negro Renaissance. As a white flapper, she also parallels the function of the white female patron collaborating with the Old Negro. Alain Locke, "To Certain of Our Philistines," *Opportunity* 3 (May 1925): 156.
47. Alain Locke, foreword to *The New Negro: An Interpretation* (New York: Alfred and Charles Boni, 1925), p. xxv. Alain Locke, "Welcome the New South," *Opportunity* 4 (1926): 375.
48. Quoted in Foley, 102.
49. Charles S. Johnson, "Women's Brains," *Opportunity* 1 (1923): 4.
50. "The Trope of a New Negro and the Reconstruction of the Image of the Black," Sally Mitchell, "New Women, Old and New," *Victorian Literature and Culture* 27, no. 2 (1999): 586.
51. Carroll, Smith-Rosenberg, "Discourses of Sexuality and Subjectivity: The New Woman, 1870-1936," in *Hidden From History: Reclaiming the Gay and Lesbian Past*, eds. Martin Bauml Duberman, Martha Vicinus, and George Chauncey, Jr. (New York: New American Library, 1989), 266.
52. Michelle Elizabeth Tusan, "Inventing the New Woman: Print Culture and Identity Politics During the *Fin-de-Siècle*," *Victorian Periodical Review* 31, no. 2 (1998): 169-182.
53. Smith-Rosenberg, 273.

54. Kevin J. Mumford, *Interzones: Black/White Sex Districts in Chicago and New York in the Early Twentieth Century* (New York: Columbia University Press, 1997), 109.

55. Hazel V. Carby, "Policing the Black Woman's Body in an Urban Context," *Critical Inquiry* 18, no. 4 (summer 1992): 741.

56. Foreword to *The New Negro: An Interpretation*, p. ix; emphasis added.

57. Charlene Avallone, "What American Renaissance? The Gendered Genealogy of a Critical Discourse," *PMLA* 112, no. 5 (1997): 1002.

58. Ralph Waldo Emerson, "Self-Reliance," in *The Norton Anthology of American Literature*, ed. Nina Baym, Volume B, 6th ed. (New York: W. W. Norton & Company, 2003), 1164, 1162.

59. For the function of the rites of passage, see Conrad Kottak, "Anthropological Analysis of Mass Enculturation," in *Researching American Culture* (Ann Arbor, MI: University of Michigan Press, 1982), 40-74. For connections between initiation rituals and masculine identity, see Elizabeth Badinter, *XY: On Masculine Identity* (New York: Columbia University Press, 1992), especially 74-75; David Gilmore, *Manhood in the Making: Cultural Concepts of Masculinity*; and Michael S. Kimmel and Michael Kaufman, "Weekend Warriors: The New Men's Movement," in *Theorizing Masculinities*, ed. Harry Brod (Thousand Oaks, CA: Sage Publications, 1994), 259-288.

60. D. H. Lawrence, *Studies in Classic American Literature* (Dallas: Penguin Books, 1985), 79.

61. See "Consuming Manhood: The Feminization of American Culture and the Recreation of the Male Body, 1832-1920" and Bederman.

62. These images also fit what Foley terms as the organic trope omnipresent in the 1920s discourse and expressed in Locke's "reliance on folk and soil as mediating categories in the signifying chain of metonymic nationalism." The organic trope is responsible for the limitations of secondary race consciousness advocated by Locke, 222.

63. "The New Negro," 4; Foreword, p. xxvii; "The New Negro," 4; emphasis added.

64. "The New Negro," 4.

65. *The New Negro*, p. viii.

66. Alain Locke to Langston Hughes, box 104, folder 1975, Langston Hughes Papers JWJ MSS 26, Beinecke Rare Book and Manuscript Library, Yale University; emphasis added.

67. *The New Negro*, p. viii.

68. Alain Locke, "Youth Speaks," *Survey Graphic* 6, no. 6 (March 1925): 659.

69. Alain Locke, "Negro Youth Speaks," in *The New Negro: An Interpretation*, 47; emphasis added.

70. "Youth Speaks," 659.

71. Alain Locke and W. E. B. Du Bois, "The Younger Literary Movement," *Crisis* 28 (February 1924): 161; Alain Locke, "Jingo, Counter-Jingo and Us: A Retrospective Review of Negro Literature," *Opportunity* 16 (January and February 1938), 11.

72. Charles S. Johnson to Alain Locke, box 164-40, folder 23-29, Alain Locke Papers, Moorland-Spingarn Research Center, Howard University; emphasis added.

73. Jessie Fauset to Alain Locke, box 164-28, folder 41, Alain Locke Papers, Moorland-Spingarn Research Center, Howard University. A similar erasure can be found in the fact that *Four Negro Poets* edited by Locke in 1927 do not include any women poets. He anthologizes Hughes, Toomer, Cullen, and McKay, and for example chooses not to include Georgia Douglas Johnson (New York: Simon and Schuster, 1927). Her absence from the volume is striking, as her publishing career follows that of McKay's publications. Her second poetry volume *Bronze* was to a large extent concerned with race issues and Locke judges that "it represents more perhaps an occasion of seeing the 'color problem' at the heart, as it affects the inner life;" "Review of Bronze: A Book of

Verse," *Crisis* 25 (February 1923): 161. Yet both Du Bois and Locke, in their reviews of *Bronze* and *An Autumn Love Cycle*, emphasize its significance mostly in terms of expressing the black woman's experience rather than the race experience in general. This labeling prevents Johnson from being included in the category of "the Negro poet."

74. Alain Locke, "The American Temperament," in *The Critical Temper of Alain Locke*, 401. Locke's concept of the national character parallels his approach to the Negro character, since he acknowledges race to be an "ethnic fiction," yet he finds it useful for the advancement of the community, cultural exchange, and the development of American culture in general. See "Who and What is Negro?," "Jingo, Counter-Jingo and Us," 7-42. One could also interpret Locke's approach to black group subjectivity as an example of Spivak's strategic essentialism, "a strategic use of positivist essentialism in a scrupulously visible political interest," a tactical, temporary, and critical deployment of the concept of the essential subject by the oppressed. Foley argues that "*secondary race consciousness* was a term Locke chose to designate this 'revised' sense of social race – the 'counter-theory' or 'counterdoctrine' – for which he was issuing his call." She quotes Locke's argument that "such race consciousness has been a feature of national revivals in European politics and European art...and in political propaganda for recognition of the right to self-determination." For a detailed discussion and critique of Locke's secondary race consciousness, see Foley, 205-213.

75. "The American Temperament," 401-402.

76. "Self-Reliance," 1161.

77. Charles S. Johnson to Alain Locke, box 164-40, folder 23-29, Alain Locke Papers, Moorland-Spingarn Research Center, Howard University.

78. Gwendolyn Bennett to Alain Locke, box 164-13, folder 30, Alain Locke Papers, Moorland-Spingarn Research Center, Howard University; emphasis added.

79. Alexander Durnham to Alain Locke, box 164-26, folders 20 and 19; Alain Locke Papers, Moorland-Spingarn Research Center, Howard University.

80. Richmond Barthe to Alain Locke, box 164-12, folder 37, Alain Locke Papers, Moorland-Spingarn Research Center, Howard University.

81. Le Roy Foster to Alain Locke, box 164-30, folder 11, Alain Locke Papers, Moorland-Spingarn Research Center, Howard University.

82. Quoted in Holmes, 85; emphasis added.

83. Alain Locke to Langston Hughes, box 104, folder 1975, Langston Hughes Papers JWJ MSS 26, Beinecke Rare Book and Manuscript Library, Yale University; emphasis added.

84. Alain Locke to Carl Van Vechten, box LO-MJ, Carl Van Vechten Correspondence JWJ, Beinecke Rare Book and Manuscript Library, Yale University.

85. Alain Locke to Countee Cullen and an untitled note, box 164-22, folder 36, Alain Locke Papers, Moorland-Spingarn Research Center, Howard University.

86. Alain Locke to Langston Hughes, box 104, folder 1975, Langston Hughes Papers JWJ MSS 26, Beinecke Rare Book and Manuscript Library, Yale University; emphasis added.

87. Alain Locke to James Weldon Johnson, box 13, folder 297, James Weldon Johnson Papers (Correspondence) JWJ MSS, Beinecke Rare Book and Manuscript Library, Yale University.

88. Albert Dunham to Alain Locke, box 164-26, folder 19, Alain Locke Papers, Moorland-Spingarn Research Center, Howard University; emphasis added.

89. Bruce Nugent to Alain Locke, box 164-75, folder 18, Alain Locke Papers, Moorland-Spingarn Research Center, Howard University.

90. Ross, 6.

91. Badinter, 68-69; emphasis added.

92. Ibid., 69.

93. Locke's references to European discourses need not be perceived as exceptional. The connections between black American culture, mainstream American culture, and Europe at the time have been discussed by North in *The Dialect of Modernism: Race, Language, and Twentieth-Century Literature* and Paul Gilroy in *Black Atlantic: Modernity and Double Consciousness* (London: Verso, 1993). A comparative analysis of Locke's discourse and transatlantic modernism would be a productive endeavor, but it is beyond the scope of this study.

94. Alain Locke to Langston Hughes, box 104, folder 1975, Langston Hughes Papers JWJ MSS 26, Beinecke Rare Book and Manuscript Library, Yale University.

95. "The Symposium," 62.

96. Ibid., 60.

97. Alain Locke to Langston Hughes, box 104, folder 1975, Langston Hughes Papers JWJ MSS 26, Beinecke Rare Book and Manuscript Library, Yale University; emphasis added.

98. Ross, 199.

99. Michel Foucault, *The Use of Pleasure: The History of Sexuality*, trans. Robert Hurley (New York: Vintage Books, 1985), 188-193, 196, 201.

100. Yvonne Ivory, "The Urning and His Own: Individualism and the *Fin-de-Siècle* Invert," *German Studies Review* 26, no. 2 (2003): 334.

101. Edward Carpenter, *Ioläus: An Anthology of Friendship*, (London and Manchester: Swan Sonnenschein & Co. Limited and S. Clarke, 1906), 37-38.

102. Alain Locke to Langston Hughes, box 104, folder 1975, Langston Hughes Papers JWJ MSS 26, Beinecke Rare Book and Manuscript Library, Yale University; emphasis added.

103. A. B. Christa Schwarz, *Gay Voices of the Harlem Renaissance* (Bloomington, IN: Indiana University Press, 2003), 12.

104. Foley, 194. She criticizes this process as "a containing centrifugal force of a reformist nationalism" and contrasts it with the receding influence of John Brown.

105. "The American Temperament," 404, 37.

106. George Hutchinson, "The Whitman Legacy and the Harlem Renaissance," in *Walt Whitman: The Centennial Essays*, ed. Ed Folsom (Iowa City, IA: University of Iowa Press, 1994), 201, 204-205.

107. Countee Cullen to Alain Locke, box 164-25, folder 35-40, Alain Locke Papers, Moorland-Spingarn Research Center, Howard University.

108. Richmond Barthe to Alain Locke, box 164-26, folder 19, Alain Locke Papers, Moorland-Spingarn Research Center, Howard University.

109. Alain Locke to Langston Hughes, box 104, folder 1975, Langston Hughes Papers JWJ MSS 26, Beinecke Rare Book and Manuscript Library, Yale University.

110. Langston Hughes to Alain Locke, box 164-38, folder 5, Alain Locke Papers, Moorland-Spingarn Research Center, Howard University.

111. M. Jimmie Killingsworth, "Whitman's 'Calamus': A Rhetorical Prehistory of the First Gay American." Presented at the Modern Language Association Convention, San Francisco, December 1998. http://www-english.tamu.edu/pubs/body/calamus.html.

112. Arnold Rampersad, *The Life of Langston Hughes: 1914-1967: I Dream a World* (New York: Oxford University Press, 2002), 69.

113. Countee Cullen to Alain Locke, box 164-25, folder 35-40, Alain Locke Papers, Moorland-Spingarn Research Center, Howard University; emphasis added.

114. See e.g. David E. Goldweber, "Cullen, Keats and the Privileged Liar," *Papers on Language & Literature* 38, no. 1 (winter 2002): 29-49.
115. Claude McKay to Alain Locke, box 164-40, folder 8-9, Alain Locke Papers, Moorland-Spingarn Research Center, Howard University.
116. For a discussion of McKay's and Hughes's critique of Locke's patronage and attack on his effeminate style, see Ross, 284-291.
117. Schwarz, 13; emphasis added; Ross, 289; George Chauncey, *Gay New York: Gender, Urban Culture, and the Making of the Gay Male World, 1890-1940* (New York: Basic Books, 1994), 264.
118. Richmond Barthe to Alain Locke, box 164-12, folder 37, Alain Locke Papers, Moorland-Spingarn Research Center, Howard University; emphasis added.
119. Albert Dunham to Alain Locke, box 164-26, folder 19, Alain Locke Papers, Moorland-Spingarn Research Center, Howard University; emphasis added.
120. Lewis Alexander to Alain Locke, box 164-12, folder 37, Alain Locke Papers, Moorland-Spingarn Research Center, Howard University.
121. Alain Locke to Scholley Pace, box 1, folder 28, Dorothy Peterson Collection JWJ, Beinecke Rare Book and Manuscript Library, Yale University.
122. Alain Locke to Langston Hughes, box 104, folder 1975, Langston Hughes Papers JWJ MSS 26, Beinecke Rare Book and Manuscript Library, Yale University.
123. Alain Locke to Rudolf Dressler, box 164-26, folder 6, Alain Locke Papers, Moorland-Spingarn Research Center, Howard University.
124. Quoted in John Alexander Williams, "Ecstasies of the Young: Sexuality, the Youth Movement, and Moral Panic in Germany on the Eve of the First World War," *Central European History* 34, no. 2 (2001): 168.
125. Quoted in Yvory, 338.
126. Ivory, 338.
127. Ibid., 333-334.
128. Johnny Washington, *Evolution, History, and Destiny, Letters to Alain Locke (1886-1954) and Others* (New York: Peter Lang Pub Inc, 2002), 136.
129. Ivory, 330.
130. Ibid., 337.
131. Von St. Ch. Waldecke, "Die Physiologische Freundschaft in der Auffassung der Grossen Amerikanischen Dichter-Denker," *Der Eigene* 9 (1924): 293-299.
132. Thijs Maasen, "Man-Boy Friendships on Trial: On the Shift in the Discourse on Boy Love in the Early Twentieth Century," *Journal of Homosexuality* 20, no. 1/2 (1990): 51.
133. Ibid., 51.
134. Quoted in Maasen, 57.
135. John Alexander Williams, "Ecstasies of the Young: Sexuality, the Youth Movement, and Moral Panic in Germany on the Eve of the First World War," *Central European History* 34, no. 2 (2001), 164.
136. Ibid.
137. "Die Lieblingsminne in der griechischen Vasenmalerei," *Der Eigene* 9 (1922): 333. Moreover, the title echoes another influential anthology of male friendship: Elisar von Kupffer's *Lieblingminne und Freundesliebe in der Weltliteratur* (1900), which celebrates the relationship between the *eromenos* and the *erastes* as masculinist, noble, and significant for Western literature and history.
138. The intertextual link between German male nudes and Locke's visualization of the black male artist can be further complicated if read in the context of Hazel V. Carby's examination of Paul Robeson's Greek-stylized nudes by Nickolas Murray. Carby claims that the image satisfied the white modernist desire for an essentialized whole-

ness, here signified by the black male body. She also argues that even though the Antique stylization was supposed to function as a de-sexualizing alibi, the photographic gaze is homoerotic and represents the white modernist desire to "recover and claim an essence of masculinity," *Race Men*, 46-64. This reading points to the fact that Locke's preoccupation with youth is parallel to hegemonic discourses of primitivism and the remaking of masculinity. Locke's peculiar primitivism will be further discussed in the next chapter.

139. Eric Garber, "T'Aint Nobody's Bizness: Homosexuality in 1920s Harlem," in *Gay Roots: Twenty Years of Gay Sunshine: An Anthology of Gay History, Sex, Politics, and Culture*, ed. Winston Leyland (San Francisco: Gay Sunshine Press, 1991), 141-148; George Chauncey, *Gay New York: Gender, Urban Culture, and the Making of the Gay Male World, 1890-1940* (New York: Basic Books, 1994).

140. Claude McKay, *Home to Harlem* (London: Black Classics, 2000), 88.

141. Langston Hughes, *The Big Sea* (New York: Knopf, 1945), 225-228.

142. Mumford, 85-86.

143. Ibid., 83.

144. Characteristically, many of these philosophical ideals were appropriated not much later by another German movement whose rhetoric was not race-blind – the fascist discourse drew on the same sources and also propagated boy bonding in the infamous *Hitlerjugend*. The issue of racial purity and mongrelization, both in Germany and in America, Locke's strategic essentialism, and their connection to modernist appropriations of black cultures appear to be a productive object for a cultural studies analysis, which is however beyond the span of this study.

145. Chauncey, 99-130; specifically on Locke, 265.

Chapter 3

1. Alain Locke, ["On Literary Stereotypes"], in *Fighting Words*, ed. Donald Ogden Stewart (New York: New Directions, 1940), 76-77.

2. Hawthorne to Ticknor, letter of February 2, 1855, in *Letters of Hawthorne to William D. Ticknor, 1851-1864* (Newark, NJ: Cateret Book Club, 1910), 75.

3. Ann Douglas, *The Feminization of American Culture* (New York: Knopf, 1977), 3-16.

4. Frederick Jackson Turner, *The Frontier in American History* (Mineola, NY: Courier Dover Publications, 1996), 37.

5. Trachtenberg, 13.

6. Robert E. Park, *Race and Culture: Essays in the Sociology of Contemporary Man* (Glencoe, NY: Free Press, 1950), 280.

7. Ann Douglas, *Terrible Honesty: Mongrel Manhattan in the 1920s* (New York: Farrar, Straus & Giroux, 1995), 6-7, 21-22, 28, 42, 53, 115, 298.

8. Another interesting link between Douglas's reading of sentimentalism and the black liberation discourse is the text of *Uncle Tom's Cabin*, which for Douglas was the epitome of the feminization of American culture, whereas in the racial discourse it is the central symbol of the white liberal patronizing position complemented with black feminine passivity.

9. The list of the articles in which sentimentalism is condemned by Locke as an artistic strategy include the following texts published in the *Opportunity*: "A Review of Goat Alley, by Ernest Howard Culbertson" (1923), "The Colonial Literature of France" (1923), "Roland Hayes: an Appreciation" (1923), "Apropos of Africa" (1924), "To Certain of Our Philistines" (1925), "Welcome the New South: A Review" (1926), "Review

of *Sex Expression in Literature*, by V. F. Calverton" (1927), "1928: A Retrospective Review" (1929), "This Year of Grace" (1931), "We Turn to Prose" (1932), "The Saving Grace of Realism" (1934), "Deep River, Deeper Sea" (1936), "Martyrdom to Glad Music: The Irony of Black Patriotism" (1936), "Jingo, Counter-Jingo and Us" (1938), "The New Negro 'New' or 'Newer'" (1939), "Negro Music Goes to Par" (1939), "Dry Fields and Green Pastures" (1940), "Of Native Sons: Real and Otherwise" (1941).

10. Alain Locke, "Jingo, Counter-Jingo and Us," 27; "Harlem: Dark Weather-Vane," *Survey Graphic* 24 (August 1936): 457.

11. *Terrible Honesty*, 32.

12. W. E. B. Du Bois, "Criteria of Negro Art," *Crisis* 32 (October 1926): 296.

13. Alain Locke, "1928: A Retrospective Review," *Opportunity* 7 (1929): 9.

14. Ross, 15.

15. Virginia Woolf, *Mr Bennet and Mrs Brown* (London: Hogarth, 1928), 4.

16. Alain Locke, "A Review of *Goat Alley*, by Ernest Howard Culbertson," *Opportunity* 1 (1923): 30.

17. "1928: A Retrospective Review," 8.

18. "Jingo, Counter-Jingo and Us," 11.

19. Alain Locke, "The Colonial Literature of France," *Opportunity* 1 (1923): 335; emphasis added.

20. Alain Locke, introduction to *Exhibition of the Art of the American Negro (1851 to 1940) Assembled by the American Negro Exposition* (Chicago: Tanner Art Galleries, 1940), 3; Alain Locke, ["On Literary Stereotypes"], in *Fighting Words*, 76.

21. *Terrible Honesty*, 33.

22. Alain Locke, *Negro Art: Past and Present*, (Washington, DC: Associates in Negro Folk Education, 1936), 2.

23. Alain Locke, "Racial Progress and Race Adjustment," *Race Contacts and Interracial Relations: Lectures on the Theory and Practice of Race*, ed. Jeffrey Stewart (Washington, D.C.: Howard University Press, 1992), 100; brackets in the original.

24. Alain Locke, "Apropos of Africa," *Opportunity* 2 (1924): 40; emphasis added.

25. North, 7, 48-52, 100-123, 175-195.

26. Alain Locke, "The Concept of Race as Applied to Social Culture," in *The Philosophy of Alain Locke: Harlem Renaissance and Beyond*, ed. Leonard Harris (Philadelphia: Temple University Press, 1989), 197.

27. *Negro Art: Past and Present*, 4; emphasis added.

28. *Race Men*, 49.

29. Bederman, 207.

30. *The Negro in Art: Past and Present*, 8.

31. Characteristically, in his project to problematize modernist primitivism, Locke positions only Antiquity, not African art, as "pagan."

32. Similarly, Carby comments on the shift in the dominance of civilization discourse: "within the framework of modernist cultural texts, the generalities of reference to a discourse of civilization are replaced by the specificities of reference to national belonging, as both black and white intellectuals and cultural producers increasingly represented the fate of the nation and black people as interdependent," *Race Men*, 47. On the other hand, Foley points out the residual traits of civilization rhetoric in the socialist discourse of the day, 87-96.

33. "To Certain of Our Philistines," 156.

34. Alain Locke, *The Negro and His Music* (Washington, DC: The Associates in Negro Folk Education, 1936), 88.

35. Langston Hughes, *The Big Sea*, 237. The term green most likely refers to the dyed-green carnation, a French symbol of decadence and homosexuality, which was often worn by Wilde.
36. Alain Locke, "Fire: A Negro Magazine," *Survey* 9 (September 1927): 563.
37. Chad Ross, *Naked Germany: Health, Race and the Nation*, (Oxford: Berg, 2005), 2.
38. Compare with Marlon B. Ross's discussion of McKay's and Hughes's attack on Locke's personal effete decadent style, 284-300.
39. ["On Literary Stereotypes"], 76-77; emphasis added.
40. Alain Locke, "Advance on the Art Front," *Opportunity* 17 (1939): 132; emphasis added.
41. Alain Locke, "Martyrdom to Glad Music: The Irony of Black Patriotism. Review of *From Harlem to the Rhine: The Story of New York's Colored Volunteers*, by Arthur W. Little," *Opportunity* 14 (1936): 381; emphasis added.
42. Alain Locke, "The Black Watch on the Rhine," *Opportunity* 2 (1924): 6-9; emphasis added. This depiction was later criticized by a French anti-colonial activist, and Locke admitted his strategic use of the subject in "French Colonial Policy." Interestingly, the latter article is also written in heavily militarized language. Locke states for example that: "our battle is on several fronts...We have perforce different immediate objectives, there are some nasty salients yet to be straightened out that at times bring us almost back to back when we should be standing shoulder to shoulder, occasionally we get caught in our own barrage and cut up with our own shrapnel." "French Colonial Policy," *Opportunity* 2 (1924): 262.

Chapter 4

1. Wallace Thurman, *Infants of the Spring* (New York: Modern Library, 1999), 79.
2. Wallace Thurman, *The Blacker the Berry* (New York: Macmillan Publishing Company, 1970), 145.
3. Wallace Thurman, "Negro Life in New York's Harlem: A Lively Picture of a Popular and Interesting Section," in *The Collected Writings of Wallace Thurman: A Harlem Renaissance Reader*, eds. Amritjit Singh and Daniel M. Scott (New Brunswick NJ: Rutgers University Press, 2003), 46.
4. Granville Ganter, "Decadence, Sexuality, and the Bohemian Vision of Wallace Thurman," *Melus* 28, no. 2 (summer 2003): 85.
5. Thus a writer such as Richard Nugent received far wider attention, because his writings and public persona enabled him to be labeled as the "Gay Rebel of the Harlem Renaissance." Moreover, Nugent, as the longest-living member of the younger generation of New Negroes, was able to assert his gay identity within the 1960s gay liberation movement, which is visible in his text "You See, I Am a Homosexual" [*Gay Rebel of the Harlem Renaissance: Selections from the Work of Richard Bruce Nugent*, ed. Thomas H. Wirth (Durham, NC: Duke University Press, 2002)].
6. Cary D. Wintz, in his *Black Culture and the Harlem Renaissance*, acknowledges that "by the mid 1920s Thurman had emerged as a leader among the writers and poets of Harlem." Nonetheless, he devotes less than two pages to "the center of Harlem's black bohemia" (Houston: Rice University Press, 1988), 88-89. Similarly, David Levering Lewis, in his seminal history of the movement *When Harlem Was in Vogue*, admits that "all the younger artists called Thurman their 'leader'" and that he was "the best-read, most brilliant, and most uncompromising of the Harlem artists." However, he devotes much more space to patrons, such as Locke, and other younger artists (New York: Penguin Books, 1997), 193, 277. In a similar vein, in his *Harlem Renaissance*, Nathan

Huggins credits Thurman with producing *Fire!!* "almost single-handedly," and yet Thurman is analyzed in his text primarily as the author of *Infants of the Spring* (New York, Oxford University Press, 2007), 191. Also more recent accounts of the movement, such as Hutchinson's *The Harlem Renaissance in Black and White*, where Thurman is mentioned four times in the space of 500 pages, pay negligible attention to his literary and journalistic activity. Hitherto, the largest analytical work devoted to Thurman's life and fiction is Eleonore van Notten's *Wallace Thurman's Harlem Renaissance* (Amsterdam: Rodopi, 1994). This very carefully researched account combines features of a biography and a literary analysis, but the autobiographical perspective oversimplifies the relation between Thurman and his fiction. Prior to the recent publication of *The Collected Writings of Wallace Thurman: A Harlem Renaissance Reader* (2003) edited by Amritjit Singh and Daniel M. Scott, a major part of Thurman's texts, including his collection of essays *Aunt Hagar's Children*, his plays *Harlem* and *Jeremiah the Magnificent*, and his last novel *The Interne* had remained either unpublished or unavailable to a wide readership. As for contradictions, according to Lewis, *The Infants* is "so poorly done" it is almost hard to believe that such a charismatic figure wrote it, whereas Huggins claims that it is "one of the best written and most readable novels of the period." Lewis, 277; Huggins, 241.

7. Wallace Thurman to William Jourdan Rapp, box 1, folder 7-8, Wallace Thurman Collection JWJ MSS 12, Beinecke Rare Book and Manuscript Library, Yale University.

8. Van Notten, 136.

9. "Negro Life in New York's Harlem," 62; Wallace Thurman, "The Negro Literary Renaissance," in *The Collected Writings of Wallace Thurman*, 244, 245.

10. *Infants of the Spring*, p. xiv.

11. Significantly, the quote refers to the youth of the female character of Ophelia, which is in stark contrast to Locke's masculinist vision of youth.

12. *Infants of the Spring*, 89; emphasis added.

13. Ibid., 91; emphasis added.

14. *Infants of the Spring*, 111, 121, 144.

15. Wallace Thurman, *The Blacker the Berry*, 148.

16. This approach is also encouraged by the editors of Thurman's collected writings, who devote one of the eight parts of the volume to Thurman's letters.

17. Wallace Thurman to Claude McKay, box 6, folder 207, Claude McKay Collection JWJ MSS 27, Beinecke Rare Book and Manuscript Library, Yale University.

18. For example, Garelick defines "dandyism as a tradition in which the real and the imaginary are closely joined" and, linking it to camp aesthetics, claims that it "blends the extratextual, biographical self with the literary or fictionally constructed hero, extending the boundaries of the latter to include the previously understood identity of the former." Rhonda K. Garelick, *Rising Star: Dandyism, Gender, and Performance in the Fin de Siècle* (Princeton, NJ: Princeton University Press, 1998), 10, 17-18. The scope of this study ends in 1945 and hence the potentially productive juxtaposition of contemporary (black) camp aesthetics and 1920s black dandyism will not be discussed.

19. David R. Jarraway, "Tales of the City: Marginality, Community, and the Problem of (Gay) Identity in Wallace Thurman's 'Harlem' Fiction," *College English* 65, no. 1 (September 2002): 36-52; Michael L. Cobb, "Insolent Racing, Rough Narrative: The Harlem Renaissance's Impolite Queers," *Callaloo* 23, no. 1 (2000): 328-51.

20. Ganter, 85.

21. Summers, 151, 156-157.

22. Wallace Thurman to Claude McKay, box 6, folder 207, Claude McKay Collection JWJ MSS 27, Beinecke Rare Book and Manuscript Library, Yale University; emphasis added.
23. *Infants of the Spring*, 146-7; emphasis added.
24. "Consuming Manhood: The Feminization of American Culture and the Recreation of the Male Body, 1832-1920," 34-37, Bederman, 1-5, 87.
25. Turner, 301.
26. Van Notten, 70.
27. Baym, 438.
28. Wallace Thurman to Harold Jackman, box 1, folder 4, Wallace Thurman Collection JWJ MSS 12, Beinecke Rare Book and Manuscript Library, Yale University.
29. Wallace Thurman to Langston Hughes, box 155, folder 2877, Langston Hughes Papers JWJ MSS 26, Beinecke Rare Book and Manuscript Library, Yale University; emphasis added.
30. Ibid., emphasis added.
31. Ibid., emphasis added.
32. Wallace Thurman to William Jourdan Rapp, box 1, folder 7-8, Wallace Thurman Collection JWJ MSS 12, Beinecke Rare Book and Manuscript Library, Yale University; emphasis added.
33. Wallace Thurman to Langston Hughes, box 155, folder 2877-2878, Langston Hughes Papers JWJ MSS 26, Beinecke Rare Book and Manuscript Library, Yale University; emphasis added.
34. Wallace Thurman to William Jourdan Rapp, box 1, folder 7-8, Wallace Thurman Collection JWJ MSS 12, Beinecke Rare Book and Manuscript Library, Yale University; emphasis added.
35. Ibid., emphasis added.
36. Ibid., emphasis added.
37. Theophilus Lewis, ["A Profile of Wallace Thurman"], NY *Amsterdam News*, box 3, folder 60, Wallace Thurman Collection JWJ MSS 12, Beinecke Rare Book and Manuscript Library, Yale University.
38. Wallace Thurman, "Frederick Douglass: The Black Emancipator," in *The Collected Writings of Wallace Thurman*, 259; emphasis added.
39. *Infants of the Spring*, 22, 35, 38-39.
40. Ibid., 35-39.
41. Paul's interpretation renders Bull's attitude analogous to the stance analyzed as central in Du Bois's representation of black gender relations and his persistent concern with the purity of black womanhood.
42. *Infants of the Spring*, 39-40.
43. Ibid., 79; emphasis added.
44. *Unforgivable Blackness: The Rise and Fall of Jack Johnson*, DVD, directed by Ken Burns, (Alexandria, VA: PBS Home Video, 2004).
45. Wallace Thurman, *Harlem: A Melodrama of Negro Life in Harlem*, in *The Collected Writings of Wallace Thurman*, 332, 347, 343, 347.
46. "A Review of Harlem: A Melodrama of Negro Life in Harlem by Wallace Thurman," box 2, folder 39, Wallace Thurman Collection JWJ MSS 12, Beinecke Rare Book and Manuscript Library, Yale University.
47. Thomas H. Pauly, "The Criminal as Culture," *American Literary History* 9, no. 4 (winter 1997): 778-779.
48. Many reviews of Harlem criticize it as a typical gangster play in black-face: "a cliché plot" "touch[ed] up with the lurid lights of local customs," "When White is Black,"

box 2, folder 39, Wallace Thurman Collection JWJ MSS 12, Beinecke Rare Book and Manuscript Library, Yale University.

49. Van Notten, 294.

50. All citations from newspaper clippings with contemporaneous reviews of the play, box 2, folder 39, Wallace Thurman Collection JWJ MSS 12, Beinecke Rare Book and Manuscript Library, Yale University.

51. "Negro Life in New York's Harlem," 56.

52. Ibid., 56-57. Thurman, in his assessment, translates the ethical level of law-breaking into the aesthetic level of "glamour," which is reminiscent of his dandyist, art-for-art's-sake attitude discussed in the following chapter.

53. "Negro Life in New York's Harlem," 57-58.

54. Pauly, in "The Criminal as Culture," claims that "by the 1920s consumer products had sufficiently proliferated and advertising had acquired enough sophistication that this means of distinction had achieved unprecedented effectiveness," which is interpreted as a major influence on the contemporaneous cultural representations of criminality (778).

55. Elaine Showalter, Sexual Anarchy: Gender and Culture at the Fin De Siècle (New York: Viking, 1990), 1-18.

56. For an analysis of the relationship between the collapse of the public/private divide and publicity, see Terrell Scott Herring's text "The Negro Artist and the Racial Manor: Infants of the Spring and the Conundrum of Publicity," African American Review 35, no. 4 (2001): 581-597. Herring correctly recreates Thurman's comments on the double bind of the black artist's predicament and its relation to publicity. In "Negro Artists and the Negro," Thurman summarizes his critique of the conditions that limit black artistic expression: "He will receive little aid from his own people unless he spends his time spouting sociological jeremiads...He will be exploited by white faddists...He will be overrated on the one hand, and under-praised on the other," ("Negro Artists and the Negro" 198). Herring further explains such a viewpoint with the emphasis on the burden of representation: "though some white journals did provide the New Negro with the freedom of artistic expression, both the black and the white press repeatedly demanded that the Negro artist represent the race. New Negro art, that is, had to forge a group identity; and the New Negro artist had to speak as and for a communal 'we'" (584). Yet, even though it is true that Thurman rejected the burden of being Race Man since it would clash with his celebrated individualism, Herring's contention that Niggerati artists in The Infants were the victims of publicity is an oversimplification and does not take into account the possibilities of self-invention and public performance of the self featured in the novel.

57. For example, Lewis, in When Harlem Was in Vogue, entitles the chapter devoted to the decline of the movement "The Fall of the Manor."

58. Infants of the Spring, 8; emphasis added.

59. Ibid., 30-31.

60. Apart from its special relation to the narrative as a whole, the importance of the scene is reinforced in the literary history of the New Negro Renaissance, since it is selected as the most masterful of Thurman's literary performances both by his contemporaries, such as Hughes, and by recent literary critics such as Huggins. Langston Hughes to Wallace Thurman, box 1, folder 3, Wallace Thurman Collection JWJ MSS 12, Beinecke Rare Book and Manuscript Library, Yale University; Huggins, 231.

61. Infants of the Spring, 53; emphasis added.

62. Ibid., 54-55; emphasis added.

63. Thorstein Veblen, *The Theory of the Leisure Class: An Economic Study of Institutions* (New York: Oxford University Press, 2007), 57.

64. *Infants of the Spring*, 77, 125, 132.

65. Ibid., 164-166.

66. "Negro Life in New York's Harlem," 53; emphasis added. For an alternative narrative on the rent party's origins and the separate spheres in the rural South, see Zora Neale Hurston, "Characteristics of Negro Expression," in *Within the Circle: An Anthology of African American Literary Criticism from The Harlem Renaissance to the Present*, ed. Angelyn Mitchell (Durham, NC: Duke University Press, 1994), 79-96.

67. *Infants of the Spring*, 109.

68. Mikhail Bakhtin, "Discourse in the Novel," in *Dialogic Imagination: Four Essays*, ed. Michael Holquist, trans. Caryl Emerson and Michael Holquist (Austin: University of Texas Press, 1981), 411.

69. Michel Foucault, "Of Other Spaces: Heterotopias," trans. Jay Miskowiec, Michel Foucault, Info http://foucault.info/documents/heteroTopia/foucault.heteroTopia.en.html. First published as "Des Espace Autres," Architecture /Mouvement/ Continuité 5 (October 1984): 46-49.

70. Ibid.

71. Thurman was not the only writer to acknowledge the democratic character of Harlem's interracial institutions. Socialist Charles Owen argues that there does not exist a more democratic institution in America than the "black and tan cabaret." This link further illuminates Thurman's espousal of counter-bourgeois ideologies. Quoted in Foley, 113.

72. *Infants of the Spring*, 114.

73. Chauncey, 108. Showalter, 111.

74. *Infants of the Spring*, 115.

75. Mikhail Bakhtin, *Rabelais and His World*, trans. Helene Iswolsky (Bloomington, IN: Indiana University Press, 1984), 368-436.

76. Ibid., 221, 373.

77. *Infants of the Spring*, 122-123.

78. Showalter, 169; emphasis added.

79. Thurman's choice of name for the black working-class boy seems significant in the light of Melville's *Billy Bud* and a homoerotic interpretation of the novella by critics such as Leslie Fiedler, *Love and Death in the American Novel* (New York: Stein and Day, 1966), 336. *Infants of the Spring*, 108, 113, 114.

80. Ibid., 108, 114.

81. "Negro Artists and the Negro," 196.

82. Ibid., 198.

83. *Infants of the Spring*, 149.

84. "Negro Life in New York's Harlem," 46.

85. Ibid., 46.

86. Compare Ross, 157.

87. Wallace Thurman to Langston Hughes, box 155, folder 2877, Langston Hughes Papers JWJ MSS 26, Beinecke Rare Book and Manuscript Library, Yale University.

88. *The Blacker the Berry*, 154, 158.

89. *Infants of the Spring*, 18.

90. John D'Emilio and Estelle B. Freedman, *Intimate Matters: A History of Sexuality in America* (Chicago: University of Chicago Press, 1997), 183-185.

91. *Harlem*, 326.

92. "Negro Life in New York's Harlem," 42-44.

93. *Infants of the Spring*, 37.
94. Characteristically, the issue of the violation of white domesticity is elided from the texts. This fact can be explained with the earlier-mentioned link between sacred domesticity, interracial intimacy, and the lynch logic. The tensions between representations of black sexual transgressions and lynch images will be discussed later on in the chapter. Another issue that is worth examining yet transcends the scope of this analysis is the relation between Thurman's assaults on the gendered public/private divide and white and black feminists interventions, which focused on this issue; from the right to vote to "personal is political."
95. *Rabelais and His World*, 10.
96. *The Blacker the Berry*, 150; emphasis added.
97. "Discourse in the Novel," 365.
98. *Infants of the Spring*, 115.
99. "Negro Life in New York's Harlem," 46.
100. *The Blacker the Berry*, 21.
101. Ibid., 145.
102. Ibid., 13.
103. "Negro Artists and the Negro," 172, 195.
104. Wallace Thurman, "Fire Burns: A Department of Comment," in *The Collected Writings of Wallace Thurman*, 194.
105. *Infants of the Spring*, 54.
106. Wallace Thurman to Langston Hughes, box 155, folder 2878, Langston Hughes Papers JWJ MSS 26, Beinecke Rare Book and Manuscript Library, Yale University; emphasis added.
107. Wallace Thurman, "High, Low, Past, and Present: Review of *The Walls of Jericho*, *Quicksand*, and *Adventures of an African Slaver*," in *Collected Writings of Wallace Thurman*, 220.
108. His conflation of Larsen and Fauset misses the significant differences, which have been discussed by critics such as Hazel V. Carby, who argues that "in direct contrast to Fauset, Larsen did not feel that the middle class were the guardians of civilized behavior and moral values...Larsen used Helga...as a figure who could question the limits of middle-class intellectual pretension." *Reconstructing Womanhood: The Emergence of the Afro-American Woman Novelist* (Oxford: Oxford University Press, 1987), 171.
109. Van Notten, 105.
110. *Infants of the Spring*, 148.
111. Ibid., 147-148.
112. Wallace Thurman, preface to *Aunt Hagar's Children*, in *The Collected Writings of Wallace Thurman*, 234; emphasis added.
113. Ibid., 235.
114. Van Notten, 108, 109.
115. Wallace Thurman to William Jourdan Rapp, box 1, folder 7-8, Wallace Thurman Collection JWJ MSS 12, Beinecke Rare Book and Manuscript Library, Yale University.

Chapter 5

1. Langston Hughes, *The Big Sea*, 238.
2. Van Notten, 179.
3. *Infants of the Spring*, 11.
4. "Fire: A Negro Magazine," 563.
5. Showalter, 169; emphasis added.

6. Other texts that point to the gender-charged notion of the dandy, as well as related to it the modern artist and *flâneur*, are: Janet Wolff, "The Invisible Flâneuse; Women and the Literature of Modernity," *Theory, Culture and Society* 2, no. 3 (1985): 37-46; and Griselda Pollock, *Vision and Difference: Femininity, Feminism and Histories of Art* (New York: Routledge, 1988), 70-71.

7. Charles Baudelaire, "Mon Coeur mis a nu," in *Oeuvres Completes*, (Paris: Bibliotheque de la Pleiade, 1961), 677. Translation after Showalter.

8. Oscar Wilde, "The Critic as an Artist: With Some Remarks upon the Importance of Discussing Everything," in *Intentions* (Charleston, SC: BiblioBazaar, 2008), 112.

9. Showalter, 170.

10. Garelick, 5.

11. Ibid., 29, 128, 3, 19, 10.

12. *The Use of Pleasure*, 10, 22-23.

13. *Infants of the Spring*, 40.

14. Ibid., 3; emphasis added.

15. For the function of "commodity-based orientalism" in the decadent discourse represented by Wilde's *Dorian Gray*, see Eve Kosofsky Sedgwick, *Epistemology of the Closet* (Berkeley, CA: University of California Press, 1990), 173-175.

16. *Infants of the Spring*, 31.

17. Ibid., 8, 10; emphasis added.

18. Garelick, 3.

19. *Infants of the Spring*, 9-10.

20. Ibid., 9; emphasis added.

21. Ibid., 174; emphasis added.

22. Ibid., 175.

23. Ibid., 139.

24. Further racial implications of this cross-dressing gesture will be discussed later in the course of the chapter. The fact that Orientalism was a prism through which European moderns perceived various differences is accurately illustrated by North's discussion of Joseph Conrad, Polish identity, and Orientalism in *The Dialect of Modernism*, 50-51.

25. Wallace Thurman to Langston Hughes, box 155, folder 2877, Langston Hughes Papers JWJ MSS 26, Beinecke Rare Book and Manuscript Library, Yale University; emphasis added.

26. David Mazella, *The Making of Modern Cynicism* (Charlottesville, VA: University of Virginia Press, 2007), 203.

27. Wallace Thurman to Claude McKay, box 6, folder 207, Claude McKay Collection JWJ MSS 27, Beinecke Rare Book and Manuscript Library, Yale University.

28. *Infants of the Spring*, 157.

29. Thurman's representation of Lucille's attitude to abortion is not necessarily a radical bohemian gesture attempted to shock. As historians of sexuality claim, although abortion was depicted in the medical and church discourse as immoral with tragic consequences, the popular opinion of the 1920s had not internalized these beliefs. See R. Sauer's "Attitudes to Abortion in America, 1800-1973," *Population Studies* 28, no. 1 (March 1974): 53-67. The lack of post-abortion trauma in the narrative also significantly parallels Thurman's repudiation of the post-passing trauma connected with the loss of one's racial roots, which is represented in the novel in Ray's attitude to Aline's decision to pass and is reiterated in his journalistic writings. Both problems represent different embodiments of Thurman's appropriation of the concept of "race suicide." This eugenic idea was popularized by Grant Madison in his *The Passing of the Great Race: Or, The Racial Basis of European History*, where he claims that "if the valuable elements in

the Nordic race mix with inferior strains or die out through race suicide, then the citadel of civilization will fall" (New York: Charles Scribner's Sons, 1921), p. xxxi. In *The Infants*, the term "race suicide" is used by Ray, who claims that it would "cure human beings of their ills" (158). In *Aunt Hagar's Children*, the vision of passing and assimilation as "race suicide" is entertained and cynically supported as a solution to the American race problem. Thus, passing for white can be identified with the passing of the (great) black race.

30. Wallace Thurman, "Stranger at the Gates: A Review of *Nigger Heaven*, by Carl Van Vechten," in *The Collected Writings of Wallace Thurman*, 192; emphasis added.

31. Paul's cross-dressing as a geisha is parallel to Thurman's experimentations with female centers of consciousness in his texts, which will be discussed later as an element of his narrative play with life and fiction.

32. This phrase is used by Thurman to refer to the fact that he wrote a cynical novel about the hospital he was later to be treated in for TB. Furthermore, in the process of the novel's publication, he visualized this possibility and commented that it would be an ironic twist of fate. Wallace Thurman to Langston Hughes, box 155, folder 2878, Langston Hughes Papers JWJ MSS 26, Beinecke Rare Book and Manuscript Library, Yale University.

33. Ganter, 87.

34. Wallace Thurman to William Jourdan Rapp, box 1, folder 7-8, Wallace Thurman Collection JWJ MSS 12, Beinecke Rare Book and Manuscript Library, Yale University.

35. Wallace Thurman, "Cordelia the Crude," in *The Collected Writings of Wallace Thurman*, 301-302.

36. Ganter, 3.

37. Interestingly, Thurman's writings express anxiety about representing women by a man. It is best illustrated by the case of Bull's pictures – this very aggressively masculine artist paints women who "were not women at all. They were huge amazons with pugilistic biceps, prominent muscular bulges, and broad shoulders. The only thing feminine about them were frilled red dresses in which all were attired." *The Blacker the Berry*, 40.

38. Van Notten, 223-238.

39. *The Blacker the Berry*, 149.

40. *Infants of the Spring*, 151.

41. Van Notten, 224; Ganter, 88.

42. Garelick, 6.

43. *Harlem*, 369.

44. *The Blacker the Berry*, 50. The name of Emma's first lover, Weldon Taylor, also interplays with Thurman's male persona from *The Infants*, Raymond Taylor, which further complicates this textual relationship.

45. Ibid., 121-122; emphasis added.

46. "Cordelia the Crude," 304; *Harlem*, 319, 328, 330.

47. *The Blacker the Berry*, 164-165.

48. Michel Foucault, "What is Enlightenment?" in *The Foucault Reader*, ed. Paul Rabinow, trans. Catherine Porter (New York: Pantheon Books, 1984), 39-42, 47.

49. Anita Seppä, "Foucault, Enlightenment and the Aesthetics of the Self," *Contemporary Aesthetics* 2, no. 4 (2004), http://www.contempaesthetics.org/ newvolume/pages/article.php?articleID=244; emphasis in original.

50. Wallace Thurman to William Jourdan Rapp, box 1, folder 7-8, Wallace Thurman Collection JWJ MSS 12, Beinecke Rare Book and Manuscript Library, Yale University; emphasis added.

51. *The Blacker the Berry*, 226.
52. Ibid., 147.
53. Pollock, 94.
54. *The Blacker the Berry*, 129.
55. In European decadent discourse there is a tension between sexual liberation and asceticism, which is ascribed to dandyism in Baudelaire's writings. Yet, in Thurman's representation of dandyism, as embodied by Paul, asceticism is downplayed and what is foregrounded is Paul's sexual indulgence. Charles Baudelaire, "On the Heroism of Modern Life," in *The Mirror of Art: Critical Studies by Charles Baudelaire*, ed. and trans. Jonathan Mayne (London: Phaidon Press, 1955), 13.
56. Wallace Thurman, "Notes on a Stepchild," in *The Collected Writings of Wallace Thurman*, 236.
57. Wallace Thurman to Dorothy West, in *The Collected Writings of Wallace Thurman*, 172.
58. *Infants of the Spring*, 51.
59. For an interesting discursive link between "communism," "commune," miscegenation, and "free love," see Maxwell, 127-129.
60. Amritjit Singh and Daniel M. Scott, *The Collected Writings of Wallace Thurman*, 307.
61. *Harlem*, 369.
62. *The Blacker the Berry*, 51, 119, 125.
63. "Stranger at the Gates: A Review of *Nigger Heaven*, by Carl Van Vechten," 192.
64. Wallace Thurman to William Jourdan Rapp, box 1, folder 7-8, Wallace Thurman Collection JWJ MSS 12, Beinecke Rare Book and Manuscript Library, Yale University.
65. Ibid.
66. "Policing the Black Woman's Body in an Urban Context," 742, 749.
67. Ross, 388.
68. Thurman's texts seem to, at least partially, avoid the trap of the mythology of the superwoman as discussed by Michele Wallace's account of Black Nationalism in her seminal work *Black Macho and the Myth of the Superwoman* (New York: Dial Press, 1979). The association between new modes of black masculinity, jazz culture, and white New Woman's threat to bourgeois manliness is acknowledged by Summers, 175.
69. Summers, 178.
70. *Infants of the Spring*, 33, 72.
71. What makes this intertextuality even more significant is the fact that the novel was popularized again at the turn of the twentieth century due to a reference made to it in Joseph Conrad's *The Nigger of the Narcissus: A Tale of the Sea* (1897). The oldest able seaman on the ship is introduced reading the novel: "[Old Singleton] was reading 'Pelham.' The popularity of Bulwer Lytton in the forecastles of Southern-going ships is a wonderful and bizarre phenomenon. What ideas do his polished and so curiously insincere sentences awaken in the simple minds of the big children who people those dark and wandering places of the earth?" (Charleston, SC: BiblioBazaar, 2007), 21. The contrast between the simple mariners and Bulwer Lytton's novel depicted as "wonderful," "bizarre," "curious," "insincere" parallels the clash between George Jones and Pelham Gaylord. Furthermore, Conrad's engagement in the discourse of darkness and Africanist presence lends itself as fruitful material for a further race and sexuality studies analysis, which is unfortunately out of the scope of this chapter. For an analysis of *The Nigger of the Narcissus* and its position in the racialized dialect of modernism, see North, 37-58.
72. For an analysis of the minstrel black dandy, see Eric Lott, *Love and Theft: Blackface Minstrelsy and the American Working Class* (New York: Oxford University Press, 1995), 50-51, 134-135.

73. *Infants of the Spring*, 153.
74. Ibid., 152.
75. "Notes on a Stepchild," 238. His relatively nonchalant attitude to the word "to lynch" is also manifest when he appropriates it in his depiction of the black bourgeoisie's assault on artistic freedom, as in "Van Vechten is about to be *lynched*, at least in effigy". "Fire Burns: A Department of Comment," 193.
76. *Infants of the Spring*, 47-48.
77. Ibid., 39.
78. Showalter, 171.
79. Van Notten, 229.
80. *Infants of the Spring*, 3, 4.
81. Ibid., 4. See also the discussion of Mumford's *Interzones* in the previous chapters.
82. Ganter, 94.
83. *Infants of the Spring*, 25.
84. Michel Foucault, *The History of Sexuality: An Introduction*, trans. Robert Hurley (New York: Vintage, 1990), 43.
85. *Epistemology of the Closet*, 173.
86. Showalter, 149; Garelick, 128-133.
87. Alan Sinfield, *The Wilde Century: Effeminacy, Oscar Wilde, and the Queer Movement* (New York: Columbia University Press, 1994), 6. Although the controversial picture most likely does not depict Wilde, for the purpose of this study, where it is used as an illustration of a certain model of masculine reinvention, the readiness with which the picture was accepted as Wilde's self-creation is more significant than its historical authenticity.
88. King James Version (Mark 6:22).
89. Wallace Thurman to William Jourdan Rapp, box 1, folder 7-8, Wallace Thurman Collection JWJ MSS 12, Beinecke Rare Book and Manuscript Library, Yale University.
90. Ibid.
91. Ganter, 86.
92. *Infants of the Spring*, 163.
93. *The Blacker the Berry*, 107; emphasis added.
94. Ibid., 186.
95. Ibid., 138, 168-169, 198; emphasis added.
96. For other analyses of literary and cultural interdependencies of racial difference, passing, and sexuality, see Judith Butler, *Bodies that Matter: On the Discursive Limits of "Sex"* (New York: Routledge, 1993), especially the chapter "Passing, Queering: Nella Larsen's Psychoanalytic Challenge," and Susan Gubar, *Racechanges: White Skin, Black Face in American Culture* (New York: Oxford University Press, 2000).
97. Ganter, 85; emphasis added. Unlike Ganter's text, this chapter focuses on Thurman's self-creations, i.e. Wallace Thurman's Wallace Thurman and his writings rather than attempts to reveal his authorial intentions.
98. *The Blacker the Berry*, 4. There are numerous other fragments that thematize the correlation between femininity and blackness.
99. Ibid., 43.
100. Ibid., 110.
101. Seppä; emphasis in original.
102. *Infants of the Spring*, 167, 161, 162.
103. "The Negro Literary Renaissance," 248.
104. Paul's "passing" suicide also significantly resonates with the earlier-mentioned depiction by Thurman of passing as a desirable race suicide. Moreover, the link between

racial passing and death is present in the semantic content of the verb to "pass," whose multiple meaning include "to die," and other uses refer to transition and ending.

105. In the light of Wilde's picture as Salome and its similarity to Paul's death, one could also speculate about the possible further links between staged death and photography; such an examination is encouraged by the central position of death in cultural theories of photography, such as Walter Benjamin's "Short History of Photography" (1931), Susan Sontag's On Photography (1977), and Roland Barthes's Camera Lucida: Reflections on Photography (1981).

106. Infants of the Spring, 151; Wallace Thurman to Langston Hughes, box 155, folder 2878, Langston Hughes Papers JWJ MSS 26, Beinecke Rare Book and Manuscript Library, Yale University.

107. Infants of the Spring, 11. The function of other painters who are mentioned by Paul could be read in an analogous way (Matisse, famous for his odalisque pictures and Gauguin, renowned primarily for his exotic representations of Tahitian women), yet Whistler's paintings most accurately illustrate the fascination with the geisha image.

108. Ibid., 135.

109. Eerdmans Dictionary of the Bible, s.vv. "Hagar." Zora Neale Hurston, "How It Feels to Be a Colored Me," in The Norton Anthology of African American Literature, eds. Nellie Y. McKay and Henry Louis Gates (New York: W. W. Norton & Company, 2003), 1009. Wallace Thurman to Claude McKay, box 6, folder 207, Claude McKay Collection JWJ MSS 27, Beinecke Rare Book and Manuscript Library, Yale University. This biblical story, and especially the name of Hagar's son, Ishmael, contains numerous significant intertextual implications. Both Thurman's contemporary and present-day American imagination would first associate this name with the narrator of the central text in American literary history, Melville's Moby Dick, and hence would constitute productive material for an extensive intertextual analysis. Yet the biblical origins also provide fruitful interpretative resonance. In the text, Ishmael is paired with Isaac. He is an illegitimate, ethnically mixed son of white Abraham in contrast to the legitimate and pure-blooded Isaac. Moreover, biblical scholars suggest that Ishmael's persona can be read as sexually transgressive, which is suggested in the sentence "And Sarah saw the son of Hagar the Egyptian, which she had born unto Abraham, mocking" (King James Bible, Genesis 21:9). Since this fragment is read as expressing a potential violation of sexual norms, it might indicate a sexual intimacy between Ishmael and Isaac. The significance of male interracial relationships in Thurman's writings is reflected in the friendship of Raymond and Stephen represented in The Infants, which, in turn, is recognized by critics as a fictionalized and desexualized version of Thurman's real life relationship with Jan Harold Stefansson. Analogously, according to Judaic teachings, God commanded Abraham to obey his wife's wishes and expel Hagar and Ishmael into the desert alone. It is believed that Sarah was motivated by Ishmael's sexually frivolous behavior at a party ("making merry" Genesis 21:9), which has been translated as a reference to idolatry, sexual immorality, or even murder; some rabbinic sources claim that Sarah worried that Ishmael would negatively influence Isaac, or that he would demand Isaac's inheritance on the grounds of being the firstborn. A Dictionary of Biblical Tradition in English Literature, s.vv. "Hagar." Yet another intertextual allusion to this name can be found in its function in Arab culture, where Ishmael is regarded as the patriarch of the Northern Arabs. This reference, in turn, significantly interplays with Orientalist elements in The Infants, especially visible in relation to Middle-Eastern Salome. Finally, the name Hagar also has an important function in Arab politics. Since the 1970s, this name has been given to newborn female babies as a controversial poli-

tical act, marking the parents as left-wing supporters of reconciliation with the Pales-
tinians and Arab World. Oren Yiftachel, "Launching Hagar: Marginality, Beer-Sheva,
Critique," *Studies in Culture, Polity, and Identities* 1, no. 1 (2000), http://hsf.bgu.ac.il/ ha-
gar/issues/ 1_1_2000/ 1120001.aspx.

110. Wallace Thurman, "Review of *Heloise and Abelard*, by George Moore," in *The Collected
Writings of Wallace Thurman*, 188; emphasis added.

111. Ibid.

112. "Negro Life in New York's Harlem, 60; emphasis added. The relevant fragment from
Rapp's article for comparison:

In short, this economic situation in Harlem, plus the large preponderance of women
over men, is, according to the authors, speedily bringing about a relationship of the
sexes akin to that among the Old Indian tribes. The men dress up, strut, talk, loaf,
smoke, gamble and fight, while the women do all the work. Any notion, they say, that
the women in general resent this order of things would be entirely erroneous. Rather,
they pride themselves on the degree of splendor they can bestow upon their men. And,
be it well remembered, many a woman prefers a half interest in a handsome man to a
full interest in an ugly one. Thus the 'sweetback,' or professional lover, has become
one of Harlem's most prominent inhabitants. He can be seen at all hours of the day
and night, dressed in flashy clothes, loafing in poolrooms, dance halls, speakeasies,
or on street corners. He never works, but always has plenty of money for liquor and
gambling. For isn't he often the pride and love of as many as a dozen hard-working
ladies?"

William Jourdan Rapp, "Sweetbacks," box 3, folder 49, Wallace Thurman Collection
JWJ MSS 12, Beinecke Rare Book and Manuscript Library, Yale University.

113. Ibid.

114. *Their Eyes Were Watching God*, 189.

115. William Jourdan Rapp, "Sweetbacks," box 3, folder 49, Wallace Thurman Collection
JWJ MSS 12, Beinecke Rare Book and Manuscript Library, Yale University.

116. "Frederick Douglass: The Black Emancipator," 268. Harlem, 332. *The Blacker the Berry*,
58.

117. Summers, 179.

118. The marketing campaign greatly overstates the significance of sweetbacks in the play.
Moreover, the only fragment discussing this issue largely parallels other excerpts discussed here: "You see, Roy wants to be a big time sweetback. He's one of these young
niggers new to city ways. Come from some little town in Virginia, got to New York,
saw these sweetbacks posing 'round these corners and pool halls and decided that
with his looks and his brains he could out-sweetback them all. Any time he gets a
girl, he 'spects her to make money for him." *Harlem*, 348.

119. *The Blacker the Berry*, 121.

120. Ibid., 176.

121. Ibid., 132, 159.

122. William Jourdan Rapp, "Sweetbacks," box 3, folder 49, Wallace Thurman Collection
JWJ MSS 12, Beinecke Rare Book and Manuscript Library, Yale University; *The Blacker
the Berry*, 173.

123. Mazella, 187, 186.

124. The earlier-mentioned phenomenon of "hot stuff" and "hot men" who deal in clothes
enables sweetbacks' colorful performance. The fact that "hot stuff" is constrained to
clothes foregrounds the performative character of consumption in Harlem in general.

125. Significantly, one of Thurman's most influential projects – *Fire!!* – was intended to
shock. Allegedly, Thurman and Nugent strategically selected prostitution and bisexu-

ality as the themes that were supposed to achieve this goal. As I have mentioned, Thurman's account cross-dresses his personal experience as narrated in a letter to Rapp. The discontents with sweetbacks expressed in his texts can be read as another possible reason to choose the female sex for the short story's protagonist.

126. Garelick, 14.
127. Christopher Lane, "The Drama of the Impostor: Dandyism and Its Double," *Cultural Critique* 28 (fall 1994): 31.
128. Mazella, 208-209.
129. *Infants of the Spring*, 30-31.
130. An issue that is beyond the scope of this analysis but seems to be worth future scholarly investigation is the relation of dandyism, sweetbacks, the leisure class, and the newly emergent advertising culture of the 1920s.
131. Garelick, 124-125.
132. Pollock, 101.
133. Significantly, whereas Du Bois wrote in defense of Jack Johnson and the freedom to engage in black male-white female relations, Thurman chooses to celebrate the earlier-mentioned Norah Holt Ray and black female-white male intimacy.

Chapter 6

1. Richard Wright, "Blueprint for Negro Writing," in *Richard Wright Reader*, eds. Michel Fabre and Ellen Wright (New York: Harper, 1978), 36.
2. Richard Wright, "Blueprint for Negro Writing," box 5, folder 76, Richard Wright Papers JWJ MSS, Beinecke Rare Book and Manuscript Library, Yale University.
3. Richard Wright, *Black Boy (American Hunger)* (New York: Harper Collins, 1993), 335.
4. The end of the movement was announced by its participants in the early 1930s: Alain Locke writes about the end of the Renaissance and the beginning of reformation in his "Harlem: Dark Weather-Vane," 457-458; whereas Langston Hughes, in his autobiography *The Big Sea*, dates spring 1931 as the end of the vogue (*The Big Sea*, 334).
5. For a more detailed discussion of Brown's use of the term "Harlem Renaissance" and his problematic identification with it and "the New Negro," see James Smethurst, *The New Red Negro: The Literary Left and African American Poetry, 1930-1946* (New York: Oxford University Press, 1999), 80.
6. Sterling Brown, *The Negro in American Fiction* (Washington, DC: The Associates in Negro Folk Education, 1937), 149; emphasis added. The Harlem Riot refers to the public unrest in Harlem in 1935.
7. *The Big Sea*, 228.
8. Sterling Brown, Arthur P. Davis, Ulysses Lee, eds., *The Negro Caravan* (New York: The Dryden Press, 1941), 281.
9. *The Negro Caravan*, 835.
10. Hugh Morris Gloster, *Negro Voices in American Fiction* (Chapel Hill, NC: The University of North Carolina Press, 1948), 164, 166, 171, 172, 195.
11. John Stokes, *In the Nineties* (Chicago: University of Chicago Press, 1989), 26.
12. Gunnar Myrdal, *An American Dilemma: The Negro Problem and Modern Democracy* (New York: Harper & Brothers, 1944), 750.
13. Myrdal, 750.
14. "The New Negro: 'New' or Newer," 4.
15. *The Negro in American Fiction*, 186.
16. *The Negro Caravan*, 144, 16-17.

17. Gloster, 233, 229.
18. Ironically, ten years later, James Baldwin would position Wright's iconic *Native Son* as analogous to *Uncle Tom's Cabin*, the epitome of sentimentalism. According to Baldwin, sentimental fiction is "always...the signal of secret and violent inhumanity, the mask of cruelty," hence Uncle Tom is "robbed of his humanity and divested of his sex." In turn, "Bigger is Uncle Tom's descendant, flesh of his flesh." These quotes prove that the issue of sentimentalism and its gendering remained central to the dialogues of black identity and masculinity for years to come. "Everybody's Protest Novel," in *Notes of a Native Son* (Boston: Beacon, 1984), 13-23.
19. "Blueprint for Negro Writing," in *Richard Wright Reader*, 36; emphasis added.
20. Ibid., 47; emphasis added.
21. Richard Wright, "Blueprint for Negro Writing," box 5, folder 76, Richard Wright Papers JWJ MSS, Beinecke Rare Book and Manuscript Library, Yale University; emphasis added.
22. *Black Boy*, 418. Also *Lawd Today*, Wright's first novel, written in the 1930s and posthumously published, criticizes black people's shortsighted gratitude for white charity in a satirical way. Richard Wright, *Lawd Today* (New York: Walker & Co, 1963).
23. "Blueprint for Negro Writing," in *Richard Wright Reader*, 48; emphasis added.
24. Ibid., 37; emphasis added. For a historical analysis of Wright's rejection of the patronage, which was so closely associated with the New Negro Renaissance, and of help from figures such as Carl Van Vechten as well as a comparison between 1920s Negrotarians and white communists, see Amy E. Carreiro, "Ghosts of the Harlem Renaissance: 'Negrotarians' in Richard Wright's *Native Son*," *The Journal of Negro History* 84, no. 3 (summer 1999): 247-259.
25. Ross, 199.
26. "Blueprint for Negro Writing," in *Richard Wright Reader*, 40; Richard Wright, "Blueprint for Negro Writing," box 5, folder 76, Richard Wright Papers JWJ MSS, Beinecke Rare Book and Manuscript Library, Yale University. Significantly, the femininely charged adjectives are used by Wright to criticize the literature of the New Negro Renaissance championed by Locke in a parallel way to Locke's criticism of sentimental fiction and propaganda. An even more interesting twist can be found in the correspondence between the two black intellectuals. In a letter from 1938, Locke criticizes *Challenge* magazine as "effete" and hopes that Wright will change it into something truly "challenging" and not "inappropriately aesthetic." Alain Locke to Richard Wright, box 100, folder 1452, Richard Wright Papers JWJ MSS, Beinecke Rare Book and Manuscript Library, Yale University.
27. "Blueprint for Negro Writing," in *Richard Wright Reader*, 49; emphasis added.
28. *Black Boy*, 335; emphasis added.
29. A potentially fruitful analysis, which is beyond the scope of this project, would be to examine Wright's attitude to the black bohemia in the light of Denning's claim that in the 1930s, "the older notions of the bohemian artist and freelance intellectual were no longer adequate to the new armies of white-collar and professional workers in cultural bureaucracies" and the "laboring" of artistic creativity in the concept of "mental labor." Michael Denning, *The Cultural Front: The Laboring of American Culture in the Twentieth Century* (New York: Verso, 1996), 49, 100.
30. "Blueprint for Negro Writing," in *Richard Wright Reader*, 40. See also *Black Boy*, 91-97, 232-233, 401.
31. Denning, 49, 97, 462.

32. Stephen Best, "Stand By Your Man: Richard Wright, Lynch Pedagogy, and Rethinking Black Male Agency," in *Representing Black Men*, eds. Marcellus Blount and George Cunningham (New York: Routledge, 1996), 112.

33. *Black Boy*, 295, 198.

34. *Lawd Today*, 62; emphasis added.

35. Best, 126.

36. *Black Boy*, 45-46.

37. Michael S. Kimmel, *The History of Men: Essays in the History of American and British Masculinities* (Albany, NY: SUNY Press, 2005), 33.

38. *Black Boy*, 151; emphasis added.

39. This episode also accurately illustrates Jane Tompkins's analysis of the emergence of the western as a literary genre that is a masculinist atheistic answer to the religious feminine literary domination in the late 19th century. Jane Tompkins, *West of Everything: The Inner Life of Westerns* (New York: Oxford University Press, 1992).

40. Both young black writers choose a white critic of American culture as their symbolic literary father instead of black critics such as Du Bois. This choice, if read purely from the perspective of race, is parallel to Washington's choice of symbolic paternity.

41. *Black Boy*, 288.

42. Ibid., 293.

43. Ibid., 298.

44. This text is significant also because it parallels the attempts of the younger generation of the Negro Renaissance to publish a magazine of their own. Wright attempted to revive *Challenge*, and "Blueprint" was published in the first issue of *New Challenge*. The outlet followed in the footsteps of *Fire!!* and *Harlem*, and was discontinued after one issue.

45. "Blueprint for Negro Writing," in *Richard Wright Reader*, 41, 48.

46. "Blueprint for Negro Writing," box 5, folder 76, Richard Wright Papers JWJ MSS, Beinecke Rare Book and Manuscript Library, Yale University; emphasis added. Wright's fiction is also often interpreted in militant metaphors. For example, in his discussion of *Native Son*, *Lawd Today*, and *The Outsider*, Denning claims that the novels are "acts of literary violence, assaults on their readers," 252.

47. Ralph Ellison to Richard Wright, box 97 folder 1314, Richard Wright Papers JWJ MSS, Beinecke Rare Book and Manuscript Library, Yale University; emphasis added.

48. Ralph Ellison, "Richard Wright's Blues," in *Shadow and Act* (New York: Quality Paperback Book Club, 1994), 93. Interestingly, later, when Ellison distances himself from Wright and his mode of writing, he argues that the primary limitation of Wright's fiction is that he treated the novel as a weapon. Ralph Ellison, "The World and the Jug," in *Shadow and Act*, 114.

49. Denning, p. xvi. Denning also claims that many artists and intellectuals who gradually broke with the Communist Party or left-wing philosophies in general remained aesthetically indebted to the left-wing aesthetic, 26.

50. *Black Boy*, 375.

51. "Blueprint for Negro Writing," in *Richard Wright Reader*, 44.

52. "Blueprint for Negro Writing," box 5, folder 76, Richard Wright Papers JWJ MSS, Beinecke Rare Book and Manuscript Library, Yale University.

53. Ibid., 44; original emphasis.

54. Richard Wright, "I Bite the Hand That Feeds Me," box 5, folder 107, Richard Wright Papers JWJ MSS, Beinecke Rare Book and Manuscript Library, Yale University.

55. Ibid.

56. Richard Wright, "On Literature," box 6, folder 128, Richard Wright Papers JWJ MSS, Beinecke Rare Book and Manuscript Library, Yale University; emphasis added.

57. "The New Negro," 7.

58. "Advance on the Art Front," 132-133.

59. *Lawd Today*, 24-25.

60. Ibid., 30, 50; emphasis original.

61. Ibid., 12; emphasis added.

62. Ibid., 26, 51.

63. For an examination of the connection between Jake's nationalism and emasculation, see Anthony Dawahare, "From No Man's Land to Mother-Land: Emasculation and Nationalism in Richard Wright's Depression Era Urban Novels," *African American Review* 33, no. 3 (autumn 1999): 451-466. One could elaborate Dawahare's largely Freudian interpretation by linking Jake's "nationalistic fantasies" constructed with images reminiscent of newspaper reports about Hitler and fascism in the novel as a totalitarian fantasy of omnipotence that is characteristic of the Lacanian imaginary realm. The function of Hilter as a trope in Wright's writing is a productive issue to explore, which is nevertheless beyond the scope of this study.

64. Since, as I have argued, the black dandy bears a strong resemblance to the sweetback, Jake could also be juxtaposed with this figure. Yet, since this chapter primarily focuses on Wright's dialogue with the previous generation and his texts do not foreground sweetback characters, such examination is not of central relevance.

65. Mary Murphy, "Picture/Story: Representing Gender in Montana Farm Security Administration Photographs," *Frontiers: A Journal of Women Studies* 22, no. 3 (2001): 94.

66. Nicholas Natanson, *The Black Image in the New Deal: The Politics of FSA Photography* (Knoxville, TN: University of Tennessee Press, 1993), 143.

67. Richard Wright, "The Future of Literary Expression," box 5, folder 87, Richard Wright Papers JWJ MSS, Beinecke Rare Book and Manuscript Library, Yale University.

68. Richard Wright, *12 Million Black Voices* (New York: Thunder's Press, 1988), p. xix. As these quotes manifest, even though Wright's approach to migrating North is parallel to Du Bois's, he clearly positions himself in opposition to the editor of the *Crisis*.

69. Natanson, 247.

70. For a positive evaluation of Wright's collective national project, see John M. Reilly "Richard Wright Preaches the Nation: *12 Million Black Voices*," *Black American Literature Forum* 16, no. 3 (autumn 1982): 116-119.

71. *12 Million Black Voices*, 13; emphasis added.

72. Ibid., 14.

73. Ibid., 36-37; emphasis added.

74. Ibid., 38; emphasis added.

75. *Lawd Today*, 138; emphasis added.

76. Dawahare, 457.

77. *Black Boy*, 3.

78. Ibid., 7-8; emphasis added.

79. See also Ralph Ellison, "Richard Wright's Blues," 85; Dale E. Peterson, "Richard Wright's Long Journey from Gorky to Dostoevsky," *African American Review* 28, no. 3 (fall 1994): 375-387; Claudia Tate, *Psychoanalysis and Black Novels: Desire and the Protocols of Race* (New York: Oxford University Press, 1998), 90. One could also compare the imagery of "fog of fear," "whiteness," and ice in this scene with the way Mrs. Dalton is represented in *Native Son*. It can be argued that the conflation of oppression and whiteness in Wright's texts is utilized to reinforce black female domination in the scene from *Black Boy*.

80. *Black Boy*, 48.
81. Ibid., 308.
82. *Lawd Today*, 97.
83. *12 Million Black Voices*, 37.
84. "Consuming Manhood: The Feminization of American Culture and the Recreation of the Male Body, 1832-1920," 13.
85. *12 Million Black Voices*, 131.
86. Ibid., 135.
87. *12 Million Black Voices*, 14.
88. For an analysis of residual nostalgia for the pastoral South in Wright's *Uncle Tom's Children*, see Maxwell, 166-178.
89. *12 Million Black Voices*, 88.
90. St. Clair Drake and Horace Roscoe Cayton, *Black Metropolis: A Study of Negro Life in a Northern City* (Chicago: University of Chicago Press, 1993), 214-262, 507-519.
91. For a parallel analysis of black national identity as necessarily "essentialist and class-collaborationist," see Foley, 80.
92. Denning, 253.
93. For an anthropological account of this African American ritual of insult see Roger D. Abrahams, "'Playing the Dozens,'" *Journal of American Folklore* 75 (1962): 209-220 and Lawrence W. Levine, *Black Culture and Black Consciousness: Afro-American Folk Thought from Slavery to Freedom* (Oxford: Oxford University Press, 1977).
94. *Lawd Today*, 79.
95. Ibid., 79-81. For an analysis of the fragment with reference to Gates's concept of Signifyin(g), see Henry Louis Gates, *The Signifying Monkey*, 96-99. Although, in his work, Gates does not refer to Bakhtin's concept of medieval laughter, there seems to be a significant parallel between the two concepts, whose exploration is, however, beyond the scope of this study.
96. *Lawd Today*, 81.
97. Ibid., 78.
98. *Rabelais and His World*, 72, 82, 92, 12.
99. The fact that Locke used modernists such as Picasso to provide legitimization for African art whereas Wright legitimizes Stein's fiction with a reference to the proletariat powerfully illustrates the cultural shift that occurred between the 1920s and the 1940s.
100. *Lawd Today*, 150.
101. Richard Wright, "A Review of *Wars I Have Seen*, by Gertrude Stein," in *Richard Wright Reader*, 78.
102. *Lawd Today*, 162.
103. *Black Boy*, 91-95.
104. Ibid., 233.
105. Ibid., 401.
106. Ibid., 298, 286.
107. Wiegman, 6.
108. *Black Boy*, 286-287; emphasis added. For more elaborate discussions of specularity, the white gaze, and the racialization of the black body, see Mikko Juhani Tuhkanen, "'[B]igger's Place': Lynching and Specularity in Richard Wright's 'Fire and Cloud' and Native Son," *African American Review* 33, no. 1 (spring 1999): 125-133; and Maurice O. Wallace, *Constructing the Black Masculine: Identity and Ideality in African American Men's Literature and Culture, 1775-1995*, 35-44.
109. James Baldwin, "Alas, Poor Richard," in *Nobody Knows My Name* (New York: Dial, 1961), 187.

110. *Lawd Today*, 96-97, 156, 318.
111. Ibid., 41.
112. Ibid., 166-167.
113. Richard Wright, *Native Son* (New York: Buccaneer Books, 1997), 34.
114. Ibid., 262.
115. Ibid., 64.
116. *Black Boy*, 233.
117. *Native Son*, 97.
118. Ibid., 97; emphasis added.
119. Ibid., 129; emphasis added.
120. "Alas, Poor Richard," 188.
121. Even in Wright's Southern fiction, lynching occurs in the narrative as a result of violence against the white man or the awakening of the black man's political consciousness, never as a consequence of the desire for the white woman, a correlation that downplays castration anxiety and emphasizes black male militancy. This pattern repeats itself in *Black Boy*, "Big Boy Leaves Home," and "Fire and Cloud," in *Uncle Tom's Children* (New York: Harper, 1965).
122. *Lawd Today*, 189.
123. *Native Son*, 273.
124. If one were to elaborate on such a reading, Eliot's allusions to Guy Fawkes and his effigy – "the stuffed men" in the poem – can be illuminated with a reference to Southern lynching spectacles, which were sometimes referred to as "barbecues" or "bonfires." The relevance of race in the poem is reinforced by the presence of a black voice from Conrad's *Heart of Darkness* in the poem's epigraph.
125. Dawahare, 458.
126. *Native Son*, 247.
127. *Black Boy*, 18.

Conclusion

1. Schwarz, 1-24.

Bibliography

Abrahams, Roger D. "'Playing the Dozens.'" *Journal of American Folklore* 75 (1962): 209-220.

Avallone, Charlene. "What American Renaissance? The Gendered Genealogy of a Critical Discourse." *PMLA* 112, no. 5 (1997): 1102-1120.

Badinter, Elizabeth. *XY: On Masculine Identity.* New York: Columbia University Press, 1992.

Baker, Houston A., Jr. *Modernism and the Harlem Renaissance.* Chicago: University of Chicago Press, 1987.

Bakhtin, Mikhail. "Discourse in the Novel." In *The Dialogic Imagination: Four Essays.*

—. *Rabelais and His World.* Translated by Helene Iswolsky. Bloomington: Indiana University Press, 1984.

—. *Speech Genres and Other Late Essays.* Translated by Vern W. McGee. Austin: University of Texas Press, 1986.

—. *The Dialogic Imagination: Four Essays.* Edited by Michael Holquist. Translated by Caryl Emerson and Michael Holquist. Austin: University of Texas Press, 1981.

Baldwin, James. "Alas, Poor Richard." In *Nobody Knows My Name.* New York: Dial, 1961.

—. "Everybody's Protest Novel." In *Notes of a Native Son.* 1955. Boston: Beacon Press, 1984.

Baudelaire, Charles. "Mon Coeur mis a nu." In *Oeuvres Completes.* Paris: Bibliotheque de la Pleiade, 1961.

—. "On the Heroism of Modern Life." In *The Mirror of Art: Critical Studies by Charles Baudelaire,* edited and translated by Jonathan Mayne. London: Phaidon Press, 1955.

Baym, Nina. "Melodramas of Beset Manhood: How Theories of American Fiction Exclude Women Authors." *American Quarterly* 33, no. 2 (summer 1981): 123-139.

Bederman, Gail. *Manliness and Civilization: A Cultural History of Gender and Race in the United States, 1880-1917.* Chicago: University of Chicago Press, 1995.

Best, Stephen. "Stand By Your Man: Richard Wright, Lynch Pedagogy, and Rethinking Black Male Agency." In *Representing Black Men,* edited by Marcellus Blount and George Cunningham. New York: Routledge, 1996.

Bloom, Harold. *The Anxiety of Influence: A Theory of Poetry.* New York: Oxford University Press, 1973.

Brown, Sterling, Arthur P. Davis, and Ulysses Lee, eds. *The Negro Caravan.* New York: The Dryden Press, 1941.

Brown, Sterling. *The Negro in American Fiction.* Washington, DC: The Associates in Negro Folk Education, 1937.

Burns, Ken. *Unforgivable Blackness: The Rise and Fall of Jack Johnson.* DVD. Directed by Ken Burns. Alexandria, VA: PBS Home Video, 2004.

Butler, Judith. *Bodies that Matter: On the Discursive Limits of "Sex."* New York: Routledge, 1993.

Carby, Hazel V. "Policing the Black Woman's Body in an Urban Context." *Critical Inquiry* 18, no. 4 (summer 1992), 738-755.

—. *Race Men: The W. E. B. Du Bois Lectures.* Cambridge, MA: Harvard University Press, 1998.

—. *Reconstructing Womanhood: The Emergence of the Afro-American Woman Novelist.* Oxford: Oxford University Press, 1987.

Carpenter, Edward. *Ioläus: An Anthology of Friendship.* London and Manchester: Swan Sonnenschein & Co. Limited and S. Clarke, 1906.

Carreiro, Amy E. "Ghosts of the Harlem Renaissance: 'Negrotarians' in Richard Wright's *Native Son.*" *The Journal of Negro History* 84, no. 3 (summer 1999): 247-259.

Cayton, Horace Roscoe, and St. Clair Drake. *Black Metropolis: A Study of Negro Life in a Northern City.* 1945. Chicago: University of Chicago Press, 1993.

Chauncey, George. *Gay New York: Gender, Urban Culture, and the Making of the Gay Male World, 1890-1940.* New York: Basic Books, 1994.

Cobb, Michael L. "Insolent Racing, Rough Narrative: The Harlem Renaissance's Impolite Queers." *Callaloo* 23, no. 1 (2000): 328-351.

Connell, Robert W. *Masculinities.* Cambridge: Polity Press, 2005.

Conrad, Joseph. *The Nigger of the Narcissus: A Tale of the Sea.* 1897. Charleston, SC: BiblioBazaar, 2007.

D'Emilio, John, and Estelle B. Freedman. *Intimate Matters: A History of Sexuality in America.* Chicago: University of Chicago Press, 1997.

Dawahare, Anthony. "From No Man's Land to Mother-Land: Emasculation and Nationalism in Richard Wright's Depression Era Urban Novels." *African American Review* 33, no. 3 (autumn 1999): 451-466.

Denning, Michael. *The Cultural Front: The Laboring of American Culture in the Twentieth Century.* New York: Verso, 1996.

Douglas, Ann. *Terrible Honesty: Mongrel Manhattan in the 1920s.* New York: Farrar, Straus & Giroux, 1995.

—. *The Feminization of American Culture.* New York: Knopf, 1977.

Douglass, Frederick. *The Life and Times of Frederick Douglass: His Early Life as a Slave, His Escape from Bondage, and His Complete History.* Edited by Rayford Whittingham Logan. 1881. Mineola, NY: Courier Dover Publications, 2003.

Du Bois, W. E. B. "An Open Letter to Woodrow Wilson." In *Writings.*

—. "Criteria of Negro Art." *Crisis* 32 (October 1926): 290-297.

—. "I Am Resolved." In *Writings.*

—. "Negroes of Farmville, Virginia." In *On Sociology and the Black Community.*

—. "Propaganda and World War." In *Writings.*

—. "Returning Soldiers." In *The Portable Harlem Renaissance,* edited by David Levering Lewis. New York: Viking, 1994.

—. "The Black North in 1901: New York." In *On Sociology and the Black Community.*

—. "The Conservation of Races." In *Writings.*

—. "The Negro American Family." In *On Sociology and the Black Community.*

—. "The Negro College." In *Writings.*

—. "The Negro Race in the United States." In *On Sociology and the Black Community.*

—. "The Negroes of Dougherty County, Georgia." In *On Sociology and the Black Community.*

—. "The Niagara Movement Statement." In *Writings.*

—. "The Philadelphia Negro." In *On Sociology and the Black Community.*

—. "The Problem of Amusement." In *On Sociology and the Black Community.*

—. "The Religion of the American Negro." In *On Sociology and the Black Community.*

—. "The Talented Tenth." In *Writings*.

—. *Darkwater: Voices from Within the Veil*. 1920. New York: Schocken Books, 1972.

—. *On Sociology and the Black Community*. Edited by Dan S. Green and Edwin D. Driver. Chicago: University of Chicago Press, 1978.

—. *The Autobiography of W. E. B. Du Bois: A Soliloquy on Viewing My Life from the Last Decade of Its First Century*. New York: International Publishers, 1968.

—. *The Souls of Black Folk*. 1903. New York: Vintage Books, 1990.

—. *Writings: The Suppression of the African Slave-Trade, The Souls of Black Folk, Dusk of Dawn, Essays and Articles*. Edited by Nathan Huggins. New York: Viking Press, 1986.

Dubbert, Joe L. "Progressivism and the Masculinity Crisis." In *The American Man*, edited by Elizabeth Pleck. Englewood Cliffs, NJ: Prentice-Hall, 1980.

Ellison, Ralph. "Richard Wright's Blues." In *Shadow and Act*.

—. "The World and the Jug." In *Shadow and Act*.

—. *Shadow and Act*. 1953. New York: Quality Paperback Book Club, 1994.

Emerson, Ralph Waldo. "Self Reliance." In *The Norton Anthology of American Literature*, edited by Nina Baym. Volume B. 6th ed. New York: Norton & Company, 2003.

Fiedler, Leslie. *Love and Death in the American Novel*. New York: Stein and Day, 1966.

Foley, Barbara. *Spectres of 1919: Class and Nation in the Making of the New Negro*. Chicago: University of Illinois Press, 2003.

Foucault, Michel. "Of Other Spaces: Heterotopias." Translated by Jay Miskowiec. Michel Foucault, Info. http://foucault.info/documents/heteroTopia/foucault.heteroTopia.en.html. First published as "Des Espace Autres." *Architecture /Mouvement/ Continuité* 5 (October 1984): 46-49.

—. "What is Enlightenment?" In *The Foucault Reader*, edited by Paul Rabinow, translated by Catherine Porter. New York: Pantheon Books, 1984.

—. *The History of Sexuality: An Introduction*. Translated by Robert Hurley. New York: Vintage, 1990.

—. *The Use of Pleasure: The History of Sexuality*. Translated by Robert Hurley. New York: Vintage Books, 1985.

Ganter, Granville. "Decadence, Sexuality, and the Bohemian Vision of Wallace Thurman." *Melus* 28, no. 2 (summer 2003): 83-106.

Garber, Eric. "T'Aint Nobody's Bizness: Homosexuality in 1920s Harlem." In *Gay Roots: Twenty Years of Gay Sunshine: An Anthology of Gay History, Sex, Politics, and Culture*, edited by Winston Leyland. San Francisco: Gay Sunshine Press, 1991.

Garelick, Rhonda K. *Rising Star: Dandyism, Gender, and Performance in the Fin de Siècle*. Princeton, NJ: Princeton University Press, 1998.

Gates, Henry Louis, and Gene Andrew Jarrett, ed. *The New Negro: Readings on Race, Representation, and African American Culture, 1892-1938*. Princeton, NJ: Princeton University Press, 2007.

Gates, Henry Louis. "The Trope of a New Negro and the Reconstruction of the Image of the Black." *Representations* 24, no. 1 (autumn 1988): 129-155.

—. *The Signifying Monkey: A Theory of African-American Literary Criticism*. New York: Oxford University Press, 1989.

Gibson, Donald. "Chapter One of Booker T. Washington's *Up From Slavery* and the Feminization of the African American Male." In *Representing Black Men*, edited by Marcellus Blount and George Philbert Cunningham. New York: Routledge, 1996.

Gilbert, Sandra M., and Susan Gubar. *The Madwoman in the Attic: The Woman Writer and the Nineteenth-Century Literary Imagination.* 2nd ed. 1979. New Haven, CT: Yale University Press, 2000.

Gilmore, David D. *Manhood in the Making: Cultural Concepts of Masculinity.* New Haven, CT: Yale University Press, 1990.

Gilroy, Paul. *Black Atlantic: Modernity and Double Consciousness.* London: Verso, 1993.

Gloster, Hugh Morris. *Negro Voices in American Fiction.* Chapel Hill, NC: The University of North Carolina Press, 1948.

Goldweber, David E. "Cullen, Keats and the Privileged Liar." *Papers on Language & Literature* 38, no. 1 (2002): 29-49.

Gubar, Susan. *Racechanges: White Skin, Black Face in American Culture.* New York: Oxford University Press, 2000.

Hall, Jacquelyn Dowd. "'The Mind that Burns in Each Body': Women, Rape, and Racial Violence." In *Powers of Desire: The Politics of Sexuality*, edited by Anne Snitow, Christine Stansell, and Sharon Thompson. New York: Monthly Review Press, 1983.

Hall, Stuart. "The Rediscovery of 'Ideology': Return of the Repressed in Media Studies." In *Culture, Society and the Media*, edited by M. Gurevitch, T. Bennett, J. Curran, and J. Woollacott. London: Methuen, 1982.

Hantover, Jeffrey P. "The Boy Scouts and the Validation of Masculinity." In *The American Man*, edited by Elizabeth Pleck. Englewood Cliffs, NJ: Prentice-Hall, 1980.

Harris, Leonard. "'Outing' Alain L. Locke: Empowering the Silenced." In *Sexual Identities, Queer Politics*, edited by Mark Blasius. Princeton, NJ: Princeton University Press, 2001.

Harris, Thomas E. *Analysis of the Clash over Issues between Booker T. Washington and W. E. B. Du Bois.* New York: Garland, 1993.

Hawthorne, Nathaniel. *Letters of Hawthorne to William D. Ticknor, 1851-1864.* Newark, NJ: Cateret Book Club, 1910.

Herring, Terrell Scott. "The Negro Artist and the Racial Manor: *Infants of the Spring* and the Conundrum of Publicity." *African American Review* 35, no. 4 (2001): 581-597.

Holmes, Eugene C. "Alain Leroy Locke: A Sketch." *The Phylon Quarterly* 20, no. 1 (1959): 82-89.

Huggins, Nathan. *Harlem Renaissance.* 1971. New York: Oxford University Press, 2007.

Hughes, Langston. *The Big Sea.* 1940. New York: Knopf, 1945.

Hull, Gloria T. *Color, Sex and Poetry: Three Women Writers of the Harlem Renaissance.* Bloomington, IN: Indiana University Press, 1987.

Hurston, Zora Neale. "Characteristics of Negro Expression." In *Within the Circle: An Anthology of African American Literary Criticism from the Harlem Renaissance to the Present*, edited by Angelyn Mitchell. North Carolina: Duke University Press, 1994.

—. "How It Feels to Be a Colored Me." In *The Norton Anthology of African American Literature*, edited by Nellie Y. McKay and Henry Louis Gates. New York: W. W. Norton & Company, 2003.

—. *Their Eyes Were Watching God.* 1937. New York: HarperCollins, 1990.

Hutchinson, George. *The Harlem Renaissance in Black and White*. New York: Belknap Press, 1997.

Hutchinson, George. "The Whitman Legacy and the Harlem Renaissance." In *Walt Whitman: The Centennial Essays*, edited by Ed Folsom. Iowa City, IA: University of Iowa Press, 1994.

Hwang, Hae Sung. *Booker T. Washington and W. E. B. Du Bois: A Study in Race Leadership 1895-1915*. Seoul: American Studies Institute, Seoul National University, 1992.

Ivory, Yvonne. "The Urning and His Own: Individualism and the Fin-de-Siècle Invert." *German Studies Review* 26, no. 2 (2003): 333-52.

Jarraway, David R. "Tales of the City: Marginality, Community, and the Problem of (Gay) Identity in Wallace Thurman's 'Harlem' Fiction." *College English* 65, no. 1 (September 2002): 36-52.

Johnson, Charles S. "Women's Brains," *Opportunity* 1 (1923): 4.

Jones, Leroi (Amiri Baraka). "The Myth of a 'Negro Literature.'" In *Within the Circle: An Anthology of African American Literary Criticism from the Harlem Renaissance to the Present*, edited by Angelyn Mitchell. Durham, NC: Duke University Press, 1994.

Kallen, Horace. "Alain Locke and Cultural Pluralism." *The Journal of Philosophy*. 54, no. 5 (February 1957): 119-127.

Killingsworth, M. Jimmie. "Whitman's 'Calamus': A Rhetorical Prehistory of the First Gay American." Presented at the Modern Language Association Convention, San Francisco, December 1998. http://www-english.tamu.edu/pubs/body/calamus.html.

Kimmel, Michael S. and Michael Kaufman. "Weekend Warriors." In *Theorizing Masculinities*, edited by Harry Brod. Thousand Oaks, CA: Sage Publications, 1994.

Kimmel, Michael S. "Consuming Manhood: The Feminization of American Culture and the Recreation of the Male Body, 1832-1920." In *The Male Body: Features, Destinies, Exposures*, edited by Leo Goldstein. Ann Arbor, MI: Michigan University Press, 1998.

—. "The Contemporary 'Crisis' of Masculinity in Historical Perspective." In *The Making of Masculinities*, edited by Harry Brod. New York: Routlege, 1987.

—. *The History of Men: Essays in the History of American and British Masculinities*. Albany, NY: SUNY Press, 2005.

Kolodny, Annette. *The Land Before Her: Fantasy and Experience of the American Frontiers, 1630-1860*. Chapel Hill, NC: University of North Carolina Press, 1984.

Kottak, Conrad. "Anthropological Analysis of Mass Enculturation." In *Researching American Culture*. Ann Arbor, MI: University of Michigan Press, 1982.

Lane, Christopher. "The Drama of the Impostor: Dandyism and Its Double." *Cultural Critique* 28 (Fall 1994): 29-52.

Lawrence, D. H. *Studies in Classic American Literature*. 1923. Dallas: Penguin Books, 1985.

Lemke, Sieglinde. *Primitivist Modernism: Black Culture and the Origins of Transatlantic Modernism*. Oxford: Oxford University Press, 1998.

Lewis, David Levering. *When Harlem Was in Vogue*. 1981. New York: Penguin Books, 1997.

Levine, Lawrence W. *Black Culture and Black Consciousness: Afro-American Folk thought from Slavery to Freedom*. Oxford: Oxford University Press, 1977.

Locke, Alain, and W.E.B. Du Bois. "The Younger Literary Movement." *Crisis* 28 (February 1924): 161-163.

Locke, Alain, ed. *The New Negro: An Interpretation*. New York: Albert and Charles Boni, 1925.

Locke, Alain. ["On Literary Stereotypes"]. In *Fighting Words*, edited by Donald Ogden Stewart. New York: New Directions, 1940.

—. "1928: A Retrospective Review." *Opportunity* 7 (1929): 8-11.

—. "A Decade of Negro Self-Expression." In *The Critical Temper of Alain Locke*.

—. "A Review of *Goat Alley*, by Ernest Howard Culbertson." *Opportunity* 1 (1923): 30.

—. "Advance on the Art Front." *Opportunity* 17 (1923): 132-36.

—. "Apropos of Africa." *Opportunity* 2 (1924): 37-40, 58.

—. "Deep River: Deeper Sea: Retrospective Review of the Literature of the Negro for 1935." *Opportunity* 14 (1936): 6-10; 42-43, 61.

—. "Dry Fields and Green Pastures: A Retrospective Review of the Literature of the Negro for 1939." *Opportunity* 18 (1940): 4-10, 28; 41-46, 53.

—. "Enter the New Negro." *Survey Graphic* 6, no. 6 (March 1925): 631-634.

—. "Fire: A Negro Magazine." *Survey* 58 (1927): 563.

—. "French Colonial Policy." *Opportunity* 2 (1924): 262-263.

—. "Harlem." *Survey Graphic* 6, no. 6 (March 1925): 629-630.

—. "Harlem: Dark Weather-Vane." *Survey Graphic* 24 (1936): 457-62, 493-95.

—. "Jingo, Counter-Jingo and Us: A Retrospective Review of Negro Literature," *Opportunity* 16 (January and February, 1938): 8-11, 27, 39-42.

—. "Martyrdom to Glad Music: The Irony of Black Patriotism." *Opportunity* 14 (1936): 381.

—. "Negro Music Goes to Par." *Opportunity* 17 (1939): 196-200.

—. "Negro Youth Speaks." In Locke, *The New Negro: An Interpretation*.

—. "Of Native Sons: Real and Otherwise: A Retrospective Review of the Literature of the Negro for 1940." *Opportunity* 19 (1941): 4-9, 48-52.

—. "Racial Progress and Race Adjustment." In *Race Contacts and Interracial Relations: Lectures on the Theory and Practice of Race*, edited by Jeffrey Stewart. Washington, DC: Howard University Press, 1992.

—. "Review of *Bronze: A Book of Verse*." *Crisis* 25 (February 1923): 161.

—. "Review of *Sex Expression in Literature*, by V. F. Calverton." *Opportunity* 5 (1927): 57-58.

—. "Roland Hayes: An Appreciation." *Opportunity* 1 (1923): 356-358.

—. "The American Temperament." In *The Critical Temper of Alain Locke*.

—. "The Black Watch on the Rhine." *Opportunity* 2 (1924): 6-9.

—. "The Colonial Literature of France." *Opportunity* 1 (1923): 331-335.

—. "The Concept of Race as Applied to Social Culture." In *The Philosophy of Alain Locke: Harlem Renaissance and Beyond*, edited by Leonard Harris. Philadelphia: Temple University Press, 1989.

—. "The Negro: 'New' or Newer: A Retrospective Review of the Literature of the Negro for 1938." *Opportunity* 17 (1939): 4-10, 36-42.

—. "The New Negro." In Locke, *The New Negro: An Interpretation*.

—. "The Saving Grace of Realism: Retrospective Review of the Literature of the Negro for 1933." *Opportunity* 12 (1934): 8-11, 30, 48-51.

—. "This Year of Grace." *Opportunity* 9 (1931): 48-50.

—. "To Certain of Our Philistines." *Opportunity* 3 (1925): 155-156.

—. "We Turn to Prose: A Retrospective Review of the Literature of the Negro for 1931." *Opportunity* 10 (1932): 40-44.

—. "Welcome the New South: A Review of *The Advancing South*, by Edwin Mims." *Opportunity* 4 (1926): 374-375.

—. "Youth Speaks." *Survey Graphic* 6, no. 6 (March 1925): 659-660.

—. Foreword to Locke, *The New Negro: An Interpretation*.

—. Introduction to *Exhibition of the Art of the American Negro (1851 to 1940) Assembled by the American Negro Exposition*. Chicago: Tanner Art Galleries, 1940.

—. *Negro Art: Past and Present*. Washington, DC: Associates in Negro Folk Education, 1936.

—. *The Critical Temper of Alain Locke*. Edited by Jeffrey Stewart. New York: Garland, 1983.

—. *The Negro and His Music*. Washington, DC: The Associates in Negro Folk Education, 1936.

—. *The Negro in Art: A Pictorial Record of the Negro Artist and of the Negro Theme in Art*. Washington, DC: Associates in Negro Folk Education, 1940.

Lomax, Louis. Introduction to *Up from Slavery*, by Booker T. Washington. New York: Dell Publishing, 1965.

Lott, Eric. *Love and Theft: Blackface Minstrelsy and the American Working Class*. New York: Oxford University Press, 1995.

Maasen, Thijs. "Man-Boy Friendships on Trial: On the Shift in the Discourse on Boy Love in the Early Twentieth Century." *Journal of Homosexuality* 20, no. 1/2 (1990): 47-70.

MacBrady, J. E. Introduction to *A New Negro for a New Century: An Accurate and Up-to-Date Record of the Upward Struggles of the Negro Race*, by Booker T. Washington.

Madison, Grant. *The Passing of the Great Race: Or, The Racial Basis of European History*. 1918. New York: Charles Scribner's Sons, 1921.

Majors, Richard, and Janet Mancini Billson. *Cool Pose: The Dilemmas of Black Manhood in America*. New York: Lexington Books, 1992.

Maxwell, William J. *New Negro Old Left: African-American Writing and Communism between the Wars*. New York: Columbia University Press, 1999.

Mazella, David. *The Making of Modern Cynicism*. Charlottesville, VA: University of Virginia Press, 2007.

McDougald, Elise Johnson. "The Task of Negro Womanhood." In Locke, *The New Negro: An Interpretation*.

McKay, Claude. *Home to Harlem*. 1928. London: Black Classics, 2000.

Meier, August, and Elliot Rudwick. *From Plantation to Ghetto*. New York: Hill and Wang, 1970.

Mercer, Kobena, and Isaac Julien. "True Confessions." In *Black Male: Representations of Masculinity in Contemporary Art*, edited by Thelma Golden. New York: Whitney Museum of Art, 1994.

Mitchell, Sally. "New Women, Old and New." *Victorian Literature and Culture* 27, no. 2 (1999): 579-88.

Moore, Jacqueline M. *Booker T. Washington, W. E. B. Du Bois, and the Struggle for Racial Uplift*. Wilmington, DE: Scholarly Resources, 2003.

Mosse, George L. *Nationalism and Sexuality: Respectability and Abnormal Sexuality in Modern Europe*. New York: Howard Fertig, 1985.

Mumford, Kevin J. *Interzones: Black/White Sex Districts in Chicago and New York in the Early Twentieth Century*. New York: Columbia University Press, 1997.

Murphy, Mary. "Picture/Story: Representing Gender in Montana Farm Security Administration Photographs." *Frontiers: A Journal of Women Studies* 22, no. 3 (2001): 93-115.

Myrdal, Gunnar. *An American Dilemma: The Negro Problem and Modern Democracy*. New York: Harper & Brothers, 1944.

Natanson, Nicholas. *The Black Image in the New Deal: The Politics of FSA Photography*. Knoxville, TN: University of Tennessee Press, 1993.

North, Michael. *The Dialect of Modernism: Race, Language, and Twentieth-Century Literature*. New York: Oxford University Press, 1994.

Nugent, Richard Bruce. *Gay Rebel of the Harlem Renaissance: Selections from the Work of Richard Bruce Nugent*. Edited by Thomas H. Wirth. Durham, NC: Duke University Press, 2002.

Park, Robert E. *Race and Culture: Essays in the Sociology of Contemporary Man*. 1919. Glencoe, NY: Free Press, 1950.

Pauly, Thomas H. "The Criminal as Culture." *American Literary History* 9, no. 4 (winter 1997): 776-785.

Perloff, Richard M. "The Press and Lynchings of African Americans." *Journal of Black Studies* 30, no. 3 (January 2000): 315-330.

Peterson, Dale E. "Richard Wright's Long Journey from Gorky to Dostoevsky." *African American Review* 28, no. 3 (fall 1994): 375-387.

Plato. "The Symposium." *The Dialogues of Plato*. Translated by Benjamin Jowett. Oxford: Clarendon Press, 1875.

Pochmara, Anna. "Are You a 'Real Man'?: the Construction of Hegemonic Masculinity in American Culture." *Polish Journal for American Studies* 2 (2009): 127-140.

Pollock, Griselda. *Vision and Difference: Femininity, Feminism, and Histories of Art*. New York: Routledge, 1988.

Putney, Clifford. *Muscular Christianity: Manhood and Sports in Protestant America, 1880-1920*. Cambridge, MA: Harvard University Press, 2003.

Quarles, Benjamin. *The Negro in the Making of America*. New York: Collier Books, 1969.

Rampersad, Arnold. "The Book That Launched the Harlem Renaissance." *The Journal of Blacks in Higher Education* 38 (winter 2002-2003): 87-91.

—. "The Founding Fathers: Frederick Douglass, W. E. B. Du Bois, Washington." In *Slavery and the Literary Imagination*, edited by Deborah E. McDowell and Arnold Rampersad. Baltimore, MD: Johns Hopkins University Press, 1989.

—. *The Life of Langston Hughes: 1914-1967: I Dream a World*. New York: Oxford University Press, 2002.

Randall, Dudley. "Booker T. and W. E. B." In *Modern and Contemporary Afro-American Poetry*, edited by Bernard W. Bell. Boston: Allyn and Bacon, 1972.

Redding, J. Saunders. *To Make a Poet Black*. Chapel Hill, NC: The University of North Carolina Press, 1939.

Reilly, John M. "Richard Wright Preaches the Nation: 12 Million Black Voices." *Black American Literature Forum* 16, no. 3 (autumn 1982): 116-119.

Ross, Chad. *Naked Germany: Health, Race and the Nation*. Oxford: Berg, 2005.

Ross, Marlon Bryan. *Manning the Race: Reforming Black Men in the Jim Crow Era*. New York: NYU Press, 2004.

Sauer, R. "Attitudes to Abortion in America, 1800-1973." *Population Studies* 28, no. 1 (March 1974): 53-67.

Schwarz, A. B. Christa. *Gay Voices of the Harlem Renaissance*. Bloomington, IN: Indiana University Press, 2003.

Sedgwick, Eve Kosofsky. *Between Men: English Literature and Male Homosocial Desire*. New York: Columbia University Press, 1985.

—. *Epistemology of the Closet*. Berkeley, CA: University of California Press, 1990.

Seppä, Anita. "Foucault, Enlightenment and the Aesthetics of the Self." *Contemporary Aesthetics* 2, no. 4 (2004) http://www.contempaesthetics.org/ newvolume/ pages/ article. php?articleID=244.

Shapiro, Herbert. *White Violence and Black Response: From Reconstruction to Montgomery*. Amherst, MA: University of Massachusetts Press, 1988.

Showalter, Elaine. *Sexual Anarchy: Gender and Culture at the Fin De Siècle*. New York: Viking, 1990.

Sinfield, Alan. *The Wilde Century: Effeminacy, Oscar Wilde, and the Queer Movement*. New York: Columbia University Press, 1994.

Singleton, Gregory Holmes. "Birth, Rebirth, and the 'New Negro' of the 1920s." *Phylon* 43, no. 1 (1982): 29-45.

Smethurst, James. *The New Red Negro: The Literary Left and African American Poetry, 1930-1946*. New York: Oxford University Press, 1999.

Smith-Rosenberg, Carroll. "Discourses of Sexuality and Subjectivity: The New Woman, 1870-1936." In *Hidden From History: Reclaiming the Gay and Lesbian Past*, edited by Martin Bauml Duberman, Martha Vicinus, and George Chauncey, Jr.. New York: New American Library, 1989.

Spillers, Hortense J. "'The Permanent Obliquity of an In(pha)llibly Straight': In the Time of the Daughters and the Fathers." In *Changing Our Own Words, Essays on Criticism, Theory, and Writing by Black Women*, edited by Cheryl A. Wall. New Brunswick, NJ: Rutgers University Press, 1989.

Stokes, John. *In the Nineties*. Chicago: The University of Chicago Press, 1989.

Sundquist, Eric J. *To Wake the Nations: Race in the Making of American Literature*. Cambridge, MA: Belknap Press, 1993.

Tate, Claudia. *Psychoanalysis and Black Novels: Desire and the Protocols of Race*. New York: Oxford University Press, 1998.

Thurman, Wallace. "Fire Burns: A Department of Comment." In *The Collected Writings of Wallace Thurman: A Harlem Renaissance Reader*.

—. "Frederick Douglass: The Black Emancipator." In *The Collected Writings of Wallace Thurman: A Harlem Renaissance Reader*.

—. "High, Low, Past, and Present: Review of *The Walls of Jericho, Quicksand*, and *Adventures of an African Slaver*." In *The Collected Writings of Wallace Thurman: A Harlem Renaissance Reader*.

—. "Negro Artists and the Negro." In *The Collected Writings of Wallace Thurman: A Harlem Renaissance Reader*.

—. "Negro Life in New York's Harlem: a Lively Picture of a Popular and Interesting Section." In *The Collected Writings of Wallace Thurman: A Harlem Renaissance Reader*.

—. "Review of *Heloise and Abelard*, by George Moore." In *The Collected Writings of Wallace Thurman: A Harlem Renaissance Reader*.

—. "Stranger at the Gates: A Review of *Nigger Heaven*, by Carl Van Vechten." In *The Collected Writings of Wallace Thurman: A Harlem Renaissance Reader*.

—. "The Negro Literary Renaissance." In *The Collected Writings of Wallace Thurman: A Harlem Renaissance Reader*.

—. "Harlem: A Melodrama of Negro Life in Harlem." In *The Collected Writings of Wallace Thurman: A Harlem Renaissance Reader*.

—. *Infants of the Spring*. 1932. New York: Modern Library, 1999.

—. Preface to *Aunt Hagar's Children*. In *The Collected Writings of Wallace Thurman: A Harlem Renaissance Reader*.

—. *The Blacker the Berry*. 1929. New York: Macmillan Publishing Company, 1970.

—. *The Collected Writings of Wallace Thurman: A Harlem Renaissance Reader*. Edited by Amritjit Singh and Daniel M. Scott. New Brunswick, NJ: Rutgers University Press, 2003.

Tompkins, Jane. *West of Everything: The Inner Life of Westerns*. New York: Oxford University Press, 1992.

Trachtenberg, Alan. *The Incorporation of America: Culture and Society in the Gilded Age*. New York: Hill and Wang, 1982.

Tuhkanen, Mikko Juhani. "'[B]igger's Place': Lynching and Specularity in Richard Wright's 'Fire and Cloud' and *Native Son*." *African American Review* 33, no. 1 (spring 1999): 125-133.

Turner, Frederick Jackson. *The Frontier in American History*. 1893. Mineola, NY: Courier Dover Publications, 1996.

Tusan, Michelle Elizabeth. "Inventing the New Woman: Print Culture and Identity Politics during the Fin-de-Siecle." *Victorian Periodical Review* 31, no. 2 (1998): 169-182.

Van Notten, Eleonore. *Wallace Thurman's Harlem Renaissance*. Amsterdam: Rodopi, 1994.

Veblen, Thorstein. *The Theory of the Leisure Class: An Economic Study of Institutions*. 1902. New York: Oxford University Press, 2007.

Waldecke, St. Ch. "Die Physiologische Freundschaft in der Auffassung der Grossen Amerikanischen Dichter-Denker." *Der Eigene* 9 (1924): 293-299.

Wall, Cheryl A. *Women of the Harlem Renaissance*. Bloomington, IN: Indiana University Press, 1995.

Wallace, Maurice O. *Constructing the Black Masculine: Identity and Ideality in African American Men's Literature 1775-1995*. Durham, NC: Duke University Press, 2002.

Wallace, Michele. *Black Macho and the Myth of the Superwoman*. New York: Dial Press, 1979.

Washington, Booker T. "The American Negro and His Economic Value." In *Negro Social and Political Thought, 1850-1920*, edited by Howard Brotz. New York: Basic Books, 1966.

—. *The Booker T. Washington Papers*. Edited by Louis R. Harlan and Raymond Smock. Urbana, IL: University of Illinois Press, 1912.

—. *Up from Slavery*. 1901. New York: Dell Publishing, 1965.

Washington, Booker T., Fannie Barrier Williams, and N. B. Wood. *A New Negro for a New Century: An Accurate and Up-to-Date Record of the Upward Struggles of the Negro Race*. Chicago: American Publishing House, 1900.

Washington, Johnny. *Evolution, History, and Destiny: Letters to Alain Locke (1886-1954) and Others*. New York: Peter Lang Pub Inc, 2002.

West, Cornel. *Race Matters*. New York: Vintage Books, 1994.

—. *The Cornel West Reader*. New York: Basic Civitas Books, 1999.

White, Walter. *Fire in the Flint*. New York: Alfred A. Knopf, 1924.

Wiegman, Robyn. *American Anatomies: Theorizing Race and Gender*. Durham, NC: Duke University Press, 1995.

Wilde, Oscar. "The Critic as an Artist: With Some Remarks upon the Importance of Discussing Everything." In *Intentions*. 1891. BiblioBazaar, 2008.

—. "The Critic as an Artist: With Some Remarks upon the Importance of Doing Nothing." In *Intentions*. 1891. Charleston, SC: BiblioBazaar, 2008.

Williams, Fannie B. "Club Movement among Colored Women." In *A New Negro for a New Century: An Accurate and Up-to-Date Record of the Upward Struggles of the Negro Race*.

Williams, John Alexander. "Ecstasies of the Young: Sexuality, the Youth Movement, and Moral Panic in Germany on the Eve of the First World War." *Central European History* 34, no. 2 (2001): 163-189.

Wintz, Cary D. *Black Culture and the Harlem Renaissance*. Houston: Rice University Press, 1988.

Wolff, Janet. "The Invisible Flâneuse; Women and the Literature of Modernity." *Theory, Culture and Society* 2, no. 3 (1985): 37-46.

Woolf, Virginia. *Mr Bennet and Mrs Brown*. London: Hogarth, 1928.

Wright, Richard. "A Review of *Wars I Have Seen*, by Gertrude Stein." In *Richard Wright Reader*.

—. "Blueprint for Negro Writing." In *Richard Wright Reader*.

—. *12 Million Black Voices*. 1941. New York: Thunder's Press, 1988.

—. *Black Boy (American Hunger)*. 1944/1977. New York: Harper Collins, 1993.

—. Foreword to *Black Metropolis: A Study of Negro Life in a Northern City*, by Horace Roscoe Cayton and St. Clair Drake. 1945. Chicago: University of Chicago Press, 1993.

—. *Lawd Today*. New York: Walker & Co, 1963.

—. *Native Son*. 1940. New York: Buccaneer Books, 1997.

—. *Richard Wright Reader*. Edited by Michel Fabre and Ellen Wright. New York: Harper, 1978.

—. *Uncle Tom's Children*. 1938. New York: Harper, 1965.

Yiftachel, Oren. "Launching Hagar: Marginality, Beer-Sheva, Critique." *Studies in Culture, Polity, and Identities* 1, no. 1 (2000). http://hsf.bgu.ac.il/ hagar/issues/ 1_1_2000/ 1120001. aspx.

Archival collections:

Alain Locke Papers, Moorland-Spingarn Research Center, Howard University.

Carl Van Vechten Correspondence JWJ, Beinecke Rare Book and Manuscript Library, Yale University.

Langston Hughes Papers JWJ MSS 26, Beinecke Rare Book and Manuscript Library, Yale University.

Dorothy Peterson Collection JWJ, Beinecke Rare Book and Manuscript Library, Yale University.

Claude McKay Collection JWJ MSS 27, Beinecke Rare Book and Manuscript Library, Yale University.

Wallace Thurman Collection JWJ MSS 12, Beinecke Rare Book and Manuscript Library, Yale University.

Richard Wright Papers JWJ MSS, Beinecke Rare Book and Manuscript Library, Yale University.

Index

A

abolition 27, 70, 120

abortion 122, 148, 158, 213, 215, 242n, 29

Abrahams, Roger D. 252n, 93

aesthetic of existence. *See* aesthetic of the self

aesthetic of the self 15, 124, 143-55, 159, 166-70, 177, 187, 194-96, 239n, 56

Africa 47, 100-5, 107, 113, 117-18, 137, 181, 198-99, 205, 221n, 4

Alexander, Lewis 74, 82

Alger, Horatio 27

ambiguous racial identity 153, 155, 162, 164-70, 177. *See also* mulatto/a *and* passing

American Boy Scouts 73, 83

American Indian 30-32, 137, 173, 202, 247n, 112

American individualism 27, 70, 73, 96-7

American North 20-1, 24, 31, 34, 43, 53, 64-7, 71, 118, 124, 127, 133, 173, 196, 198-203

American Renaissance 15, 69-70, 73, 79, 85-6, 90, 92, 182, 219, 228n, 13

American South 14, 19-21, 24-25, 28-32, 34, 37, 46, 52-3, 65-7, 71, 76, 118, 127, 137, 189-90, 196, 198-203, 240n, 66, 252n, 88

American West 21, 71, 118-19, 122, 148. *See also* frontier

Ancient Greece 15, 76-83, 85- 92, 103-4, 107, 144, 154, 161-62, 219

anxiety of authorship 9-10, 27, 38, 59-60, 90, 95, 97, 126-27, 141, 176, 179, 181, 189, 215, 217-19

anxiety of influence 9-10, 38, 59, 90, 95, 108, 114, 141, 179, 184, 188, 215, 217-19

Armstrong, Samuel Chapman 26, 28

arts of existence. *See* aesthetic of the self

Asia 147

Atlanta 43

Atlanta Constitution 24

Atlanta Exposition Address 23-4, 32-3, 203

Atlantic ocean 79

authorship 9-10, 27, 38, 59-60, 90, 95, 97, 108, 112-14, 126-27, 141, 172, 179-81, 188-91, 215-18

Avallone, Charlene 69

B

Badinter, Elizabeth 75, 230n, 59

Baker, Houston 33, 223n, 4

Bakhtin, Mikhail 114, 128-130, 135, 198, 206-7, 252n, 95

Baldwin, James 48, 210, 212, 249n, 18

Baltimore 120

Balzac, Honoré de 175

Baraka, Amiri 9

Barthe, Richmond 74, 79, 81

bastardy 10, 41-2, 44, 47-9, 60, 81, 111, 121, 137, 165, 246n, 109

Baudelaire, Charles 142-43, 153-54, 161, 244n, 55

Baym, Nina 118

India 96, 147
interpellation 67
interracial intimacy. *See* miscegenation
intertextual bonding 58-9, 89-93, 218
intertextuality 15, 58-69, 76-80, 82,
 85-7, 90-3, 95, 105, 119, 130, 139-43,
 147, 150, 153, 159, 162-69, 195-96,
 219, 233n, 138, 244n, 71, 246n, 109
interzones 91-2, 161, 164
intraracial discrimination 113, 136-37,
 151, 154-55, 165, 167-68
inversion (sexual) 84, 104, 107, 129-30,
 187
Ireland 67
Ivory, Yvonne 84-5

J

Jackman, Harold 80
Jansen, Wilhelm 83-84
Japan 147
jazz 101, 105, 130, 136, 183, 244n, 68
Jazz Age 97, 180
Jim Crow. *See* segregation
Johnson, Charles S. 57, 67, 72-5
Johnson, Georgia Douglas 230n, 73
Johnson, Jack 121-22, 248n, 133
Johnson, James Weldon 57, 59
Jones, Leroi 9
Joyce, James 119
Jugendkultur. See German Youth
 Movements
Julien, Isaac 12-13

K

Kallen, Horace 64, 107
Kansas City Call 62
Killingsworth, M. Jimmie 80
Kimmel, Michael S. 10-11, 28, 43, 58,
 201
Koch, Max 89
Kottak, Conrad 230n, 59
Ku Klux Klan 23-4, 37

L

L'Ouverture, Touissant 60
Lane, Christopher 175
Larsen, Nella 137-38, 241n, 108, 245n,
 96
laughter 205-7, 210, 252n, 95
Lawrence, D. H. 70
Lee, Robert E. 49
Lee, Russell 197
left-wing 62, 105, 138-39, 180-81, 183,
 185, 187, 191-92, 197, 216, 247n, 109,
 250n, 49. *See also* communism,
 Communist Party, *and* Marxism
Lemke, Sieglinde 222n, 11
lesbian 165
Levine, Lawrence 252n, 93
Lewis, David Levering 222n, 11, 236n, 6,
 239n, 57
Liberator 62
Locke, Alain 9, 14-15, 18, 54, 57-108,
 110-119, 123, 129, 132, 137-44, 157-
 58, 160-62, 171, 173,180-81, 183-84,
 186, 188, 191, 193, 196, 198-99,
 203-4, 214, 216-19, 229n,43, 229n,
 46, 230n, 62, 230n, 73, 231n, 74,
 232n, 93, 233n, 116, 233n, 138,
 234n, 144, 235n, 31, 236n, 38, 236n,
 42, 236n, 6, 237n, 11, 248n, 4, 249n,
 26, 252n, 99
Loeb, Ralph 80
Los Angeles 116, 151
Lott, Eric 244n, 72
Louis, Joe 190-91
lynch logic 13-4, 20-1, 25, 31, 45-9,
 52-4, 93, 121, 159-60, 166, 177, 180,
 217, 219
lynching 19-20, 22, 24-5, 33, 49-52, 121,
 125, 160, 180, 190, 199-201, 204, 210-
 12, 214-15

M

M.G.M. 154
Maasen, Thijs 86
MacBrady, J. E. 60

Curriculum Vitae

Anna Pochmara is Assistant Professor at the Institute of English Studies, the University of Warsaw. She holds a double M.A. degree in American literature and culture. As a graduate student, she received a Fulbright Junior Grant to do research for her doctoral project at the African American Studies Department, Yale University, for which she earned a Ph.D. in 2009. Her interests include American fiction, gender and sexuality studies, and African American studies. She has published a number of articles on American literature and culture.